Yuto Tsukuda

The month this volume goes on ...pan), I will turn thirty— ...ee-oh. I like to think ...transform a man into ...r gentleman, so I will ...What was that saying ...ng independent ...ty? It was something Confucius said, I think.

Shun Saeki

Just look at that flexible little monster!

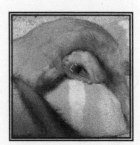

About the authors

Yuto Tsukuda won the 34th Jump Juniketsu Newcomers' Manga Award for his one-shot story *Kiba ni Naru*. He made his *Weekly Shonen Jump* debut in 2010 with the series *Shonen Shikku*. His follow-up series, *Food Wars!: Shokugeki no Soma*, is his first English-language release.

Shun Saeki made his *Jump NEXT!* debut in 2011 with the one-shot story *Kimi to Watashi no Renai Soudan*. *Food Wars!: Shokugeki no Soma* is his first *Shonen Jump* series.

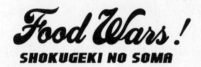

Food Wars!
SHOKUGEKI NO SOMA

Volume 17
Shonen Jump Advanced Manga Edition
Story by Yuto Tsukuda, Art by Shun Saeki
Contributor Yuki Morisaki

Translation: Adrienne Beck
Touch-Up Art & Lettering: Mara Coman
Design: Alice Lewis
Editor: Jennifer LeBlanc

Printed in the U.S.A.

Published by VIZ Media, LLC
P.O. Box 77010
San Francisco, CA 94107

10 9 8 7 6 5 4 3 2 1
First printing, April 2017

www.viz.com

THE WORLD'S MOST CUTTING-EDGE MANGA
SHONEN JUMP ADVANCED
www.shonenjump.com

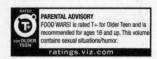

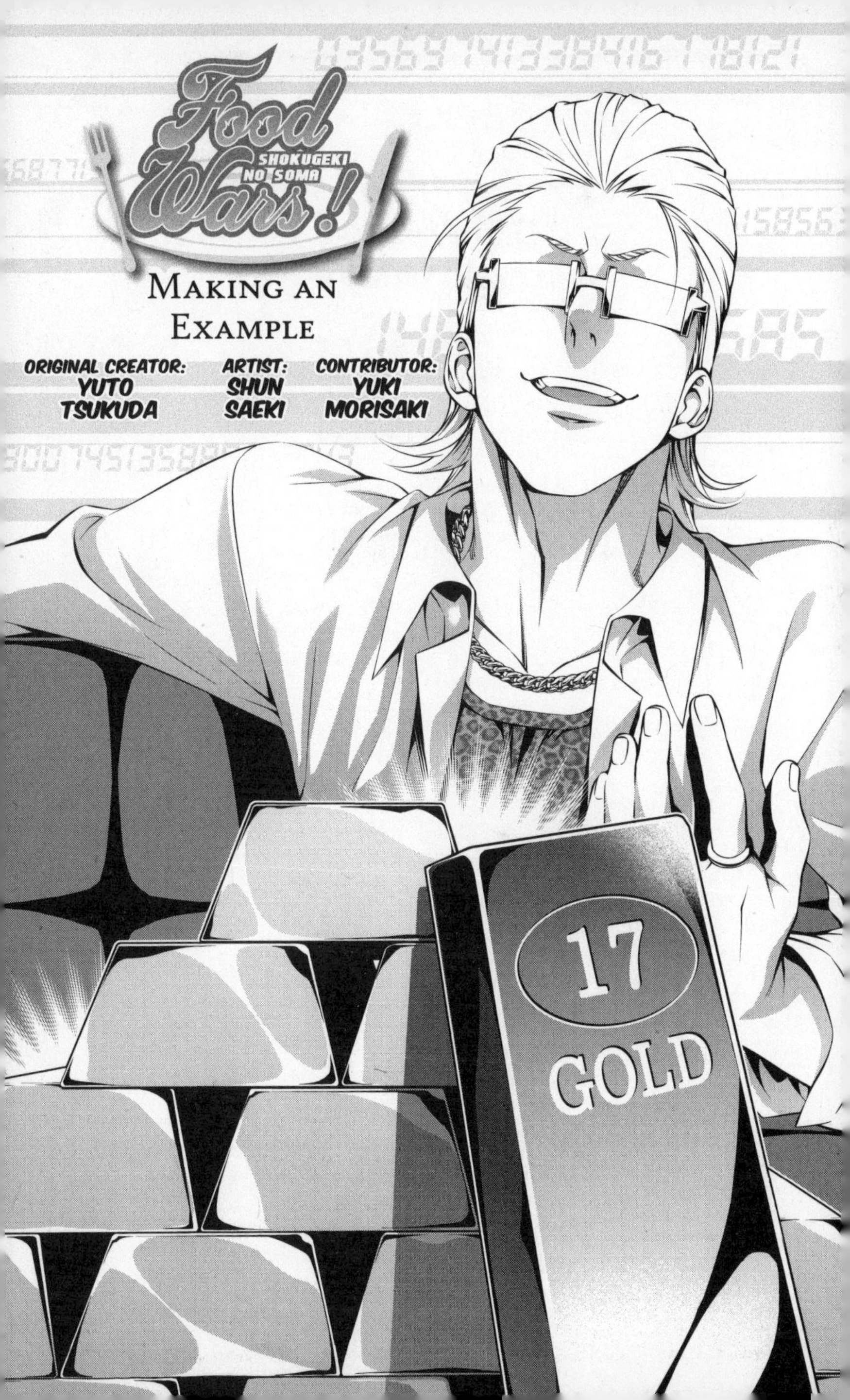
Food Wars!
SHOKUGEKI NO SOMA
MAKING AN EXAMPLE
ORIGINAL CREATOR: YUTO TSUKUDA
ARTIST: SHUN SAEKI
CONTRIBUTOR: YUKI MORISAKI
17
GOLD

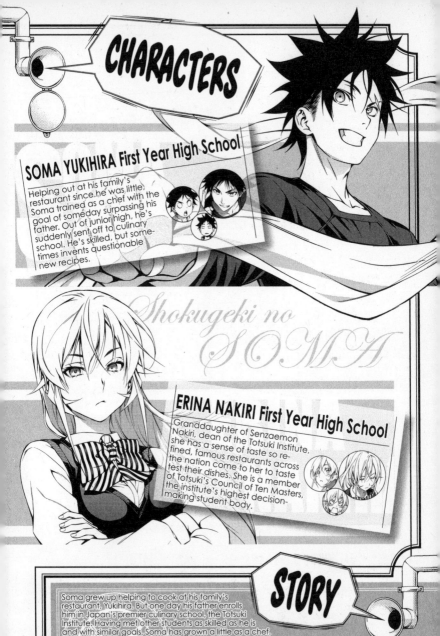

CHARACTERS

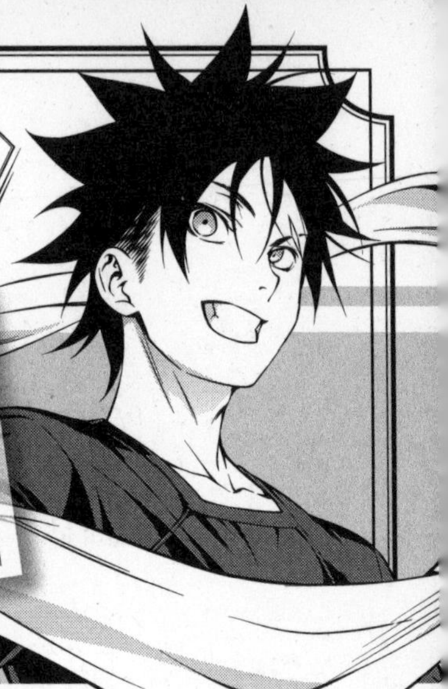

SOMA YUKIHIRA First Year High School

Helping out at his family's restaurant since he was little, Soma trained as a chef with the goal of someday surpassing his father. Out of junior high, he's suddenly sent off to culinary school. He's skilled, but sometimes invents questionable new recipes.

Shokugeki no SOMA

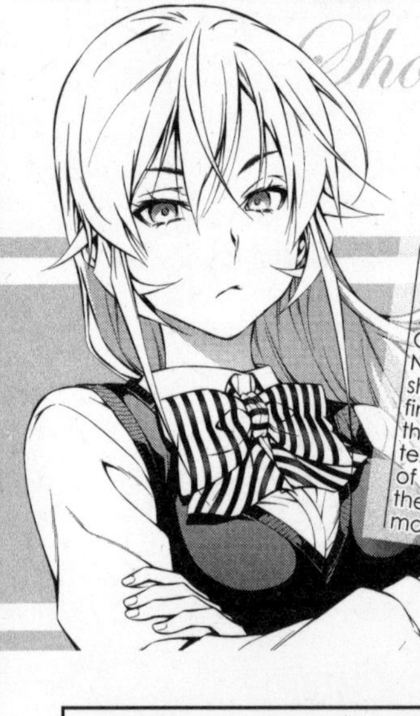

ERINA NAKIRI First Year High School

Granddaughter of Senzaemon Nakiri, dean of the Totsuki Institute, she has a sense of taste so refined, famous restaurants across the nation come to her to taste test their dishes. She is a member of Totsuki's Council of Ten Masters, the institute's highest decision-making student body.

STORY

Soma grew up helping to cook at his family's restaurant, Yukihira. But one day his father enrolls him in Japan's premier culinary school, the Totsuki Institute. Having met other students as skilled as he is and with similar goals, Soma has grown a little as a chef.

Even though Soma's tiny food cart finally tops Kuga's restaurant in profits on day four of the Moon Festival, Kuga still comes out ahead in overall profit. Soma doesn't have long to think over his loss, though, because Erina's father—Azami Nakiri—suddenly appears at Erina's restaurant on the evening of day five, even though he'd been banished from the institute. In a bold move, he declares himself the new dean by having a majority of the Council of Ten back him! With Senzaemon forced into retirement and a new administration taking over, what are Soma and the others to do?!

Shokugeki no SOMA

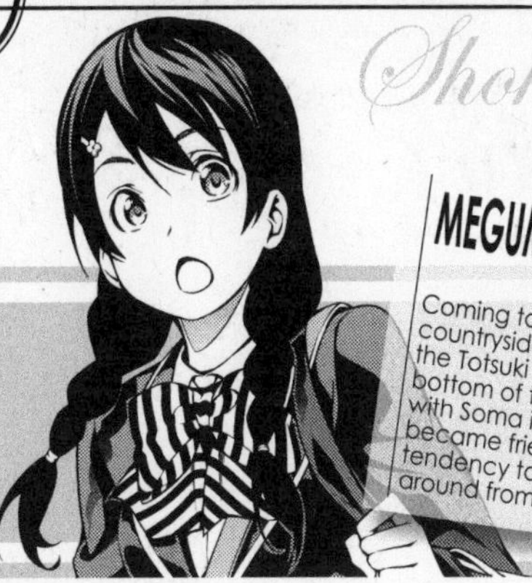

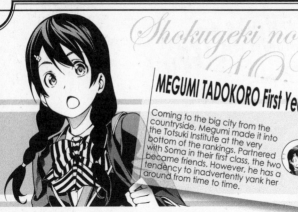

MEGUMI TADOKORO First Year High School

Coming to the big city from the countryside, Megumi made it into the Totsuki Institute at the very bottom of the rankings. Partnered with Soma in their first class, the two became friends. However, he has a tendency to inadvertently yank her around from time to time.

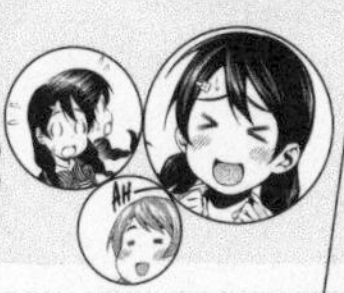
AH

ALICE NAKIRI First Year High School

Erina's cousin, she has spent much of her life overseas with her parents learning cooking from a scientific perspective through molecular gastronomy.

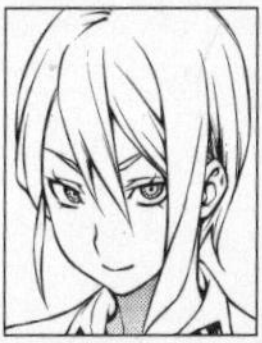

RYO KUROKIBA First Year High School

Alice's aide, he specializes in powerful, savory seafood dishes. His personality changes drastically when he puts on his bandanna.

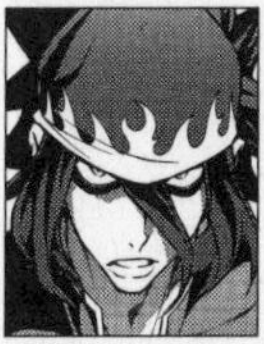

HISAKO ARATO First Year High School

Erina's exceptionally loyal and devoted aide, she is skilled in medicinal cooking. Her current worry is the proliferation of her nickname, Secretary Girl.

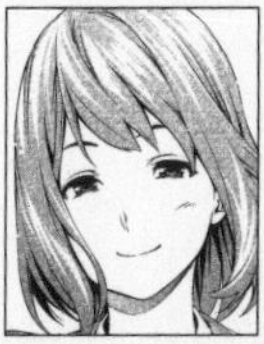

EISHI TSUKASA Third Year High School

The current first seat on Totsuki's Council of Ten. He comes off as meek and weak-willed at first, but he has absolute confidence in his skills as a chef.

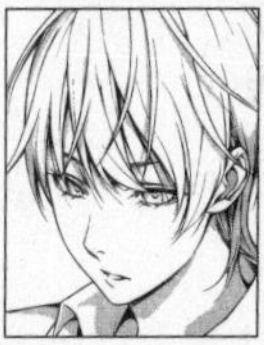

RINDO KOBAYASHI Third Year High School

The current second seat on Totsuki's Council of Ten, Rindo is friendly, sociable and easy-going. She met Soma during the Moon Festival and finds him intriguing.

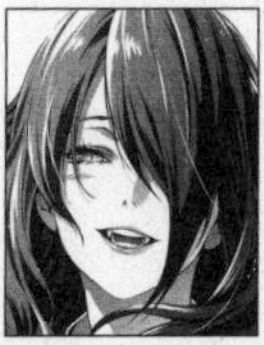

AZAMI NAKIRI

Erina's father, he imposed an unspeakably harsh training regimen on his daughter in her youth. It was so bad Senzaemon banished him from the institute.

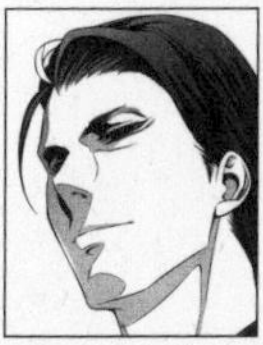

Food Wars! Shokugeki no Soma

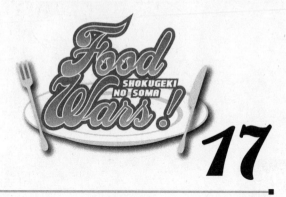

17

Table of Contents

#137 A FLAME OF HOPE

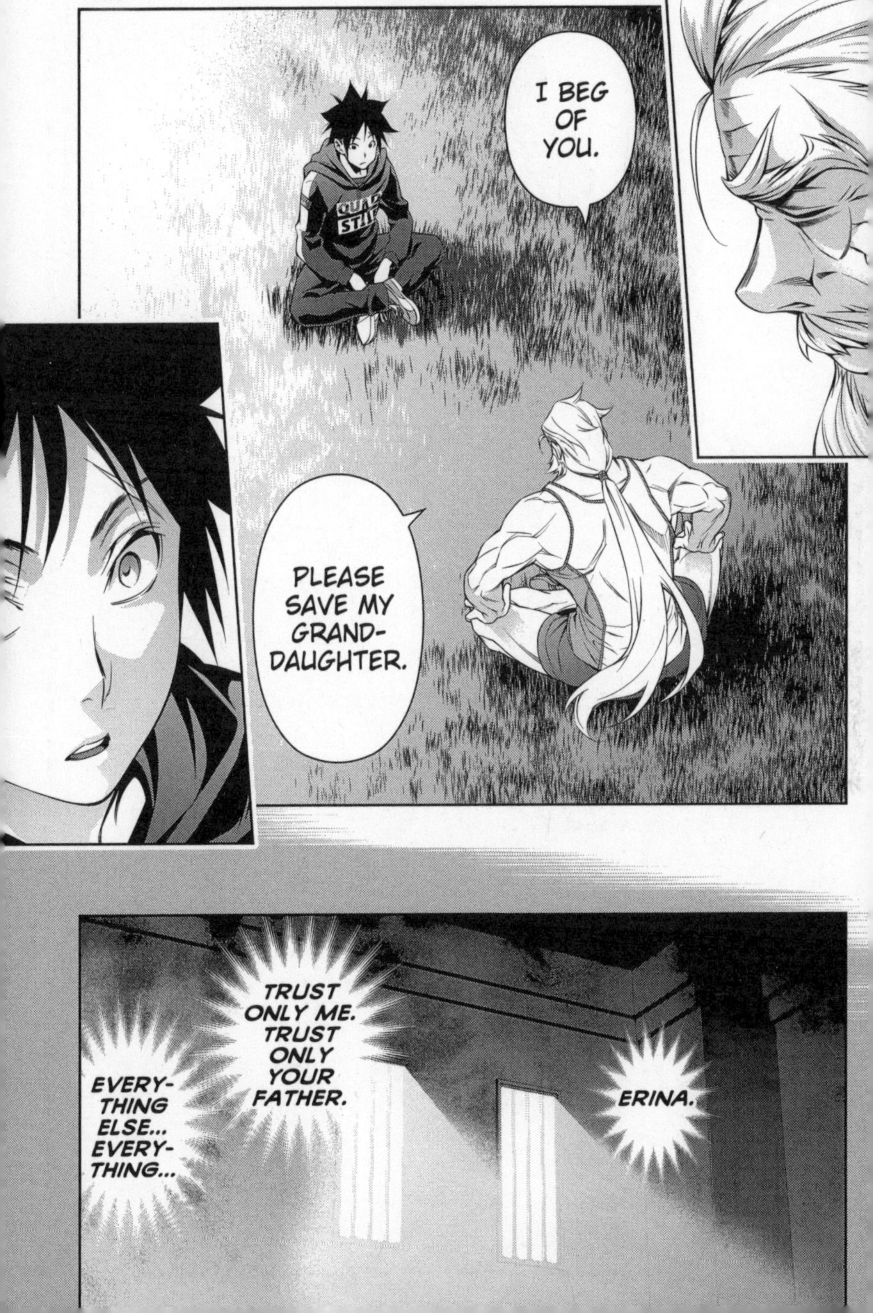
I BEG OF YOU.
PLEASE SAVE MY GRAND-DAUGHTER.
ERINA.
TRUST ONLY ME. TRUST ONLY YOUR FATHER.
EVERY-THING ELSE... EVERY-THING...

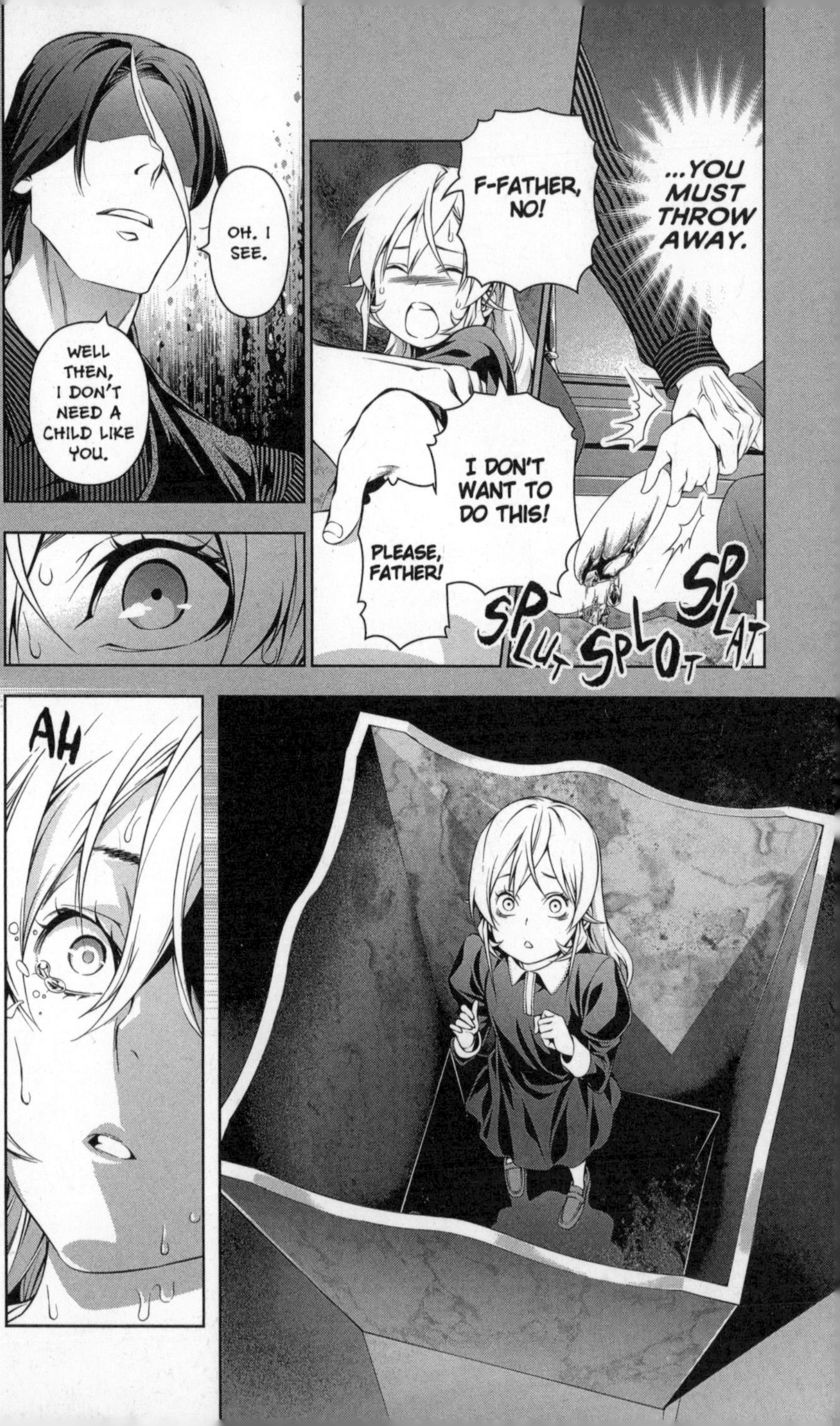
...YOU MUST THROW AWAY.
F-FATHER, NO!
I DON'T WANT TO DO THIS!
PLEASE, FATHER!
SPLUT SPLOT SPLAT
OH. I SEE.
WELL THEN, I DON'T NEED A CHILD LIKE YOU.
AH

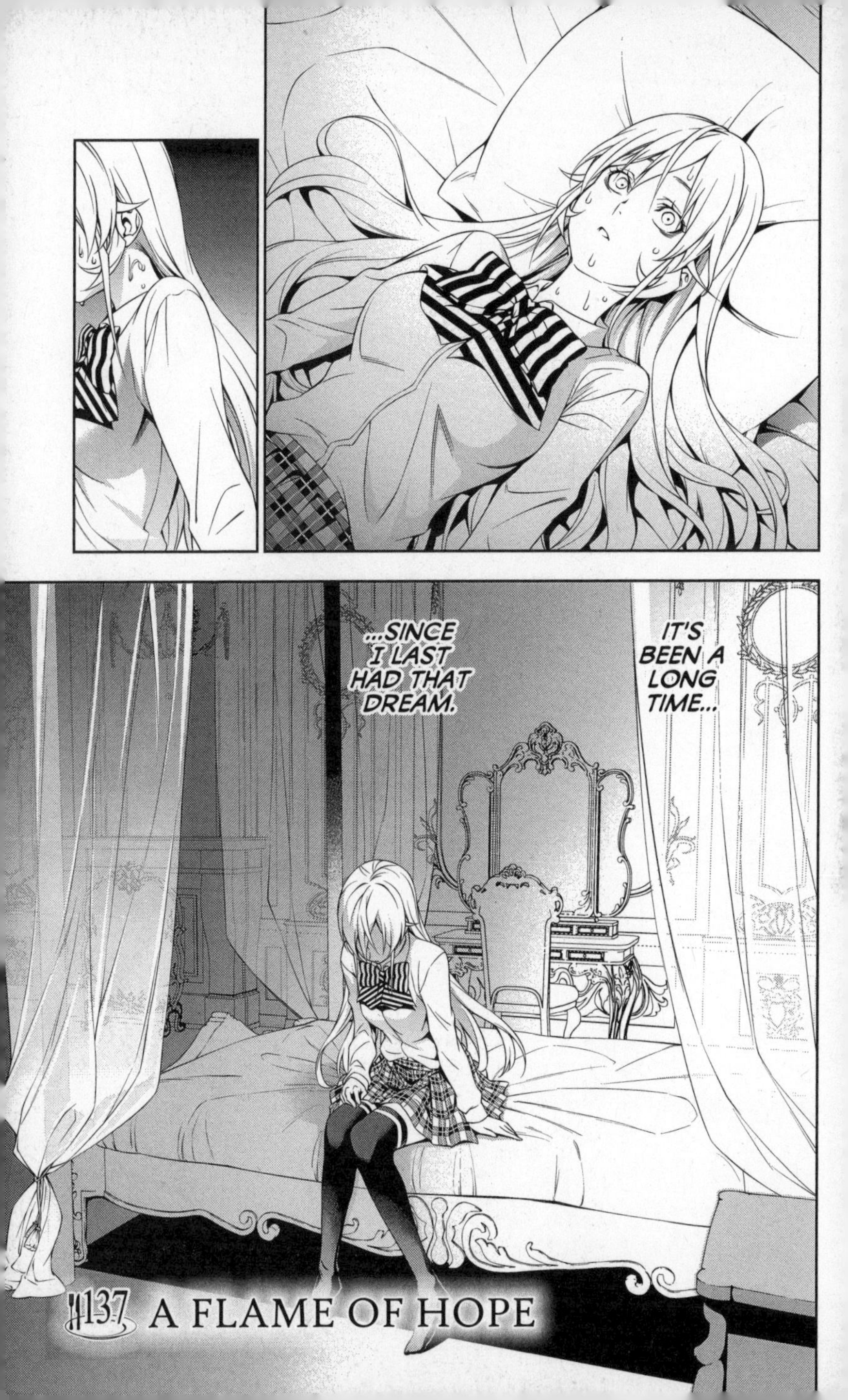
IT'S BEEN A LONG TIME...
...SINCE I LAST HAD THAT DREAM.
137 A FLAME OF HOPE

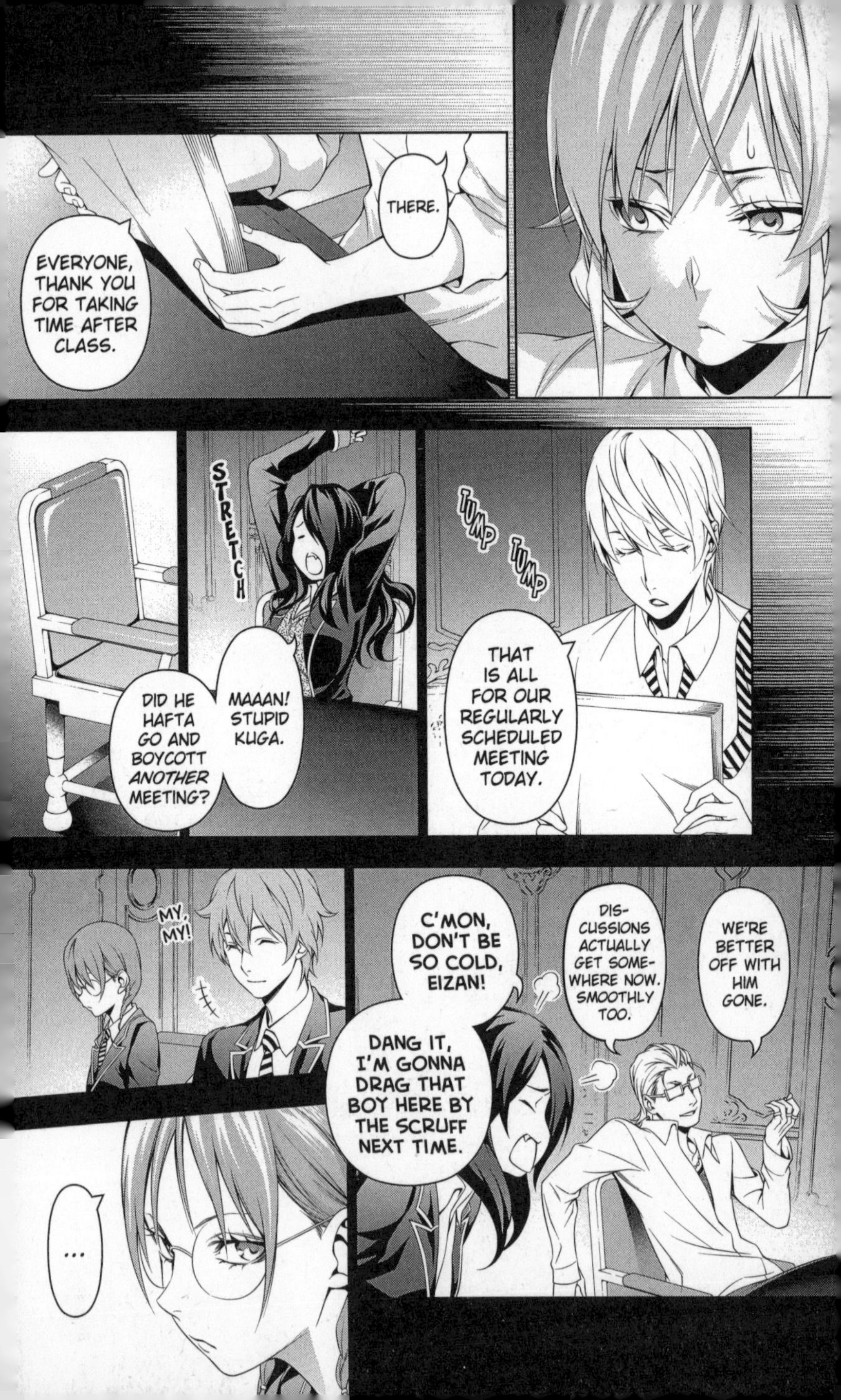
THERE.
EVERYONE, THANK YOU FOR TAKING TIME AFTER CLASS.
TUMP TUMP
THAT IS ALL FOR OUR REGULARLY SCHEDULED MEETING TODAY.
STRETCH
MAAAN! STUPID KUGA.
DID HE HAFTA GO AND BOYCOTT *ANOTHER* MEETING?
WE'RE BETTER OFF WITH HIM GONE.
DIS-CUSSIONS ACTUALLY GET SOME-WHERE NOW. SMOOTHLY TOO.
C'MON, DON'T BE SO COLD, EIZAN!
DANG IT, I'M GONNA DRAG THAT BOY HERE BY THE SCRUFF NEXT TIME.
MY, MY!
...

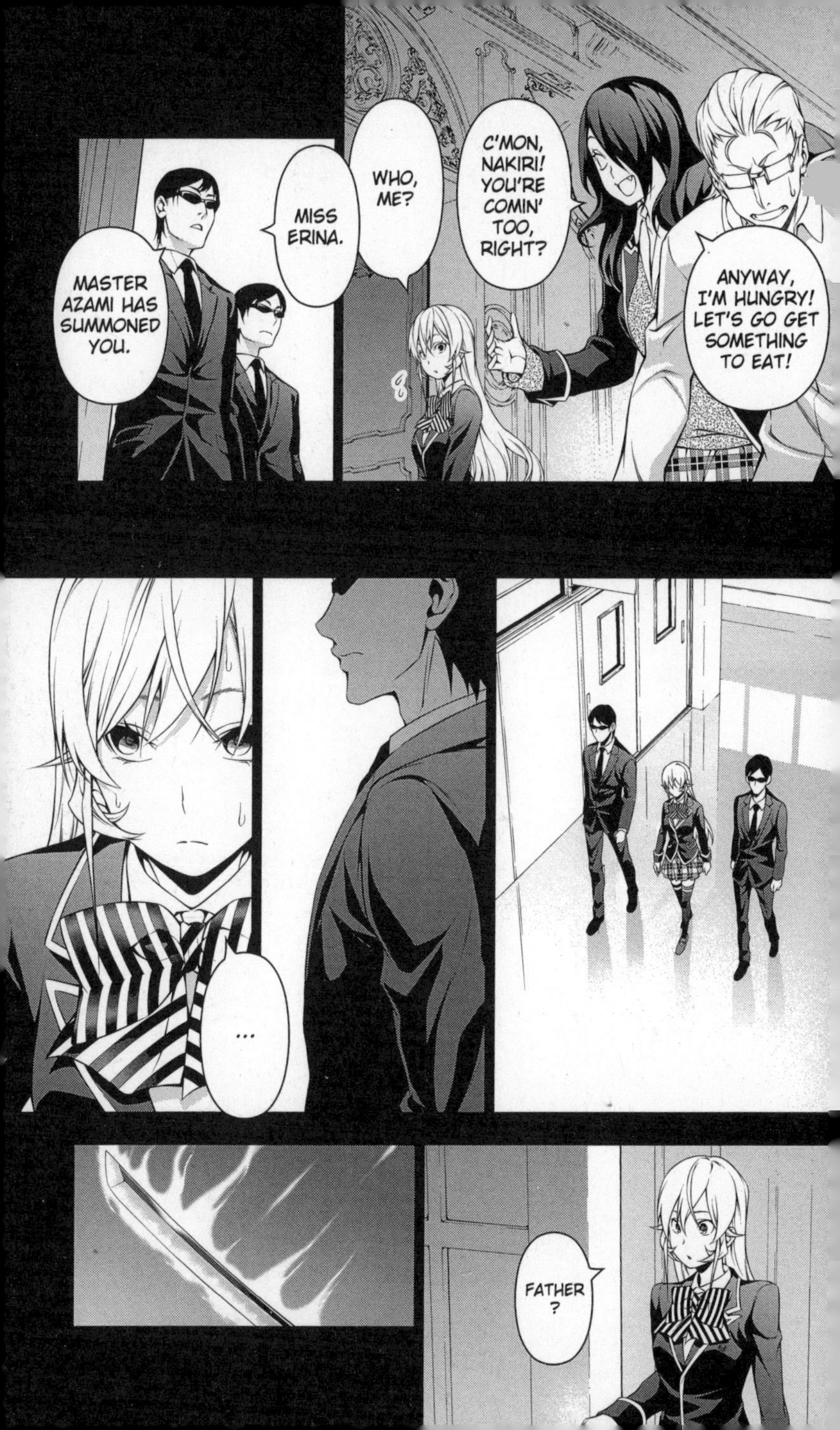
ANYWAY, I'M HUNGRY! LET'S GO GET SOMETHING TO EAT!
C'MON, NAKIRI! YOU'RE COMIN' TOO, RIGHT?
WHO, ME?
MISS ERINA.
MASTER AZAMI HAS SUMMONED YOU.
...
FATHER?

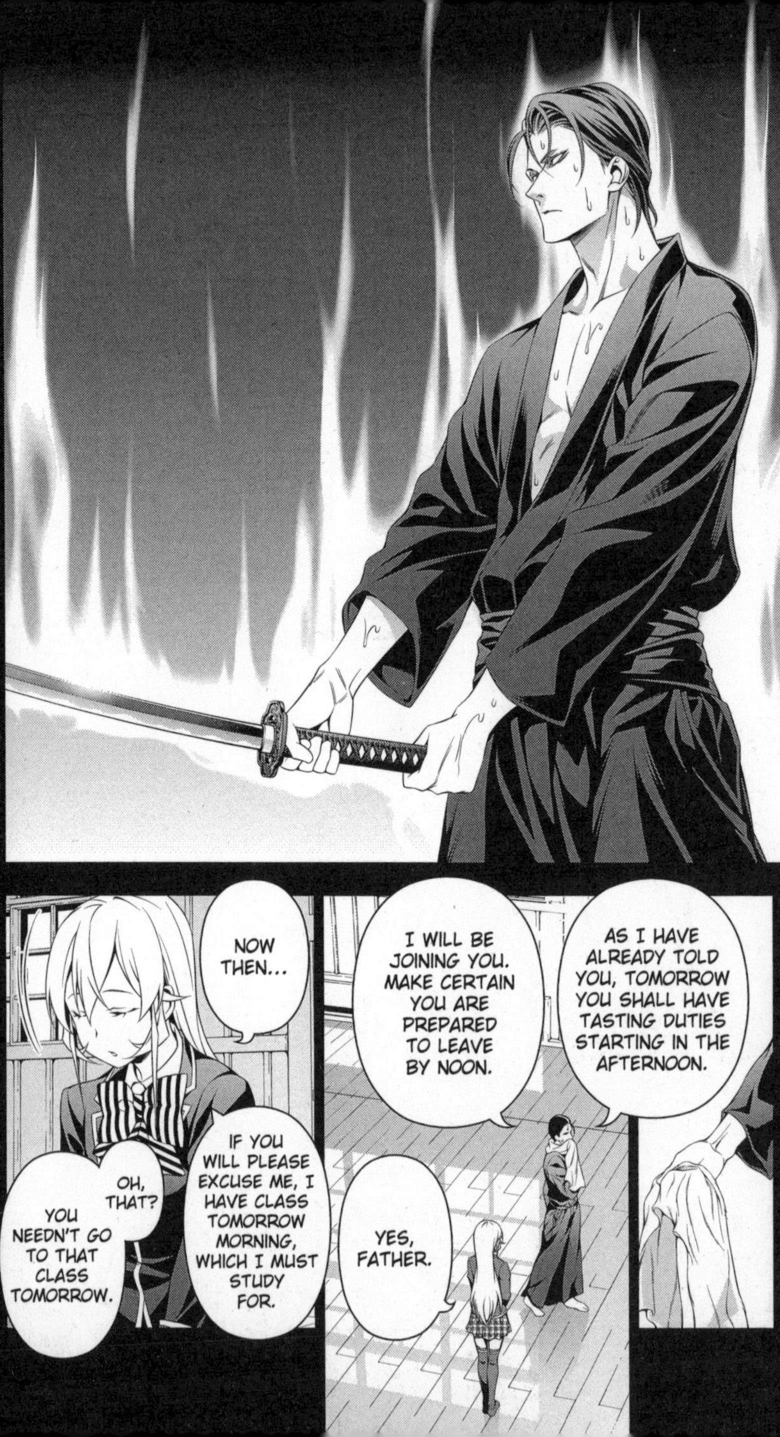
AS I HAVE ALREADY TOLD YOU, TOMORROW YOU SHALL HAVE TASTING DUTIES STARTING IN THE AFTERNOON.
I WILL BE JOINING YOU. MAKE CERTAIN YOU ARE PREPARED TO LEAVE BY NOON.
YES, FATHER.
NOW THEN...
IF YOU WILL PLEASE EXCUSE ME, I HAVE CLASS TOMORROW MORNING, WHICH I MUST STUDY FOR.
OH, THAT?
YOU NEEDN'T GO TO THAT CLASS TOMORROW.

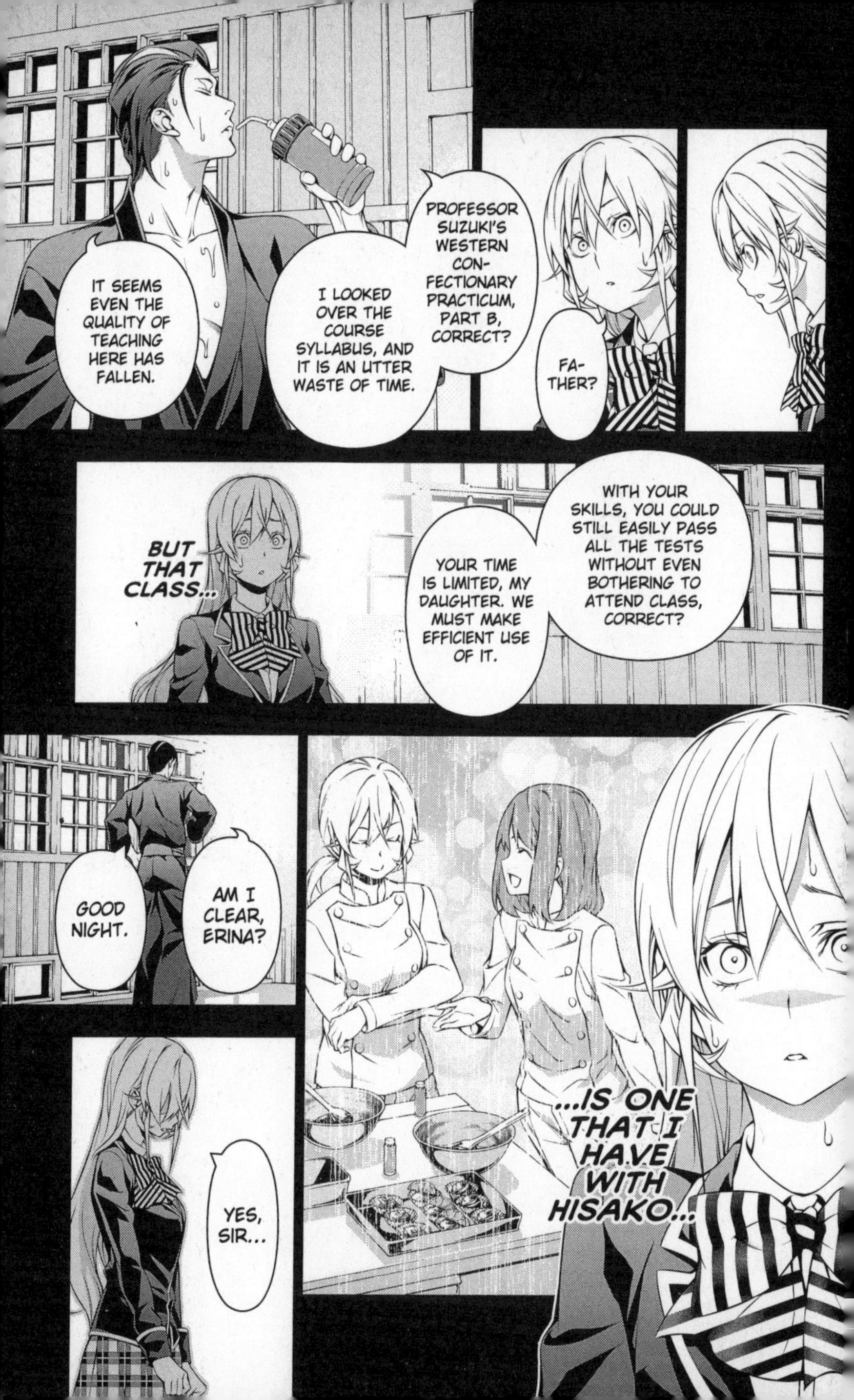
FA-THER?
PROFESSOR SUZUKI'S WESTERN CON-FECTIONARY PRACTICUM, PART B, CORRECT?
I LOOKED OVER THE COURSE SYLLABUS, AND IT IS AN UTTER WASTE OF TIME.
IT SEEMS EVEN THE QUALITY OF TEACHING HERE HAS FALLEN.
WITH YOUR SKILLS, YOU COULD STILL EASILY PASS ALL THE TESTS WITHOUT EVEN BOTHERING TO ATTEND CLASS, CORRECT?
YOUR TIME IS LIMITED, MY DAUGHTER. WE MUST MAKE EFFICIENT USE OF IT.
BUT THAT CLASS...
...IS ONE THAT I HAVE WITH HISAKO...
AM I CLEAR, ERINA?
GOOD NIGHT.
YES, SIR...

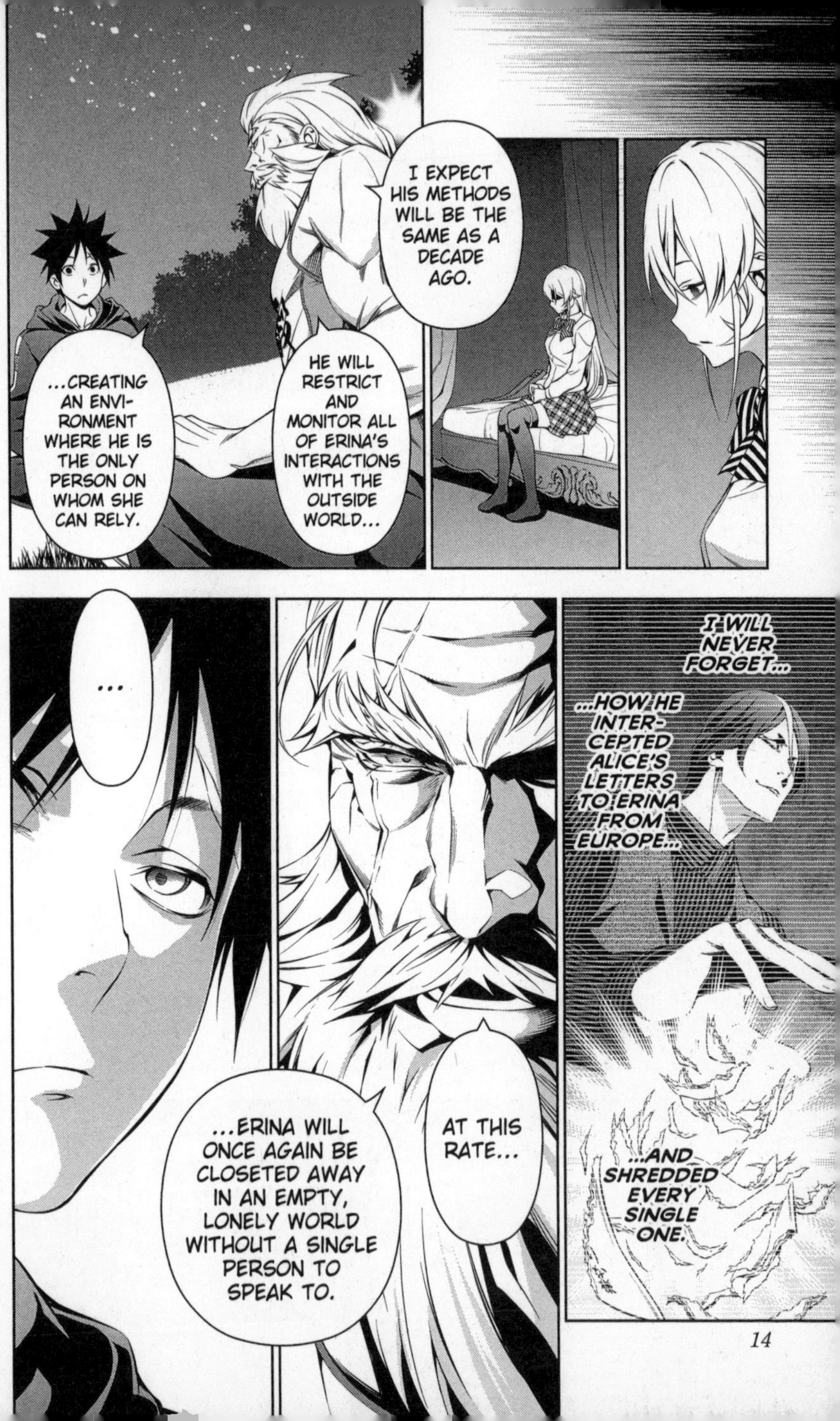
I EXPECT HIS METHODS WILL BE THE SAME AS A DECADE AGO.
HE WILL RESTRICT AND MONITOR ALL OF ERINA'S INTERACTIONS WITH THE OUTSIDE WORLD...
...CREATING AN ENVI-RONMENT WHERE HE IS THE ONLY PERSON ON WHOM SHE CAN RELY.
I WILL NEVER FORGET...
...HOW HE INTER-CEPTED ALICE'S LETTERS TO ERINA FROM EUROPE...
...AND SHREDDED EVERY SINGLE ONE.
AT THIS RATE...
...ERINA WILL ONCE AGAIN BE CLOSETED AWAY IN AN EMPTY, LONELY WORLD WITHOUT A SINGLE PERSON TO SPEAK TO.
...

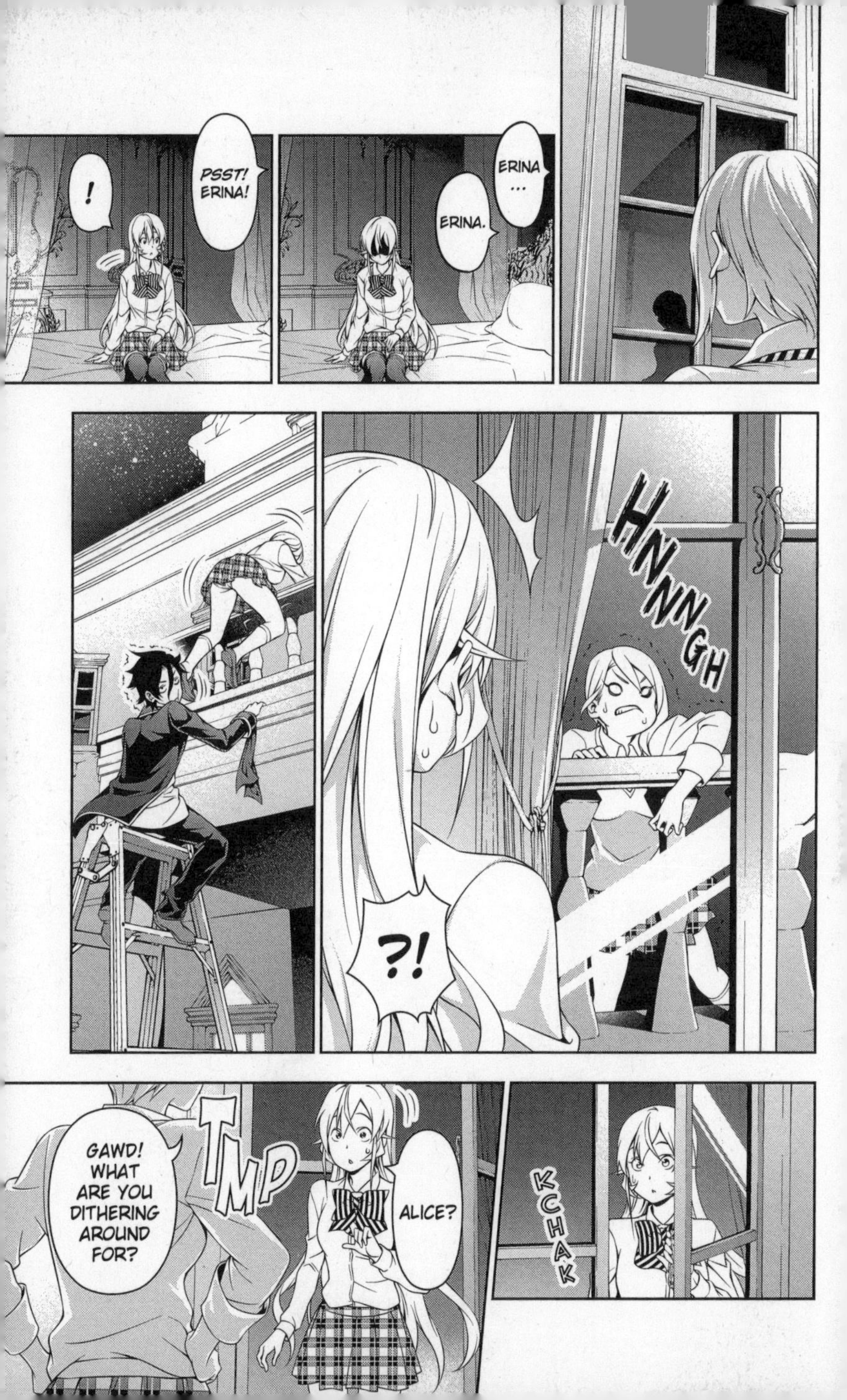
ERINA ...
ERINA.
PSST! ERINA!
!
HNNNGH
?!
KCHAK
ALICE?
TMP
GAWD! WHAT ARE YOU DITHERING AROUND FOR?

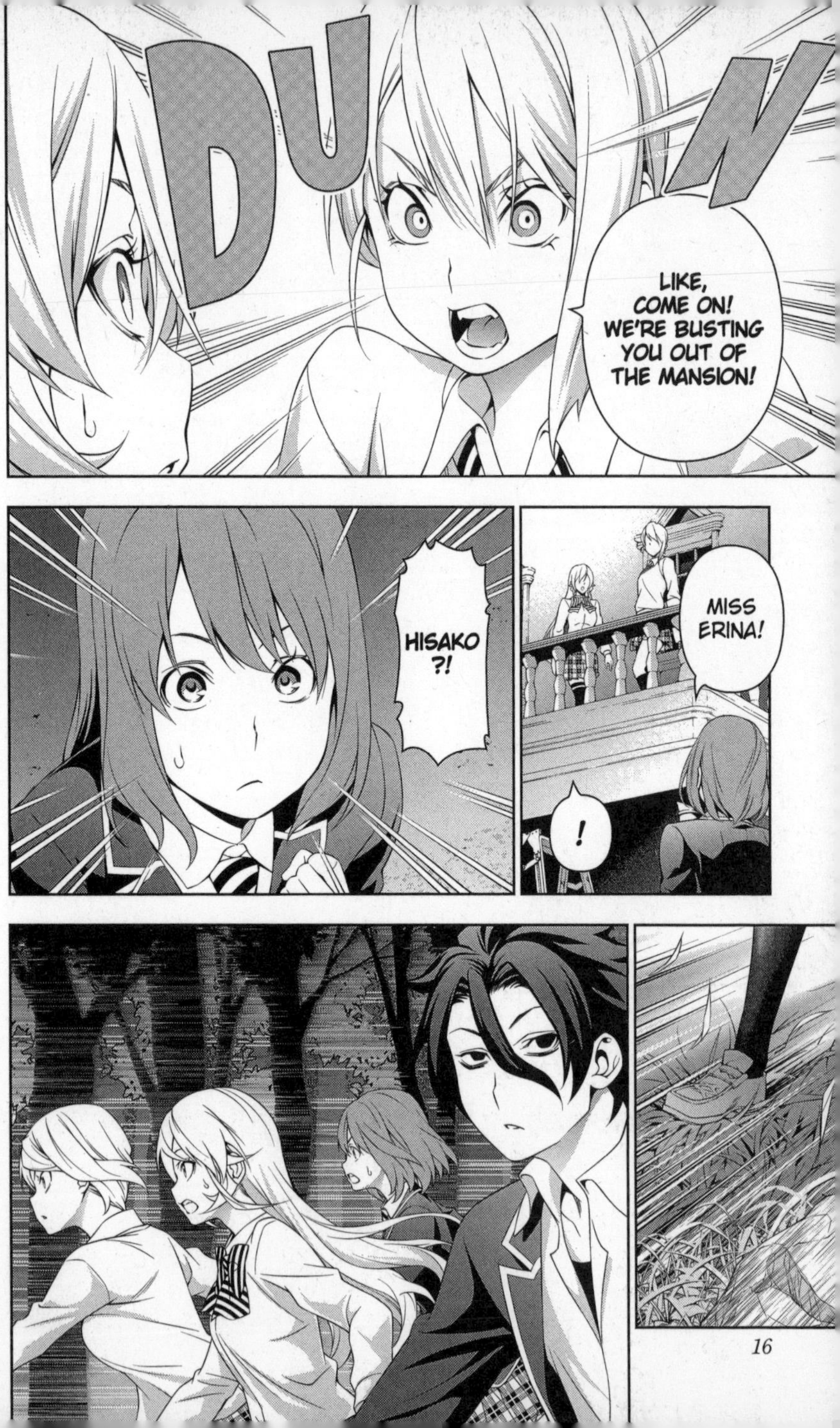
DUN
LIKE, COME ON! WE'RE BUSTING YOU OUT OF THE MANSION!
MISS ERINA!
!
HISAKO ?!

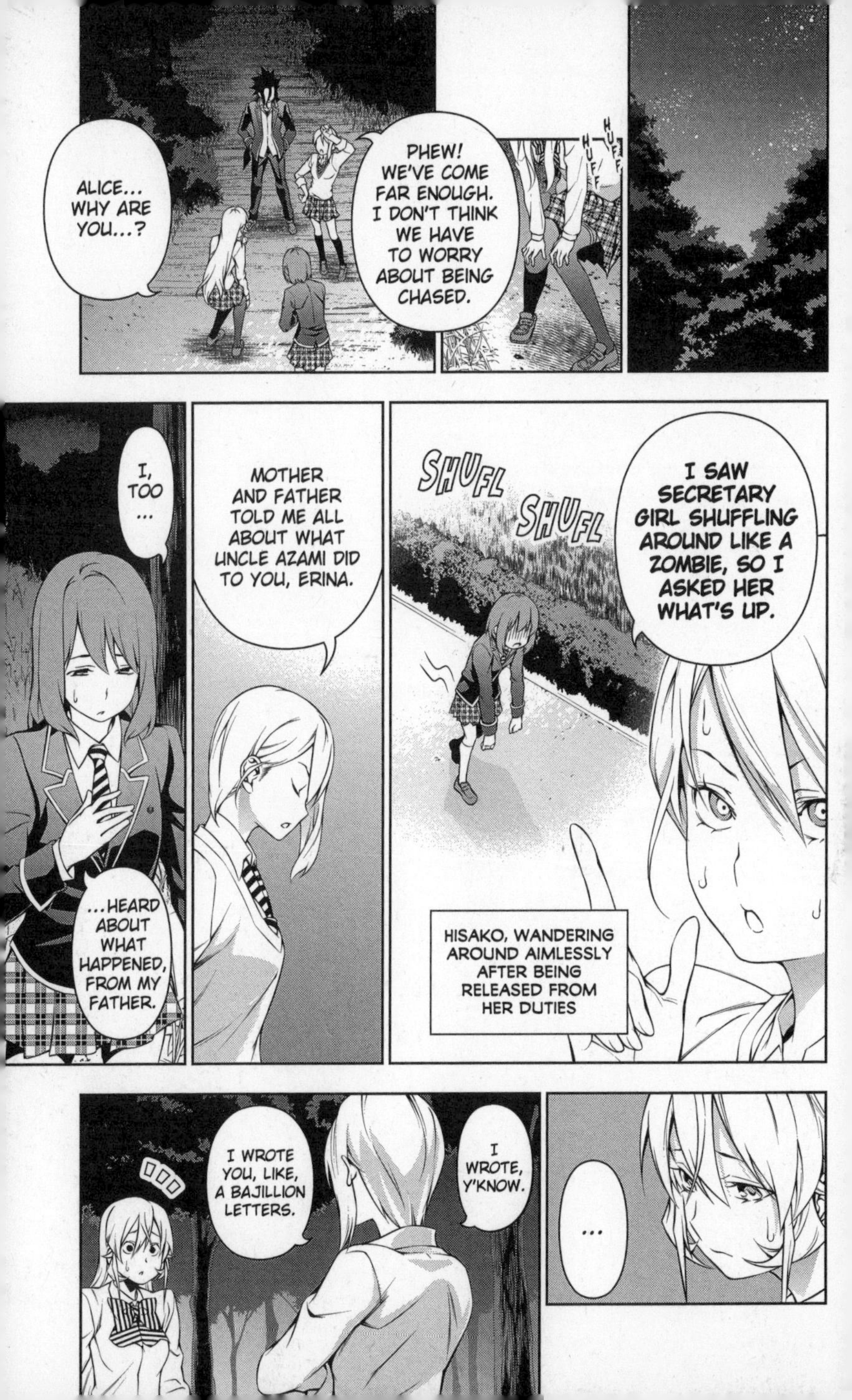
HUFF HUFF
PHEW! WE'VE COME FAR ENOUGH. I DON'T THINK WE HAVE TO WORRY ABOUT BEING CHASED.
ALICE... WHY ARE YOU...?
SHUFL SHUFL
I SAW SECRETARY GIRL SHUFFLING AROUND LIKE A ZOMBIE, SO I ASKED HER WHAT'S UP.
HISAKO, WANDERING AROUND AIMLESSLY AFTER BEING RELEASED FROM HER DUTIES
MOTHER AND FATHER TOLD ME ALL ABOUT WHAT UNCLE AZAMI DID TO YOU, ERINA.
I, TOO...
...HEARD ABOUT WHAT HAPPENED, FROM MY FATHER.
...
I WROTE, Y'KNOW.
I WROTE YOU, LIKE, A BAJILLION LETTERS.

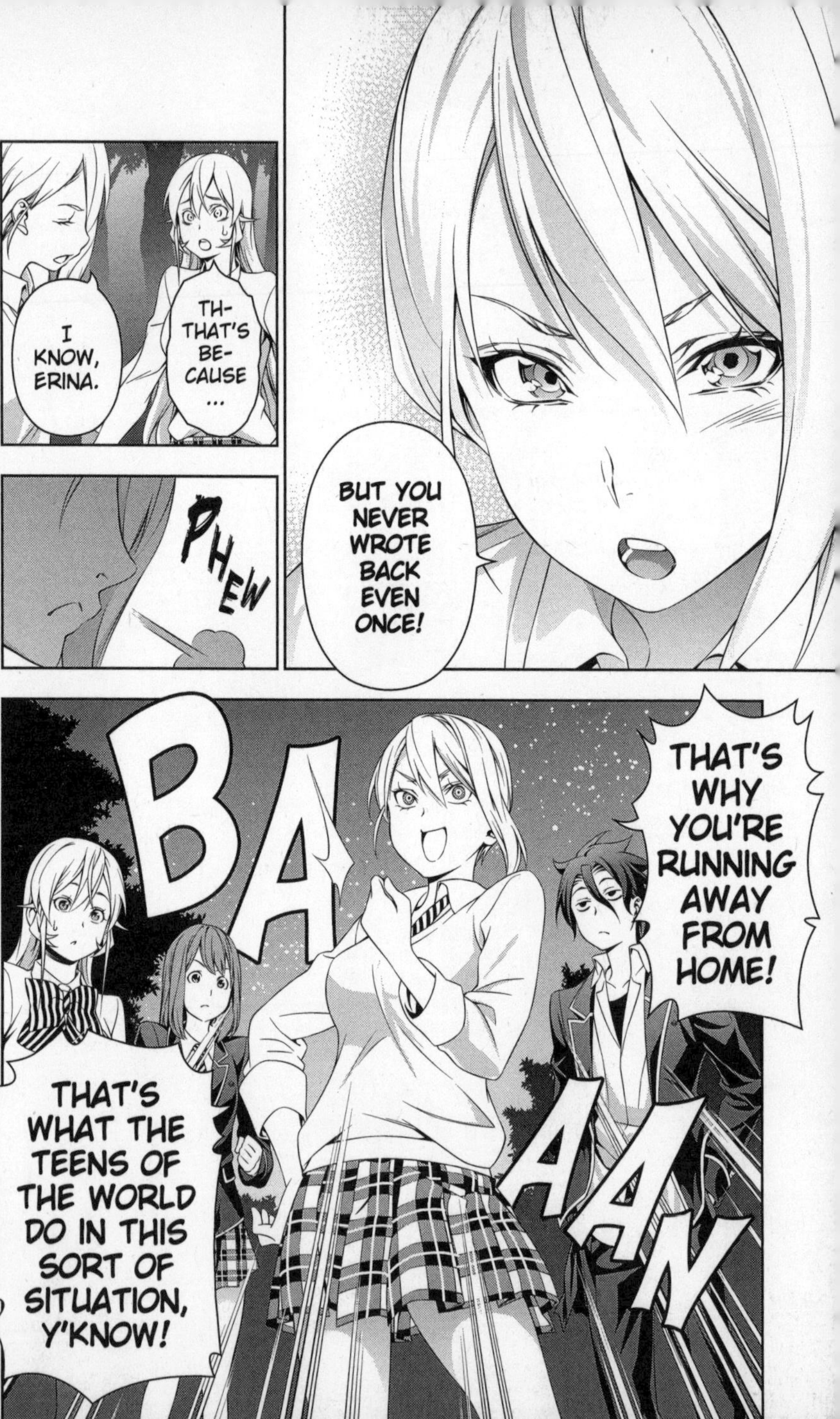
BUT YOU NEVER WROTE BACK EVEN ONCE!
TH-THAT'S BE-CAUSE...
I KNOW, ERINA.
PHEW
BA
THAT'S WHY YOU'RE RUNNING AWAY FROM HOME!
AAN
THAT'S WHAT THE TEENS OF THE WORLD DO IN THIS SORT OF SITUATION, Y'KNOW!

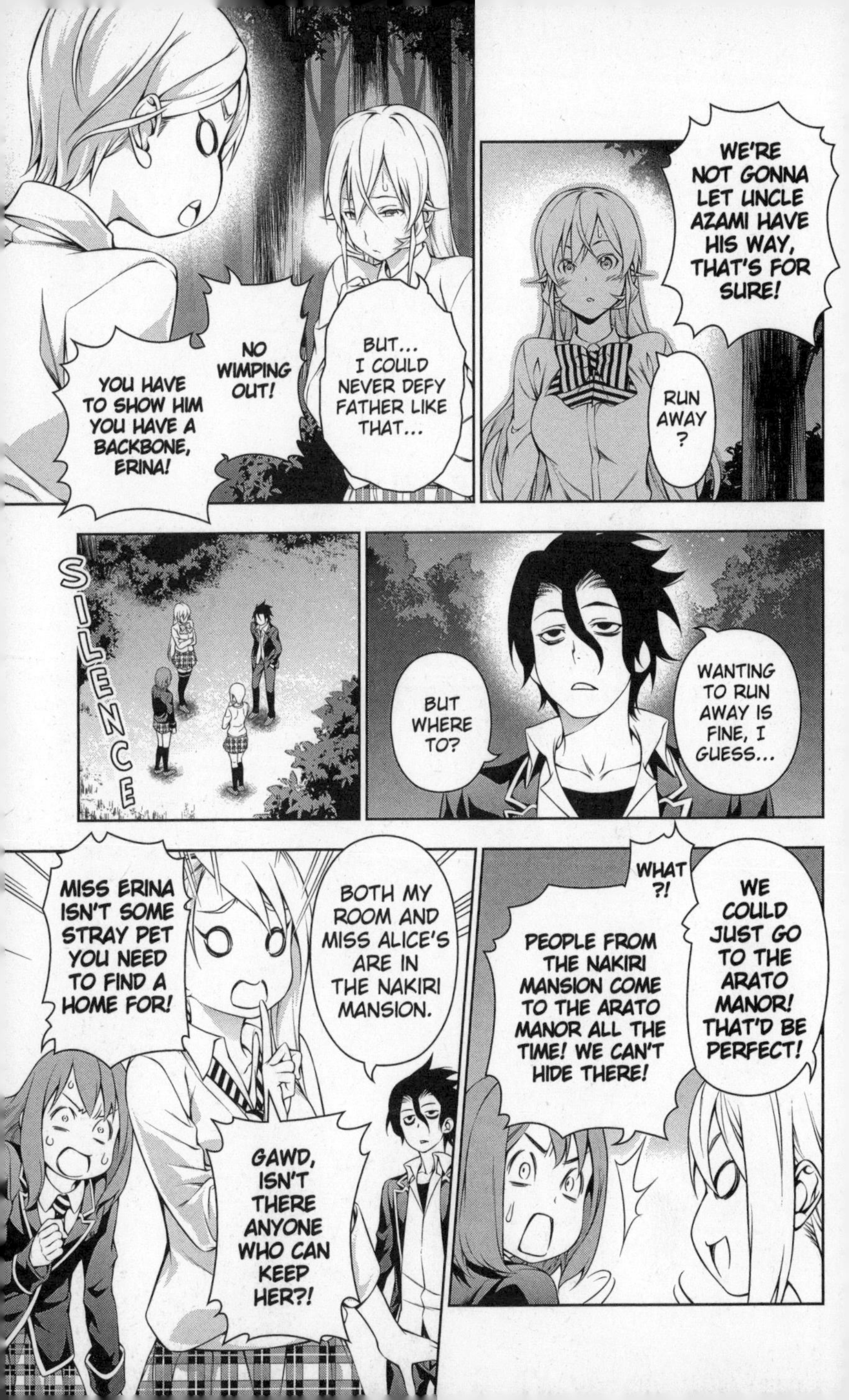
WE'RE NOT GONNA LET UNCLE AZAMI HAVE HIS WAY, THAT'S FOR SURE!
RUN AWAY?
BUT... I COULD NEVER DEFY FATHER LIKE THAT...
NO WIMPING OUT!
YOU HAVE TO SHOW HIM YOU HAVE A BACKBONE, ERINA!
WANTING TO RUN AWAY IS FINE, I GUESS...
BUT WHERE TO?
SILENCE
WE COULD JUST GO TO THE ARATO MANOR! THAT'D BE PERFECT!
WHAT?!
PEOPLE FROM THE NAKIRI MANSION COME TO THE ARATO MANOR ALL THE TIME! WE CAN'T HIDE THERE!
BOTH MY ROOM AND MISS ALICE'S ARE IN THE NAKIRI MANSION.
MISS ERINA ISN'T SOME STRAY PET YOU NEED TO FIND A HOME FOR!
GAWD, ISN'T THERE ANYONE WHO CAN KEEP HER?!

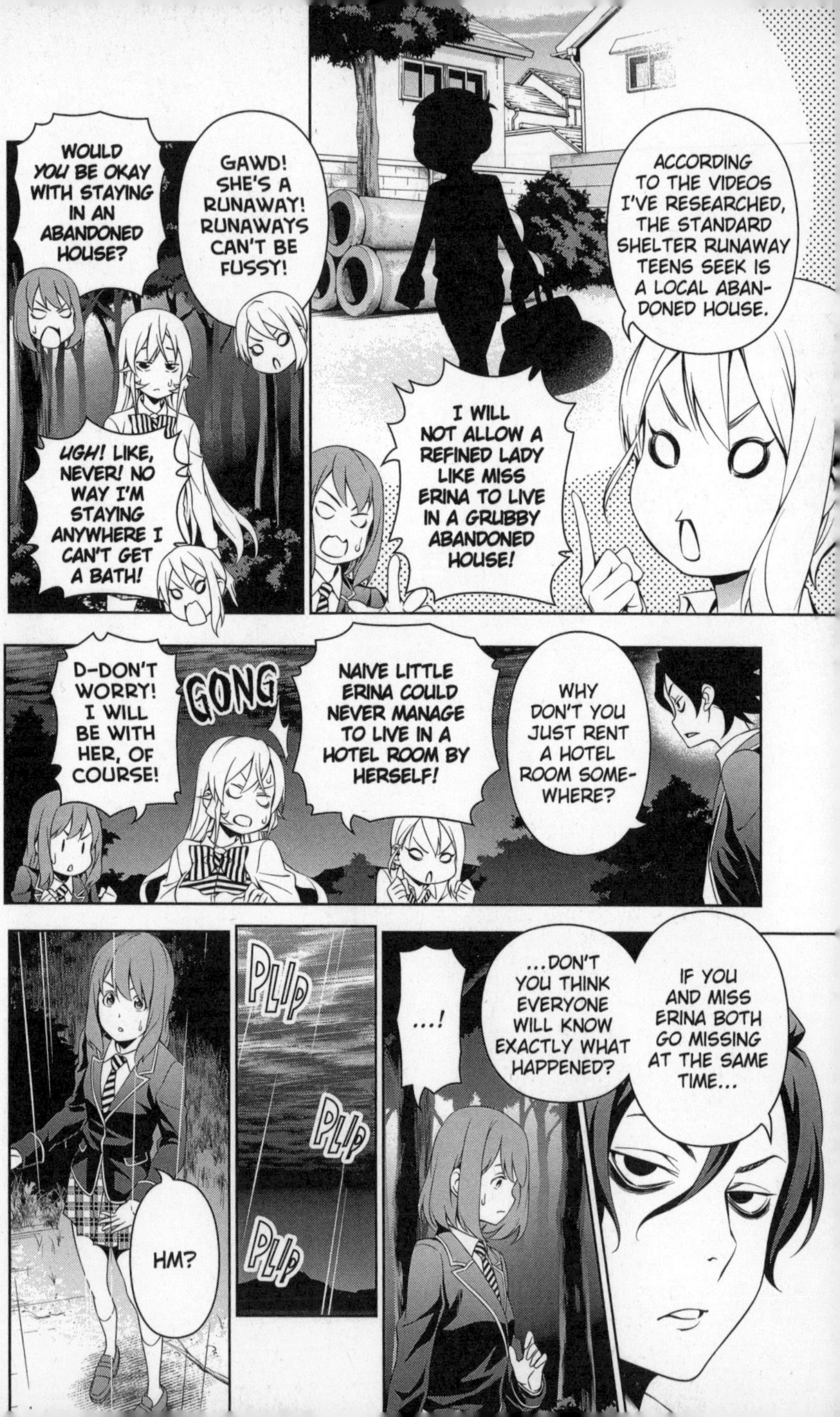
ACCORDING TO THE VIDEOS I'VE RESEARCHED, THE STANDARD SHELTER RUNAWAY TEENS SEEK IS A LOCAL ABAN-DONED HOUSE.
I WILL NOT ALLOW A REFINED LADY LIKE MISS ERINA TO LIVE IN A GRUBBY ABANDONED HOUSE!
GAWD! SHE'S A RUNAWAY! RUNAWAYS CAN'T BE FUSSY!
WOULD *YOU* BE OKAY WITH STAYING IN AN ABANDONED HOUSE?
UGH! LIKE, NEVER! NO WAY I'M STAYING ANYWHERE I CAN'T GET A BATH!
WHY DON'T YOU JUST RENT A HOTEL ROOM SOME-WHERE?
NAIVE LITTLE ERINA COULD NEVER MANAGE TO LIVE IN A HOTEL ROOM BY HERSELF!
GONG
D-DON'T WORRY! I WILL BE WITH HER, OF COURSE!
IF YOU AND MISS ERINA BOTH GO MISSING AT THE SAME TIME...
...DON'T YOU THINK EVERYONE WILL KNOW EXACTLY WHAT HAPPENED?
...!
PLIP
PLIP
PLIP
HM?

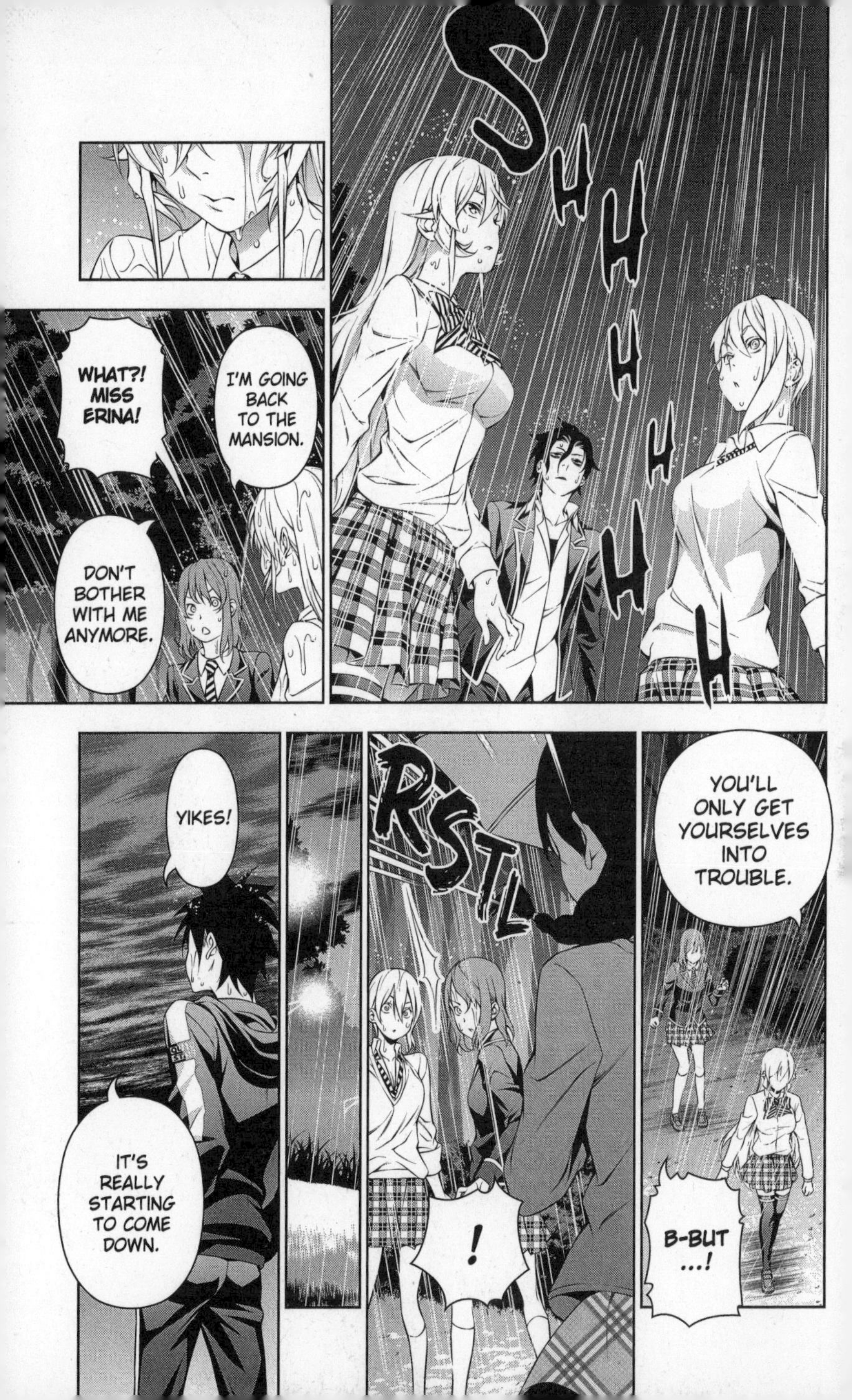
SHHHHHHH
I'M GOING BACK TO THE MANSION.
WHAT?! MISS ERINA!
DON'T BOTHER WITH ME ANYMORE.
YOU'LL ONLY GET YOURSELVES INTO TROUBLE.
B-BUT ...!
RSTL
!
YIKES!
IT'S REALLY STARTING TO COME DOWN.

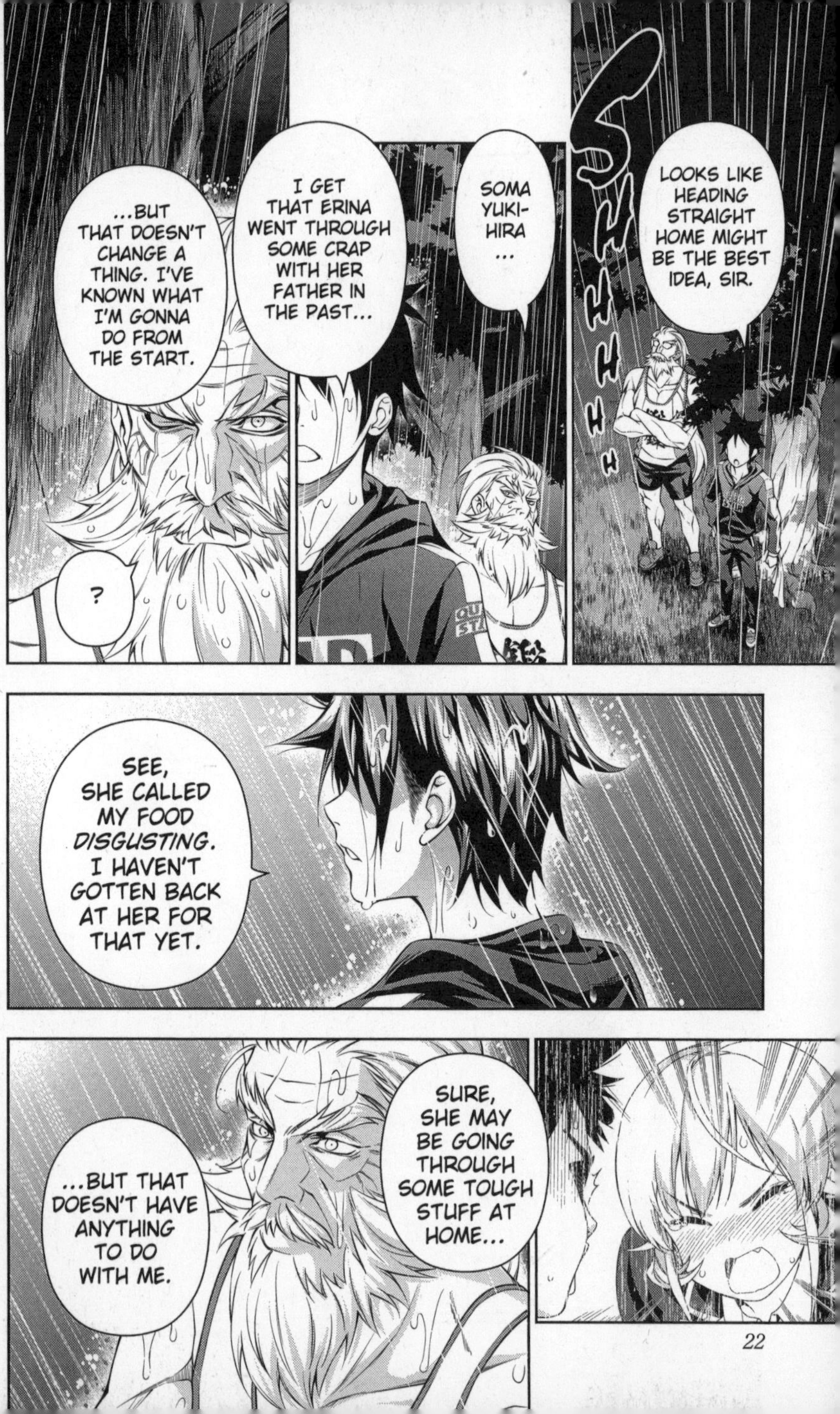
SHHHHHHH
LOOKS LIKE HEADING STRAIGHT HOME MIGHT BE THE BEST IDEA, SIR.
SOMA YUKI-HIRA...
I GET THAT ERINA WENT THROUGH SOME CRAP WITH HER FATHER IN THE PAST...
...BUT THAT DOESN'T CHANGE A THING. I'VE KNOWN WHAT I'M GONNA DO FROM THE START.
?
SEE, SHE CALLED MY FOOD *DISGUSTING*. I HAVEN'T GOTTEN BACK AT HER FOR THAT YET.
SURE, SHE MAY BE GOING THROUGH SOME TOUGH STUFF AT HOME...
...BUT THAT DOESN'T HAVE ANYTHING TO DO WITH ME.

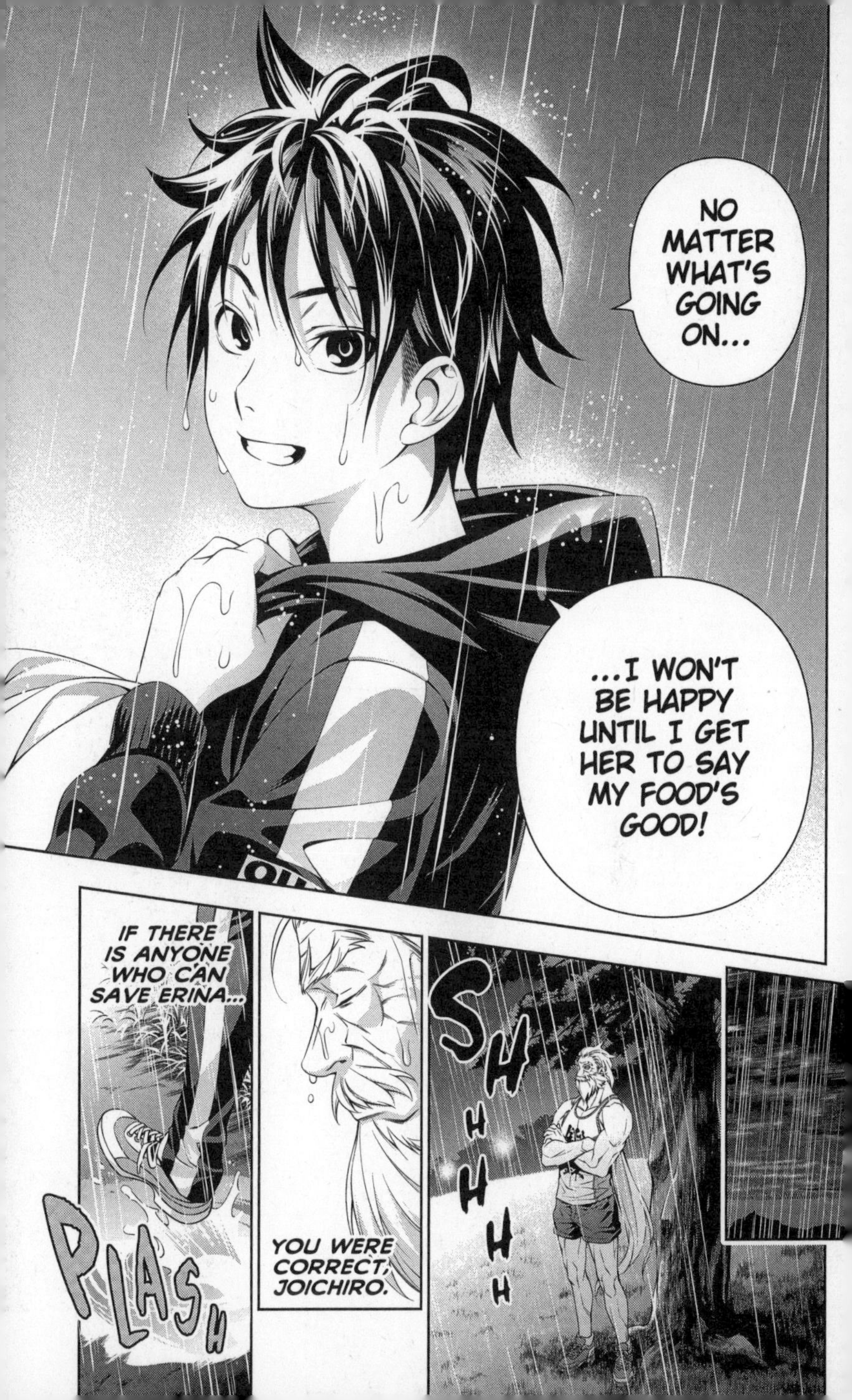
NO MATTER WHAT'S GOING ON...
...I WON'T BE HAPPY UNTIL I GET HER TO SAY MY FOOD'S GOOD!
SHHHHHH
YOU WERE CORRECT, JOICHIRO.
IF THERE IS ANYONE WHO CAN SAVE ERINA...
PLASH

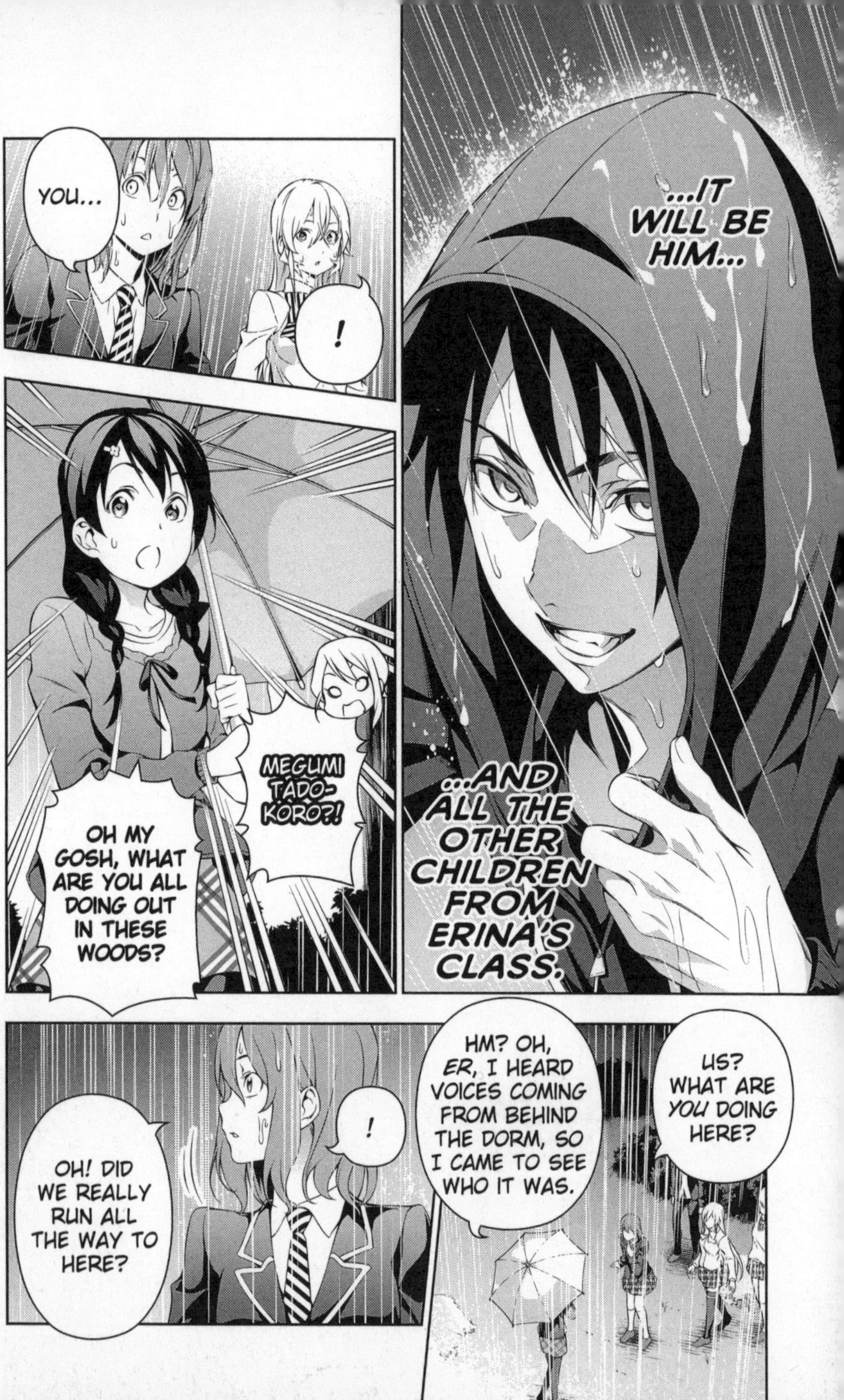
...IT WILL BE HIM...
...AND ALL THE OTHER CHILDREN FROM ERINA'S CLASS.
YOU...
!
MEGUMI TADO-KORO?!
OH MY GOSH, WHAT ARE YOU ALL DOING OUT IN THESE WOODS?
US? WHAT ARE *YOU* DOING HERE?
HM? OH, *ER*, I HEARD VOICES COMING FROM BEHIND THE DORM, SO I CAME TO SEE WHO IT WAS.
!
OH! DID WE REALLY RUN ALL THE WAY TO HERE?

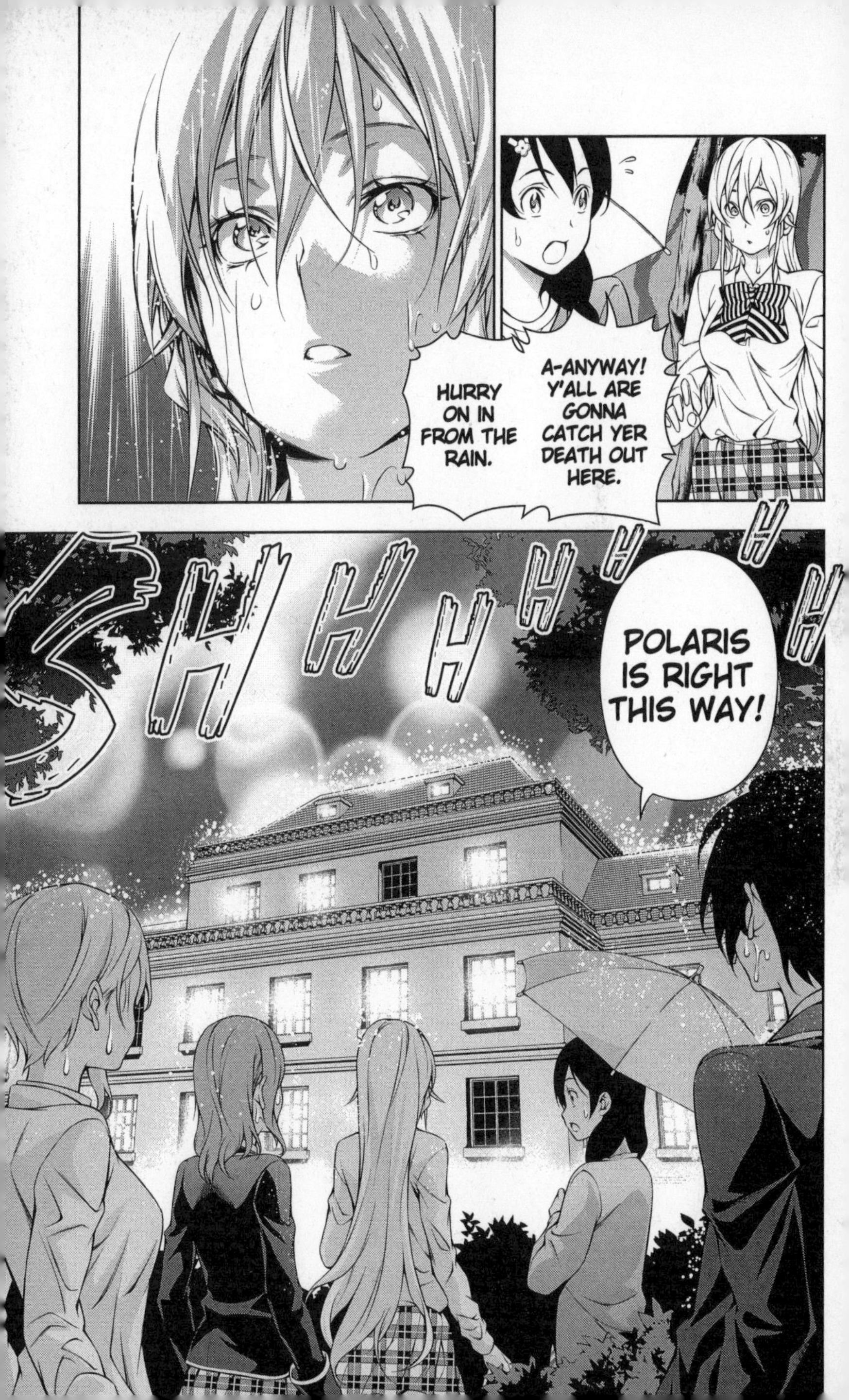
A-ANYWAY! Y'ALL ARE GONNA CATCH YER DEATH OUT HERE.
HURRY ON IN FROM THE RAIN.
SHHHHHHHHH
POLARIS IS RIGHT THIS WAY!

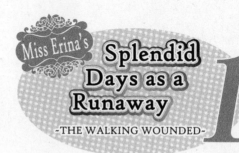

Miss Erina's Splendid Days as a Runaway 1

~THE WALKING WOUNDED~

HISAKO, LOST AND ALONE
MISS ERINA... MISS ERINA...
WOW. THAT IS, LIKE, ONE AMAZING ZOMBIE IMPRESSION.

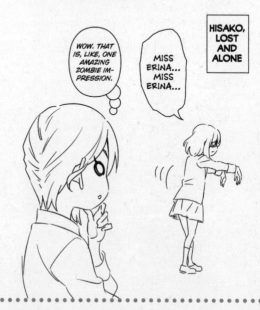

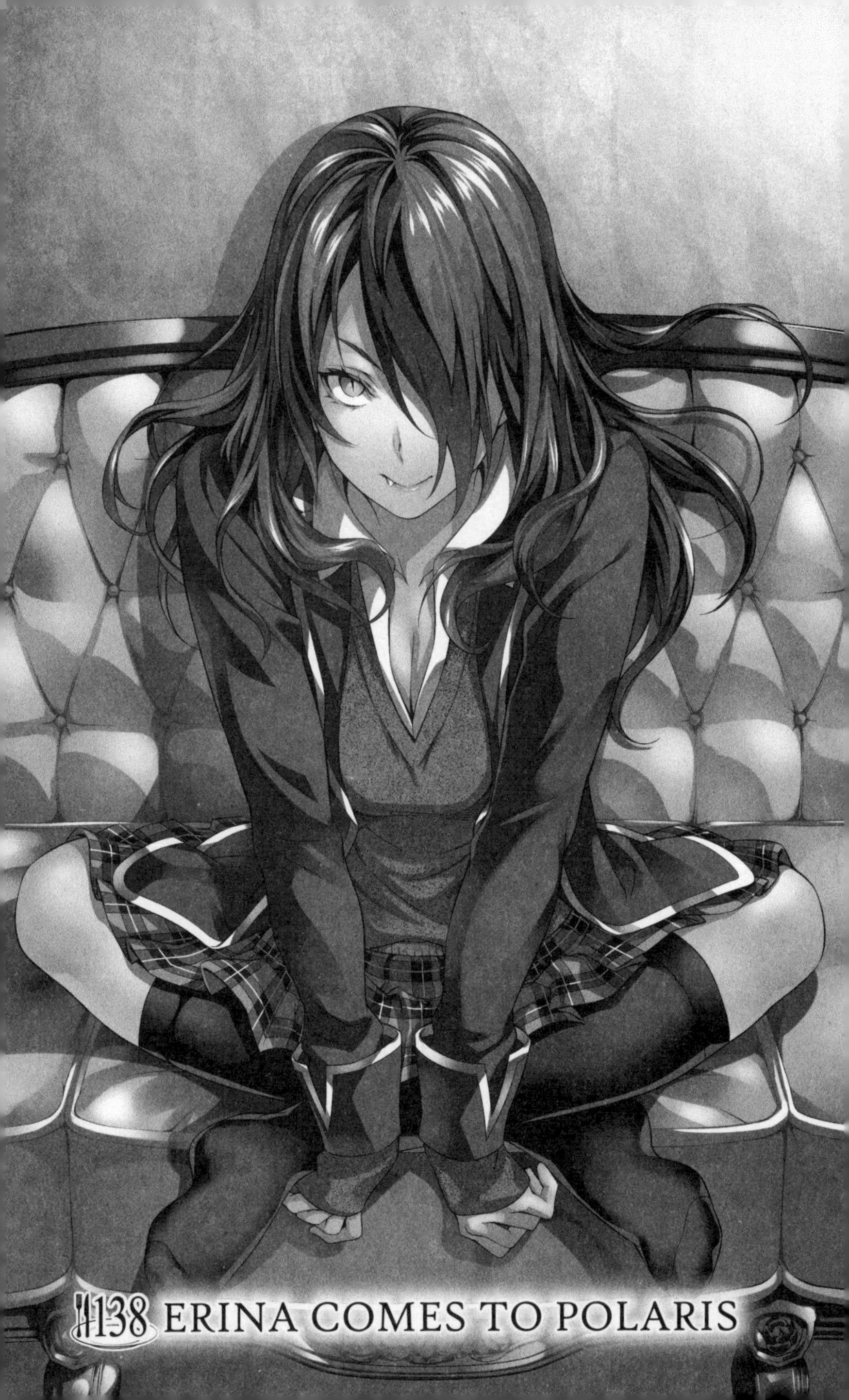

#138 ERINA COMES TO POLARIS

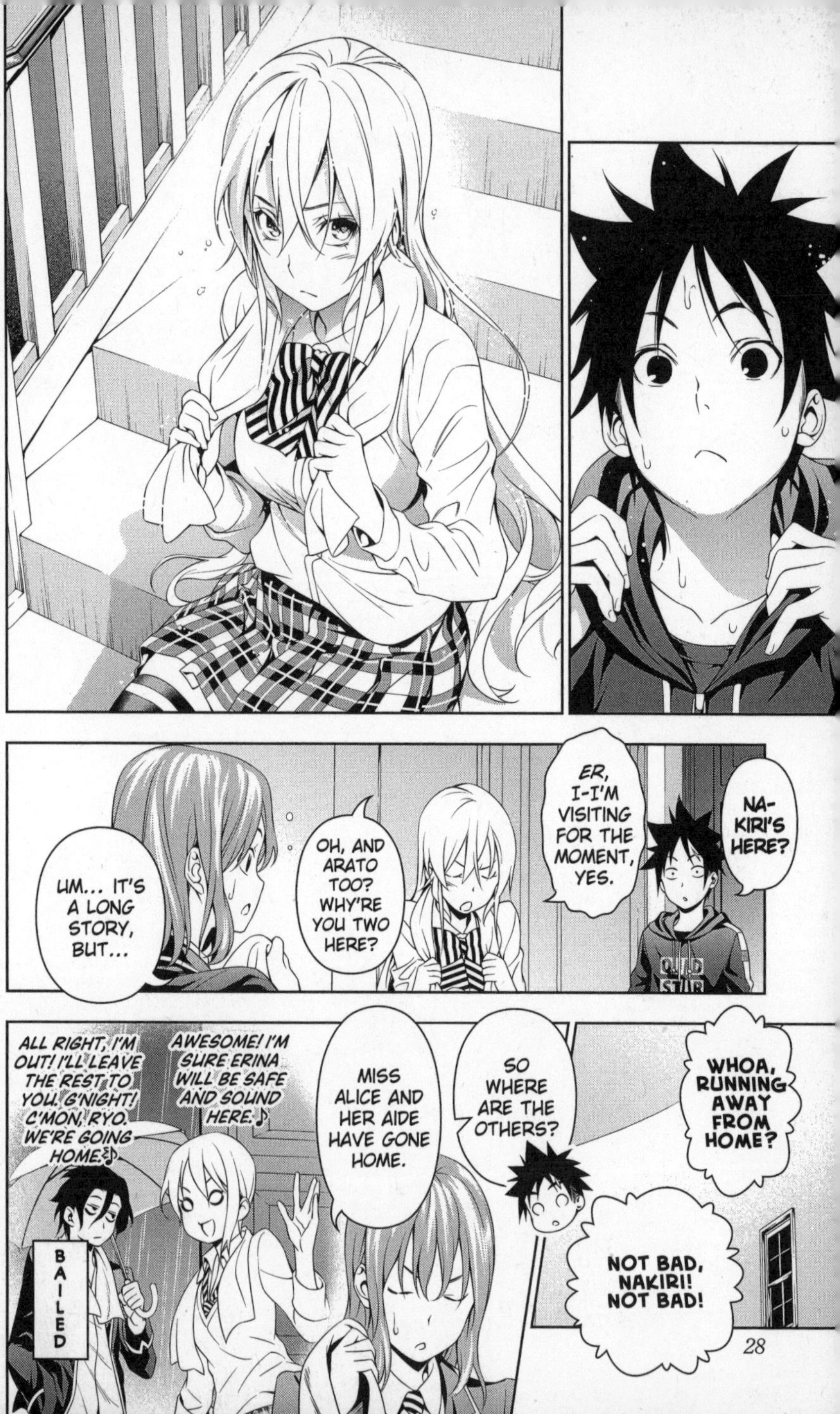
NA-KIRI'S HERE?
ER, I-I'M VISITING FOR THE MOMENT, YES.
OH, AND ARATO TOO? WHY'RE YOU TWO HERE?
UM... IT'S A LONG STORY, BUT...
WHOA, RUNNING AWAY FROM HOME?
NOT BAD, NAKIRI! NOT BAD!
SO WHERE ARE THE OTHERS?
MISS ALICE AND HER AIDE HAVE GONE HOME.
AWESOME! I'M SURE ERINA WILL BE SAFE AND SOUND HERE.♪
ALL RIGHT, I'M OUT! I'LL LEAVE THE REST TO YOU. G'NIGHT! C'MON, RYO. WE'RE GOING HOME.♪
BAILED

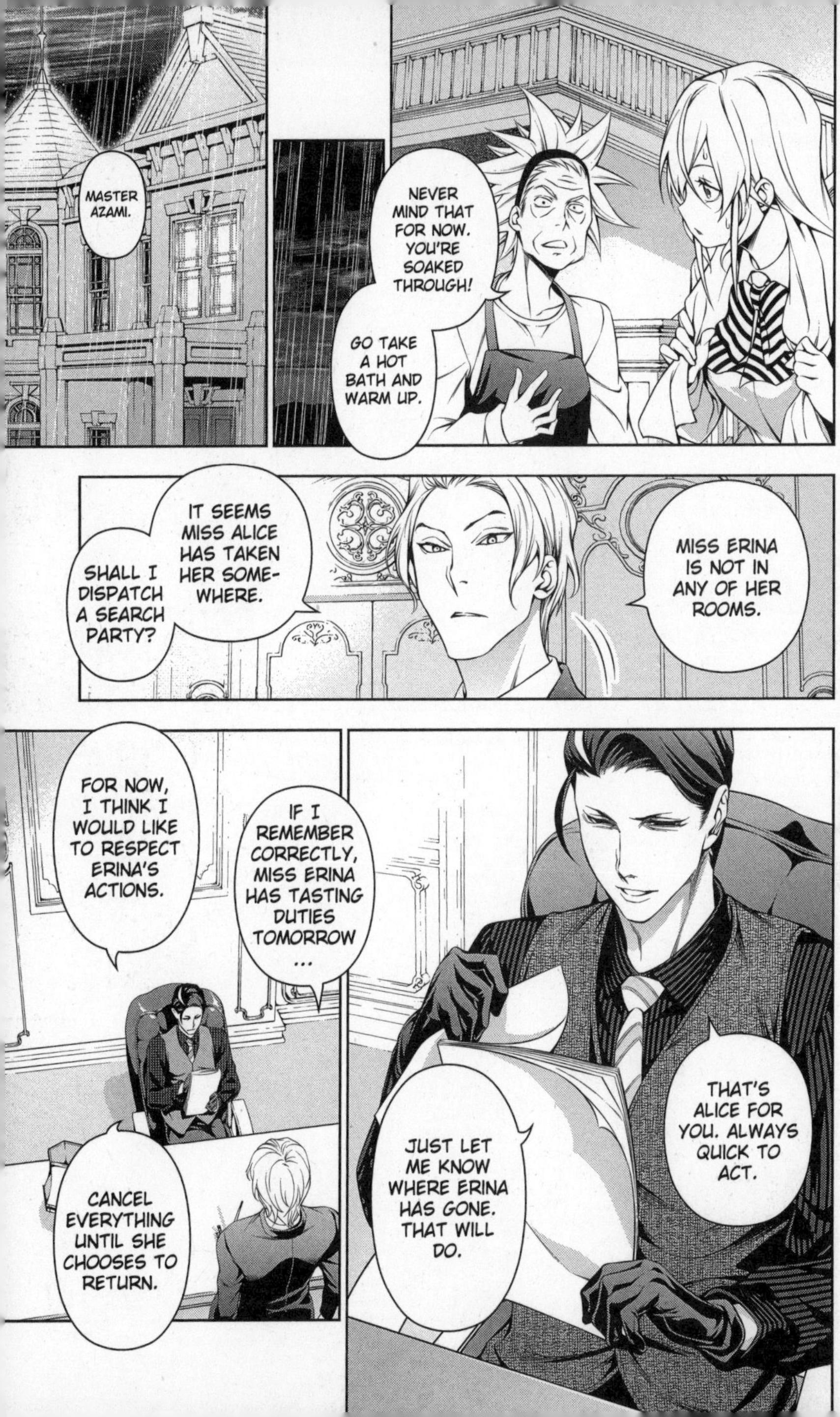
NEVER MIND THAT FOR NOW. YOU'RE SOAKED THROUGH!
GO TAKE A HOT BATH AND WARM UP.
MASTER AZAMI.
MISS ERINA IS NOT IN ANY OF HER ROOMS.
IT SEEMS MISS ALICE HAS TAKEN HER SOME-WHERE.
SHALL I DISPATCH A SEARCH PARTY?
THAT'S ALICE FOR YOU. ALWAYS QUICK TO ACT.
JUST LET ME KNOW WHERE ERINA HAS GONE. THAT WILL DO.
IF I REMEMBER CORRECTLY, MISS ERINA HAS TASTING DUTIES TOMORROW...
FOR NOW, I THINK I WOULD LIKE TO RESPECT ERINA'S ACTIONS.
CANCEL EVERYTHING UNTIL SHE CHOOSES TO RETURN.

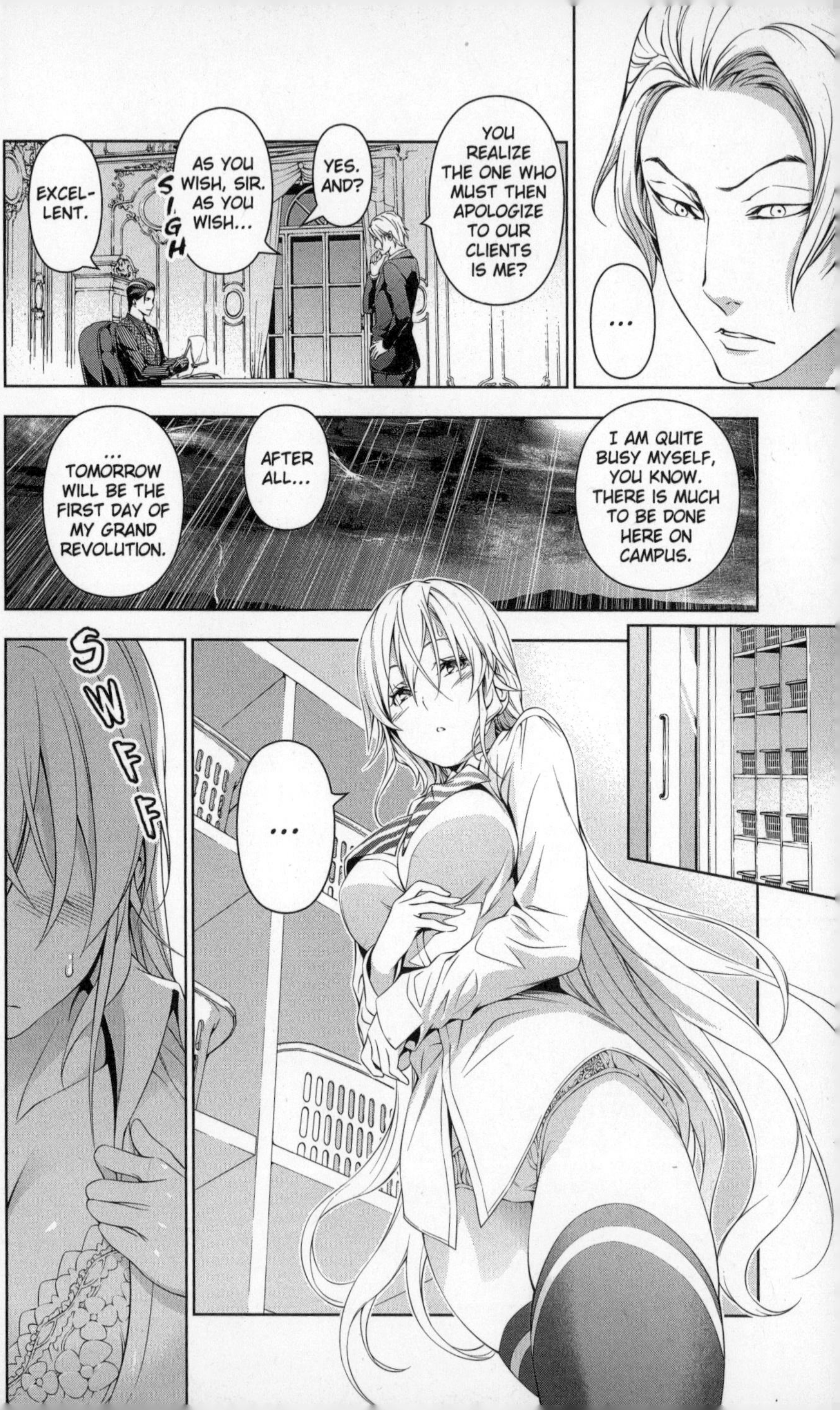
...
YOU REALIZE THE ONE WHO MUST THEN APOLOGIZE TO OUR CLIENTS IS ME?
YES. AND?
SIGH
AS YOU WISH, SIR. AS YOU WISH...
EXCEL-LENT.
I AM QUITE BUSY MYSELF, YOU KNOW. THERE IS MUCH TO BE DONE HERE ON CAMPUS.
AFTER ALL...
... TOMORROW WILL BE THE FIRST DAY OF MY GRAND REVOLUTION.
...
SWFF

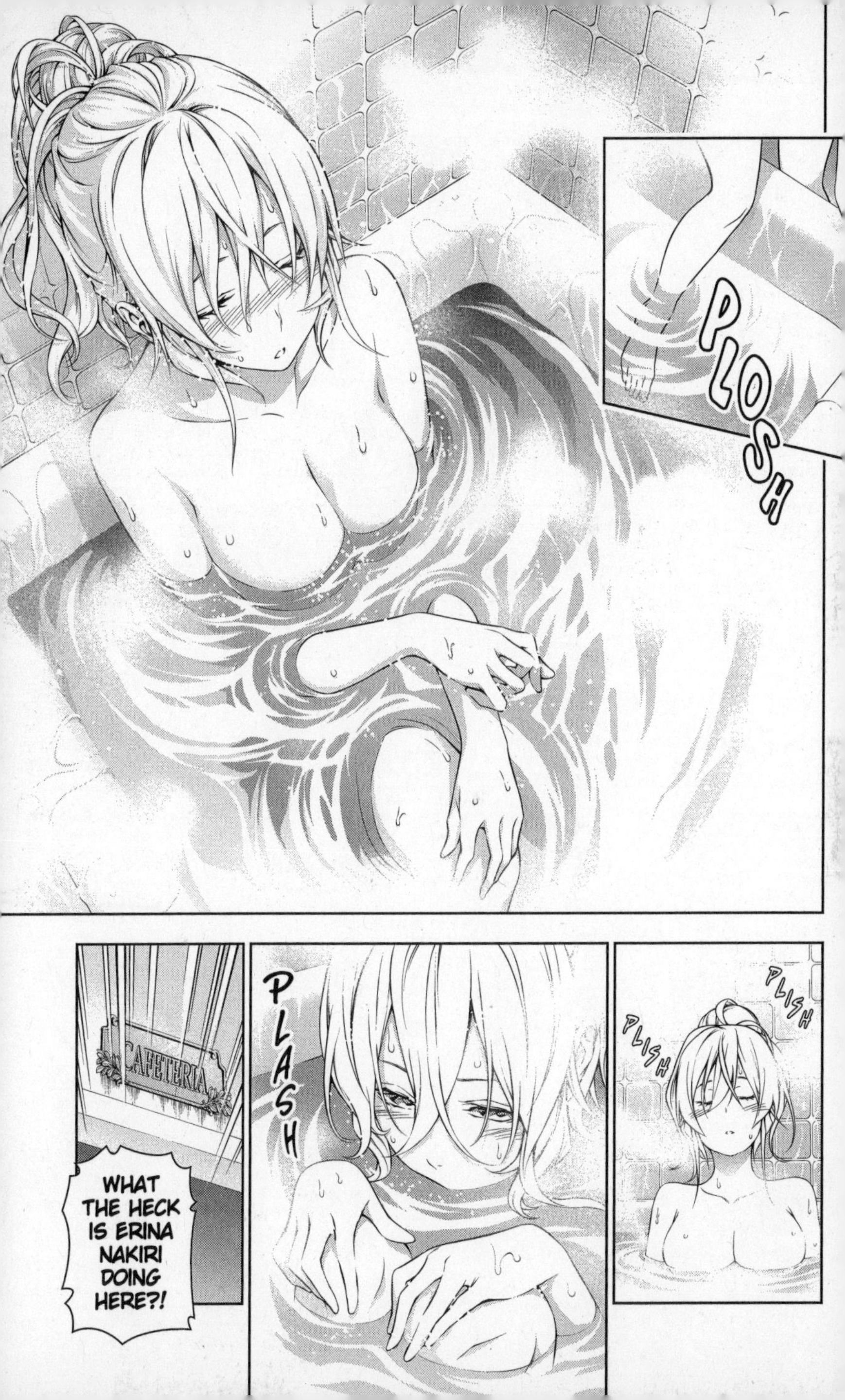
PLOSH
PLISH
PLISH
PLASH
CAFETERIA
WHAT THE HECK IS ERINA NAKIRI DOING HERE?!

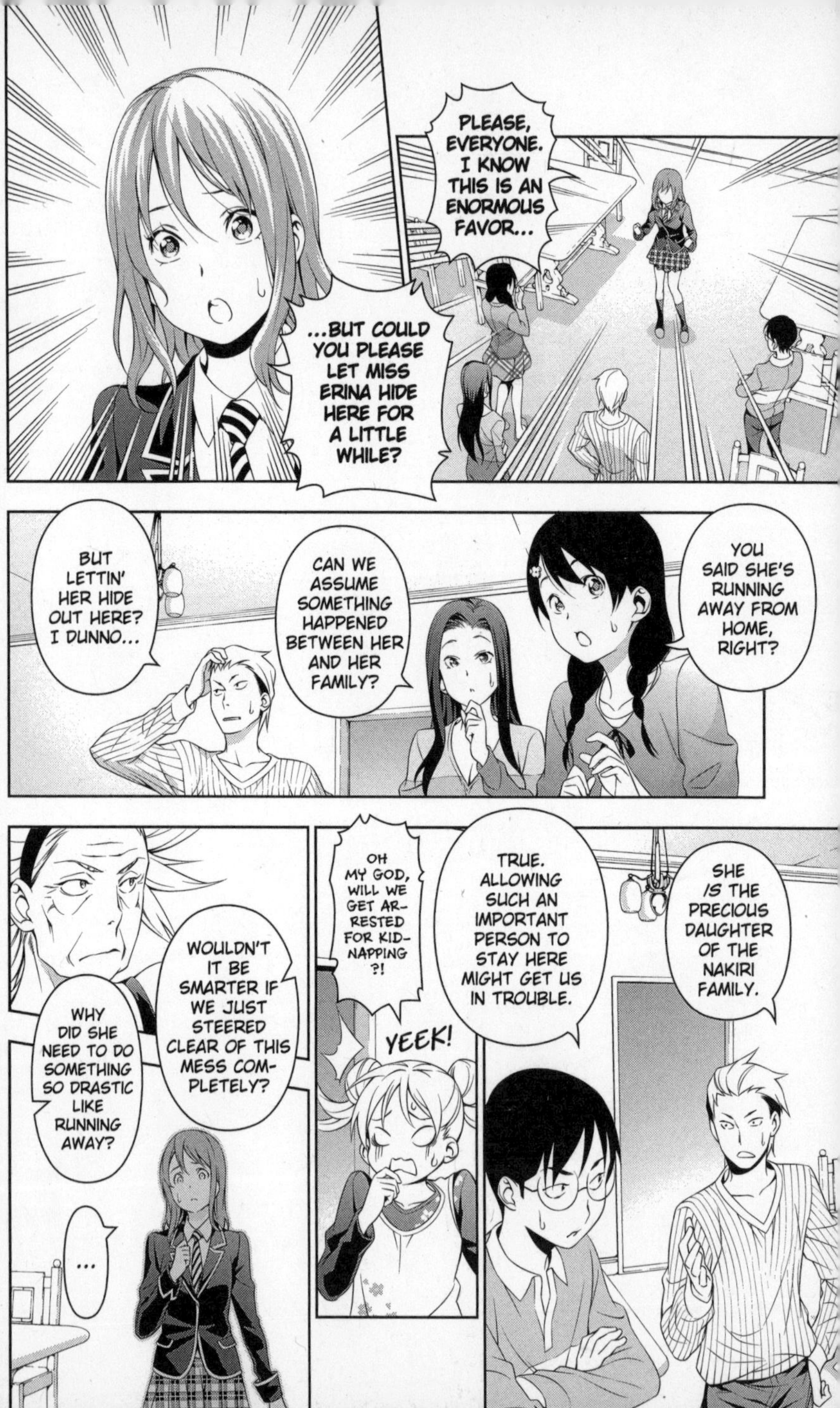

PLEASE, EVERYONE. I KNOW THIS IS AN ENORMOUS FAVOR...
...BUT COULD YOU PLEASE LET MISS ERINA HIDE HERE FOR A LITTLE WHILE?
YOU SAID SHE'S RUNNING AWAY FROM HOME, RIGHT?
CAN WE ASSUME SOMETHING HAPPENED BETWEEN HER AND HER FAMILY?
BUT LETTIN' HER HIDE OUT HERE? I DUNNO...
SHE IS THE PRECIOUS DAUGHTER OF THE NAKIRI FAMILY.
TRUE. ALLOWING SUCH AN IMPORTANT PERSON TO STAY HERE MIGHT GET US IN TROUBLE.
OH MY GOD, WILL WE GET ARRESTED FOR KIDNAPPING?!
YEEK!
WOULDN'T IT BE SMARTER IF WE JUST STEERED CLEAR OF THIS MESS COMPLETELY?
WHY DID SHE NEED TO DO SOMETHING SO DRASTIC LIKE RUNNING AWAY?
...

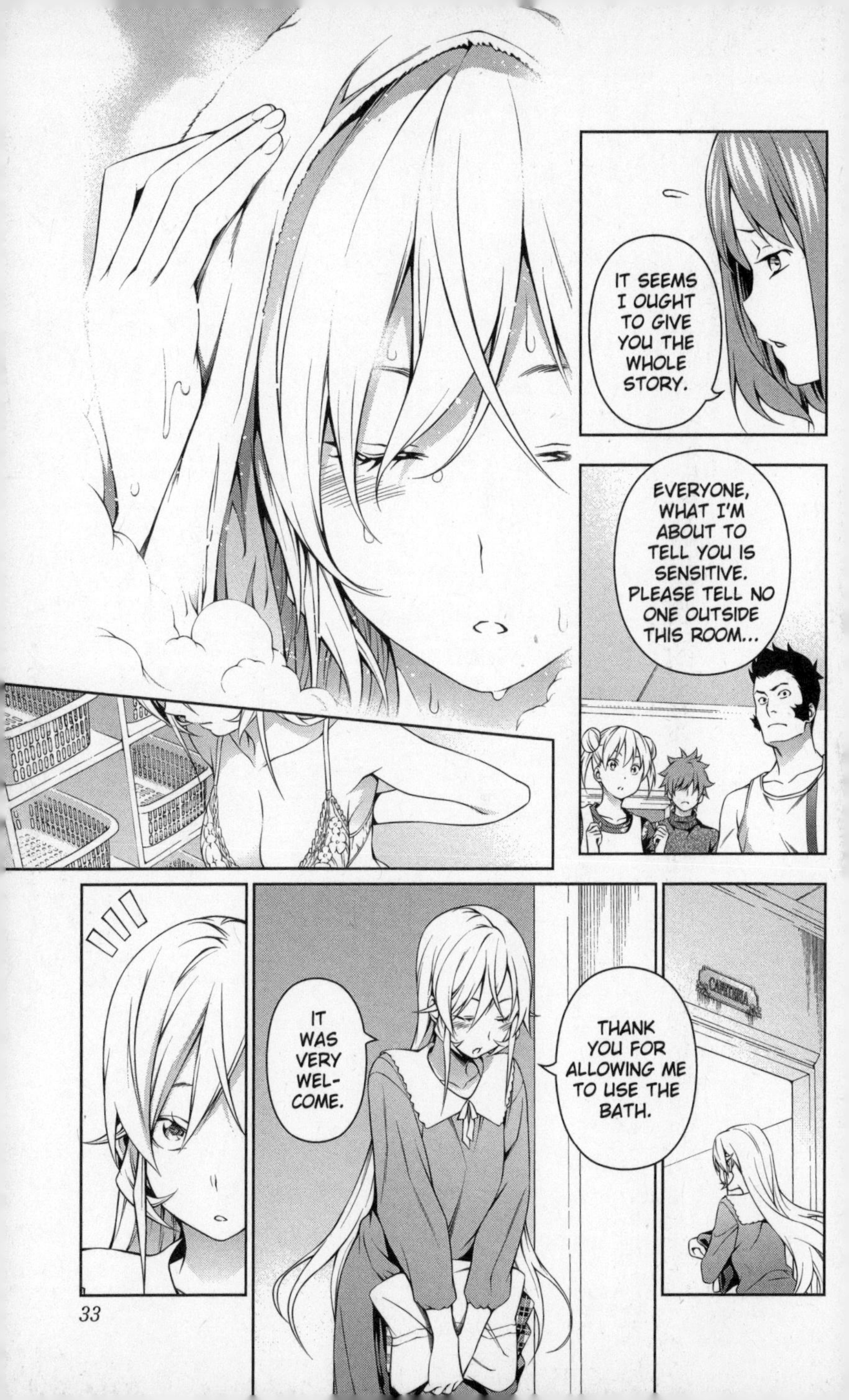
IT SEEMS I OUGHT TO GIVE YOU THE WHOLE STORY.
EVERYONE, WHAT I'M ABOUT TO TELL YOU IS SENSITIVE. PLEASE TELL NO ONE OUTSIDE THIS ROOM...
THANK YOU FOR ALLOWING ME TO USE THE BATH.
IT WAS VERY WEL-COME.

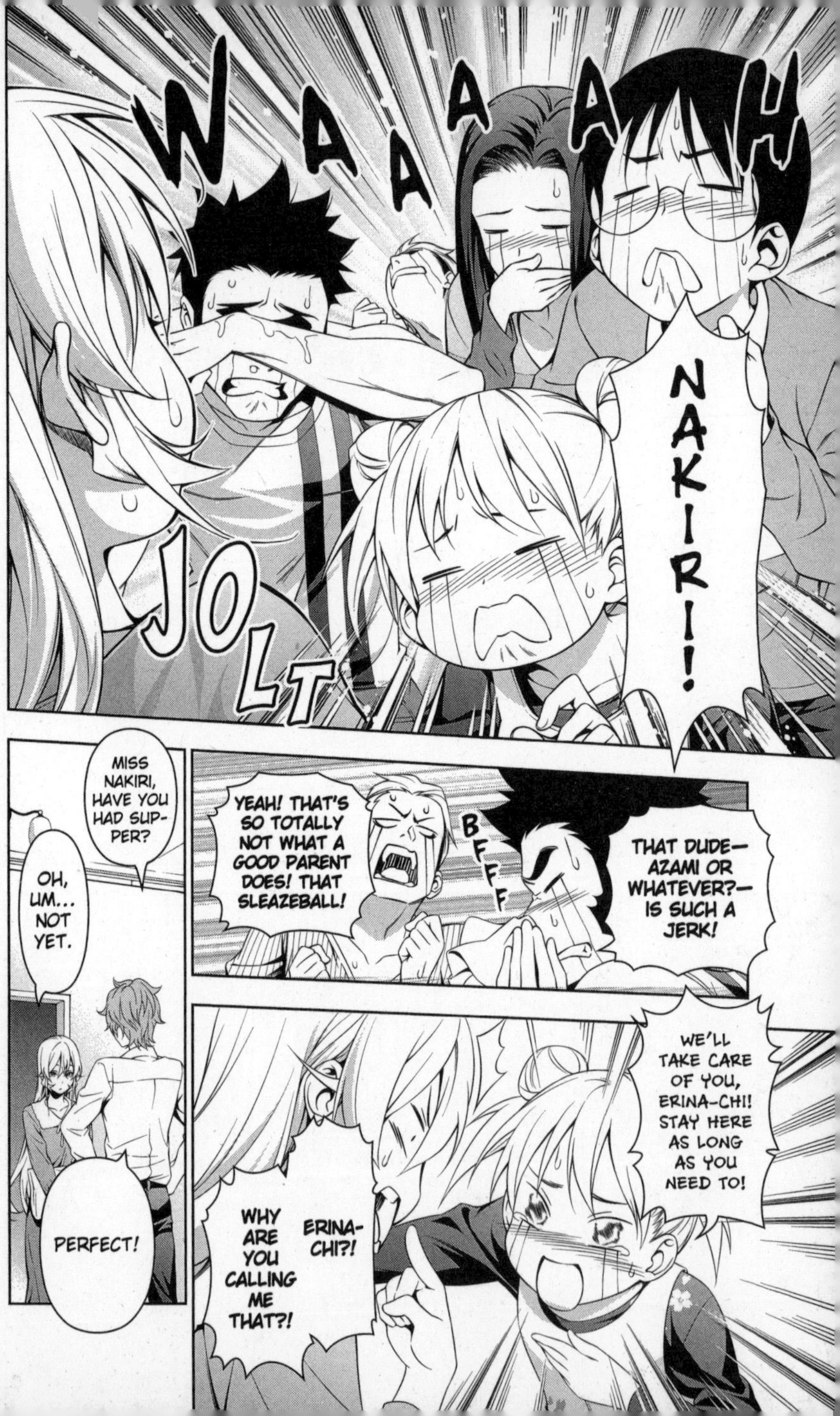
WAAAAH
NAKIRI!
JOLT
THAT DUDE—AZAMI OR WHATEVER?—IS SUCH A JERK!
BFFF
YEAH! THAT'S SO TOTALLY NOT WHAT A GOOD PARENT DOES! THAT SLEAZEBALL!
WE'LL TAKE CARE OF YOU, ERINA-CHI! STAY HERE AS LONG AS YOU NEED TO!
ERINA-CHI?!
WHY ARE YOU CALLING ME THAT?!
MISS NAKIRI, HAVE YOU HAD SUP-PER?
OH, UM... NOT YET.
PERFECT!

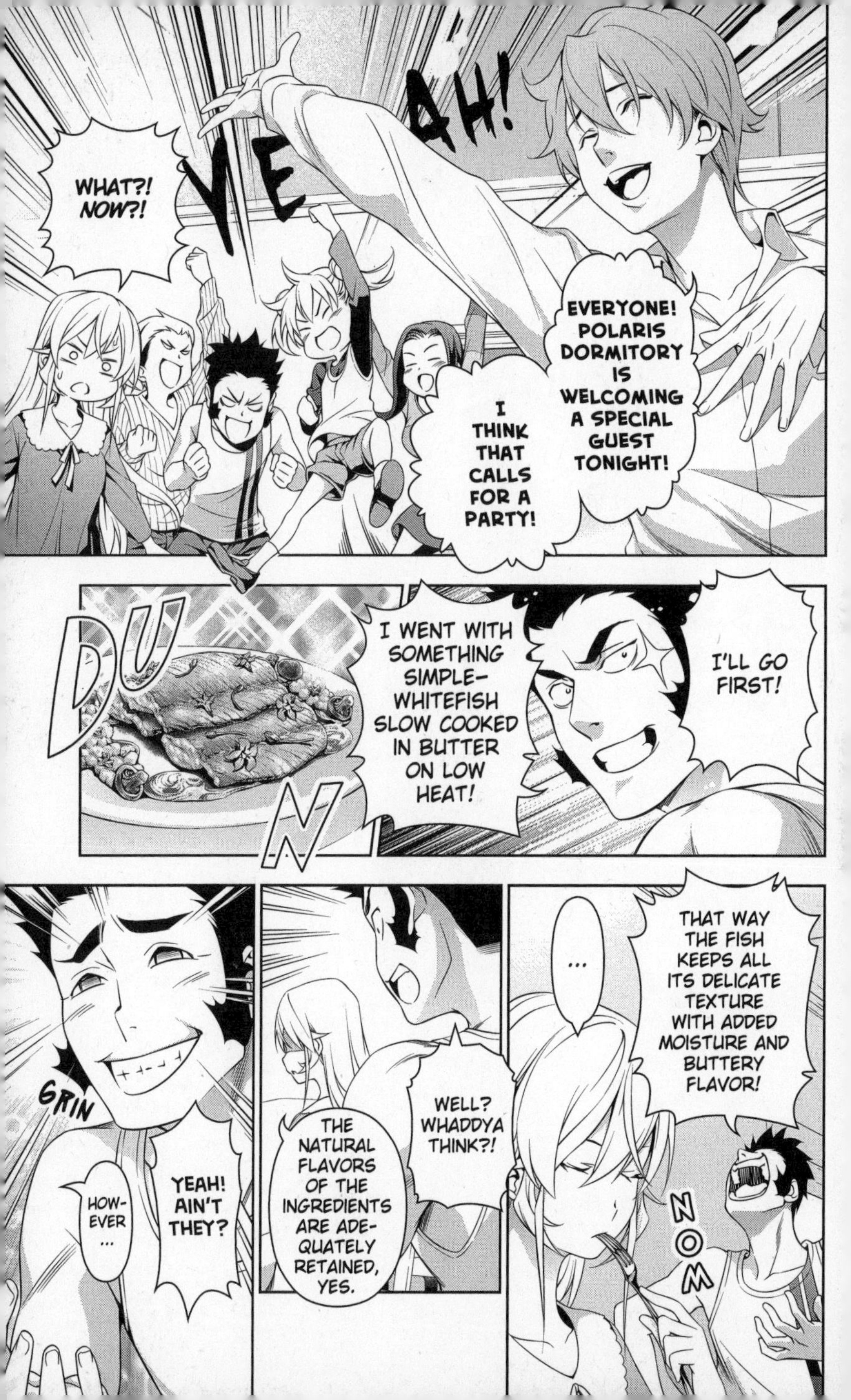
YEAH!
EVERYONE! POLARIS DORMITORY IS WELCOMING A SPECIAL GUEST TONIGHT!
I THINK THAT CALLS FOR A PARTY!
WHAT?! NOW?!
I'LL GO FIRST!
I WENT WITH SOMETHING SIMPLE-WHITEFISH SLOW COOKED IN BUTTER ON LOW HEAT!
DUN
THAT WAY THE FISH KEEPS ALL ITS DELICATE TEXTURE WITH ADDED MOISTURE AND BUTTERY FLAVOR!
...
NOM
WELL? WHADDYA THINK?!
THE NATURAL FLAVORS OF THE INGREDIENTS ARE ADEQUATELY RETAINED, YES.
GRIN
YEAH! AIN'T THEY?
HOW-EVER ...

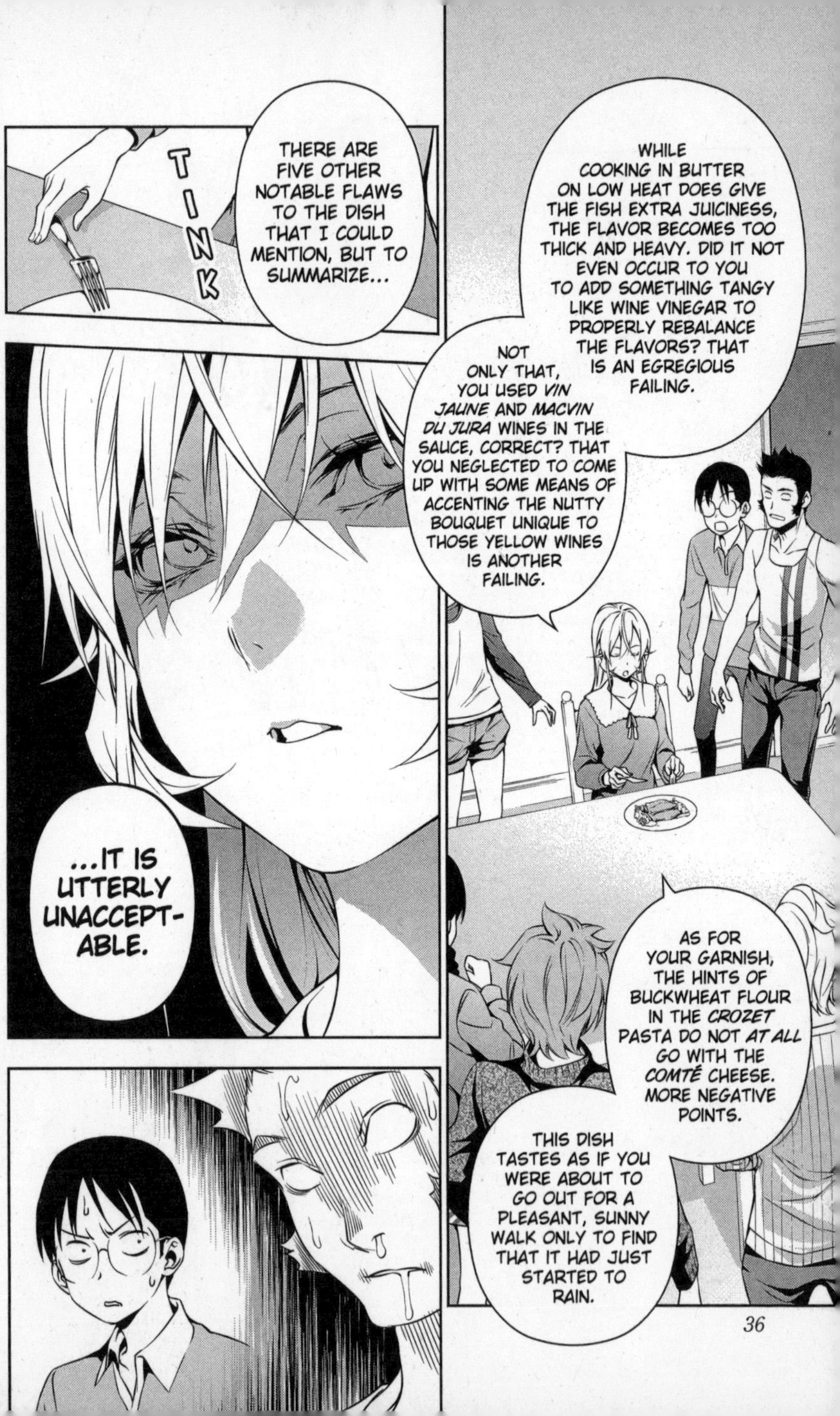
WHILE COOKING IN BUTTER ON LOW HEAT DOES GIVE THE FISH EXTRA JUICINESS, THE FLAVOR BECOMES TOO THICK AND HEAVY. DID IT NOT EVEN OCCUR TO YOU TO ADD SOMETHING TANGY LIKE WINE VINEGAR TO PROPERLY REBALANCE THE FLAVORS? THAT IS AN EGREGIOUS FAILING.
NOT ONLY THAT, YOU USED *VIN JAUNE* AND *MACVIN DU JURA* WINES IN THE SAUCE, CORRECT? THAT YOU NEGLECTED TO COME UP WITH SOME MEANS OF ACCENTING THE NUTTY BOUQUET UNIQUE TO THOSE YELLOW WINES IS ANOTHER FAILING.
AS FOR YOUR GARNISH, THE HINTS OF BUCKWHEAT FLOUR IN THE *CROZET* PASTA DO NOT *AT ALL* GO WITH THE *COMTÉ* CHEESE. MORE NEGATIVE POINTS.
THIS DISH TASTES AS IF YOU WERE ABOUT TO GO OUT FOR A PLEASANT, SUNNY WALK ONLY TO FIND THAT IT HAD JUST STARTED TO RAIN.
TINK
THERE ARE FIVE OTHER NOTABLE FLAWS TO THE DISH THAT I COULD MENTION, BUT TO SUMMARIZE...
...IT IS UTTERLY UNACCEPTABLE.

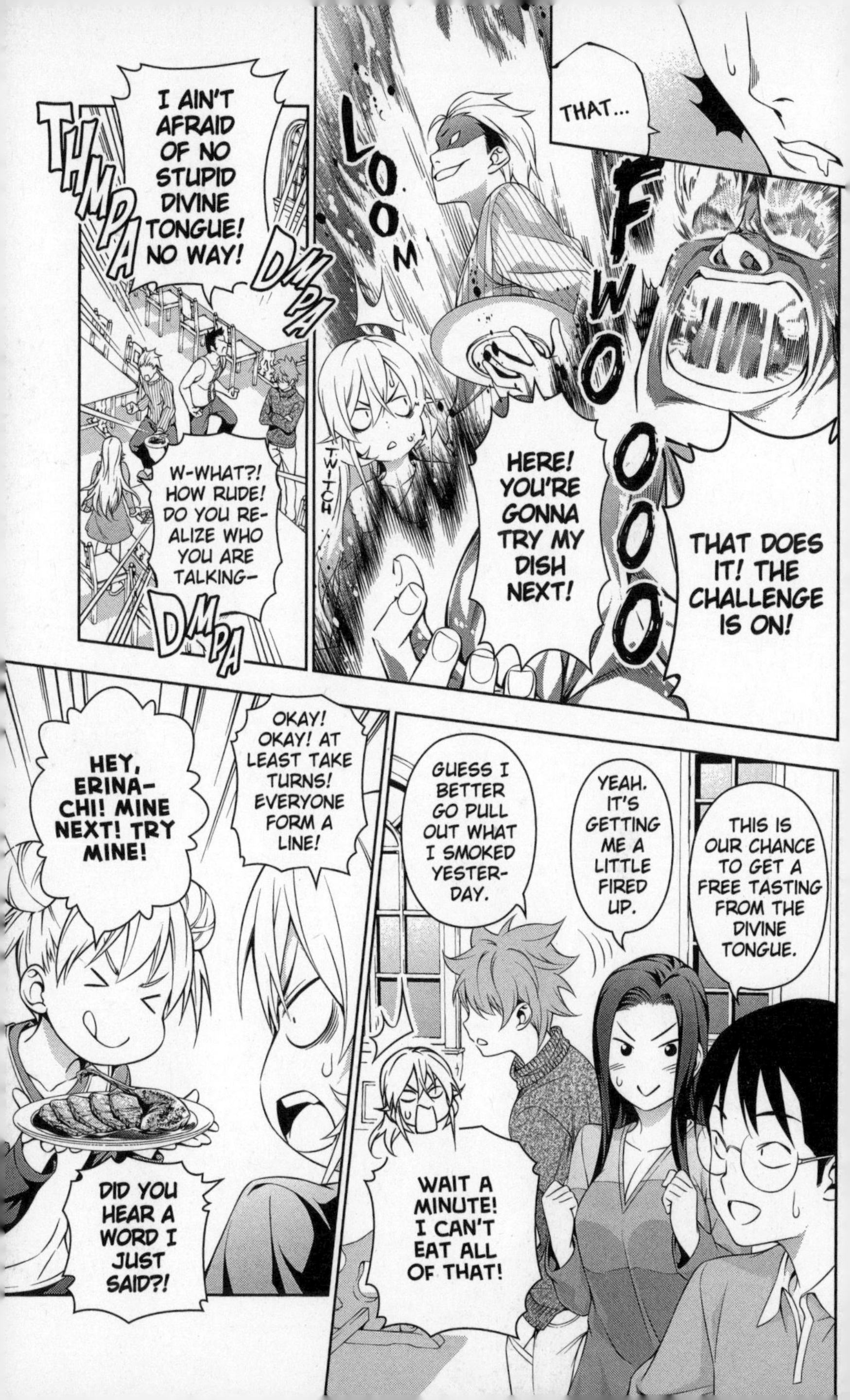
THAT...
FWOOOOOO
THAT DOES IT! THE CHALLENGE IS ON!
LOOM
HERE! YOU'RE GONNA TRY MY DISH NEXT!
TWITCH
I AIN'T AFRAID OF NO STUPID DIVINE TONGUE! NO WAY!
THMPA
DMPA
W-WHAT?! HOW RUDE! DO YOU RE-ALIZE WHO YOU ARE TALKING-
DMPA
THIS IS OUR CHANCE TO GET A FREE TASTING FROM THE DIVINE TONGUE.
YEAH. IT'S GETTING ME A LITTLE FIRED UP.
GUESS I BETTER GO PULL OUT WHAT I SMOKED YESTER-DAY.
WAIT A MINUTE! I CAN'T EAT ALL OF THAT!
OKAY! OKAY! AT LEAST TAKE TURNS! EVERYONE FORM A LINE!
HEY, ERINA-CHI! MINE NEXT! TRY MINE!
DID YOU HEAR A WORD I JUST SAID?!

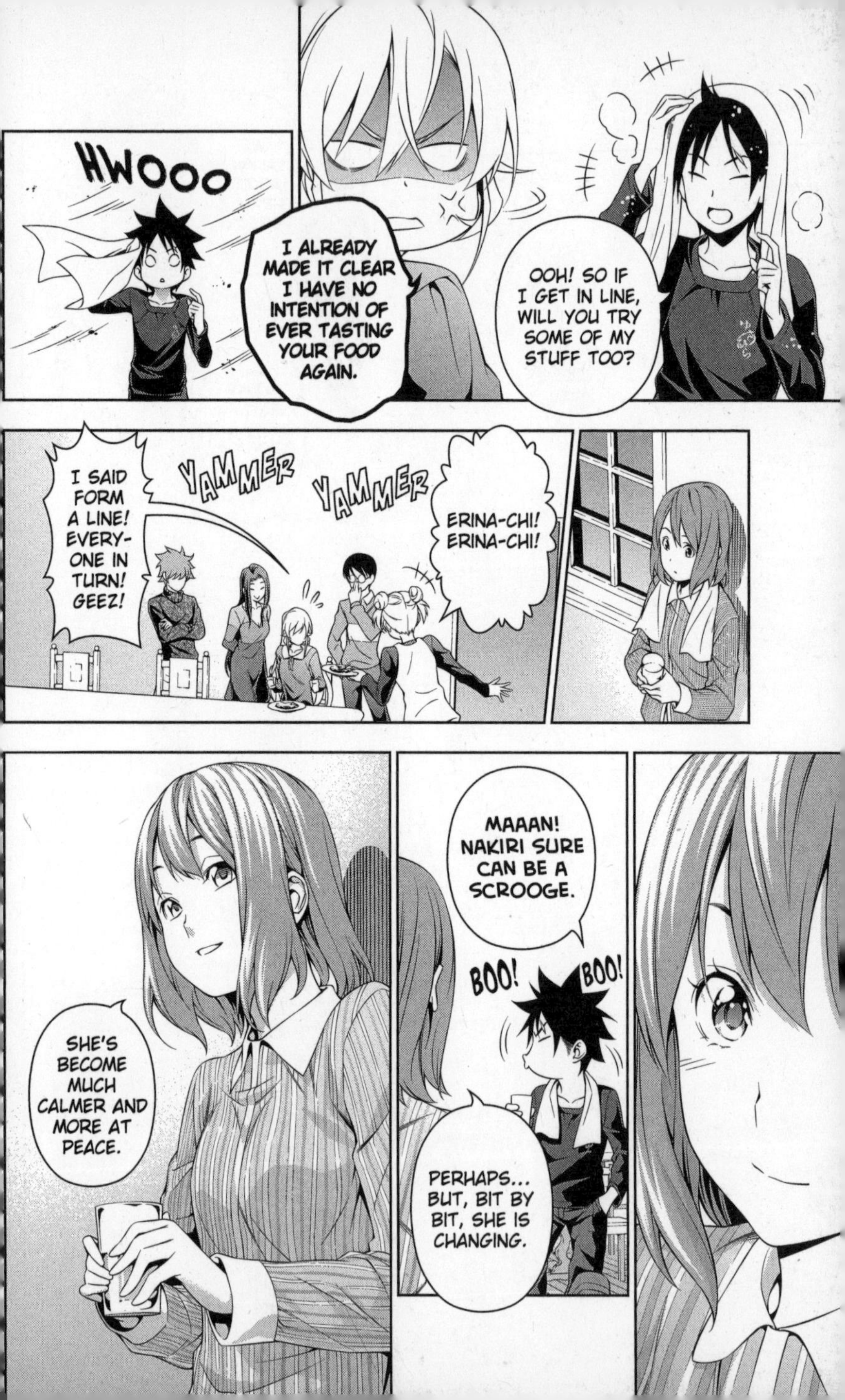
OOH! SO IF I GET IN LINE, WILL YOU TRY SOME OF MY STUFF TOO?
I ALREADY MADE IT CLEAR I HAVE NO INTENTION OF EVER TASTING YOUR FOOD AGAIN.
HWOOO
ERINA-CHI! ERINA-CHI!
YAMMER
YAMMER
I SAID FORM A LINE! EVERY-ONE IN TURN! GEEZ!
MAAAN! NAKIRI SURE CAN BE A SCROOGE.
BOO!
BOO!
PERHAPS... BUT, BIT BY BIT, SHE IS CHANGING.
SHE'S BECOME MUCH CALMER AND MORE AT PEACE.

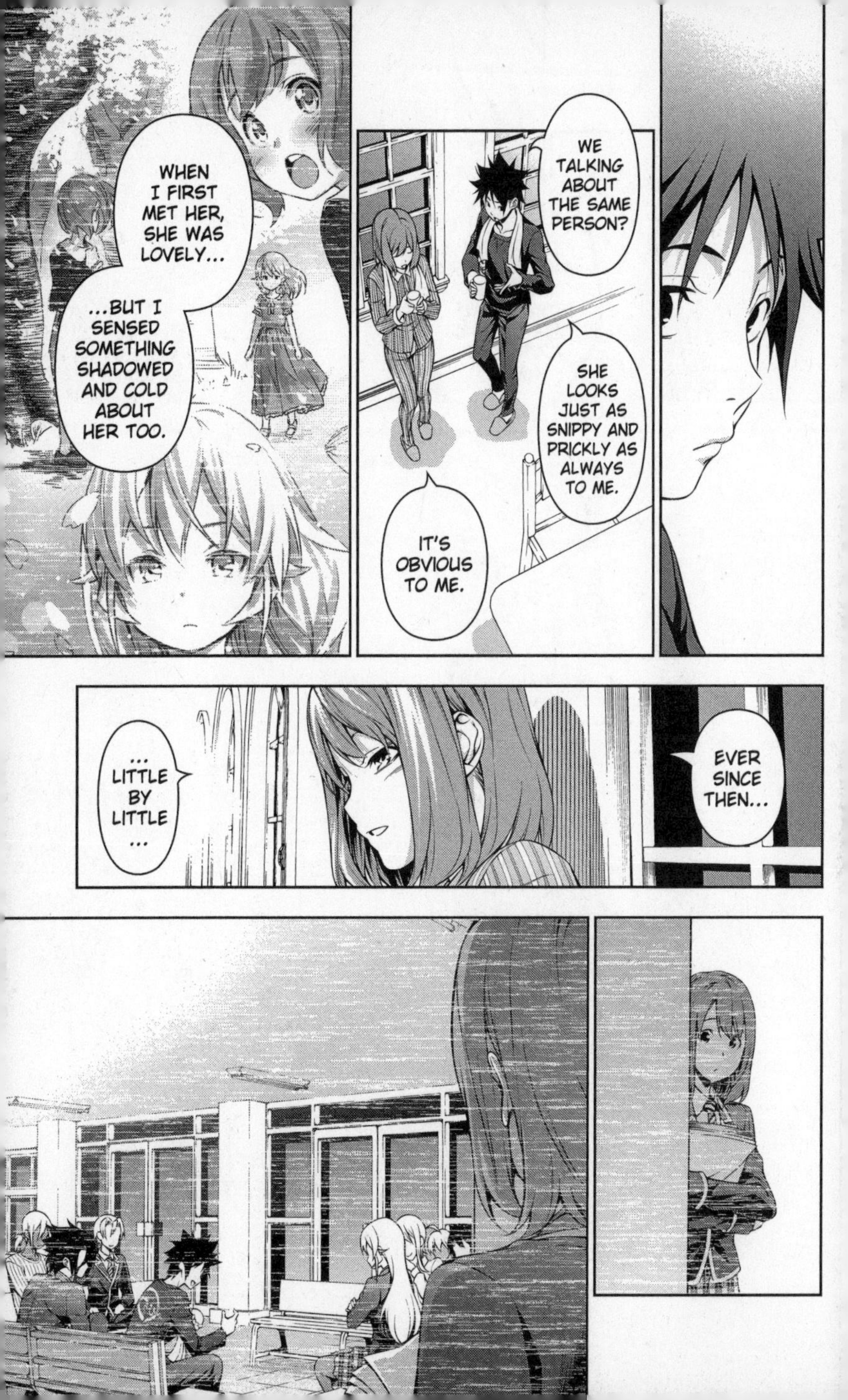
WE TALKING ABOUT THE SAME PERSON?
SHE LOOKS JUST AS SNIPPY AND PRICKLY AS ALWAYS TO ME.
IT'S OBVIOUS TO ME.
WHEN I FIRST MET HER, SHE WAS LOVELY...
...BUT I SENSED SOMETHING SHADOWED AND COLD ABOUT HER TOO.
EVER SINCE THEN...
... LITTLE BY LITTLE ...

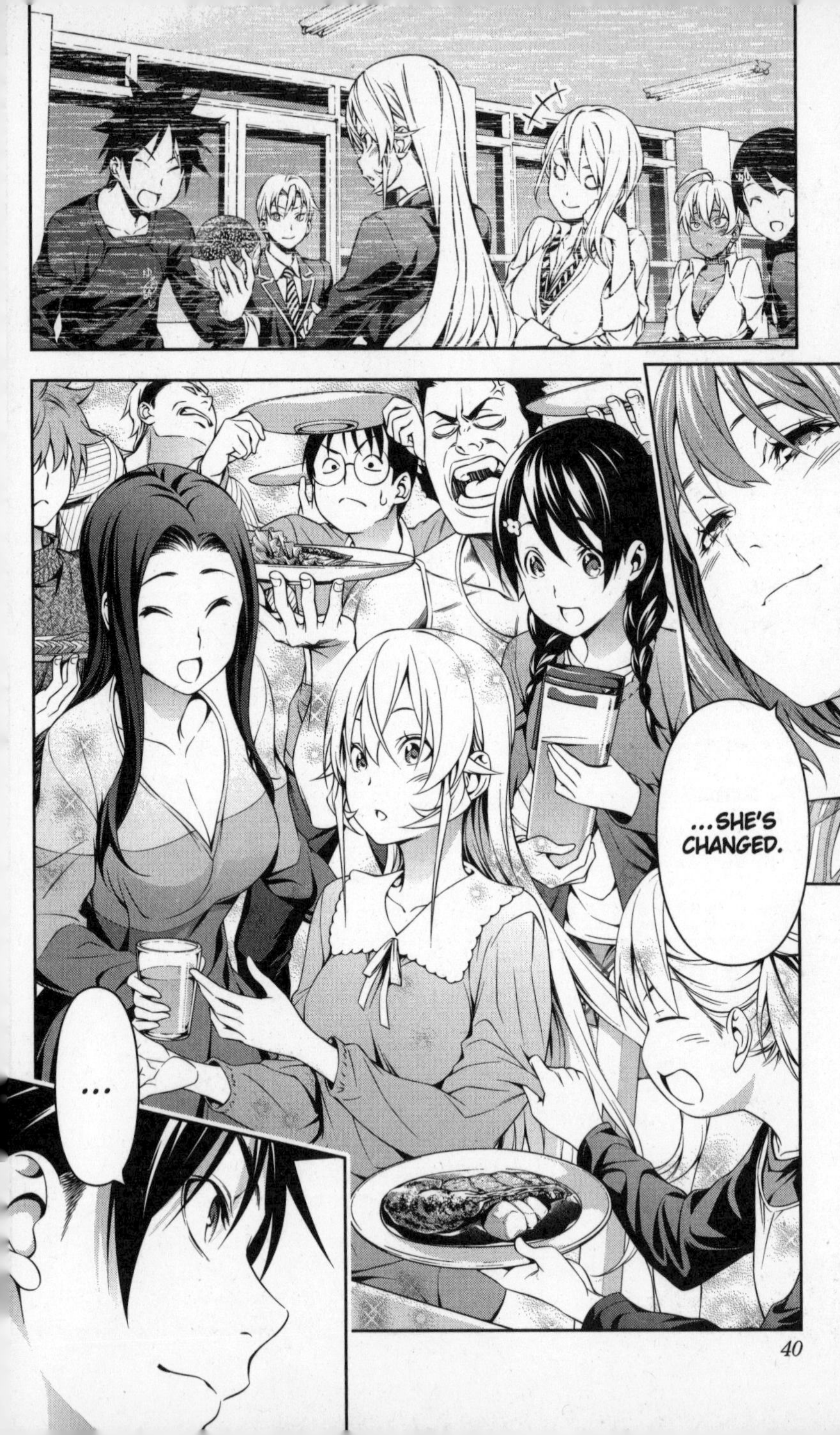
...SHE'S CHANGED.
...

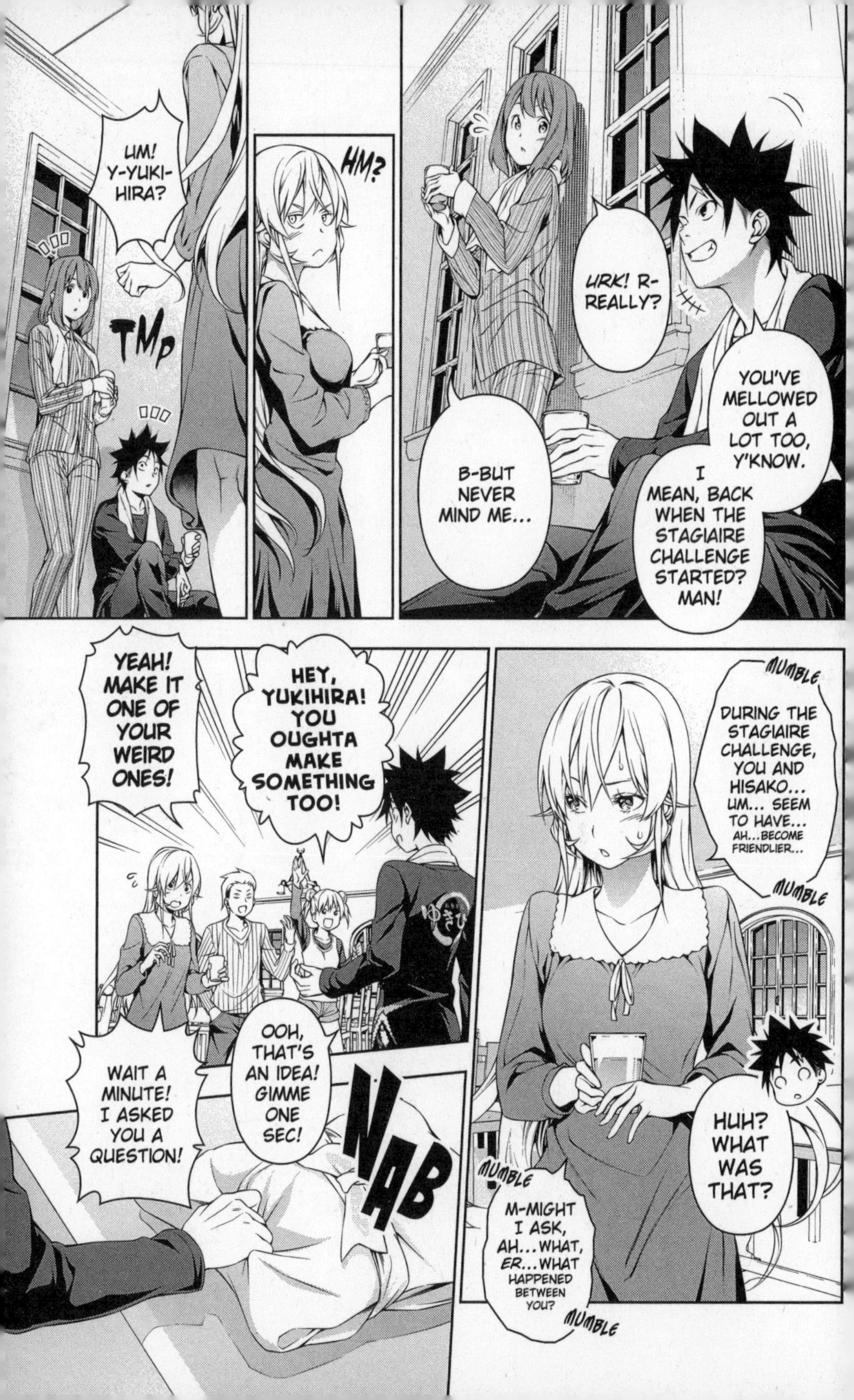
YOU'VE MELLOWED OUT A LOT TOO, Y'KNOW.
I MEAN, BACK WHEN THE STAGIAIRE CHALLENGE STARTED? MAN!
URK! R-REALLY?
B-BUT NEVER MIND ME...
HM?
UM! Y-YUKI-HIRA?
TMP
MUMBLE
DURING THE STAGIAIRE CHALLENGE, YOU AND HISAKO... UM... SEEM TO HAVE... AH...BECOME FRIENDLIER...
MUMBLE
MUMBLE
M-MIGHT I ASK, AH...WHAT, ER...WHAT HAPPENED BETWEEN YOU?
MUMBLE
HUH? WHAT WAS THAT?
HEY, YUKIHIRA! YOU OUGHTA MAKE SOMETHING TOO!
YEAH! MAKE IT ONE OF YOUR WEIRD ONES!
OOH, THAT'S AN IDEA! GIMME ONE SEC!
NAB
WAIT A MINUTE! I ASKED YOU A QUESTION!

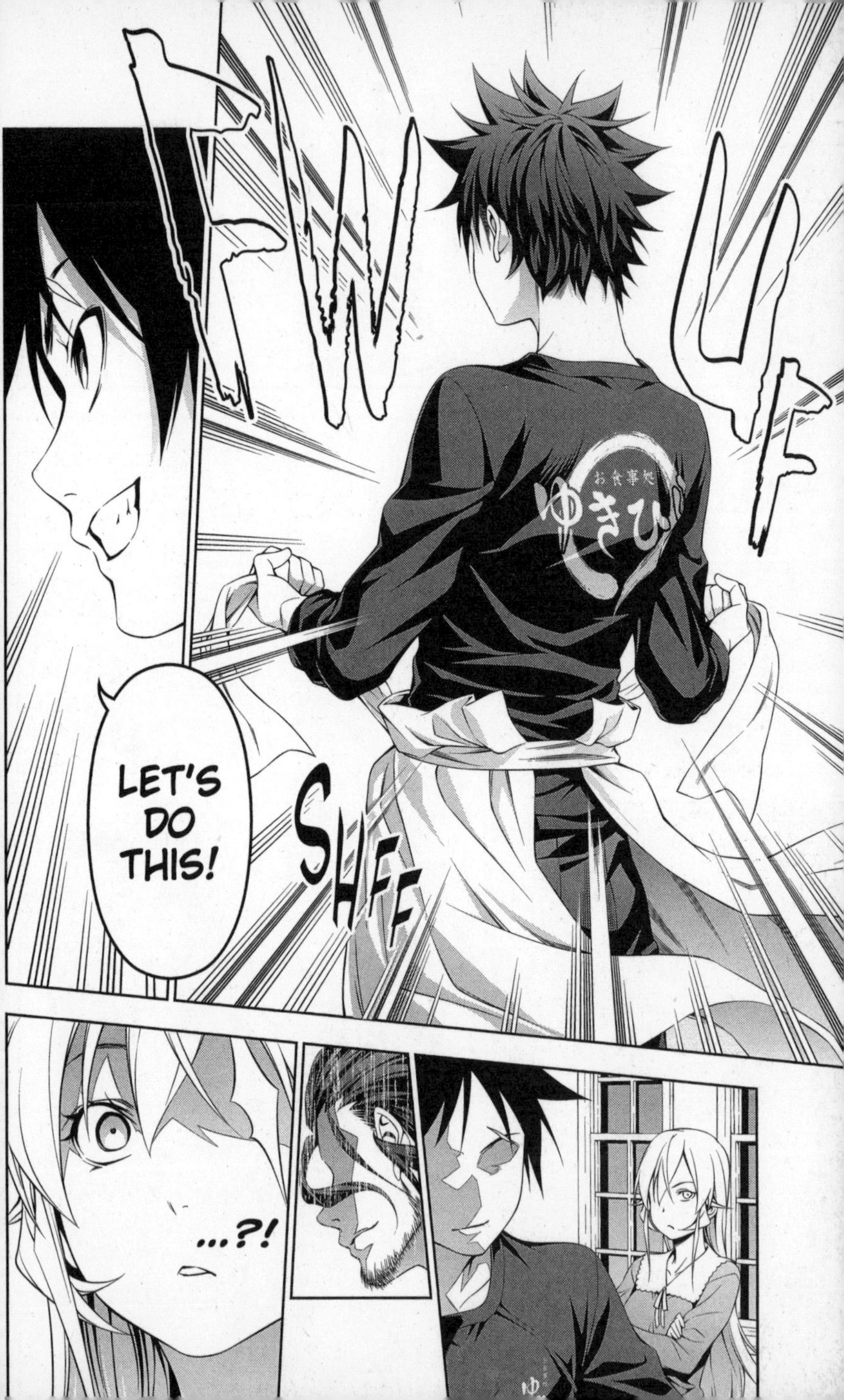
FWUF
LET'S DO THIS!
SHFF
...?!

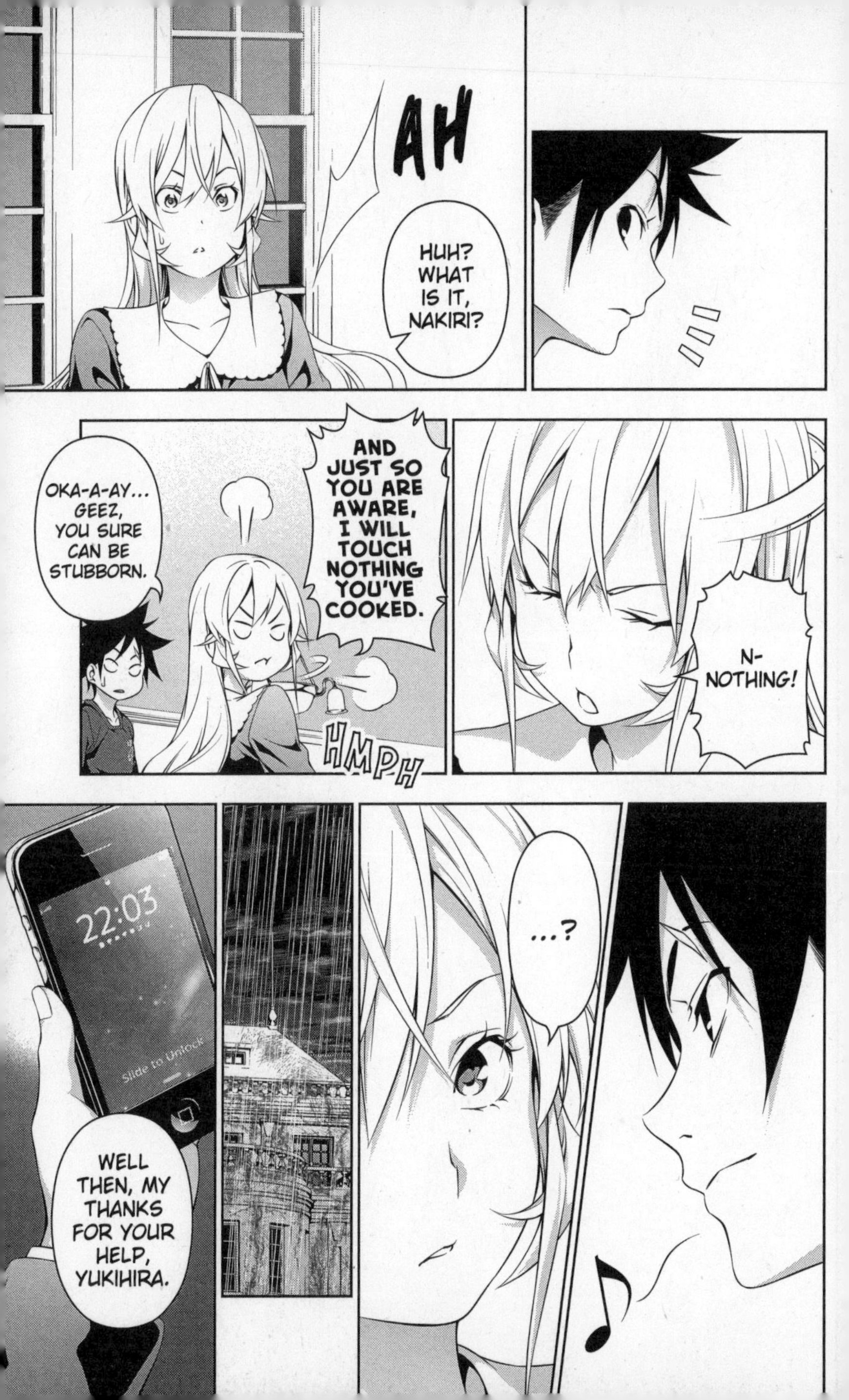
AH
HUH? WHAT IS IT, NAKIRI?
N-NOTHING!
AND JUST SO YOU ARE AWARE, I WILL TOUCH NOTHING YOU'VE COOKED.
OKA-A-AY... GEEZ, YOU SURE CAN BE STUBBORN.
HMPH
...?
22:03
Slide to Unlock
WELL THEN, MY THANKS FOR YOUR HELP, YUKIHIRA.

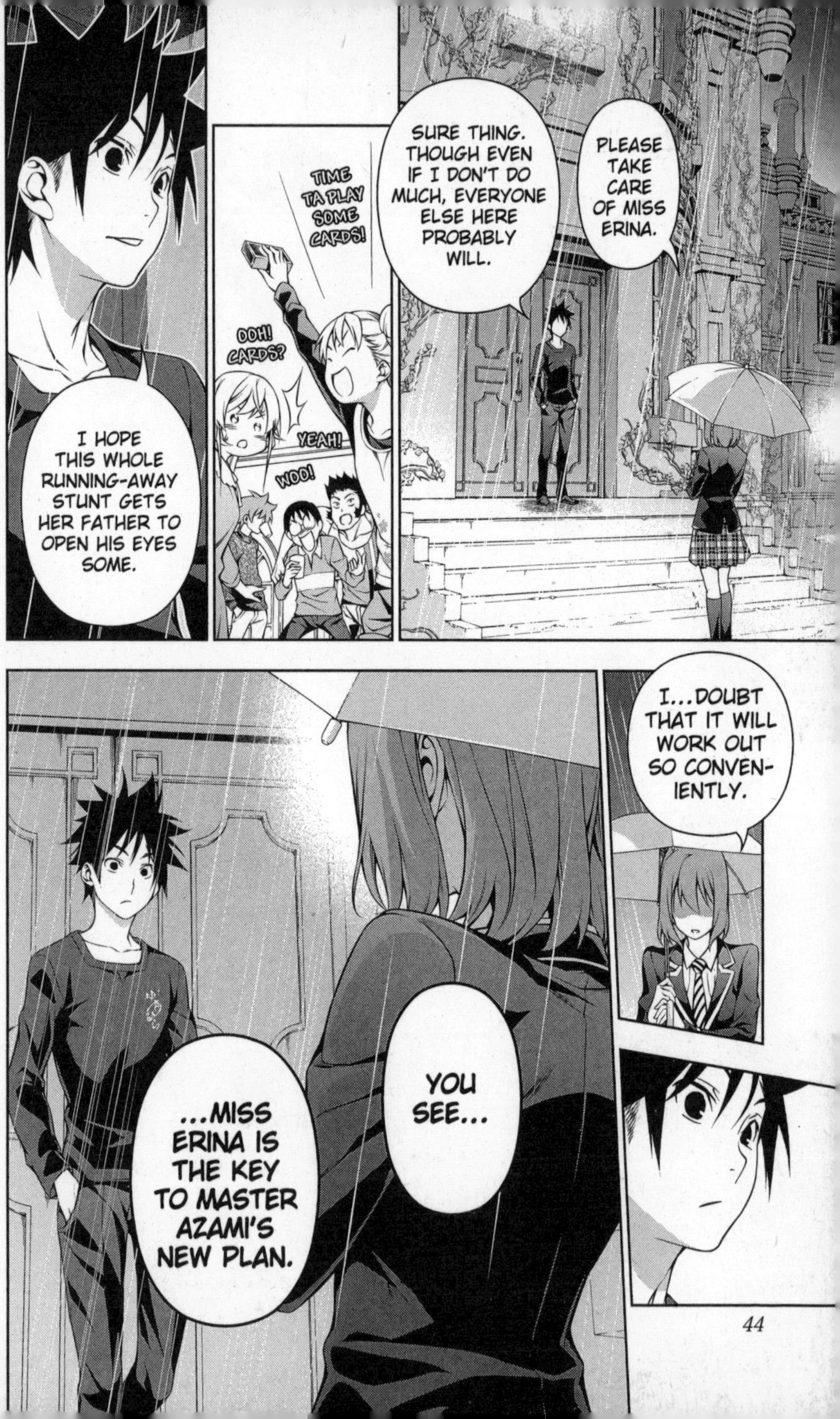
PLEASE TAKE CARE OF MISS ERINA.
SURE THING. THOUGH EVEN IF I DON'T DO MUCH, EVERYONE ELSE HERE PROBABLY WILL.
TIME TA PLAY SOME CARDS!
OOH! CARDS?
YEAH!
WOO!
I HOPE THIS WHOLE RUNNING-AWAY STUNT GETS HER FATHER TO OPEN HIS EYES SOME.
I...DOUBT THAT IT WILL WORK OUT SO CONVEN-IENTLY.
YOU SEE...
...MISS ERINA IS THE KEY TO MASTER AZAMI'S NEW PLAN.

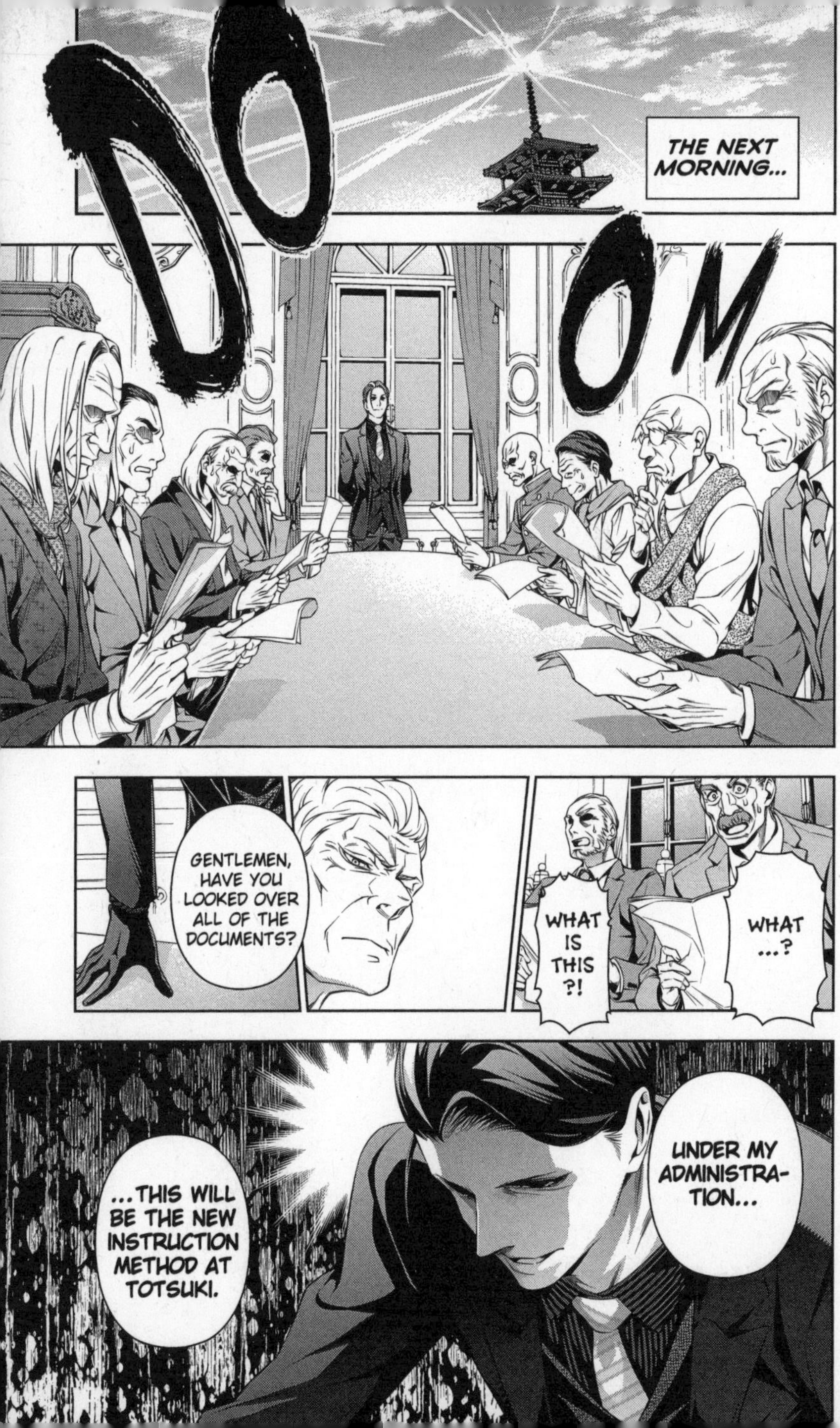
THE NEXT MORNING...
DOOM
WHAT ...?
WHAT IS THIS ?!
GENTLEMEN, HAVE YOU LOOKED OVER ALL OF THE DOCUMENTS?
UNDER MY ADMINISTRA-TION...
...THIS WILL BE THE NEW INSTRUCTION METHOD AT TOTSUKI.

Miss Erina's Splendid Days as a Runaway 2

-THE PAINFUL TRUTH-

RYOKO, BE A DEAR AND LEND HER SOME OF YOUR CLOTHES, WOULD YOU?

HER UNIFORM NEEDS TO BE WASHED.

OKAY! I'LL GO GRAB SOME FROM MY ROOM.

THAT'S WEIRD. WHY DIDN'T SHE ASK ONE OF US?

?

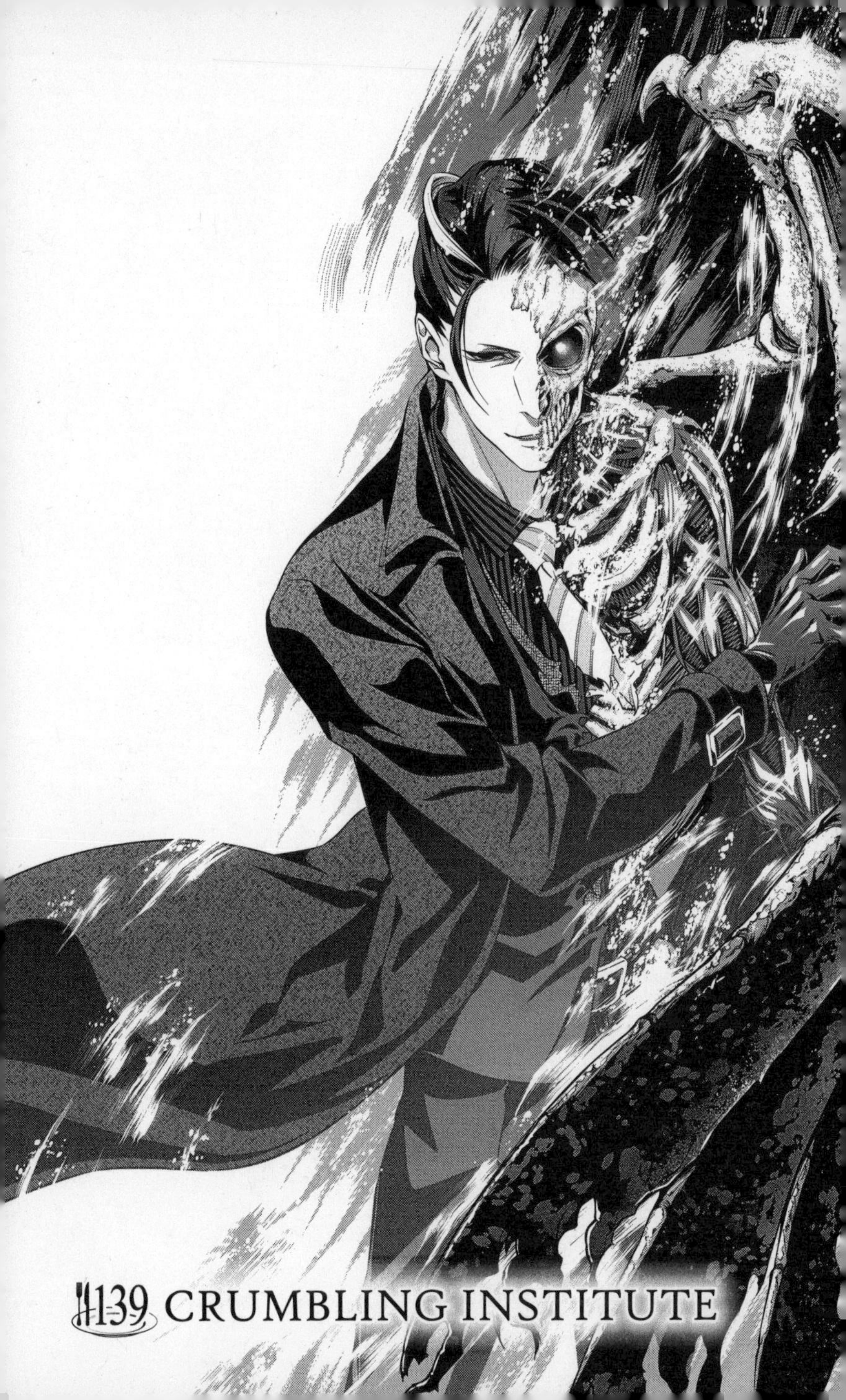

139 CRUMBLING INSTITUTE

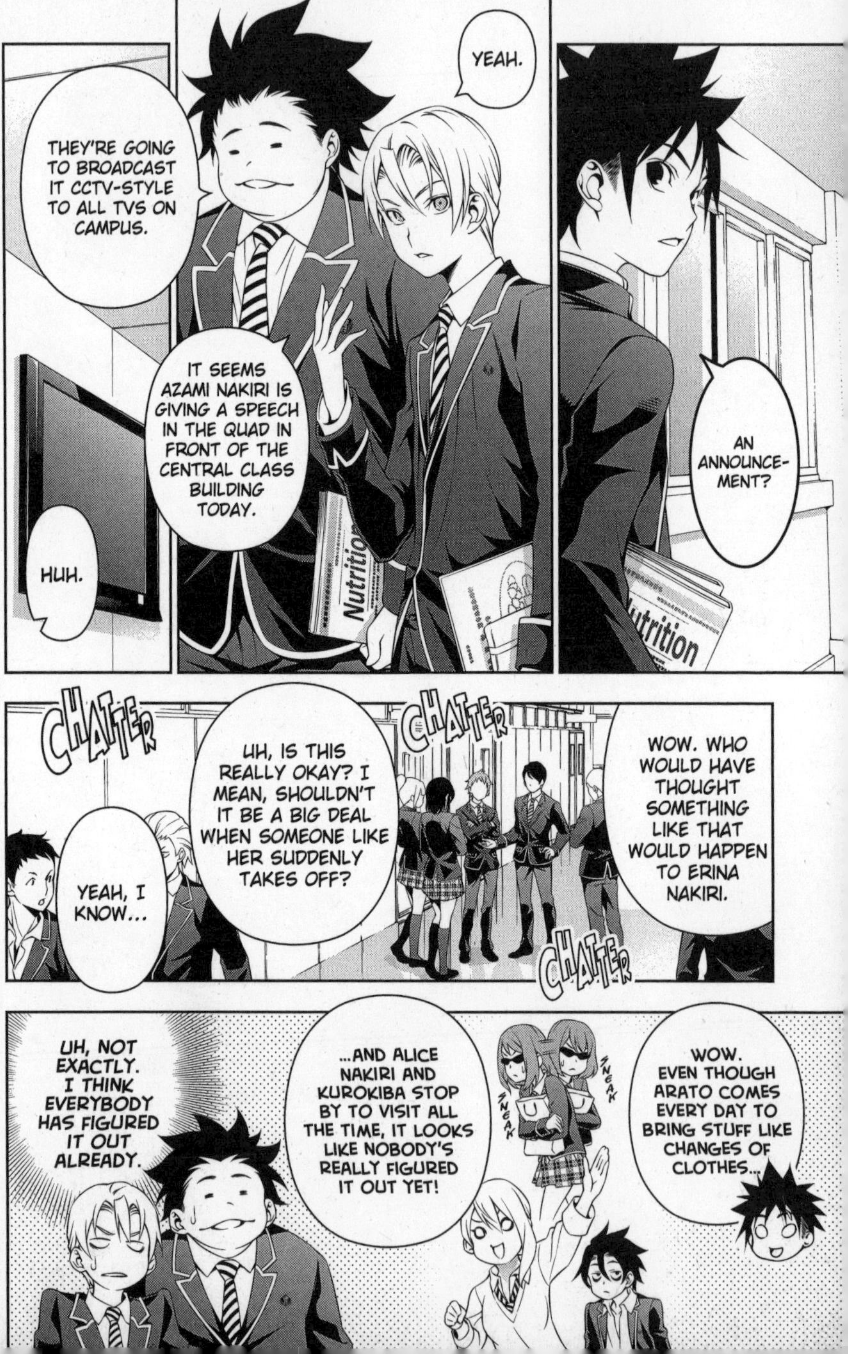
AN ANNOUNCEMENT?
YEAH.
IT SEEMS AZAMI NAKIRI IS GIVING A SPEECH IN THE QUAD IN FRONT OF THE CENTRAL CLASS BUILDING TODAY.
THEY'RE GOING TO BROADCAST IT CCTV-STYLE TO ALL TVS ON CAMPUS.
HUH.
WOW. WHO WOULD HAVE THOUGHT SOMETHING LIKE THAT WOULD HAPPEN TO ERINA NAKIRI.
CHATTER
CHATTER
UH, IS THIS REALLY OKAY? I MEAN, SHOULDN'T IT BE A BIG DEAL WHEN SOMEONE LIKE HER SUDDENLY TAKES OFF?
CHATTER
YEAH, I KNOW...
WOW. EVEN THOUGH ARATO COMES EVERY DAY TO BRING STUFF LIKE CHANGES OF CLOTHES...
SNEAK
SNEAK
...AND ALICE NAKIRI AND KUROKIBA STOP BY TO VISIT ALL THE TIME, IT LOOKS LIKE NOBODY'S REALLY FIGURED IT OUT YET!
UH, NOT EXACTLY. I THINK EVERYBODY HAS FIGURED IT OUT ALREADY.

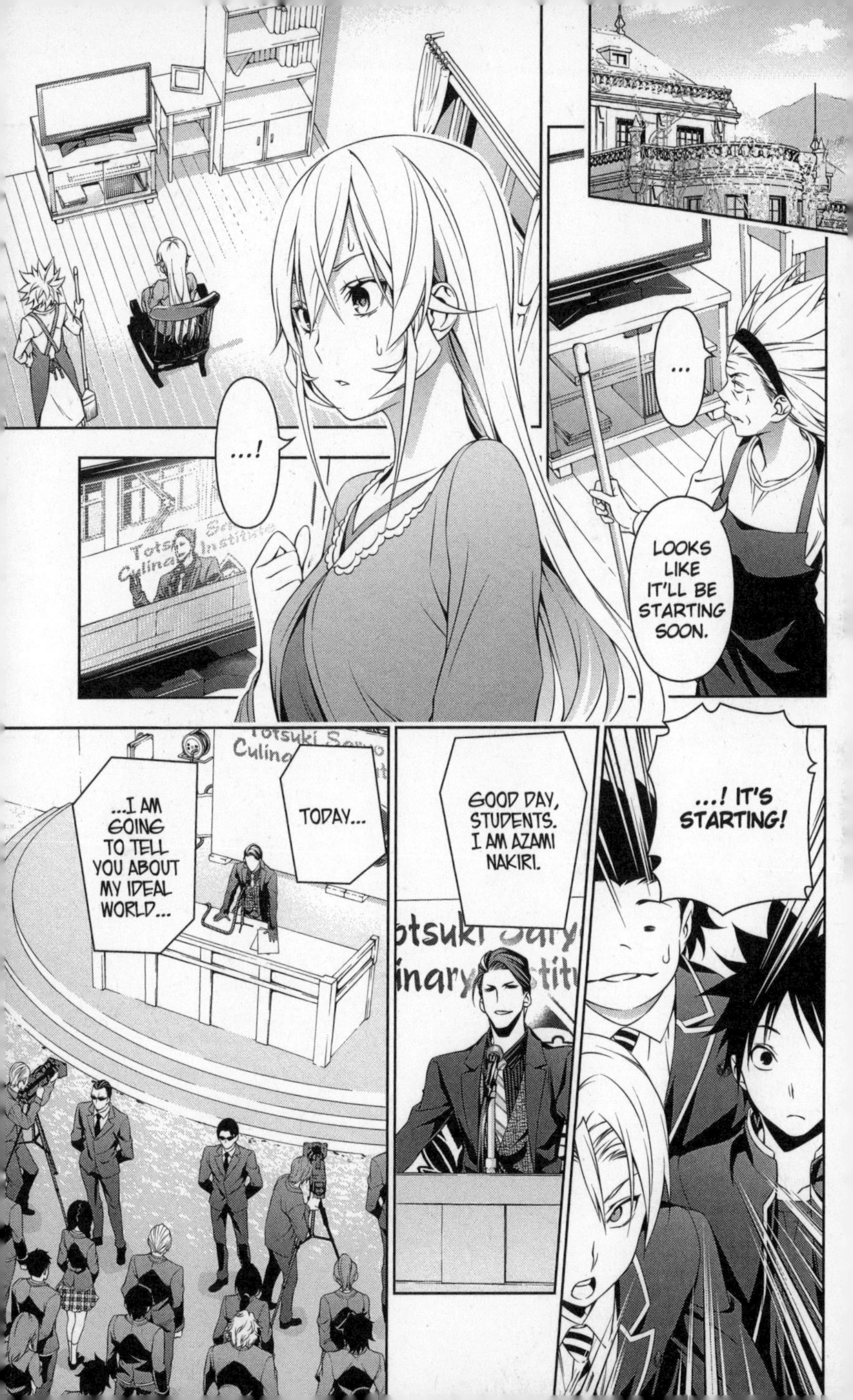
...
LOOKS LIKE IT'LL BE STARTING SOON.
...!
...! IT'S STARTING!
GOOD DAY, STUDENTS. I AM AZAMI NAKIRI.
TODAY...
...I AM GOING TO TELL YOU ABOUT MY IDEAL WORLD...

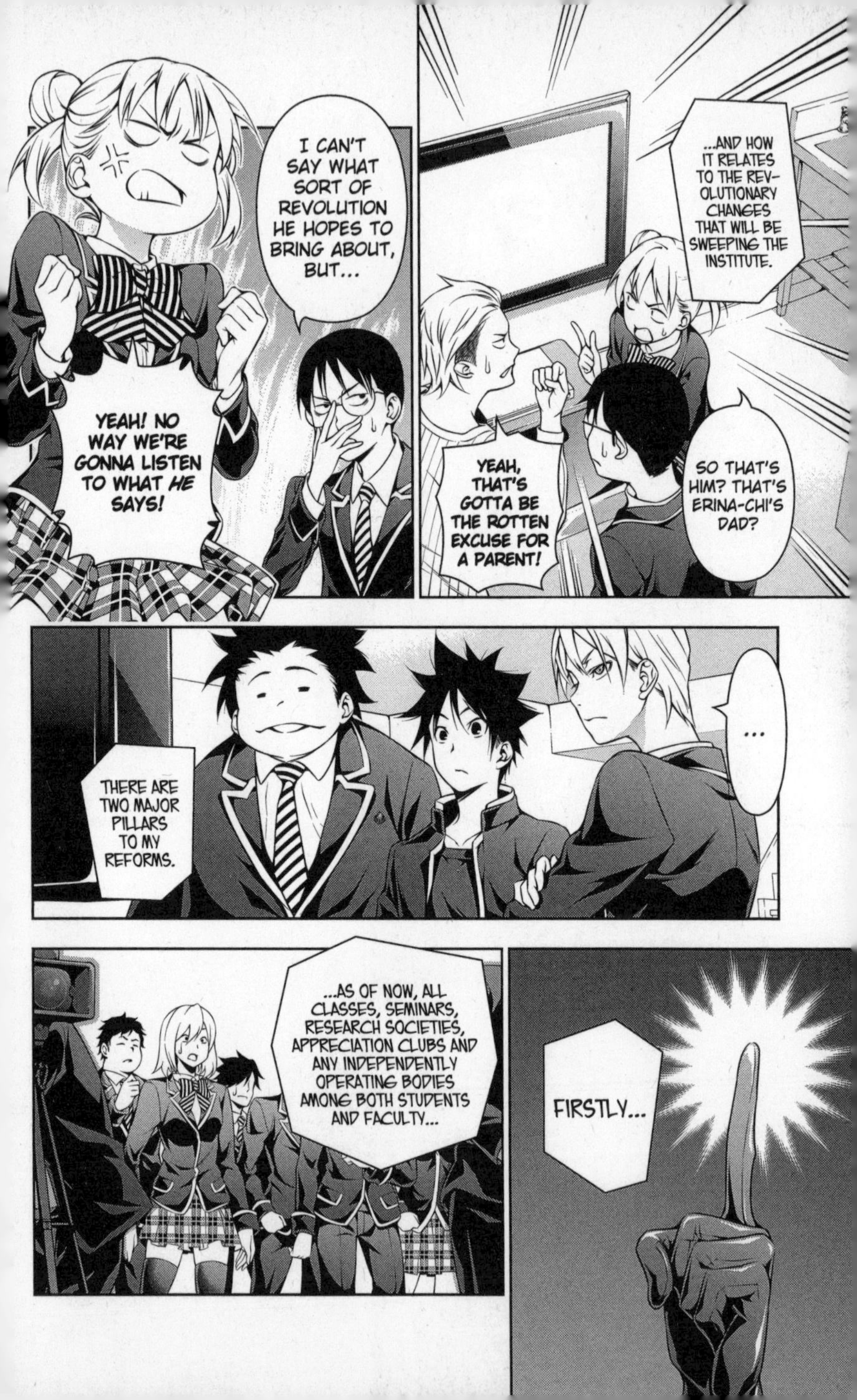
...AND HOW IT RELATES TO THE REV-OLUTIONARY CHANGES THAT WILL BE SWEEPING THE INSTITUTE.
SO THAT'S HIM? THAT'S ERINA-CHI'S DAD?
YEAH, THAT'S GOTTA BE THE ROTTEN EXCUSE FOR A PARENT!
I CAN'T SAY WHAT SORT OF REVOLUTION HE HOPES TO BRING ABOUT, BUT...
YEAH! NO WAY WE'RE GONNA LISTEN TO WHAT *HE* SAYS!
...
THERE ARE TWO MAJOR PILLARS TO MY REFORMS.
FIRSTLY...
...AS OF NOW, ALL CLASSES, SEMINARS, RESEARCH SOCIETIES, APPRECIATION CLUBS AND ANY INDEPENDENTLY OPERATING BODIES AMONG BOTH STUDENTS AND FACULTY...

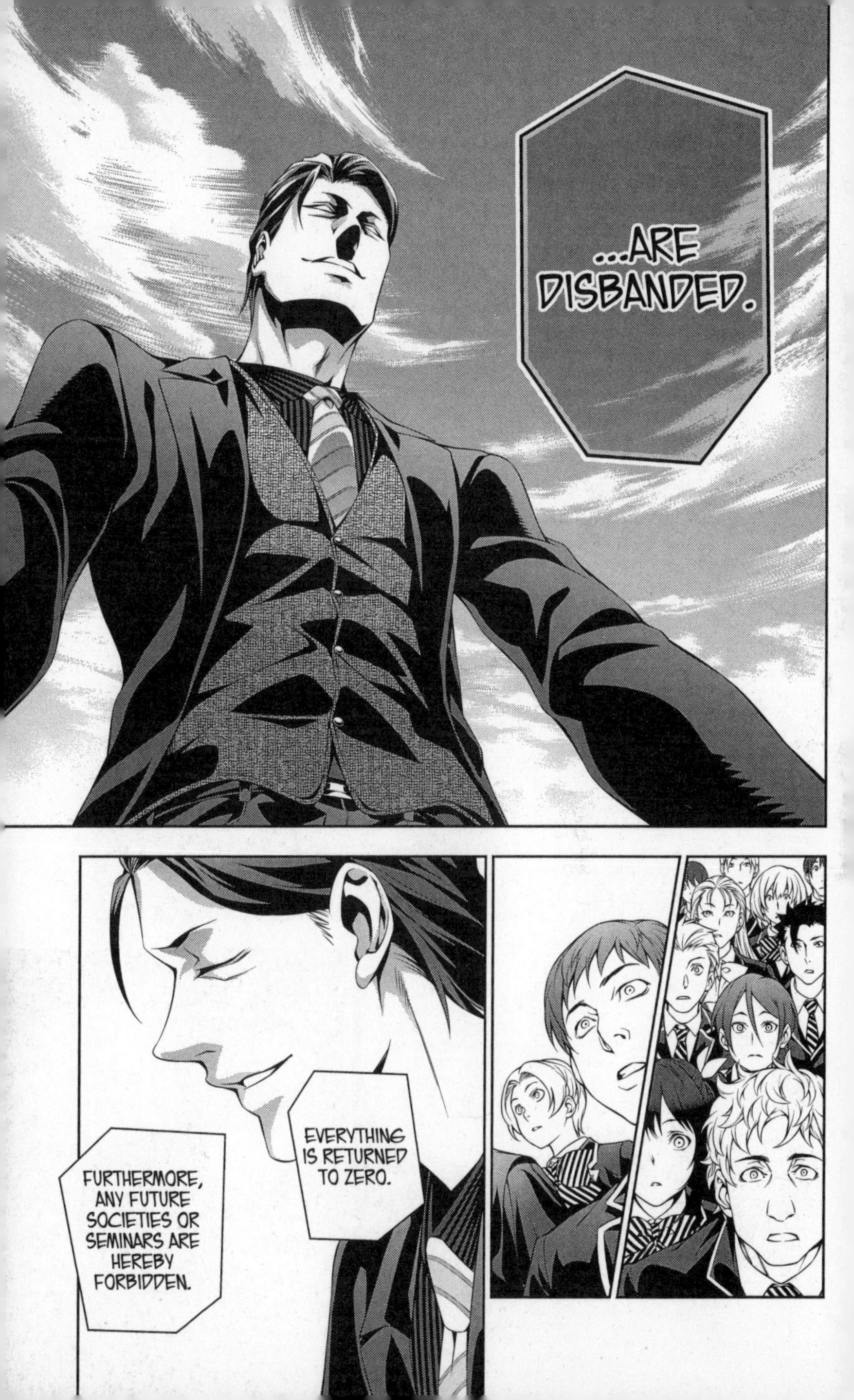
...ARE DISBANDED.
EVERYTHING IS RETURNED TO ZERO.
FURTHERMORE, ANY FUTURE SOCIETIES OR SEMINARS ARE HEREBY FORBIDDEN.

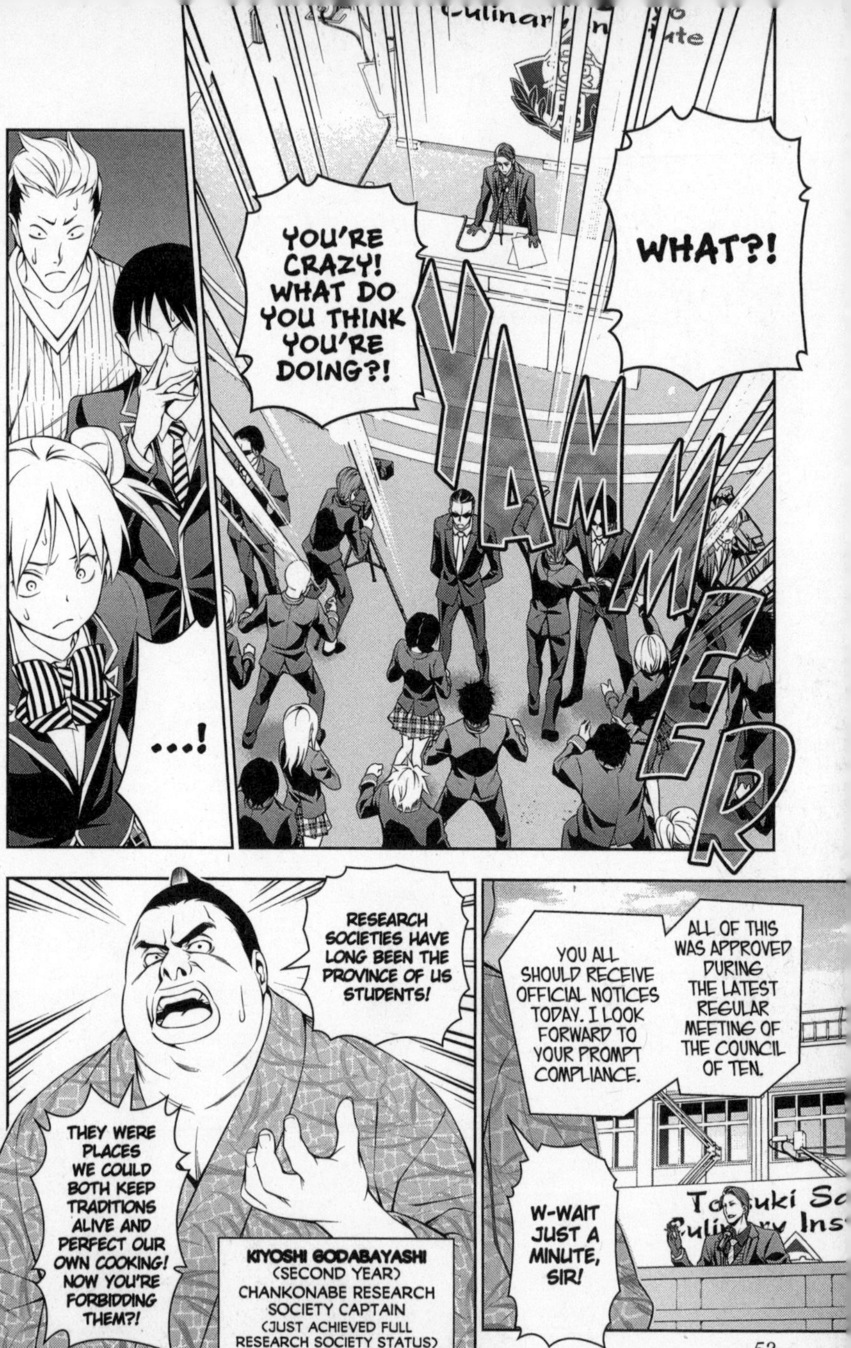
WHAT?!
YOU'RE CRAZY! WHAT DO YOU THINK YOU'RE DOING?!
YAMMER
...!
ALL OF THIS WAS APPROVED DURING THE LATEST REGULAR MEETING OF THE COUNCIL OF TEN.
YOU ALL SHOULD RECEIVE OFFICIAL NOTICES TODAY. I LOOK FORWARD TO YOUR PROMPT COMPLIANCE.
W-WAIT JUST A MINUTE, SIR!
RESEARCH SOCIETIES HAVE LONG BEEN THE PROVINCE OF US STUDENTS!
KIYOSHI GODABAYASHI (SECOND YEAR) CHANKONABE RESEARCH SOCIETY CAPTAIN (JUST ACHIEVED FULL RESEARCH SOCIETY STATUS)
THEY WERE PLACES WE COULD BOTH KEEP TRADITIONS ALIVE AND PERFECT OUR OWN COOKING! NOW YOU'RE FORBIDDING THEM?!

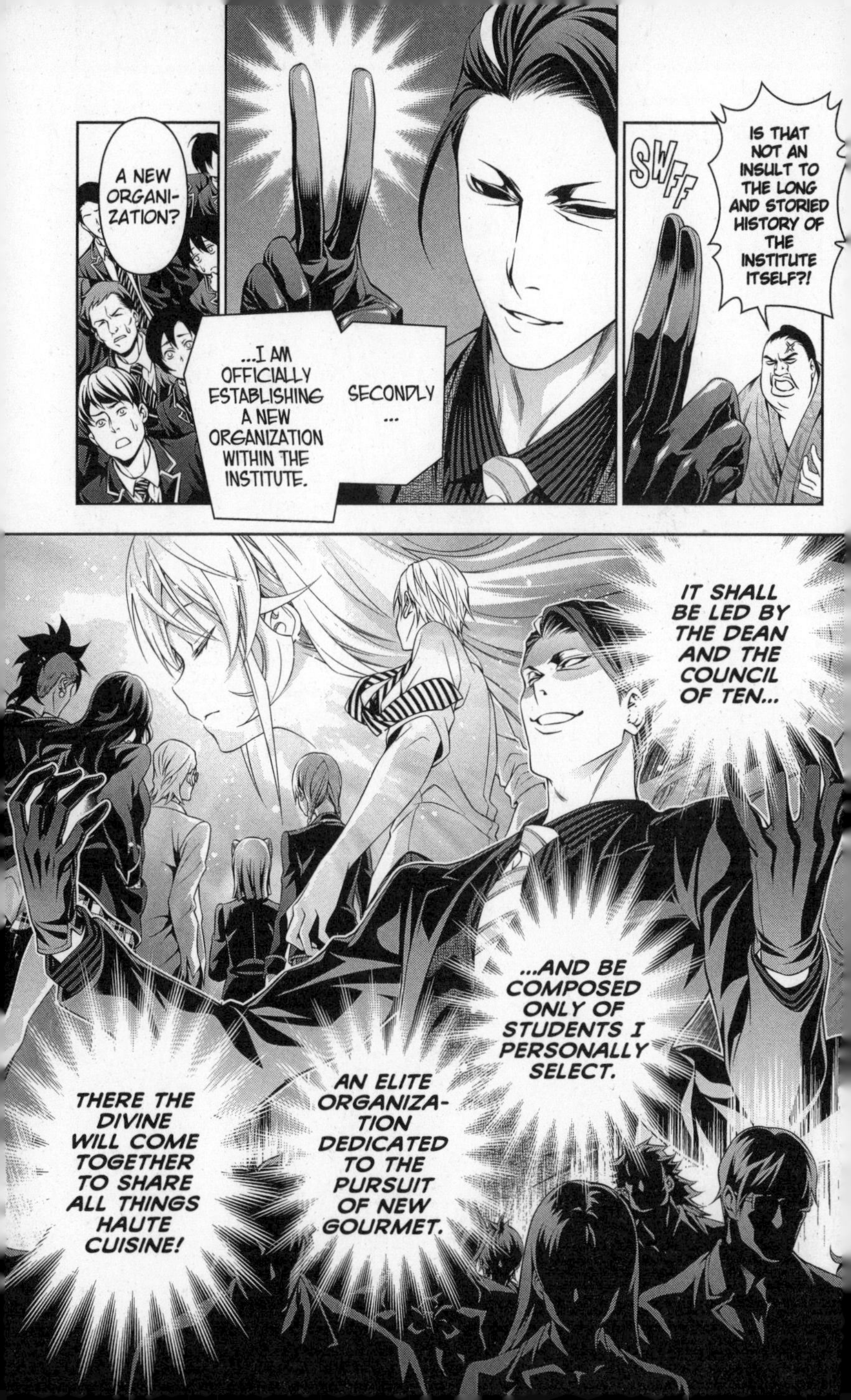
SWFF
IS THAT NOT AN INSULT TO THE LONG AND STORIED HISTORY OF THE INSTITUTE ITSELF?!
SECONDLY...
...I AM OFFICIALLY ESTABLISHING A NEW ORGANIZATION WITHIN THE INSTITUTE.
A NEW ORGANI-ZATION?
IT SHALL BE LED BY THE DEAN AND THE COUNCIL OF TEN...
...AND BE COMPOSED ONLY OF STUDENTS I PERSONALLY SELECT.
AN ELITE ORGANIZA-TION DEDICATED TO THE PURSUIT OF NEW GOURMET.
THERE THE DIVINE WILL COME TOGETHER TO SHARE ALL THINGS HAUTE CUISINE!

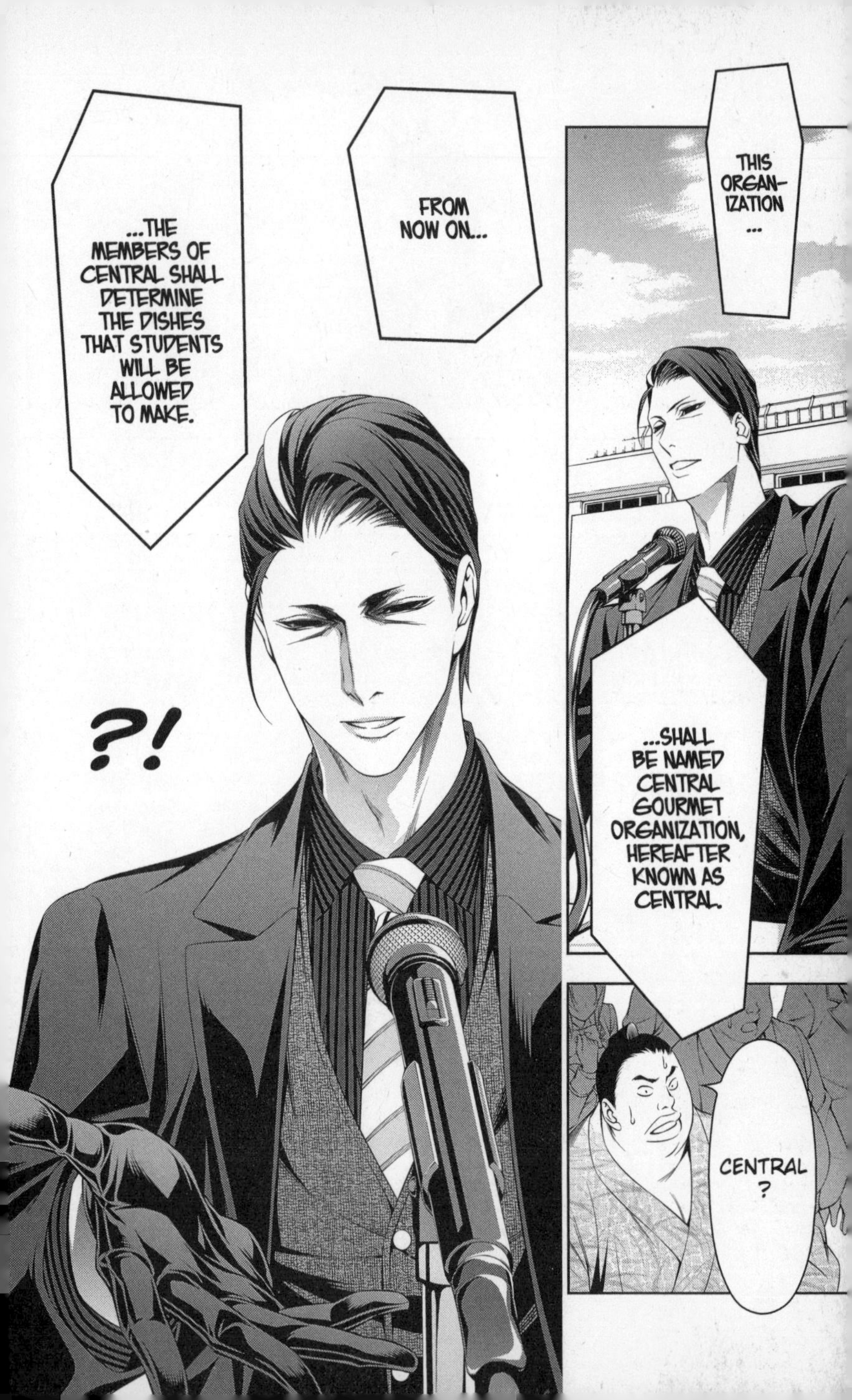
THIS ORGAN-IZATION ...
...SHALL BE NAMED CENTRAL GOURMET ORGANIZATION, HEREAFTER KNOWN AS CENTRAL.
CENTRAL ?
FROM NOW ON...
...THE MEMBERS OF CENTRAL SHALL DETERMINE THE DISHES THAT STUDENTS WILL BE ALLOWED TO MAKE.
?!

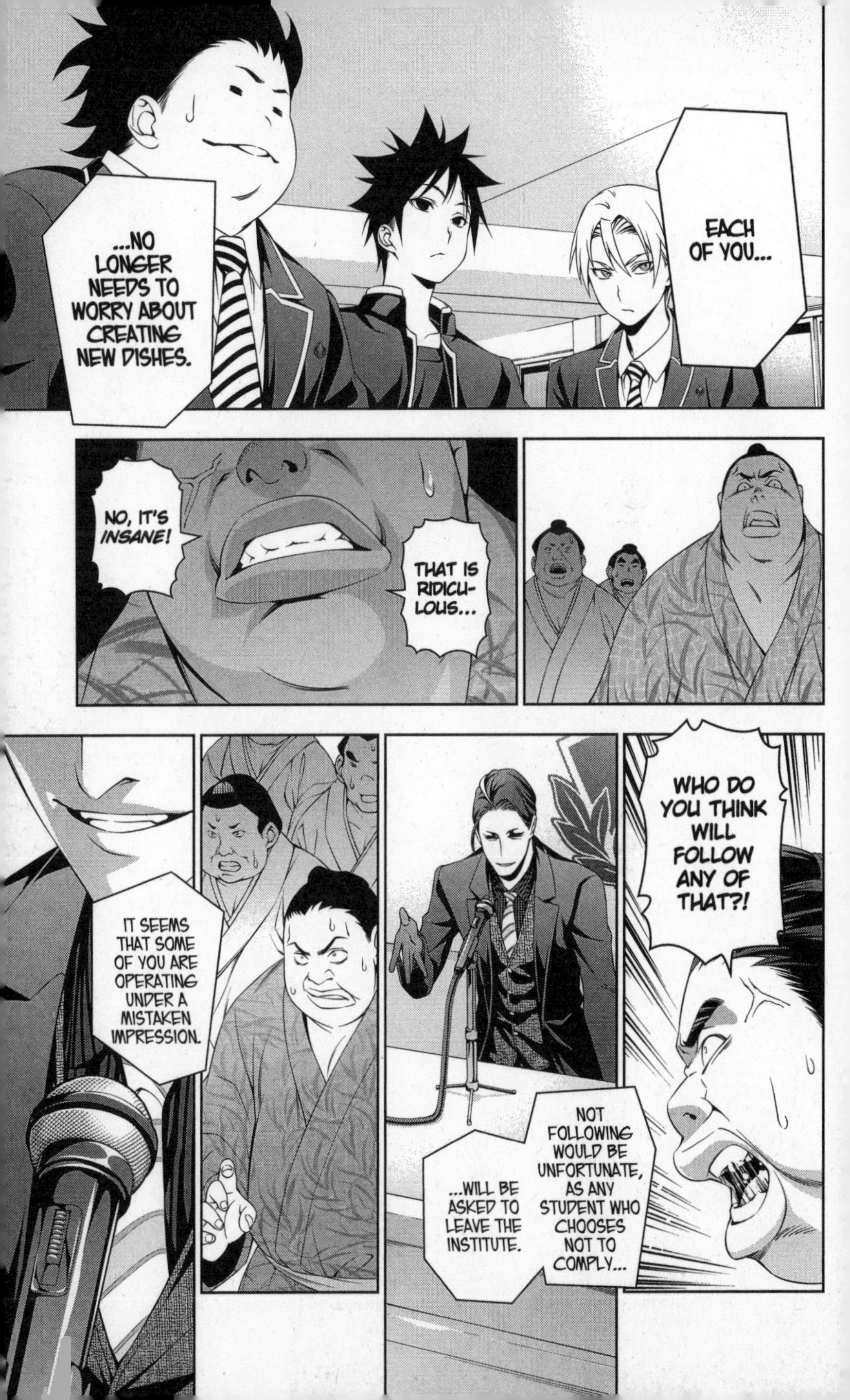
EACH OF YOU...
...NO LONGER NEEDS TO WORRY ABOUT CREATING NEW DISHES.
THAT IS RIDICULOUS...
NO, IT'S *INSANE!*
WHO DO YOU THINK WILL FOLLOW ANY OF THAT?!
NOT FOLLOWING WOULD BE UNFORTUNATE, AS ANY STUDENT WHO CHOOSES NOT TO COMPLY...
...WILL BE ASKED TO LEAVE THE INSTITUTE.
IT SEEMS THAT SOME OF YOU ARE OPERATING UNDER A MISTAKEN IMPRESSION.

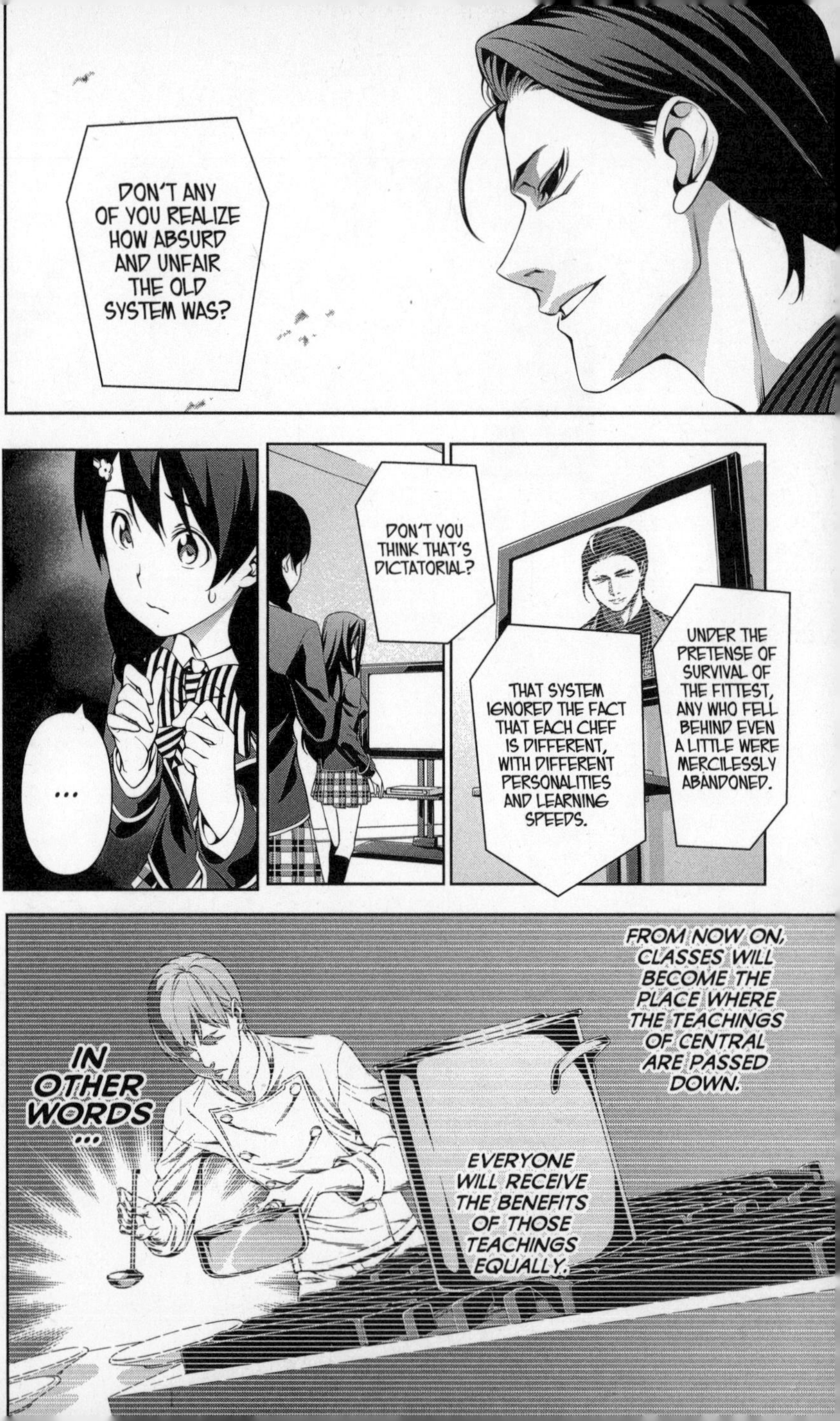
DON'T ANY OF YOU REALIZE HOW ABSURD AND UNFAIR THE OLD SYSTEM WAS?
UNDER THE PRETENSE OF SURVIVAL OF THE FITTEST, ANY WHO FELL BEHIND EVEN A LITTLE WERE MERCILESSLY ABANDONED.
THAT SYSTEM IGNORED THE FACT THAT EACH CHEF IS DIFFERENT, WITH DIFFERENT PERSONALITIES AND LEARNING SPEEDS.
DON'T YOU THINK THAT'S DICTATORIAL?
...
FROM NOW ON, CLASSES WILL BECOME THE PLACE WHERE THE TEACHINGS OF CENTRAL ARE PASSED DOWN.
IN OTHER WORDS...
EVERYONE WILL RECEIVE THE BENEFITS OF THOSE TEACHINGS EQUALLY.

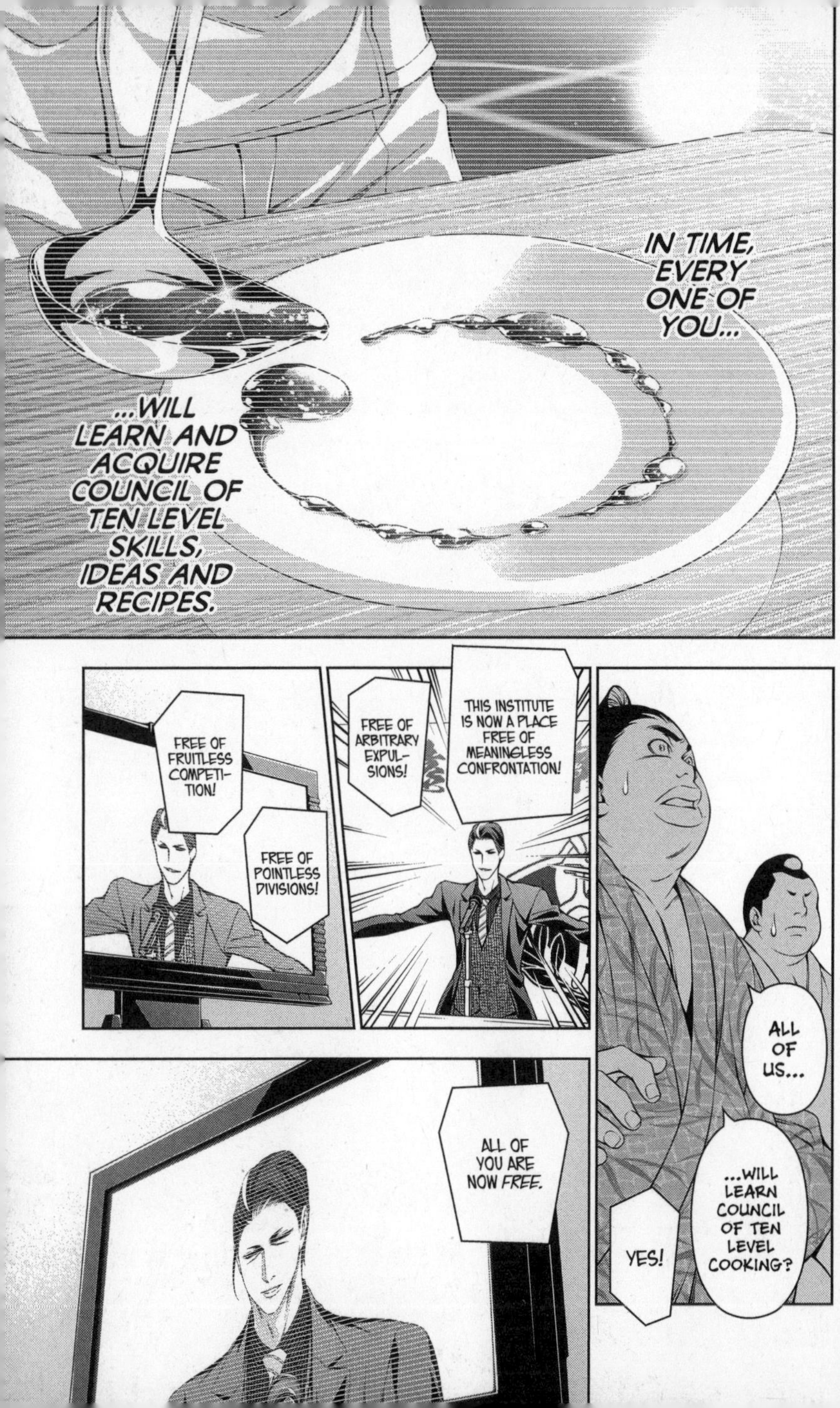
IN TIME, EVERY ONE OF YOU...
...WILL LEARN AND ACQUIRE COUNCIL OF TEN LEVEL SKILLS, IDEAS AND RECIPES.
ALL OF US...
...WILL LEARN COUNCIL OF TEN LEVEL COOKING?
YES!
THIS INSTITUTE IS NOW A PLACE FREE OF MEANINGLESS CONFRONTATION!
FREE OF ARBITRARY EXPULSIONS!
FREE OF FRUITLESS COMPETITION!
FREE OF POINTLESS DIVISIONS!
ALL OF YOU ARE NOW *FREE.*

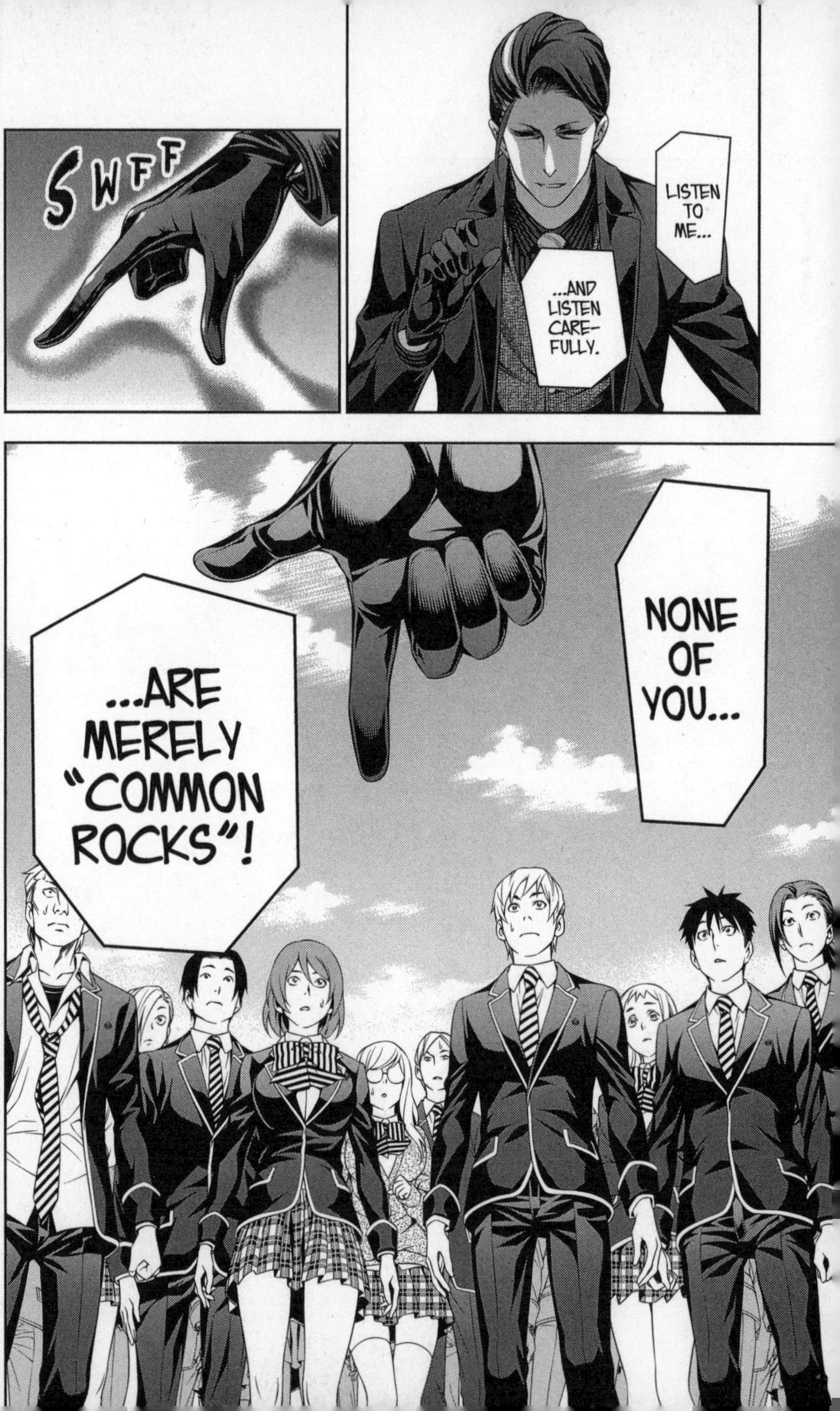
LISTEN TO ME...
...AND LISTEN CARE-FULLY.
SWFF
NONE OF YOU...
...ARE MERELY "COMMON ROCKS"!

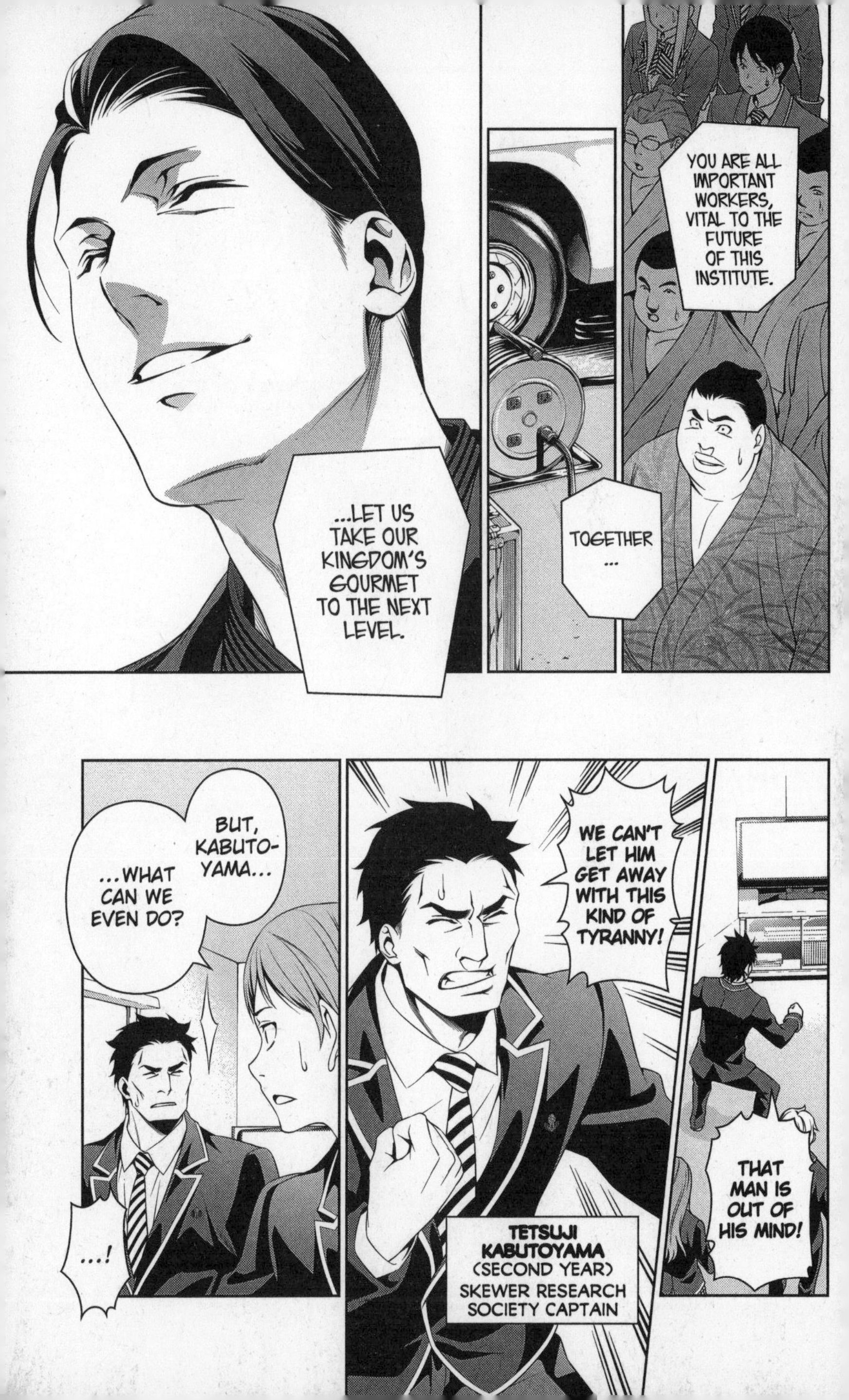
YOU ARE ALL IMPORTANT WORKERS, VITAL TO THE FUTURE OF THIS INSTITUTE.
TOGETHER...
...LET US TAKE OUR KINGDOM'S GOURMET TO THE NEXT LEVEL.
THAT MAN IS OUT OF HIS MIND!
WE CAN'T LET HIM GET AWAY WITH THIS KIND OF TYRANNY!
TETSUJI KABUTOYAMA (SECOND YEAR) SKEWER RESEARCH SOCIETY CAPTAIN
BUT, KABUTOYAMA...
...WHAT CAN WE EVEN DO?
...!

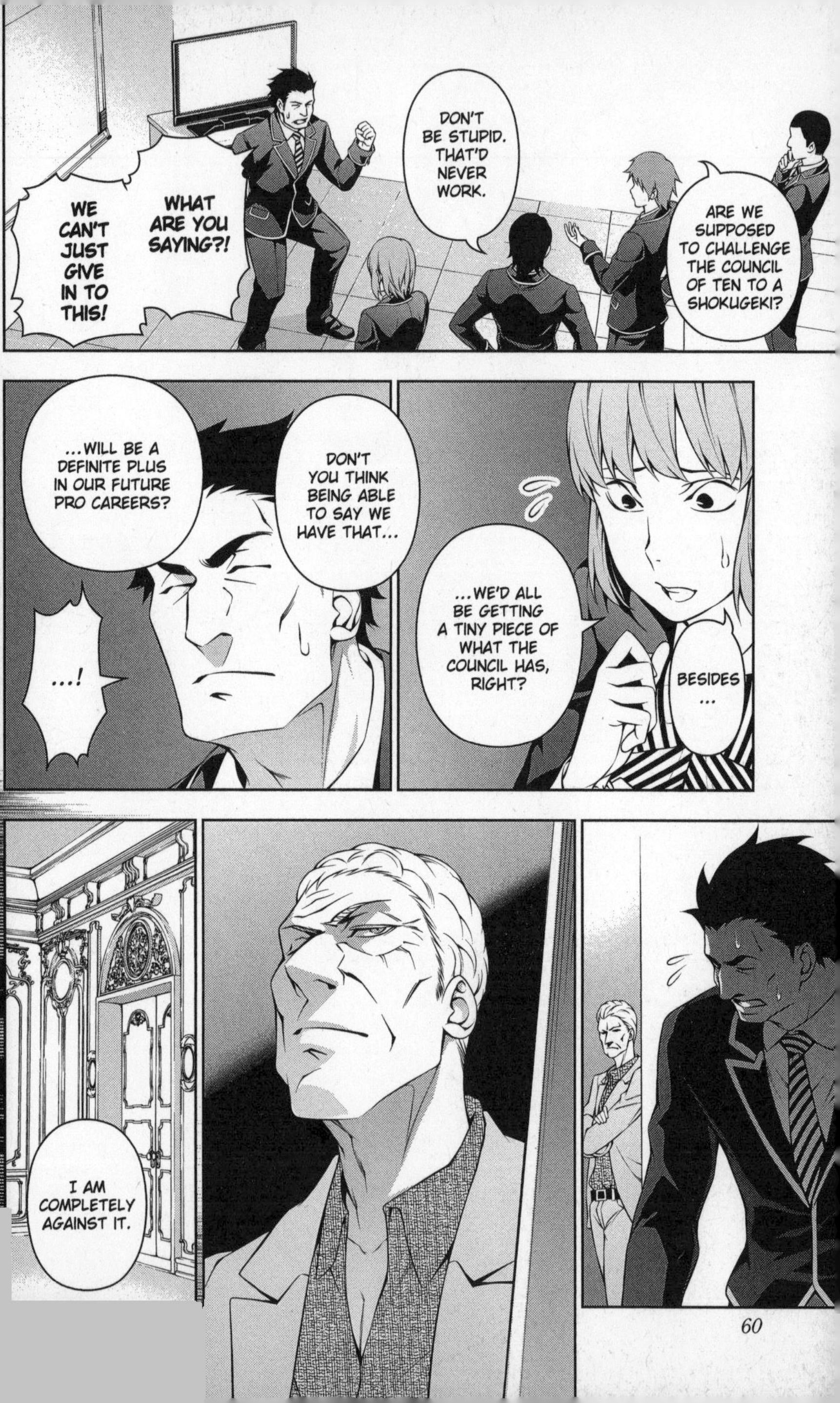
ARE WE SUPPOSED TO CHALLENGE THE COUNCIL OF TEN TO A SHOKUGEKI?
DON'T BE STUPID. THAT'D NEVER WORK.
WHAT ARE YOU SAYING?!
WE CAN'T JUST GIVE IN TO THIS!
BESIDES...
...WE'D ALL BE GETTING A TINY PIECE OF WHAT THE COUNCIL HAS, RIGHT?
DON'T YOU THINK BEING ABLE TO SAY WE HAVE THAT...
...WILL BE A DEFINITE PLUS IN OUR FUTURE PRO CAREERS?
...!
I AM COMPLETELY AGAINST IT.

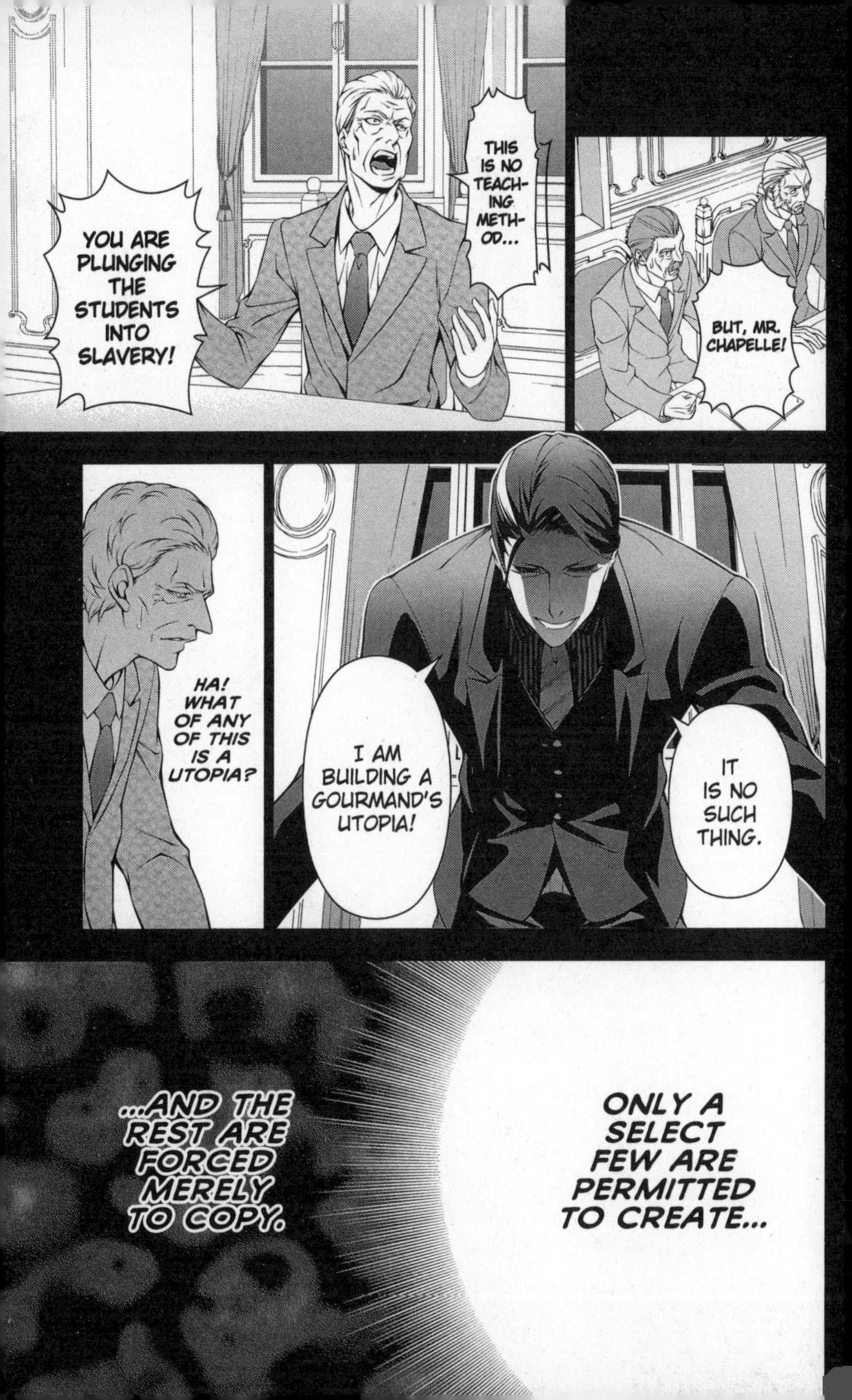
BUT, MR. CHAPELLE!
THIS IS NO TEACHING METHOD...
YOU ARE PLUNGING THE STUDENTS INTO SLAVERY!
IT IS NO SUCH THING.
I AM BUILDING A GOURMAND'S UTOPIA!
HA! WHAT OF ANY OF THIS IS A UTOPIA?
ONLY A SELECT FEW ARE PERMITTED TO CREATE...
...AND THE REST ARE FORCED MERELY TO COPY.

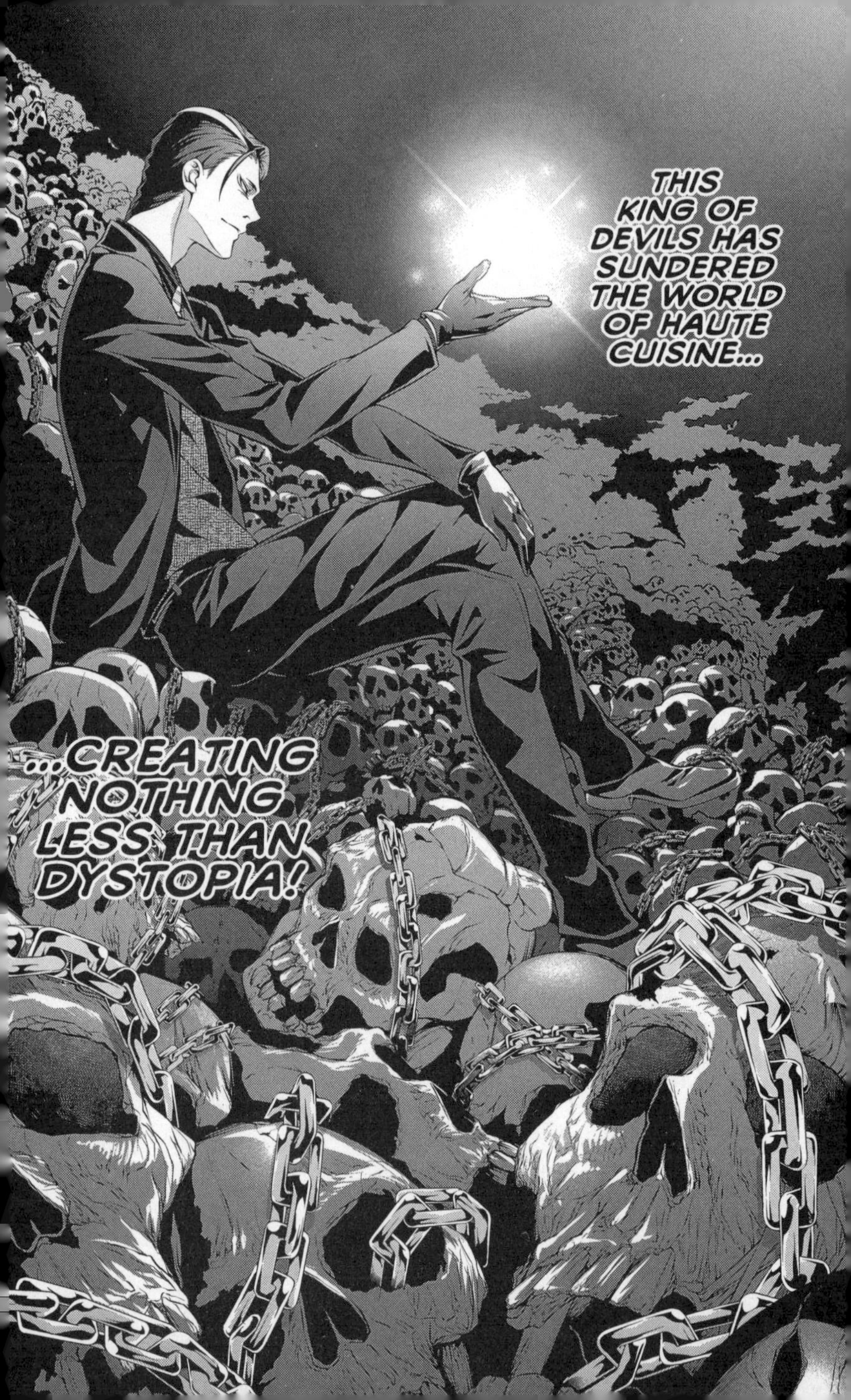
THIS KING OF DEVILS HAS SUNDERED THE WORLD OF HAUTE CUISINE...
...CREATING NOTHING LESS THAN DYSTOPIA!

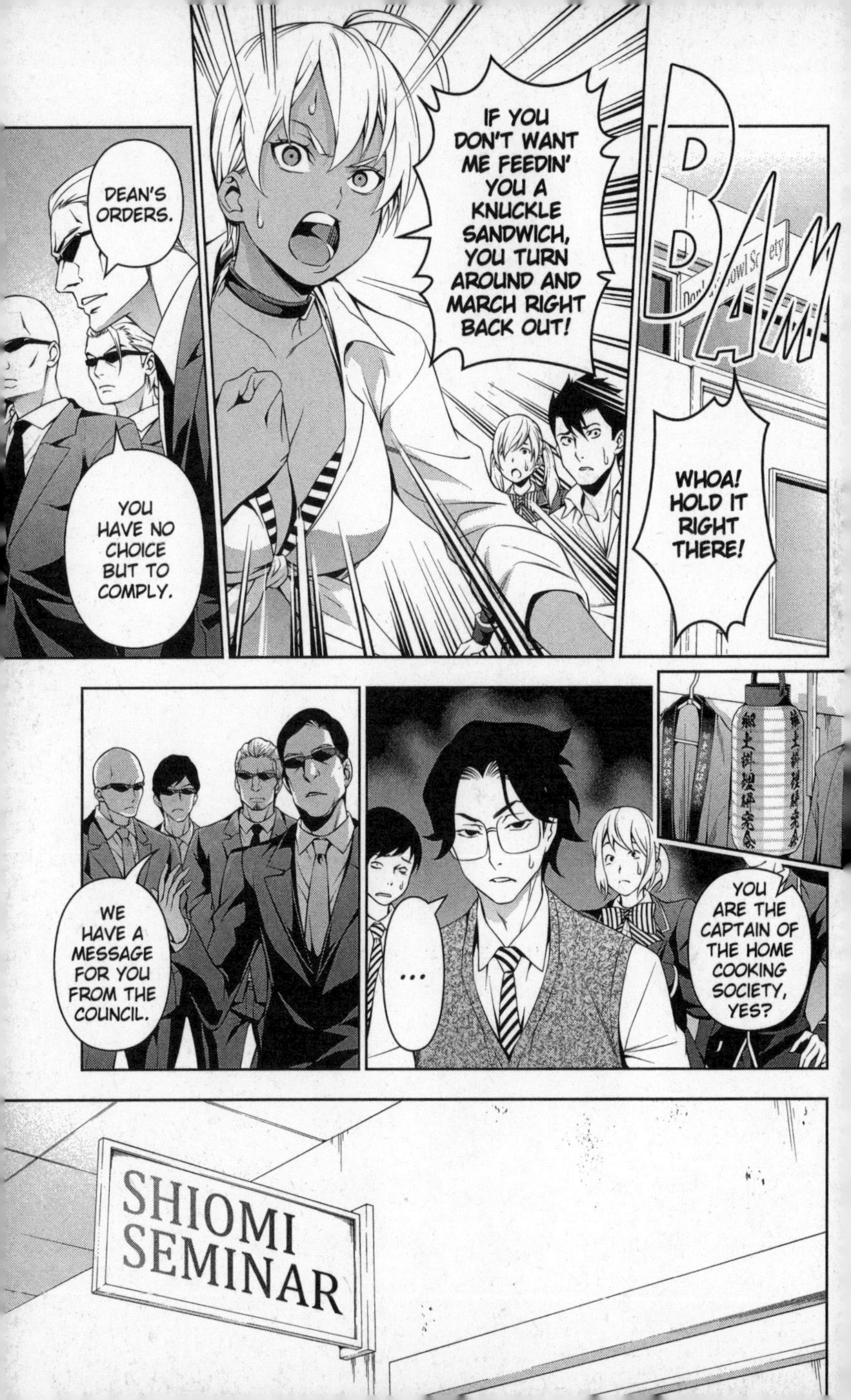
BAM
WHOA! HOLD IT RIGHT THERE!
IF YOU DON'T WANT ME FEEDIN' YOU A KNUCKLE SANDWICH, YOU TURN AROUND AND MARCH RIGHT BACK OUT!
DEAN'S ORDERS.
YOU HAVE NO CHOICE BUT TO COMPLY.
YOU ARE THE CAPTAIN OF THE HOME COOKING SOCIETY, YES?
...
WE HAVE A MESSAGE FOR YOU FROM THE COUNCIL.
SHIOMI SEMINAR

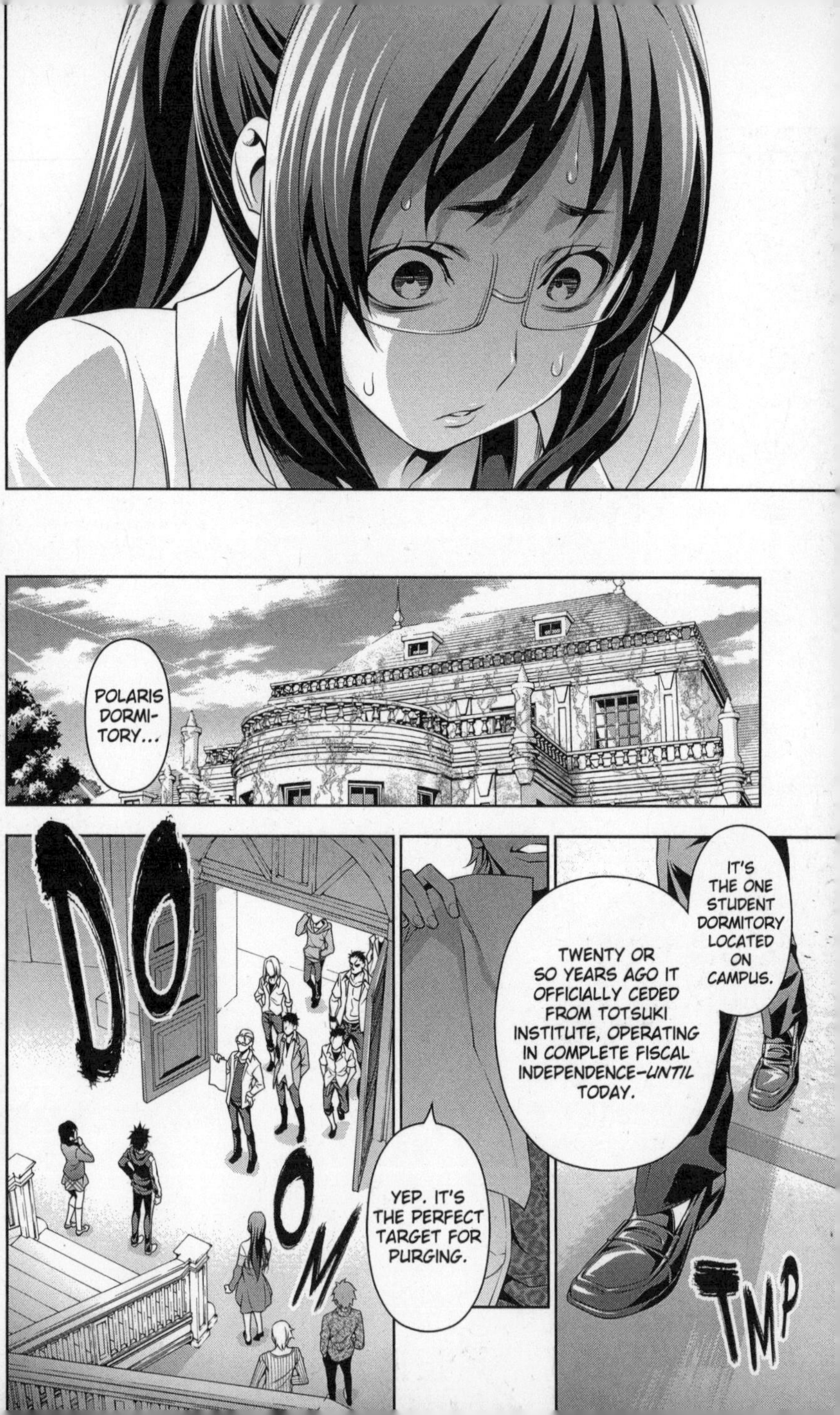
POLARIS DORMITORY...
IT'S THE ONE STUDENT DORMITORY LOCATED ON CAMPUS.
TMP
TWENTY OR SO YEARS AGO IT OFFICIALLY CEDED FROM TOTSUKI INSTITUTE, OPERATING IN COMPLETE FISCAL INDEPENDENCE–*UNTIL* TODAY.
YEP. IT'S THE PERFECT TARGET FOR PURGING.
DOOM

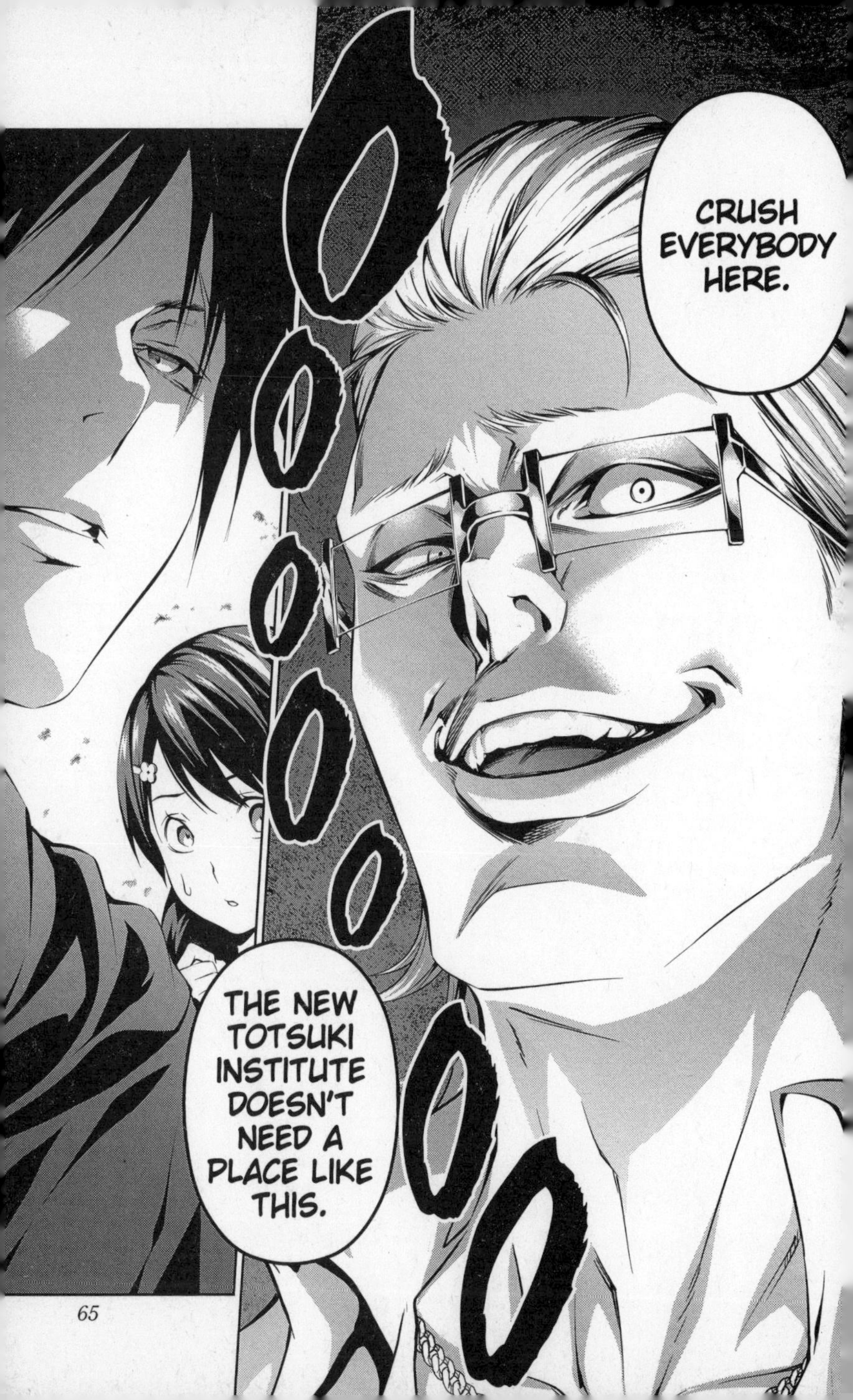
CRUSH EVERYBODY HERE.
THE NEW TOTSUKI INSTITUTE DOESN'T NEED A PLACE LIKE THIS.

Miss Erina's Splendid Days as a Runaway 3

~A SAFE HAVEN~

BY THE WAY, MISS ERINA WAS ASSIGNED ROOM 301.

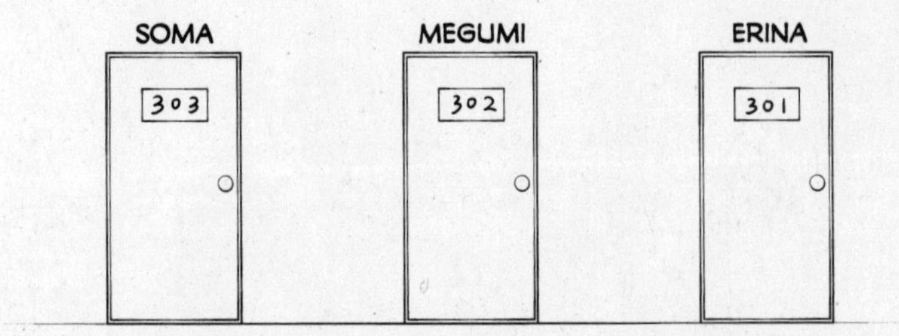

SOMA

303

MEGUMI

302

ERINA

301

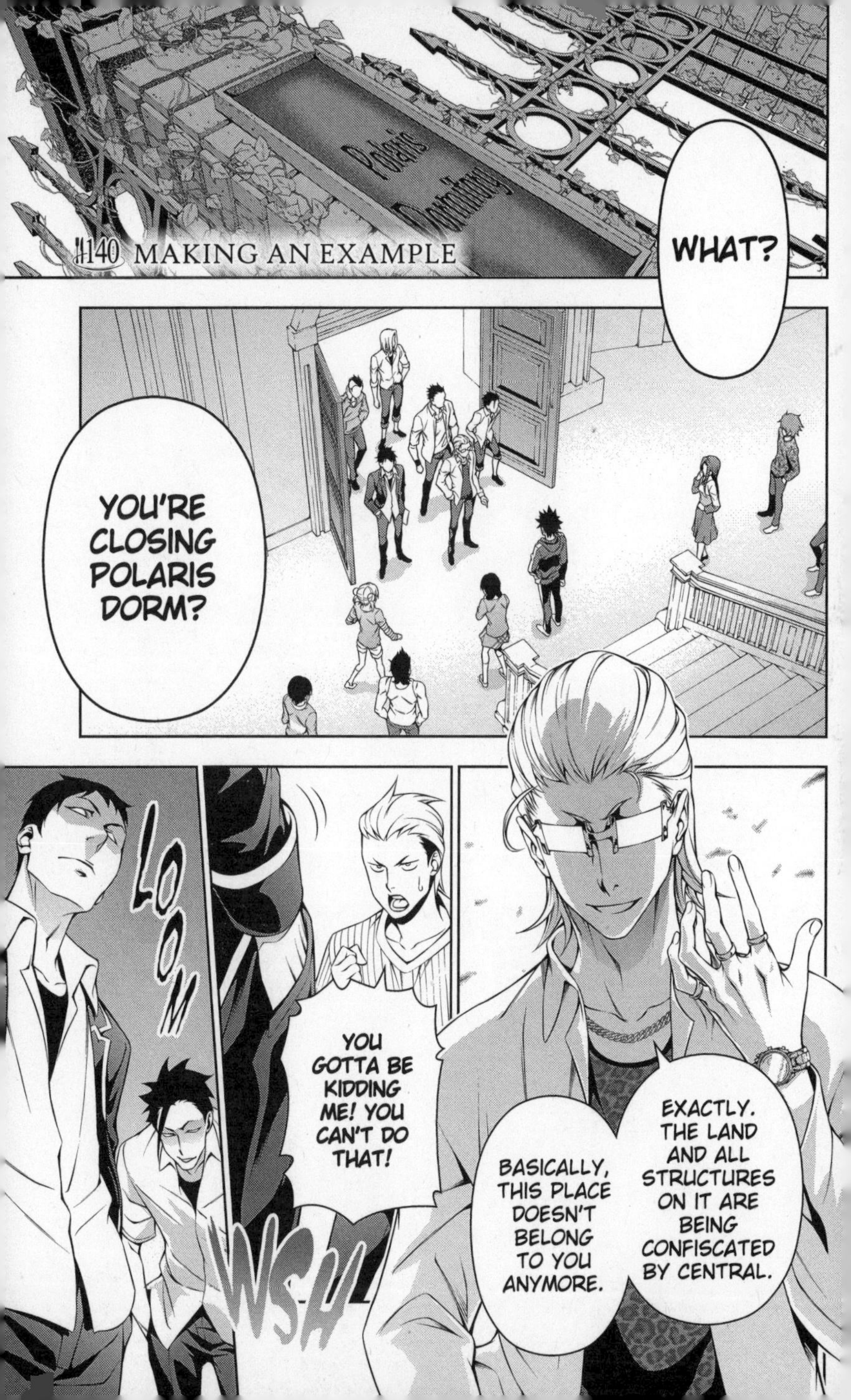
#140 MAKING AN EXAMPLE
Polaris
WHAT?
YOU'RE CLOSING POLARIS DORM?
EXACTLY. THE LAND AND ALL STRUCTURES ON IT ARE BEING CONFISCATED BY CENTRAL.
BASICALLY, THIS PLACE DOESN'T BELONG TO YOU ANYMORE.
YOU GOTTA BE KIDDING ME! YOU CAN'T DO THAT!
LOOM
WSH

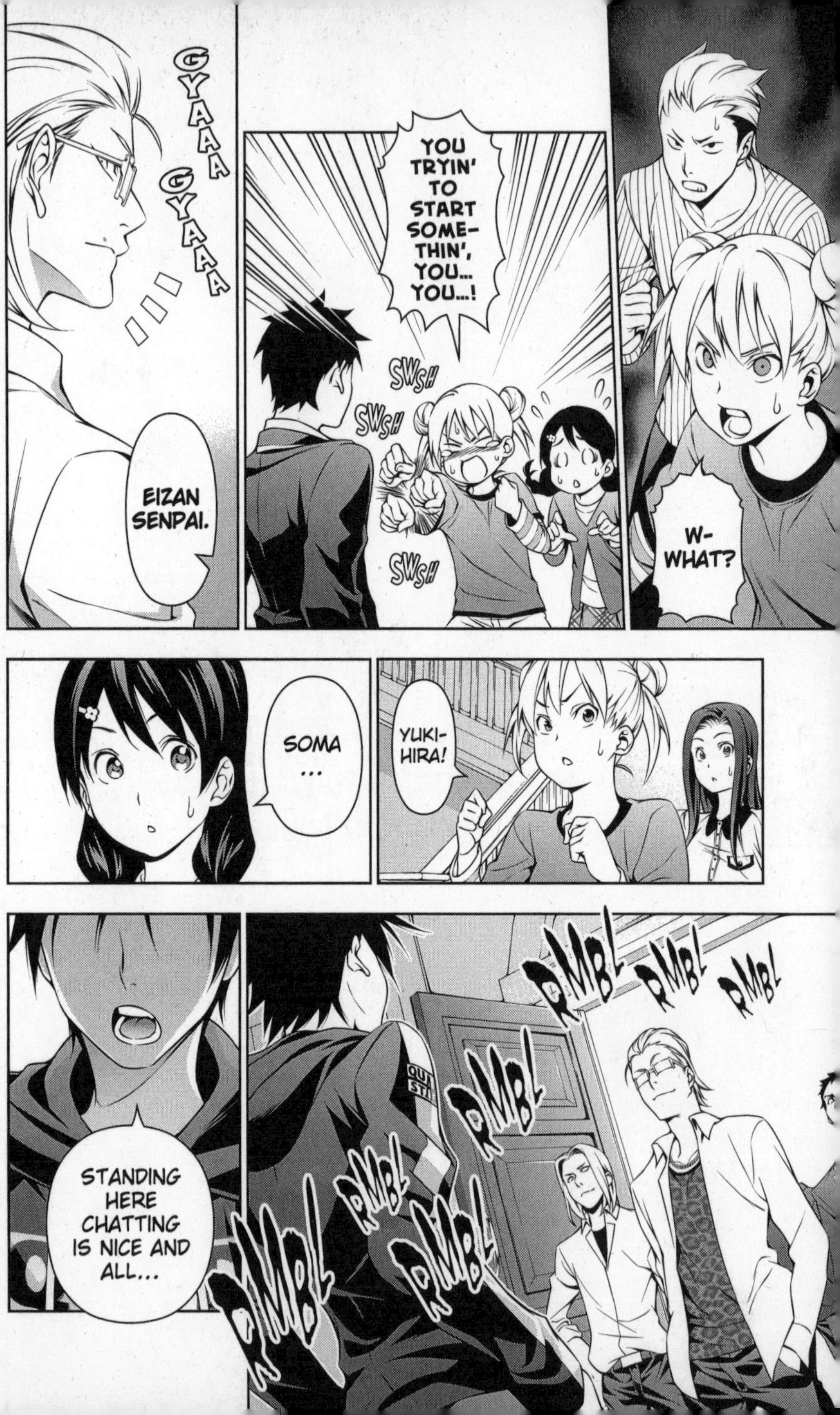
W-WHAT?
YOU TRYIN' TO START SOMETHIN', YOU... YOU...!
SWSH
SWSH
SWSH
GYAAAA
GYAAAA
...
EIZAN SENPAI.
YUKI-HIRA!
SOMA ...
RMBL
RMBL
RMBL
RMBL
RMBL
RMBL
RMBL
RMBL
RMBL
STANDING HERE CHATTING IS NICE AND ALL...

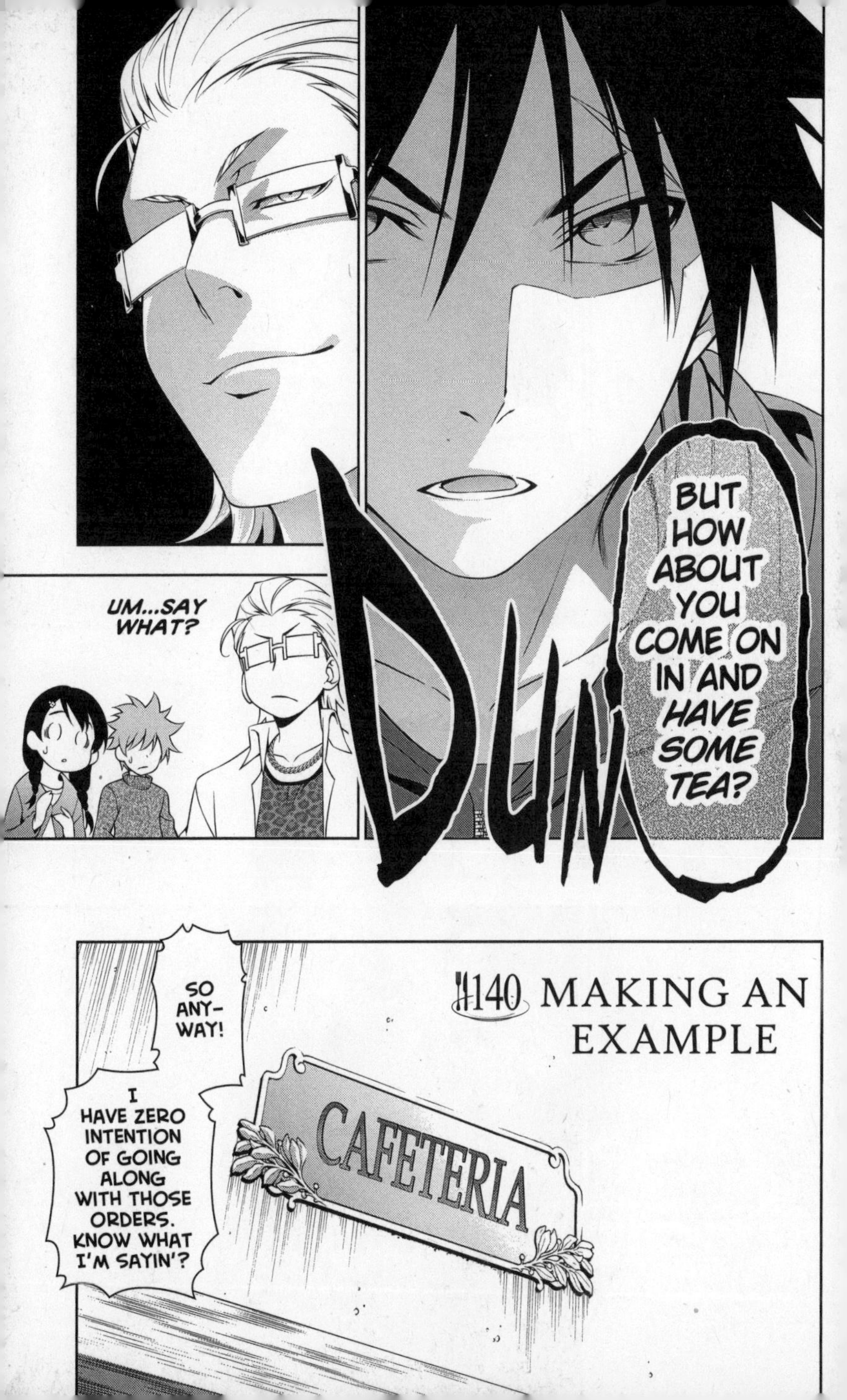
BUT HOW ABOUT YOU COME ON IN AND HAVE SOME TEA?
DUN
UM...SAY WHAT?
140 MAKING AN EXAMPLE
CAFETERIA
SO ANY-WAY!
I HAVE ZERO INTENTION OF GOING ALONG WITH THOSE ORDERS. KNOW WHAT I'M SAYIN'?

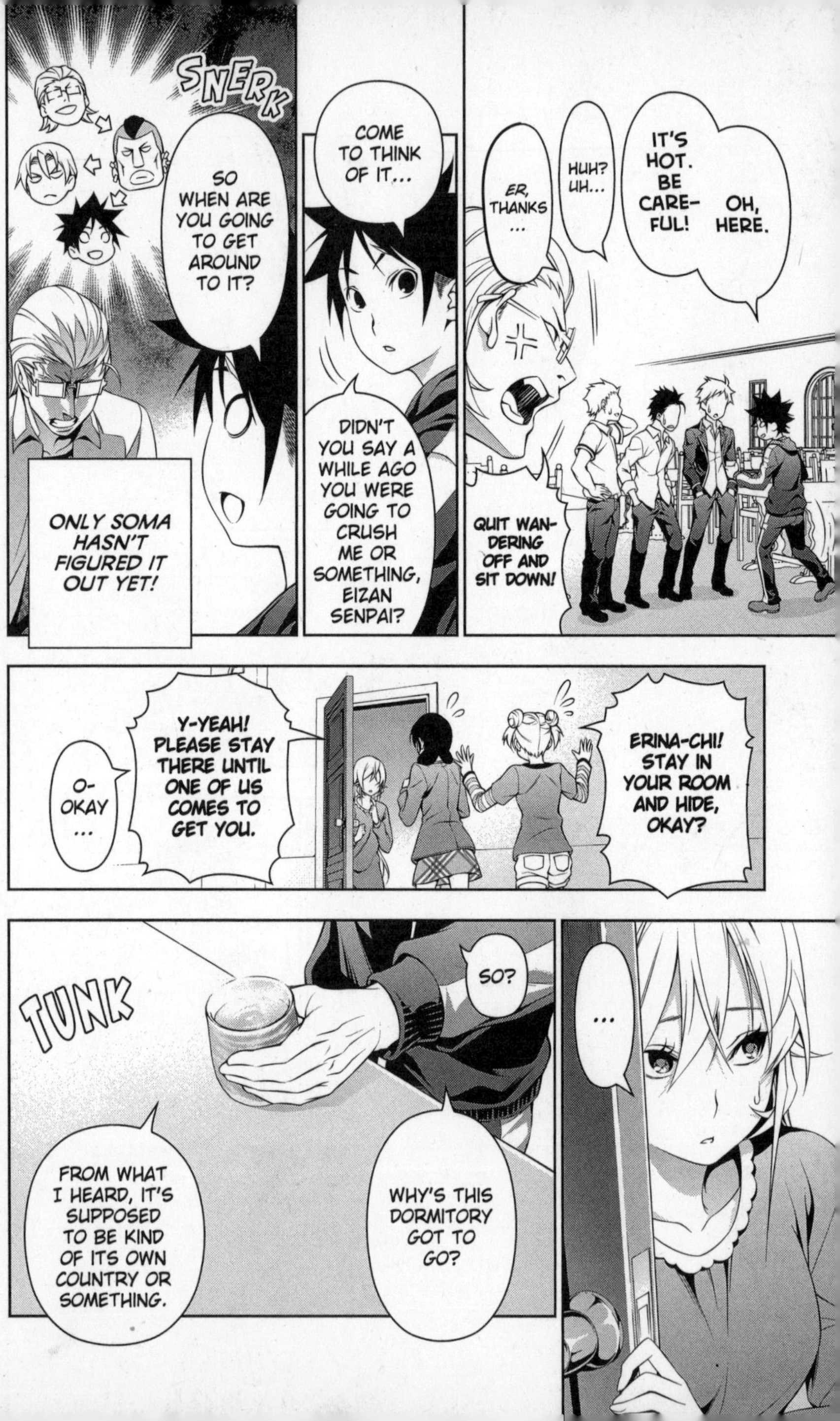
OH, HERE.
IT'S HOT. BE CARE-FUL!
HUH? UH...
ER, THANKS...
QUIT WAN-DERING OFF AND SIT DOWN!
COME TO THINK OF IT...
DIDN'T YOU SAY A WHILE AGO YOU WERE GOING TO CRUSH ME OR SOMETHING, EIZAN SENPAI?
SNERK
SO WHEN ARE YOU GOING TO GET AROUND TO IT?
ONLY SOMA HASN'T FIGURED IT OUT YET!
ERINA-CHI! STAY IN YOUR ROOM AND HIDE, OKAY?
Y-YEAH! PLEASE STAY THERE UNTIL ONE OF US COMES TO GET YOU.
O-OKAY...
...
SO?
WHY'S THIS DORMITORY GOT TO GO?
FROM WHAT I HEARD, IT'S SUPPOSED TO BE KIND OF ITS OWN COUNTRY OR SOMETHING.
TUNK

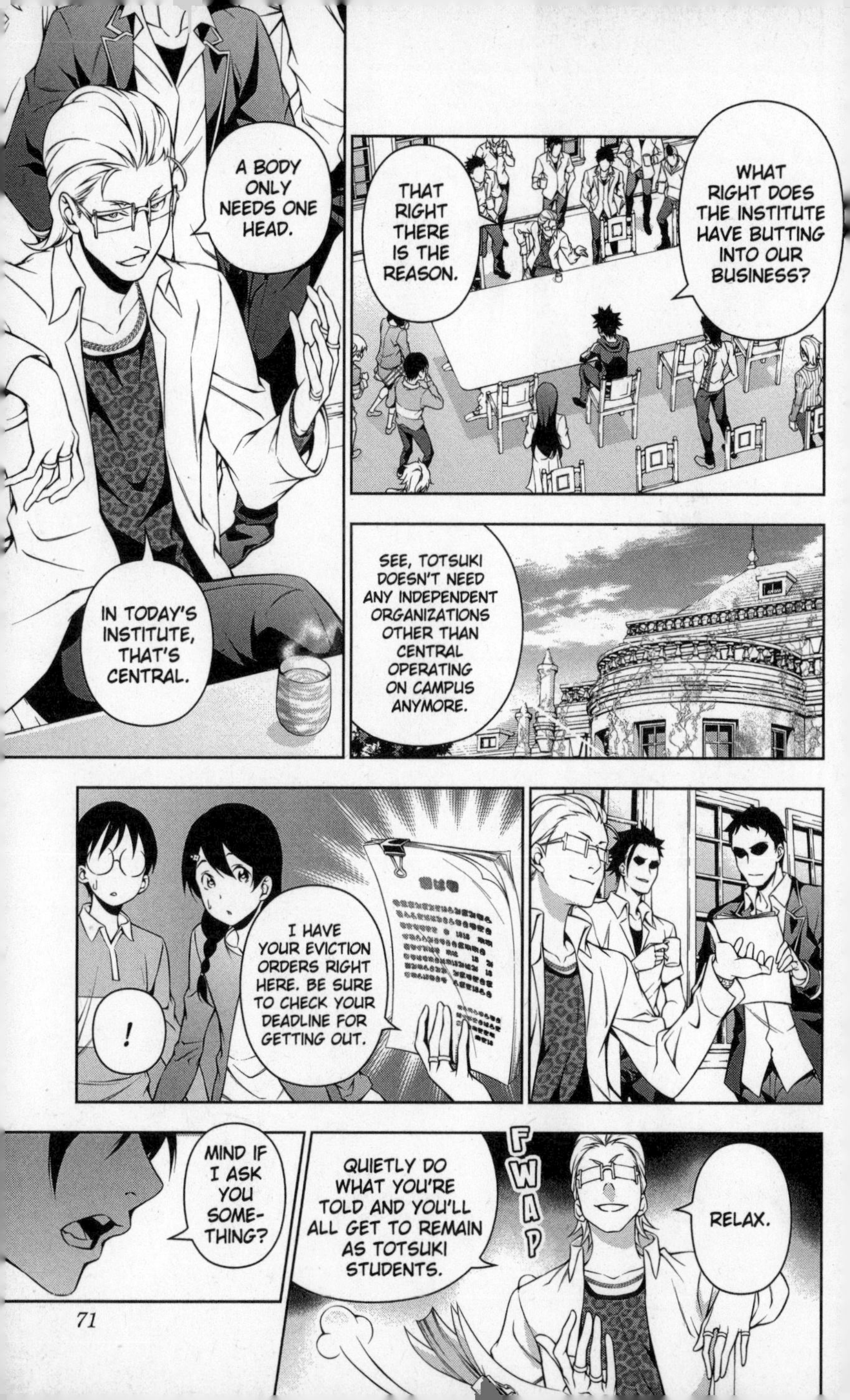
WHAT RIGHT DOES THE INSTITUTE HAVE BUTTING INTO OUR BUSINESS?
THAT RIGHT THERE IS THE REASON.
SEE, TOTSUKI DOESN'T NEED ANY INDEPENDENT ORGANIZATIONS OTHER THAN CENTRAL OPERATING ON CAMPUS ANYMORE.
A BODY ONLY NEEDS ONE HEAD.
IN TODAY'S INSTITUTE, THAT'S CENTRAL.
I HAVE YOUR EVICTION ORDERS RIGHT HERE. BE SURE TO CHECK YOUR DEADLINE FOR GETTING OUT.
!
RELAX.
FWAP
QUIETLY DO WHAT YOU'RE TOLD AND YOU'LL ALL GET TO REMAIN AS TOTSUKI STUDENTS.
MIND IF I ASK YOU SOME-THING?

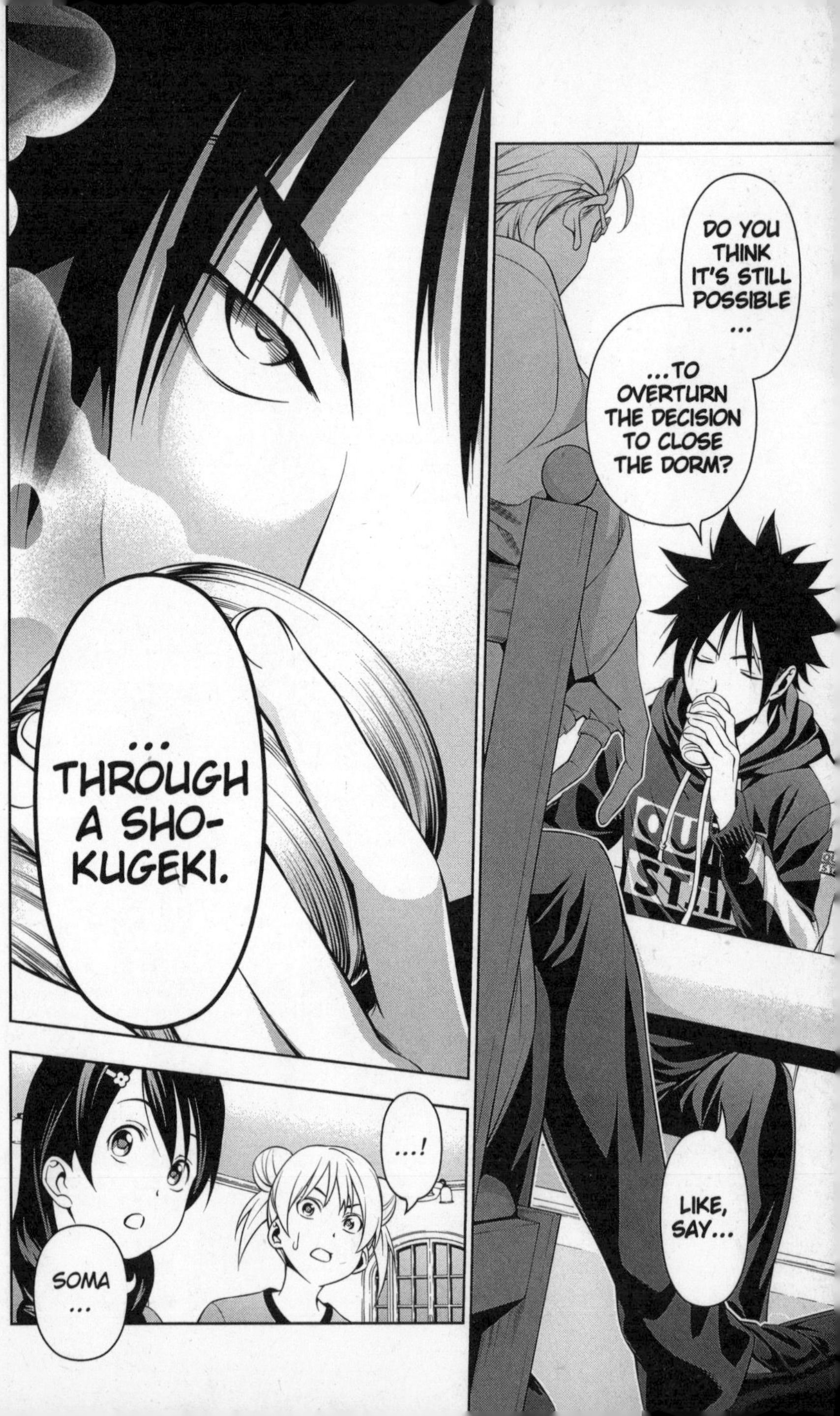
DO YOU THINK IT'S STILL POSSIBLE ...
...TO OVERTURN THE DECISION TO CLOSE THE DORM?
LIKE, SAY...
... THROUGH A SHO-KUGEKI.
...!
SOMA ...

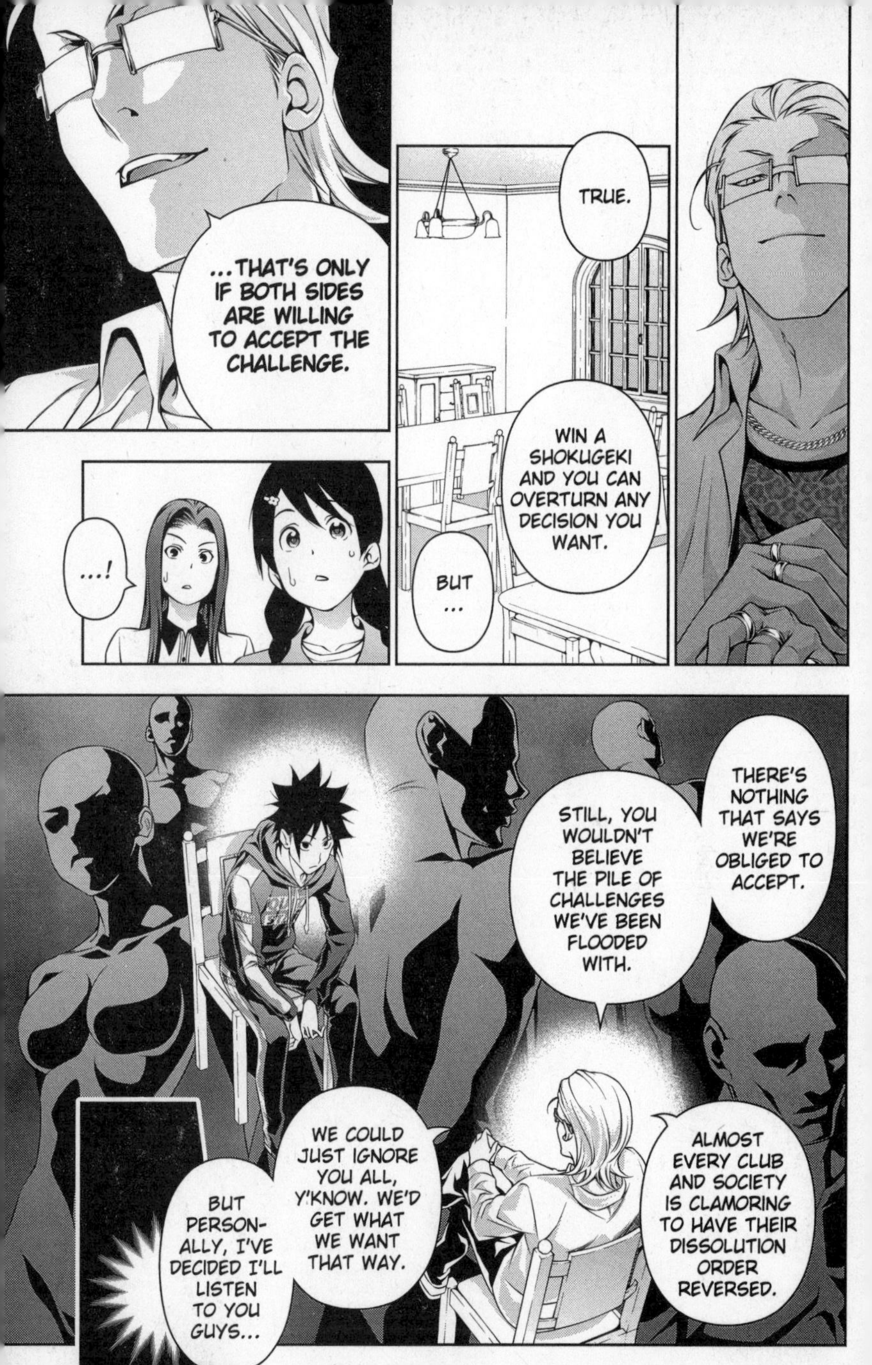
TRUE.
WIN A SHOKUGEKI AND YOU CAN OVERTURN ANY DECISION YOU WANT.
BUT ...
...THAT'S ONLY IF BOTH SIDES ARE WILLING TO ACCEPT THE CHALLENGE.
...!
THERE'S NOTHING THAT SAYS WE'RE OBLIGED TO ACCEPT.
STILL, YOU WOULDN'T BELIEVE THE PILE OF CHALLENGES WE'VE BEEN FLOODED WITH.
ALMOST EVERY CLUB AND SOCIETY IS CLAMORING TO HAVE THEIR DISSOLUTION ORDER REVERSED.
WE COULD JUST IGNORE YOU ALL, Y'KNOW. WE'D GET WHAT WE WANT THAT WAY.
BUT PERSON-ALLY, I'VE DECIDED I'LL LISTEN TO YOU GUYS...

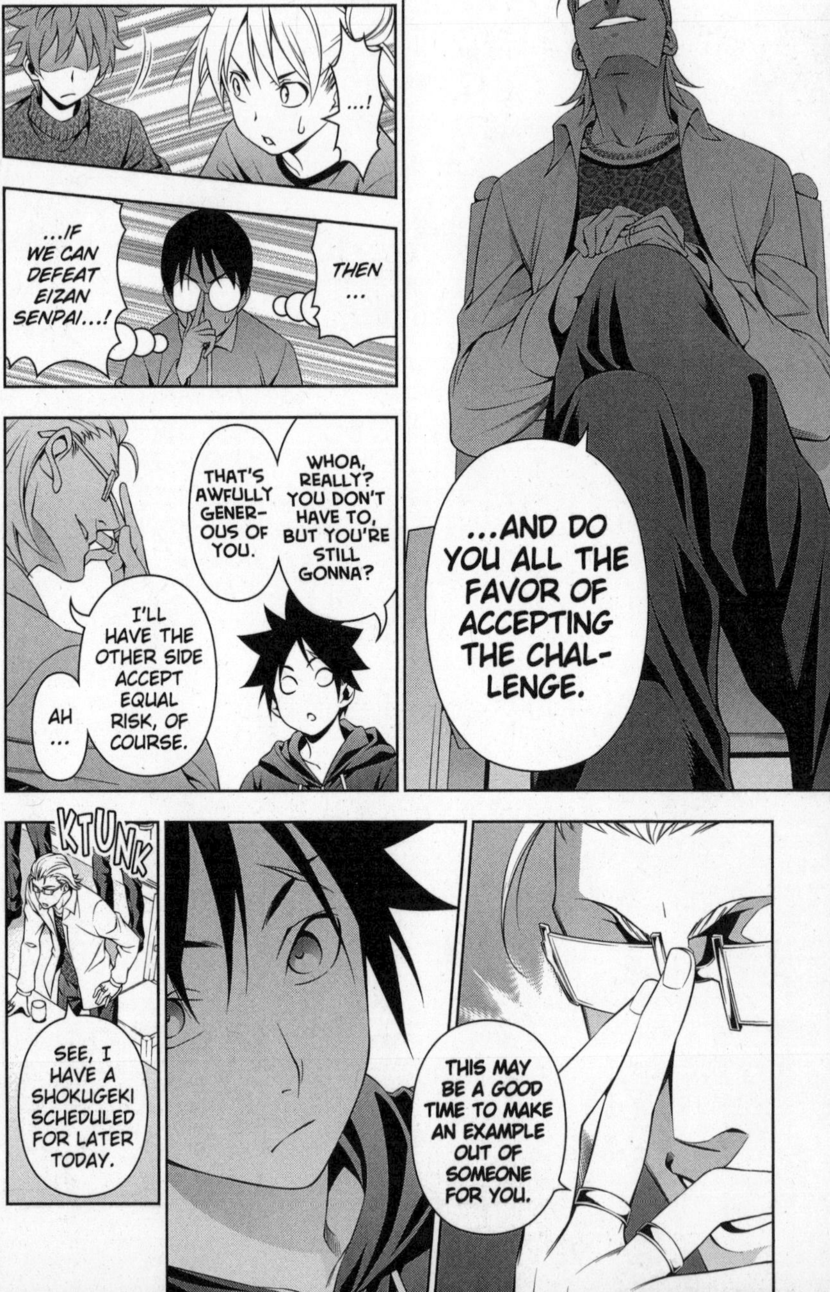
...AND DO YOU ALL THE FAVOR OF ACCEPTING THE CHAL-LENGE.
...!
THEN ...
...IF WE CAN DEFEAT EIZAN SENPAI...!
WHOA, REALLY? YOU DON'T HAVE TO, BUT YOU'RE STILL GONNA?
THAT'S AWFULLY GENER-OUS OF YOU.
I'LL HAVE THE OTHER SIDE ACCEPT EQUAL RISK, OF COURSE.
AH ...
THIS MAY BE A GOOD TIME TO MAKE AN EXAMPLE OUT OF SOMEONE FOR YOU.
KTUNK
SEE, I HAVE A SHOKUGEKI SCHEDULED FOR LATER TODAY.

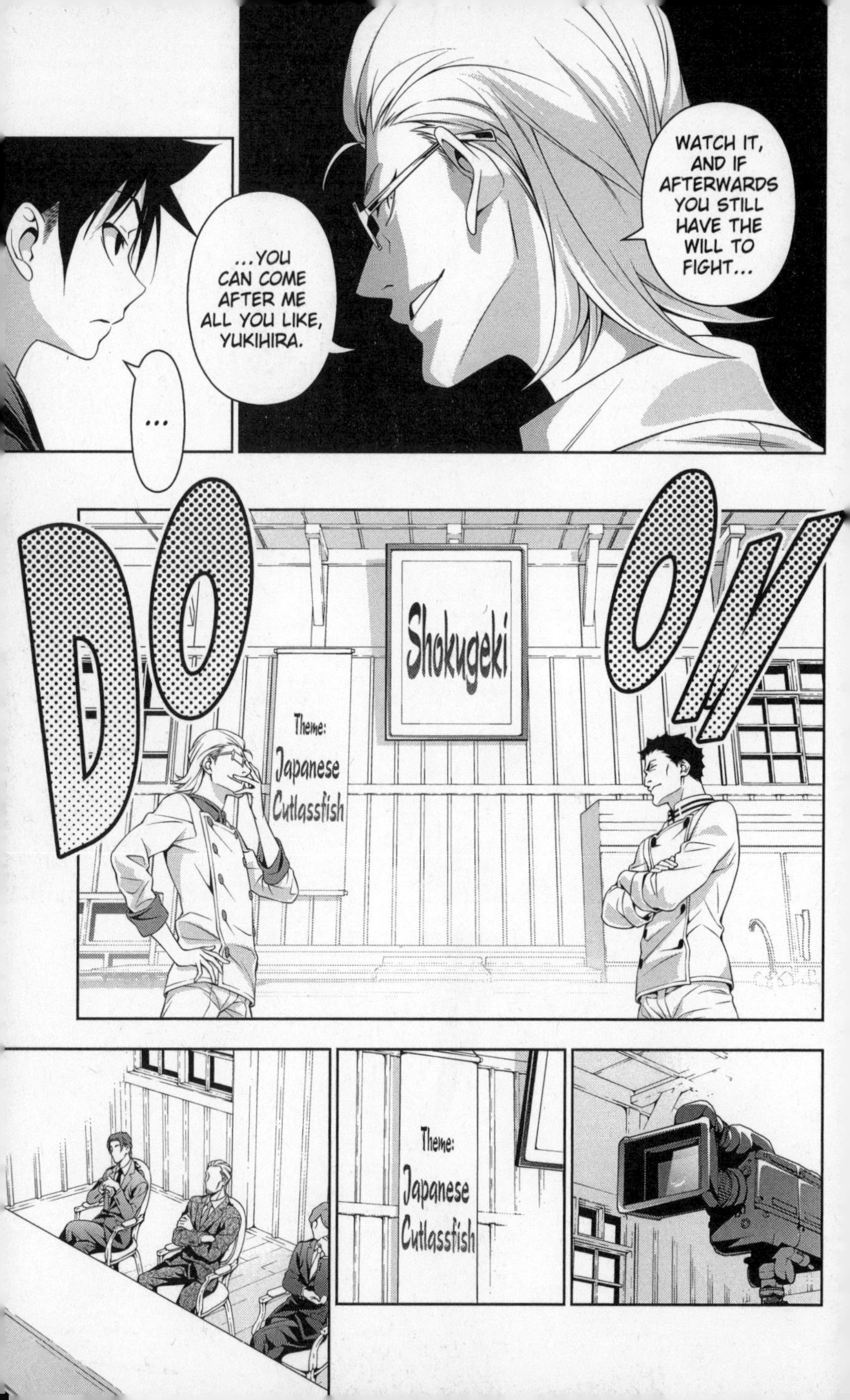
WATCH IT, AND IF AFTERWARDS YOU STILL HAVE THE WILL TO FIGHT...
...YOU CAN COME AFTER ME ALL YOU LIKE, YUKIHIRA.
...
DOOM
Shokugeki
Theme:
Japanese Cutlassfish
Theme:
Japanese Cutlassfish

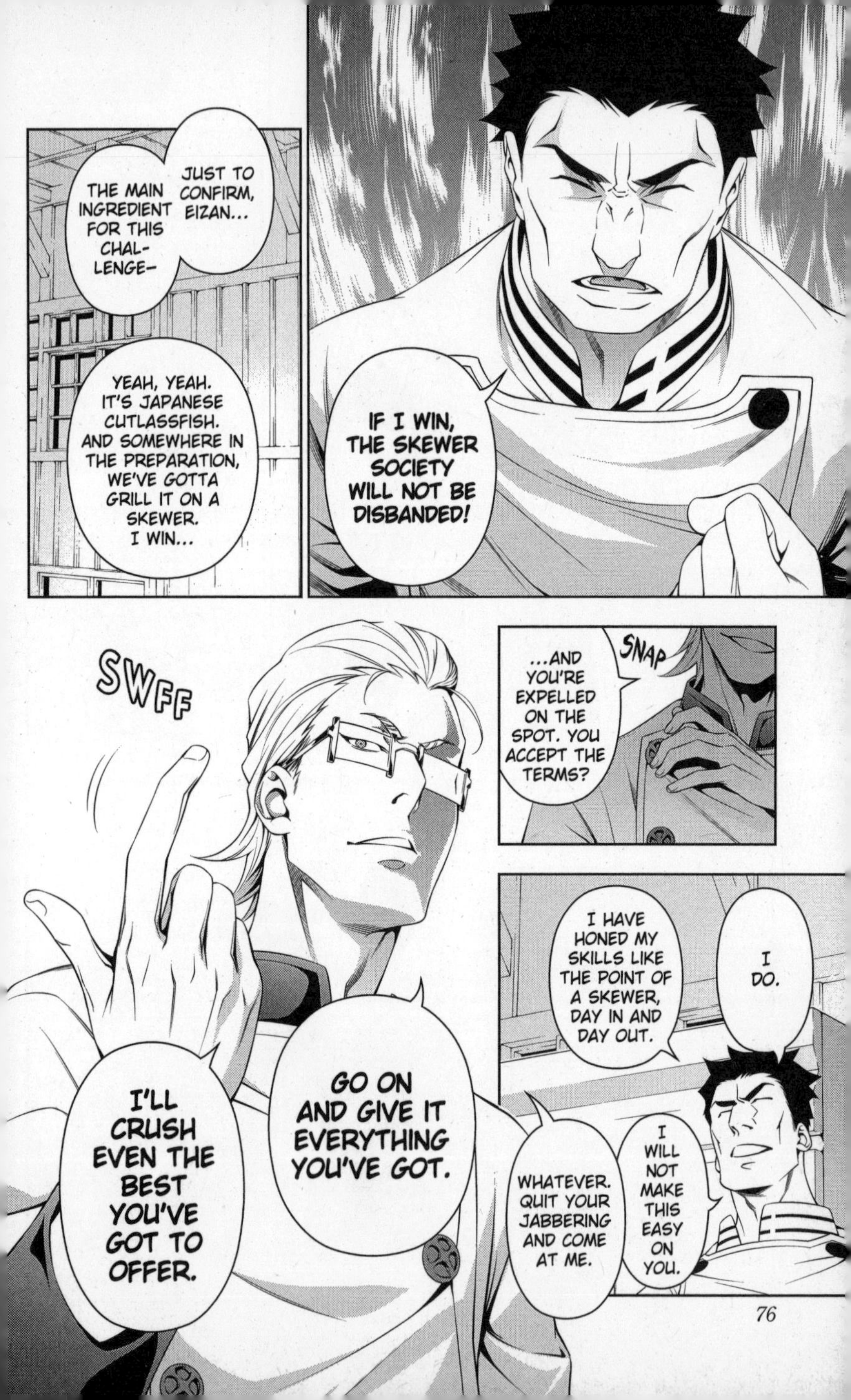
IF I WIN, THE SKEWER SOCIETY WILL NOT BE DISBANDED!
JUST TO CONFIRM, EIZAN... THE MAIN INGREDIENT FOR THIS CHAL-LENGE—
YEAH, YEAH. IT'S JAPANESE CUTLASSFISH. AND SOMEWHERE IN THE PREPARATION, WE'VE GOTTA GRILL IT ON A SKEWER. I WIN...
SNAP
...AND YOU'RE EXPELLED ON THE SPOT. YOU ACCEPT THE TERMS?
I DO.
I HAVE HONED MY SKILLS LIKE THE POINT OF A SKEWER, DAY IN AND DAY OUT.
I WILL NOT MAKE THIS EASY ON YOU.
WHATEVER. QUIT YOUR JABBERING AND COME AT ME.
SWFF
GO ON AND GIVE IT EVERYTHING YOU'VE GOT.
I'LL CRUSH EVEN THE BEST YOU'VE GOT TO OFFER.

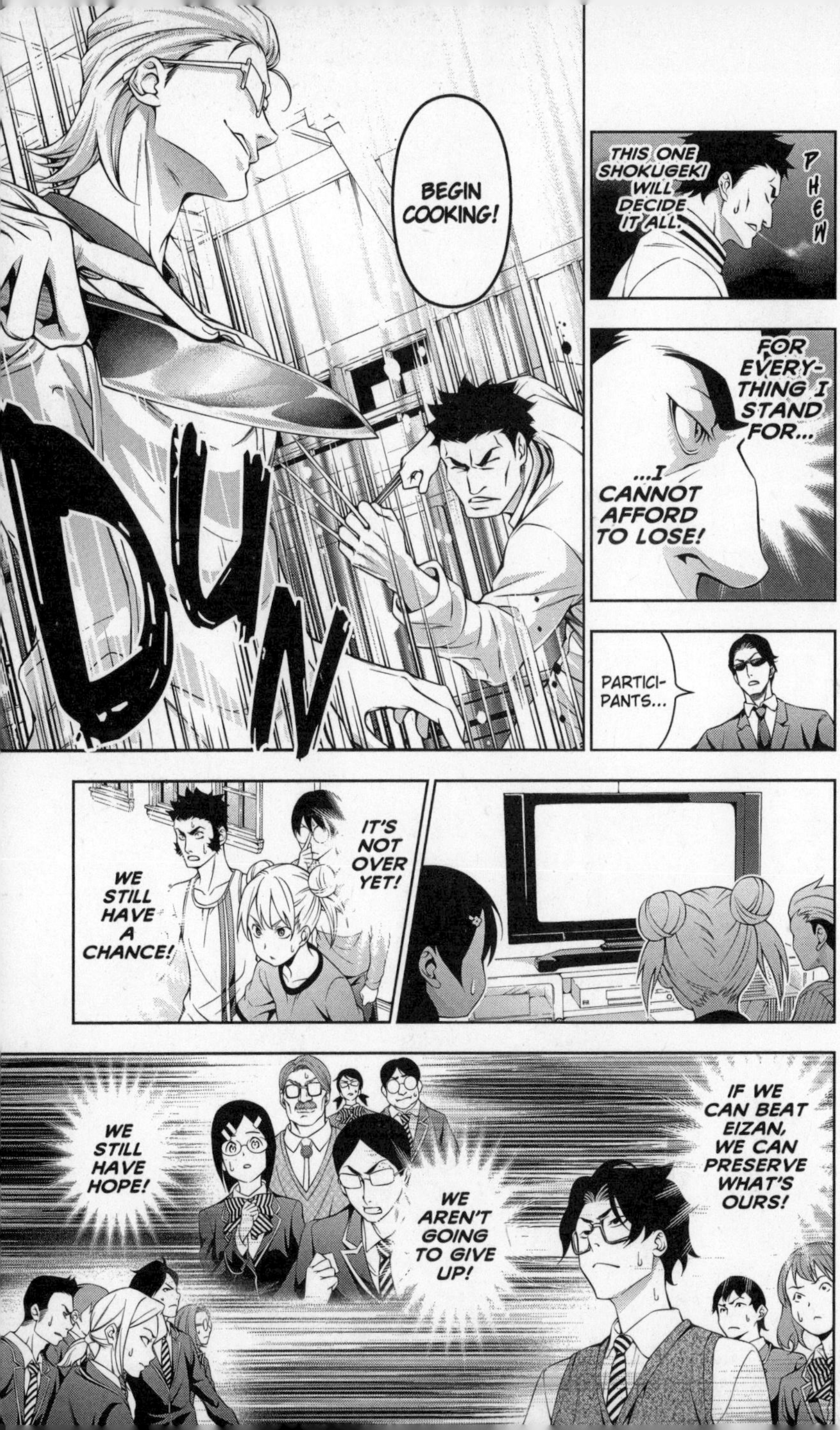
THIS ONE SHOKUGEKI WILL DECIDE IT ALL.
PHEW
FOR EVERYTHING I STAND FOR...
...I CANNOT AFFORD TO LOSE!
PARTICIPANTS...
BEGIN COOKING!
DUN
IT'S NOT OVER YET!
WE STILL HAVE A CHANCE!
IF WE CAN BEAT EIZAN, WE CAN PRESERVE WHAT'S OURS!
WE AREN'T GOING TO GIVE UP!
WE STILL HAVE HOPE!

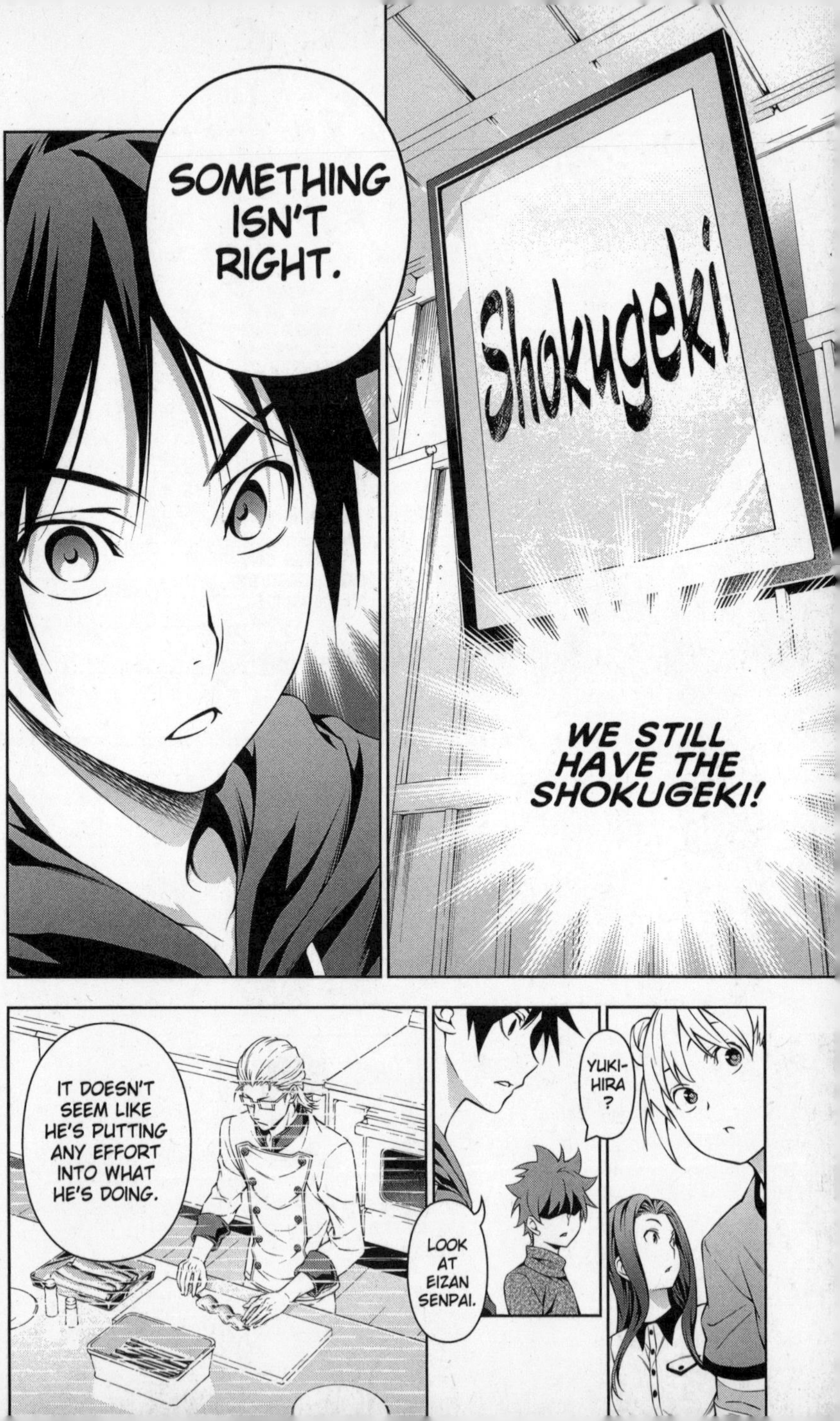
Shokugeki
WE STILL HAVE THE SHOKUGEKI!
SOMETHING ISN'T RIGHT.
YUKI-HIRA?
LOOK AT EIZAN SENPAI.
IT DOESN'T SEEM LIKE HE'S PUTTING ANY EFFORT INTO WHAT HE'S DOING.

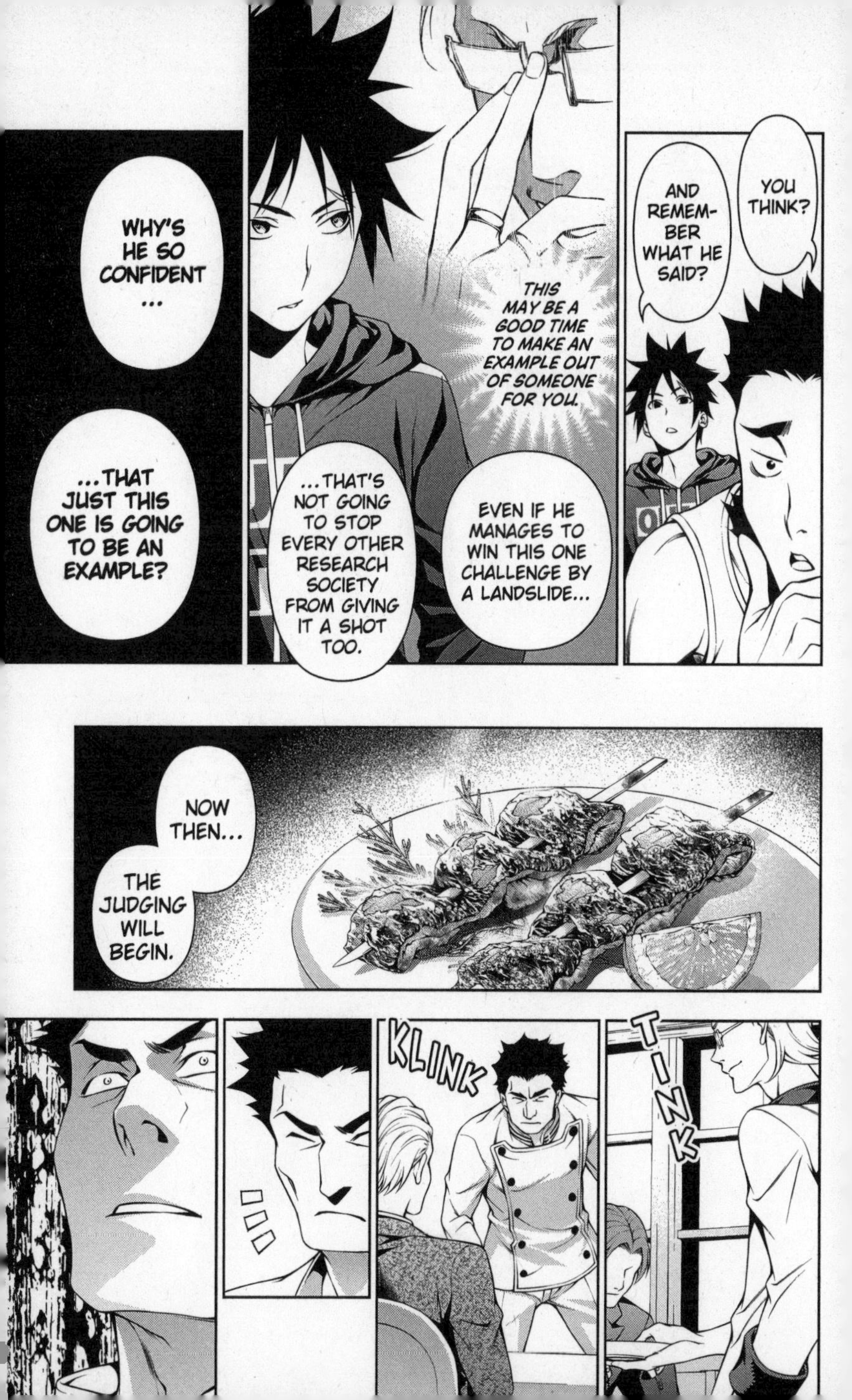
YOU THINK?
AND REMEMBER WHAT HE SAID?
THIS MAY BE A GOOD TIME TO MAKE AN EXAMPLE OUT OF SOMEONE FOR YOU.
EVEN IF HE MANAGES TO WIN THIS ONE CHALLENGE BY A LANDSLIDE...
...THAT'S NOT GOING TO STOP EVERY OTHER RESEARCH SOCIETY FROM GIVING IT A SHOT TOO.
WHY'S HE SO CONFIDENT...
...THAT JUST THIS ONE IS GOING TO BE AN EXAMPLE?
NOW THEN...
THE JUDGING WILL BEGIN.
TINK
KLINK

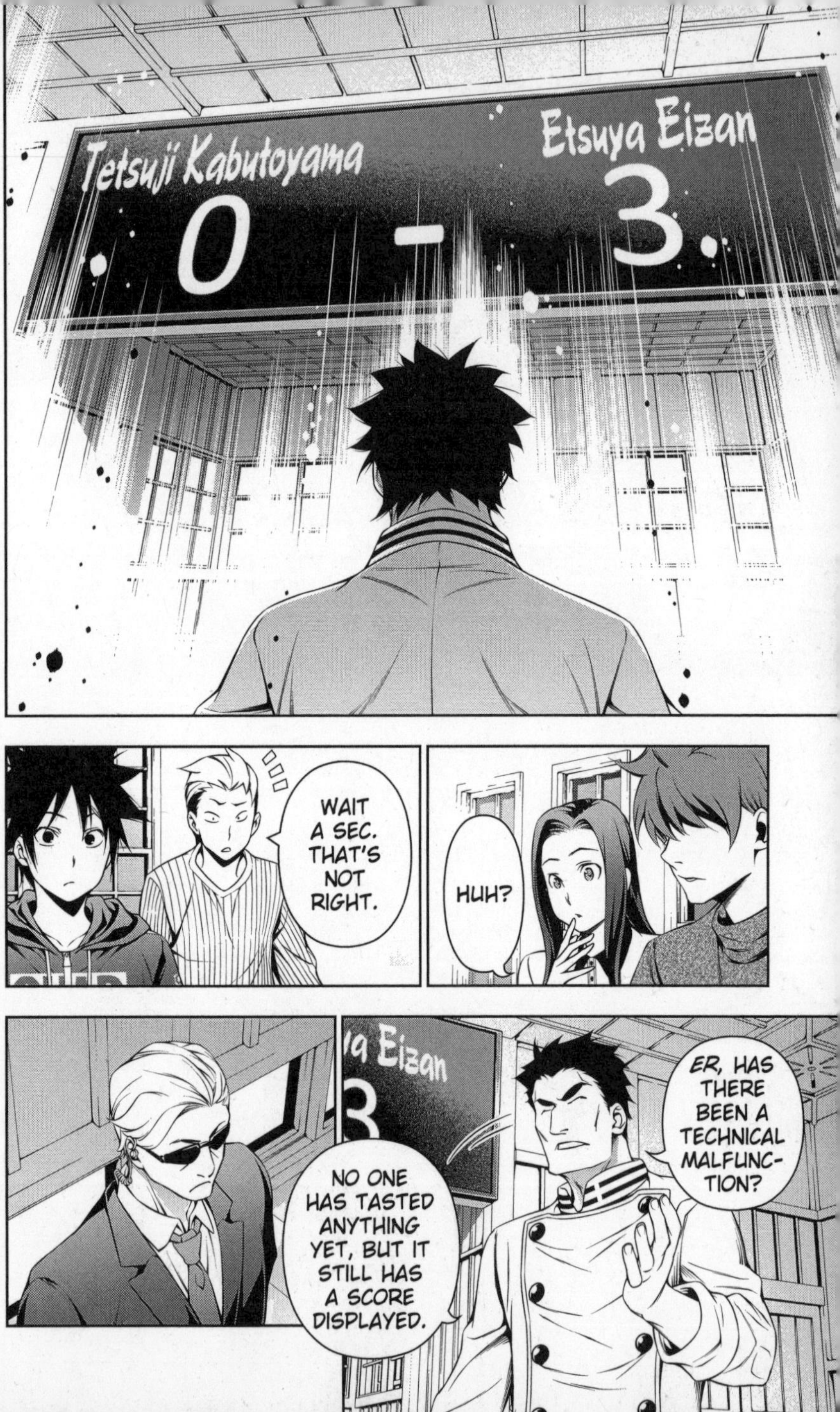
Tetsuji Kabutoyama
Etsuya Eizan
0 - 3
HUH?
WAIT A SEC. THAT'S NOT RIGHT.
ER, HAS THERE BEEN A TECHNICAL MALFUNCTION?
NO ONE HAS TASTED ANYTHING YET, BUT IT STILL HAS A SCORE DISPLAYED.

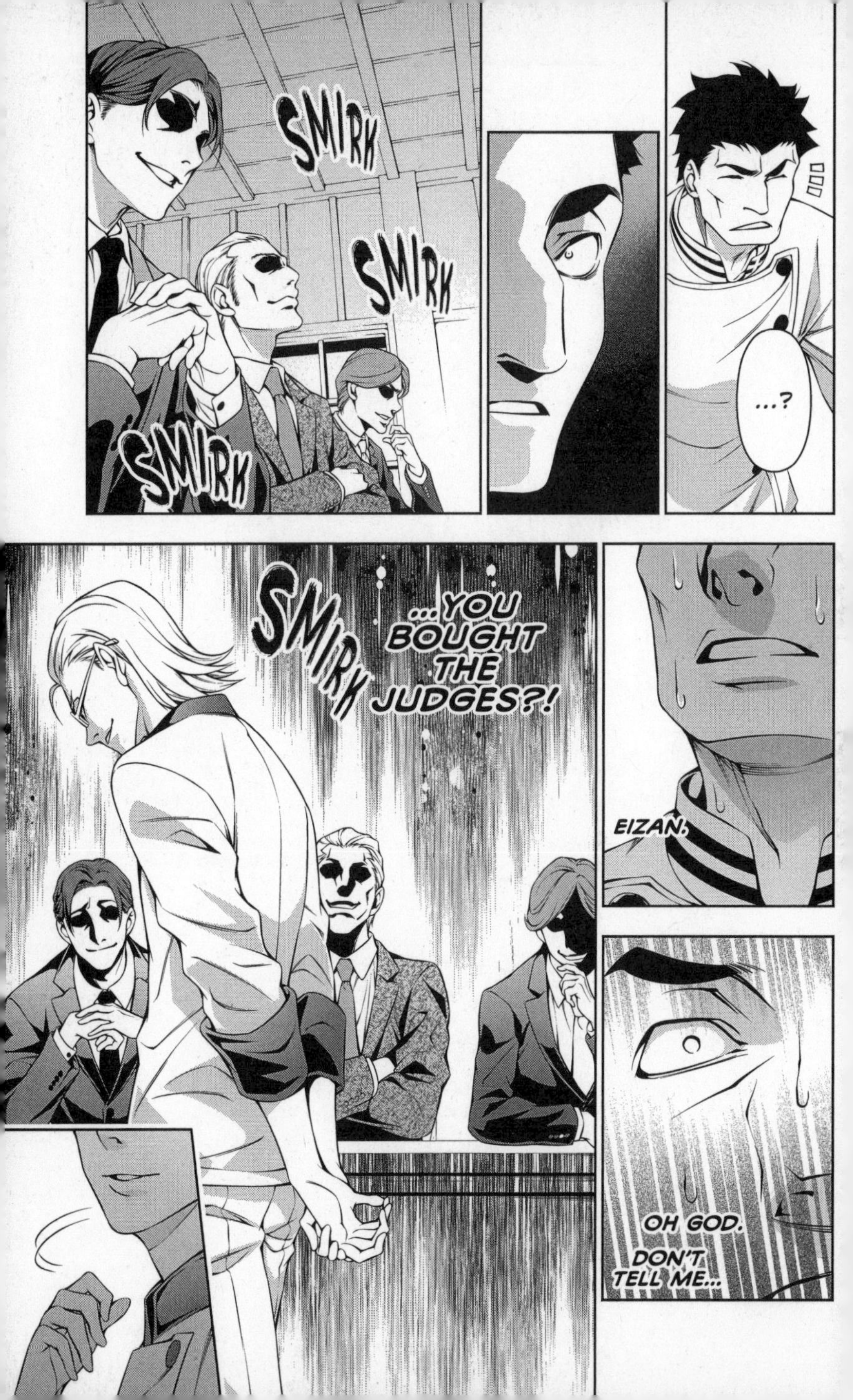
...?
SMIRK
SMIRK
SMIRK
EIZAN.
OH GOD.
DON'T TELL ME...
SMIRK
...YOU BOUGHT THE JUDGES?!

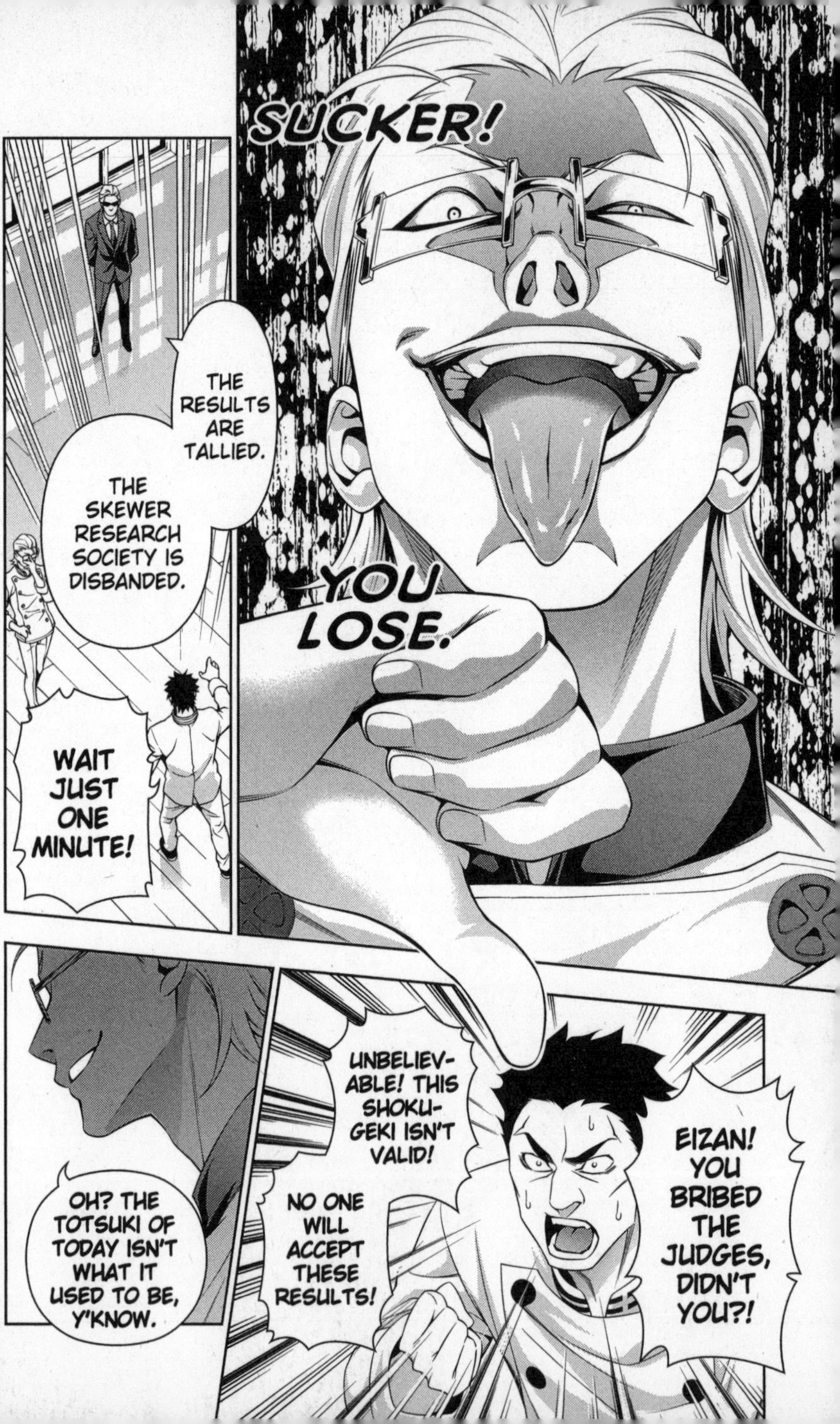
SUCKER!
YOU LOSE.
THE RESULTS ARE TALLIED.
THE SKEWER RESEARCH SOCIETY IS DISBANDED.
WAIT JUST ONE MINUTE!
EIZAN! YOU BRIBED THE JUDGES, DIDN'T YOU?!
UNBELIEV-ABLE! THIS SHOKU-GEKI ISN'T VALID!
NO ONE WILL ACCEPT THESE RESULTS!
OH? THE TOTSUKI OF TODAY ISN'T WHAT IT USED TO BE, Y'KNOW.

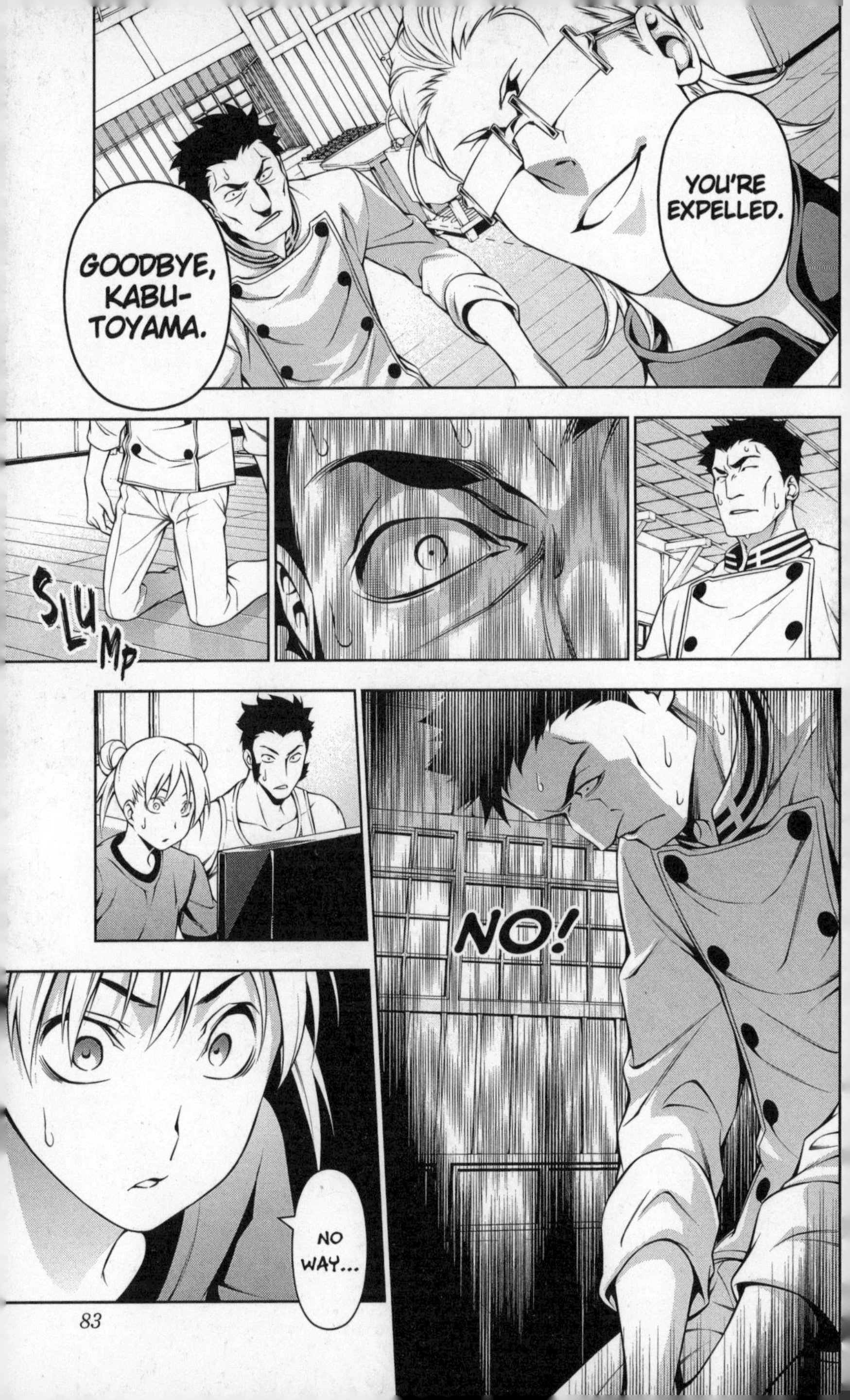
YOU'RE EXPELLED.
GOODBYE, KABU-TOYAMA.
SLUMP
NO!
NO WAY...

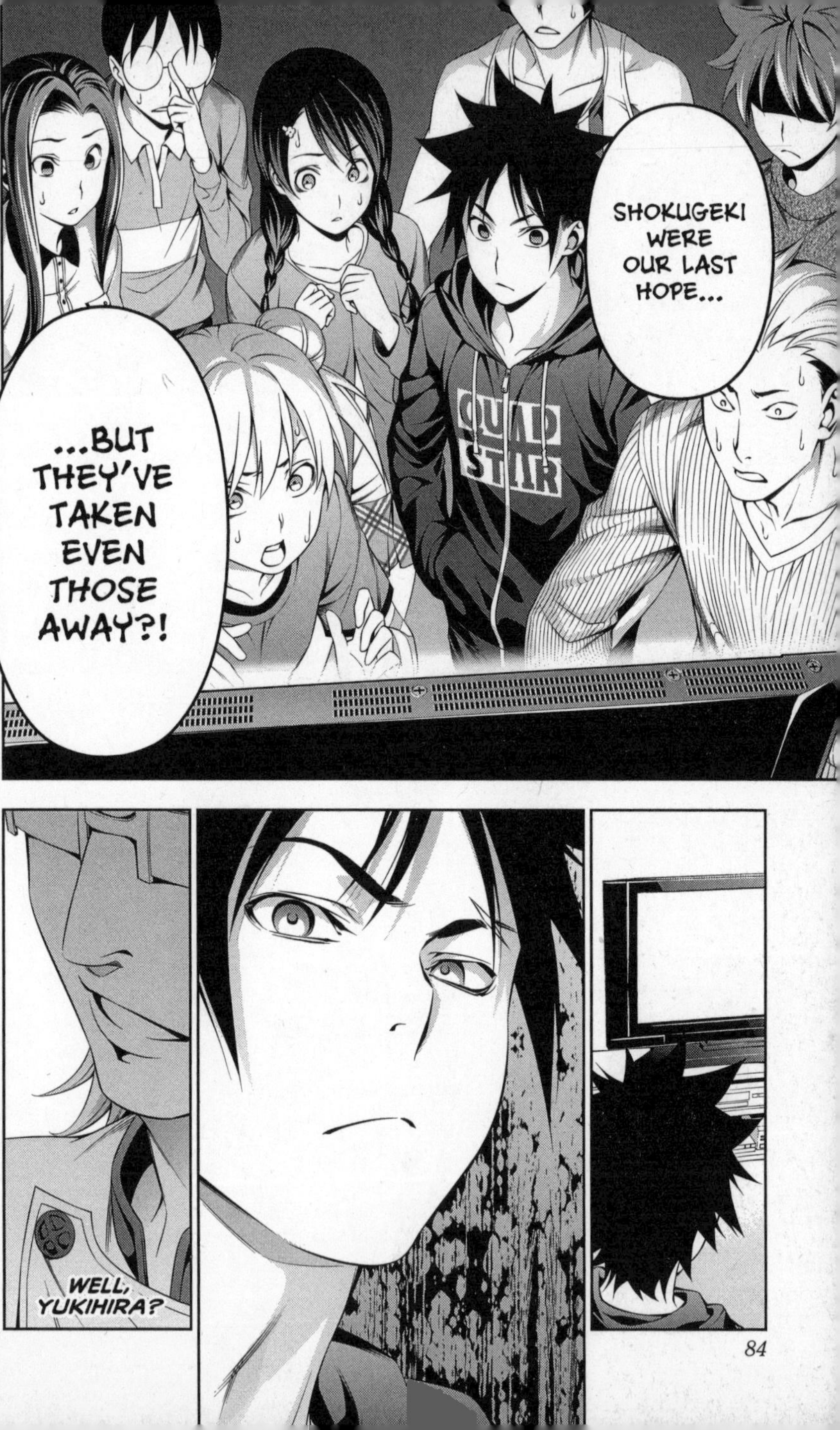
SHOKUGEKI WERE OUR LAST HOPE...
QUAD STAR
...BUT THEY'VE TAKEN EVEN THOSE AWAY?!
WELL, YUKIHIRA?

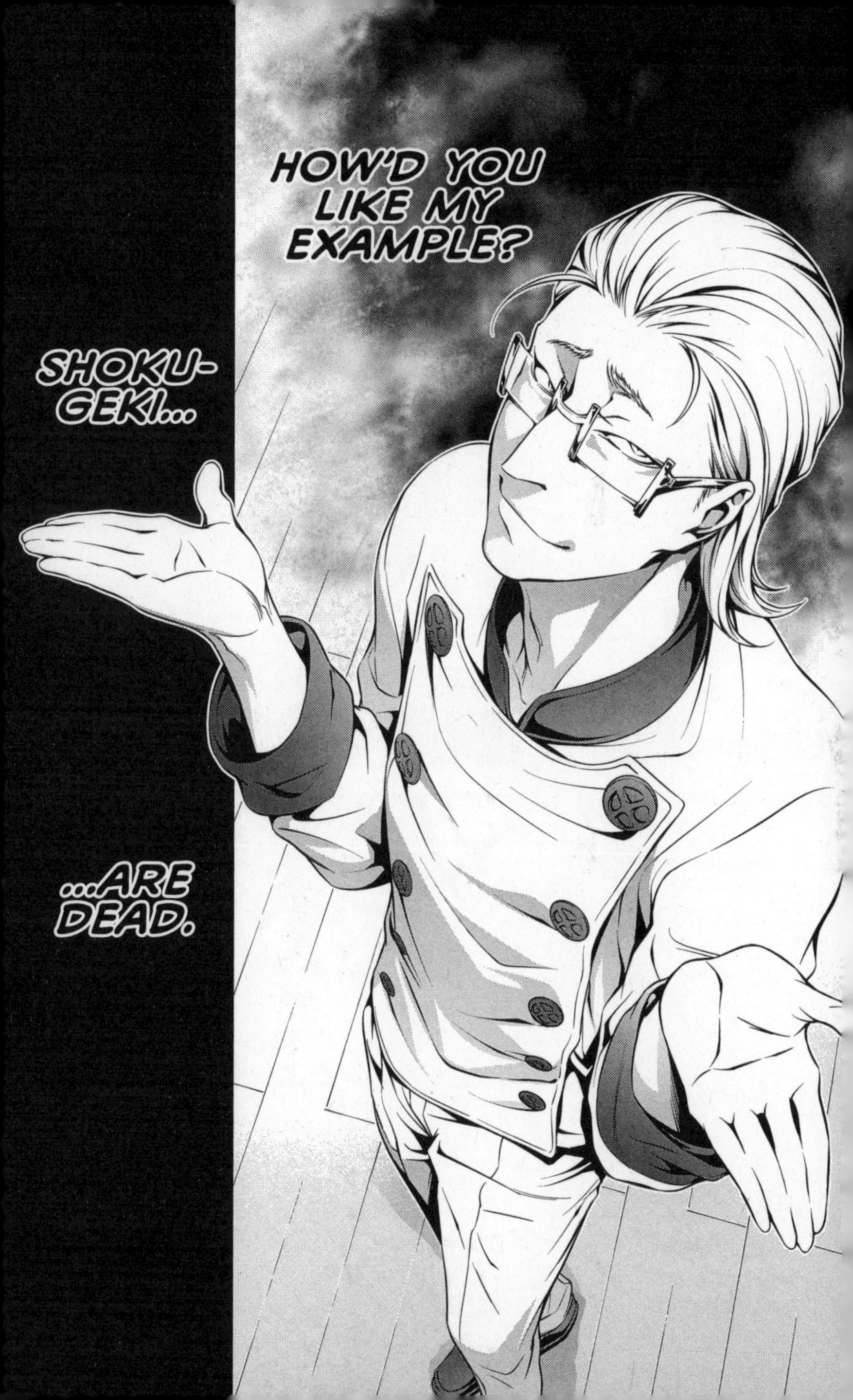
HOW'D YOU LIKE MY EXAMPLE?
SHOKU-GEKI...
...ARE DEAD.

Miss Erina's Splendid Days as a Runaway 4

~ALONG THE LONG AND WINDING ROAD~

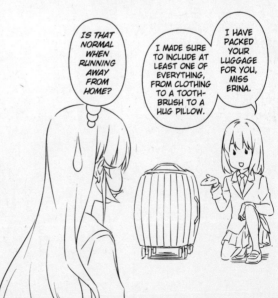

I HAVE PACKED YOUR LUGGAGE FOR YOU, MISS ERINA.
I MADE SURE TO INCLUDE AT LEAST ONE OF EVERYTHING, FROM CLOTHING TO A TOOTH-BRUSH TO A HUG PILLOW.
IS THAT NORMAL WHEN RUNNING AWAY FROM HOME?

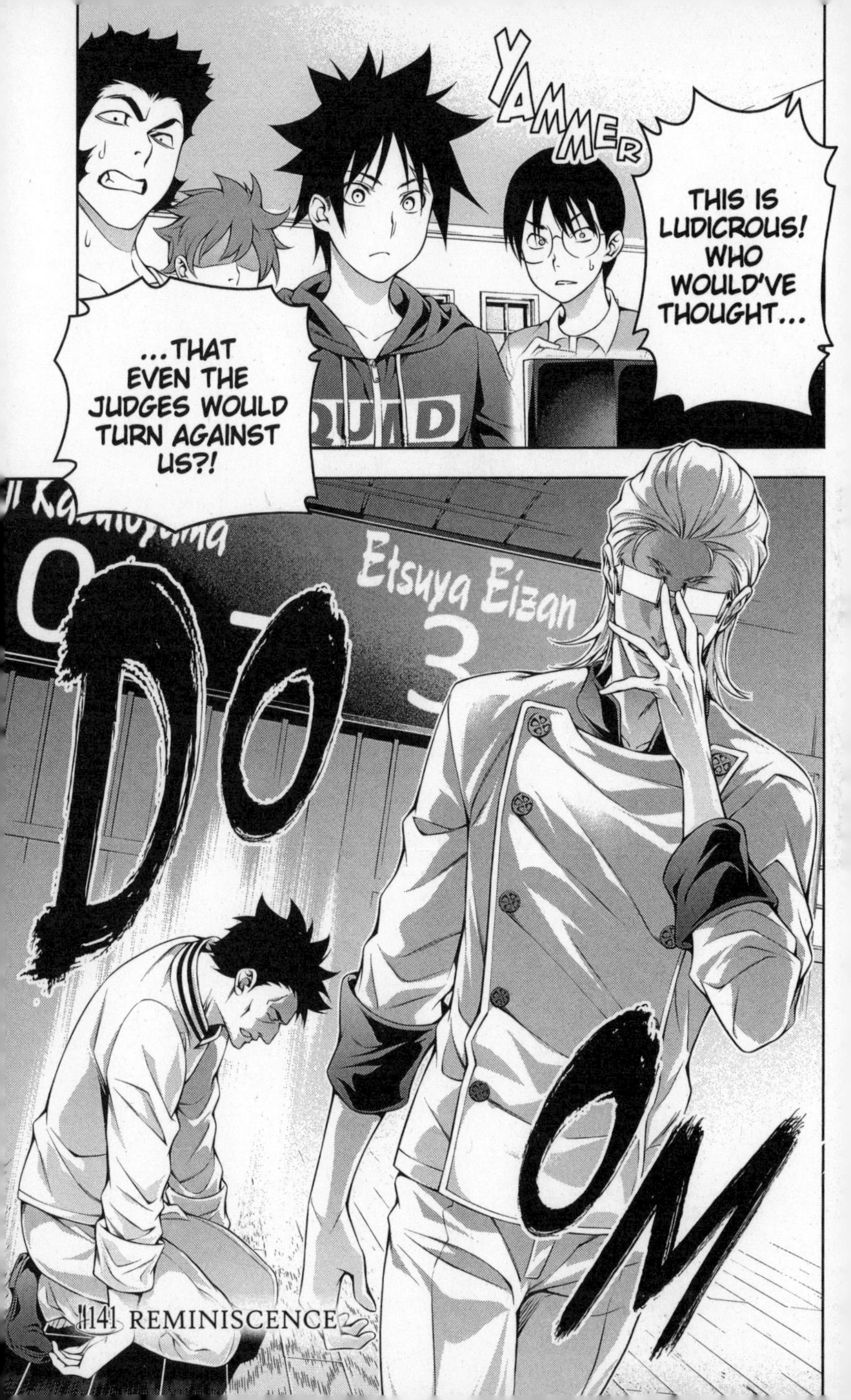
YAMMER
THIS IS LUDICROUS! WHO WOULD'VE THOUGHT...
...THAT EVEN THE JUDGES WOULD TURN AGAINST US?!
Etsuya Eizan
3
DOOOM

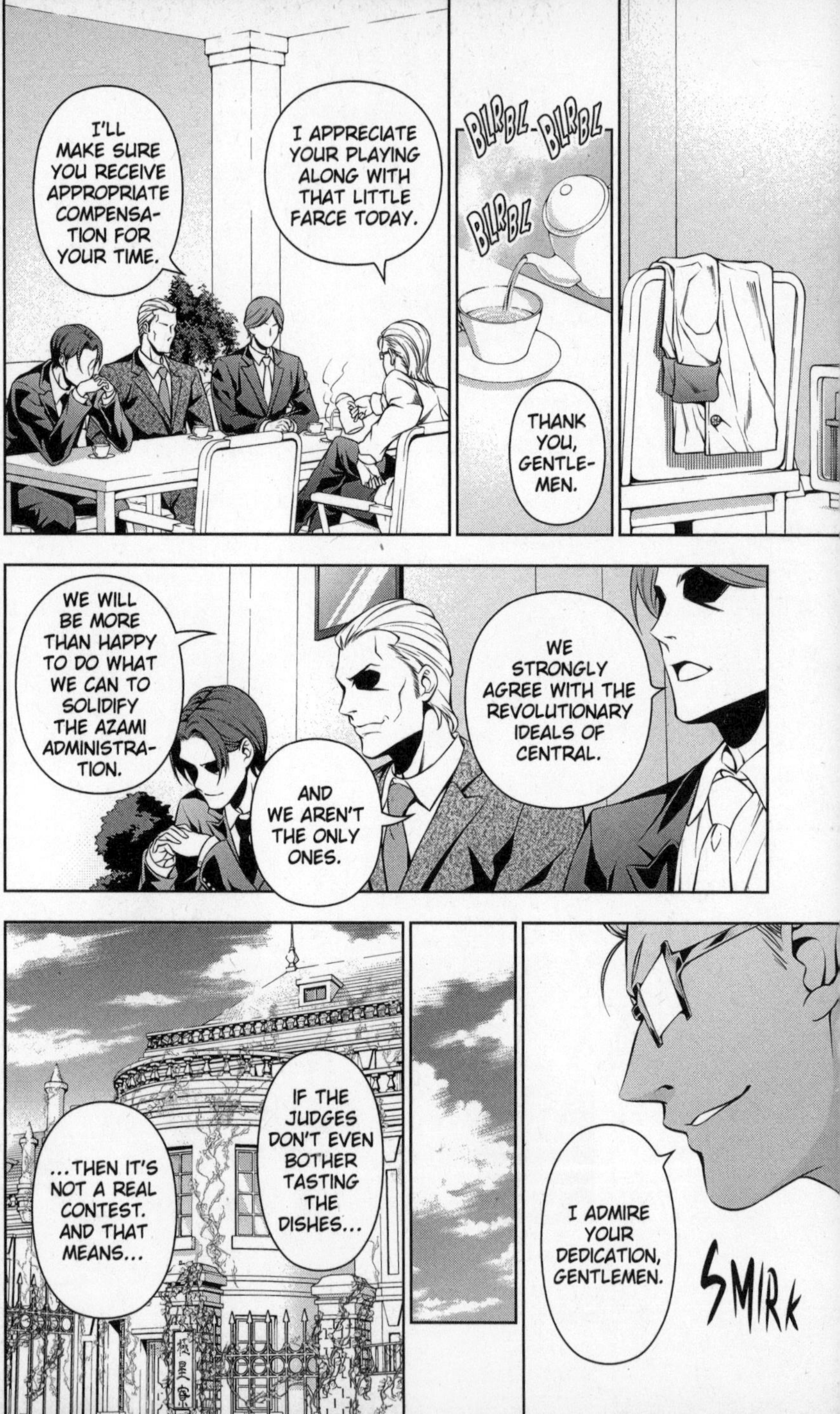
BLRBL-BLRBL
BLRBL
THANK YOU, GENTLEMEN.
I APPRECIATE YOUR PLAYING ALONG WITH THAT LITTLE FARCE TODAY.
I'LL MAKE SURE YOU RECEIVE APPROPRIATE COMPENSATION FOR YOUR TIME.
WE STRONGLY AGREE WITH THE REVOLUTIONARY IDEALS OF CENTRAL.
AND WE AREN'T THE ONLY ONES.
WE WILL BE MORE THAN HAPPY TO DO WHAT WE CAN TO SOLIDIFY THE AZAMI ADMINISTRATION.
I ADMIRE YOUR DEDICATION, GENTLEMEN.
SMIRK
IF THE JUDGES DON'T EVEN BOTHER TASTING THE DISHES...
...THEN IT'S NOT A REAL CONTEST. AND THAT MEANS...

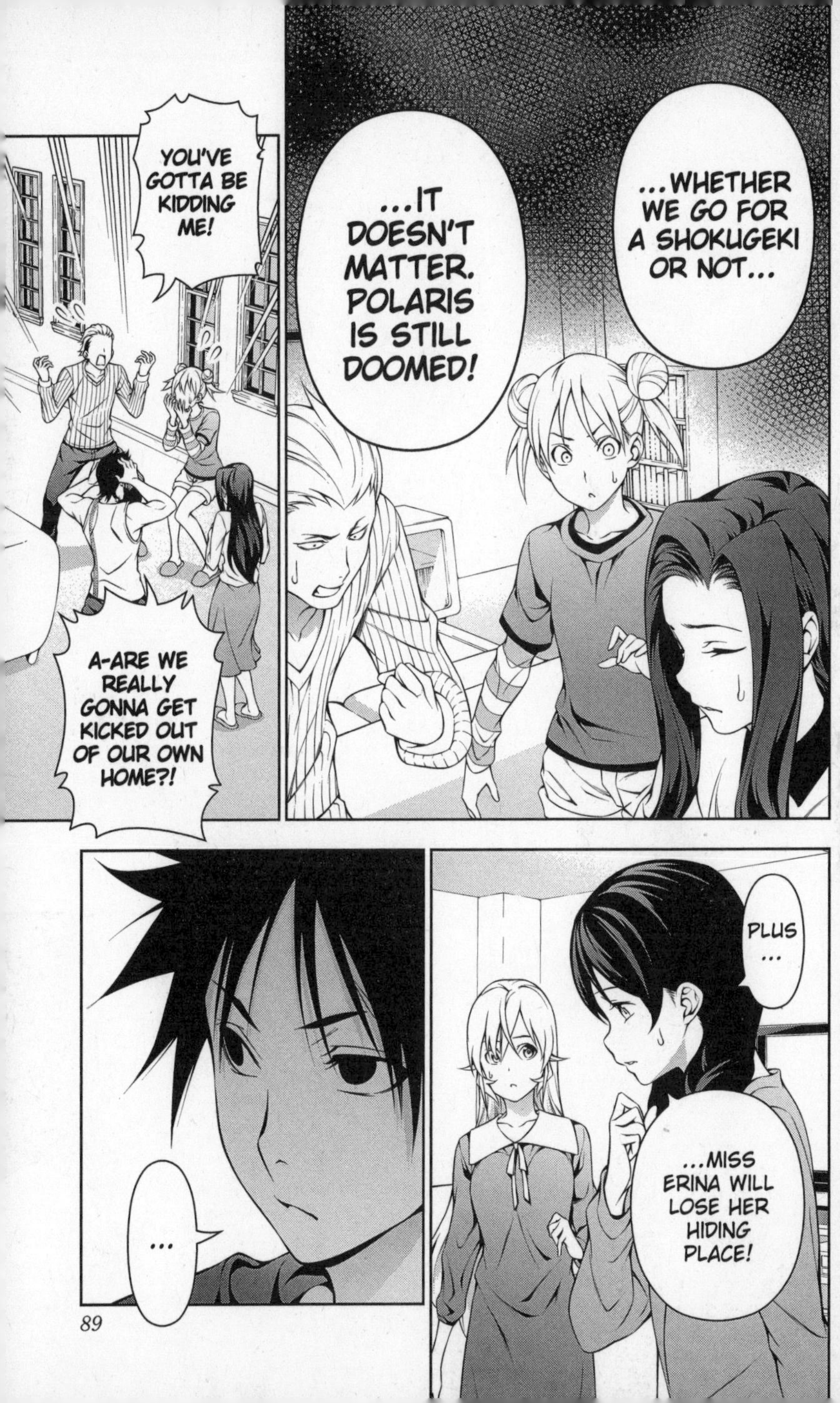
...WHETHER WE GO FOR A SHOKUGEKI OR NOT...
...IT DOESN'T MATTER. POLARIS IS STILL DOOMED!
YOU'VE GOTTA BE KIDDING ME!
A-ARE WE REALLY GONNA GET KICKED OUT OF OUR OWN HOME?!
PLUS...
...MISS ERINA WILL LOSE HER HIDING PLACE!
...

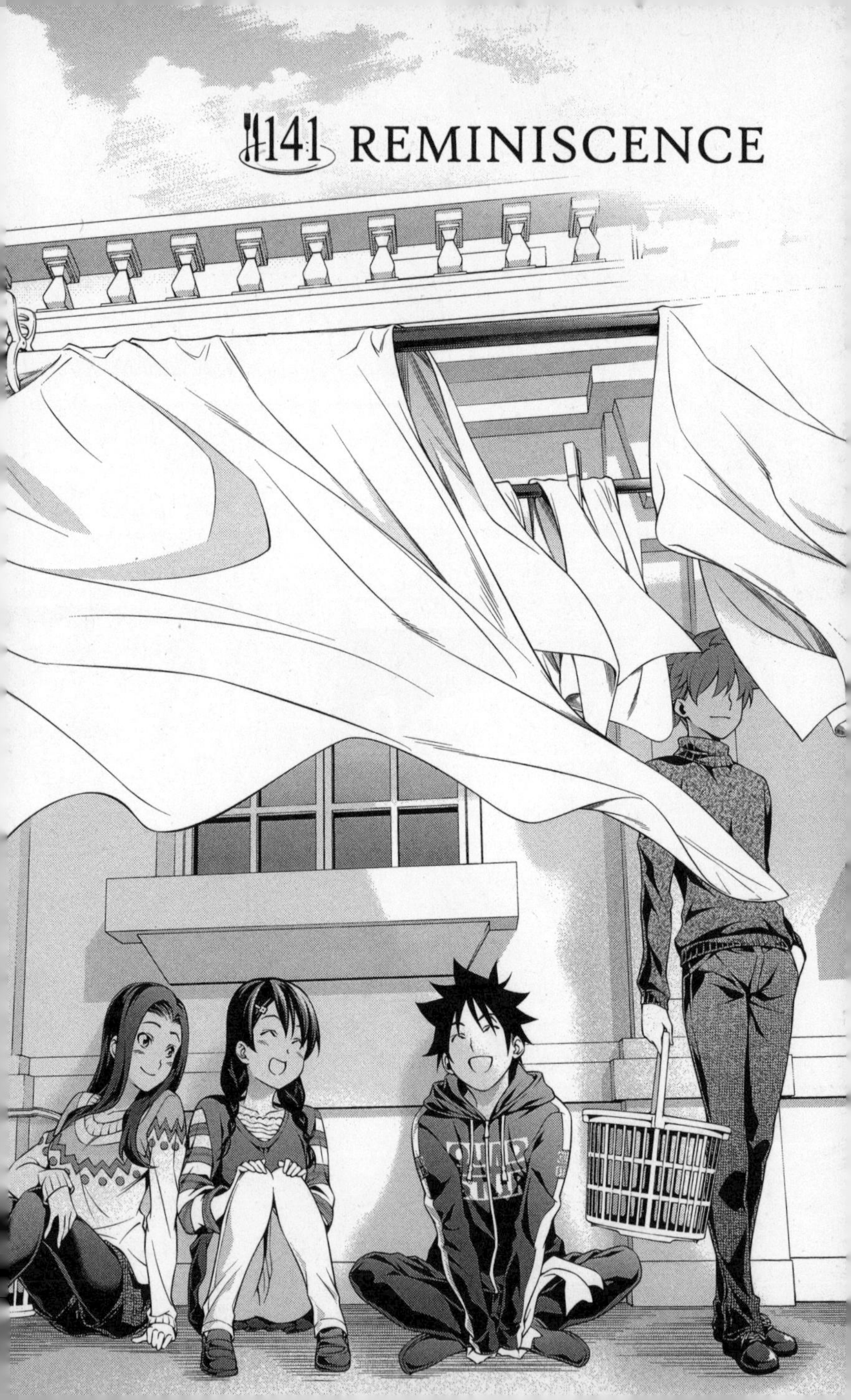
141 REMINISCENCE

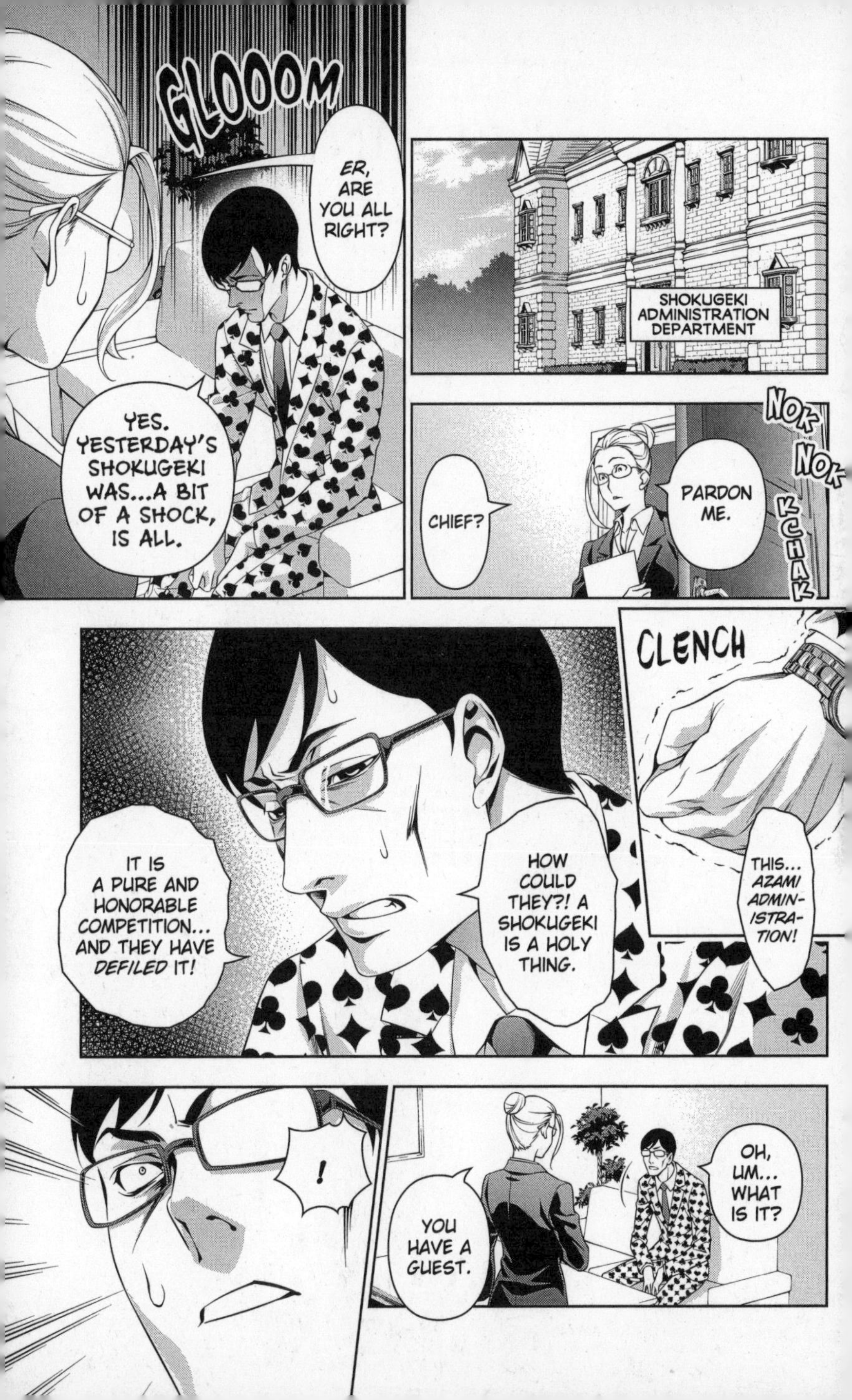
SHOKUGEKI ADMINISTRATION DEPARTMENT
NOK NOK
KCHAK
PARDON ME.
CHIEF?
GLOOOM
ER, ARE YOU ALL RIGHT?
YES. YESTERDAY'S SHOKUGEKI WAS...A BIT OF A SHOCK, IS ALL.
CLENCH
THIS... *AZAMI* ADMINISTRATION!
HOW COULD THEY?! A SHOKUGEKI IS A HOLY THING.
IT IS A PURE AND HONORABLE COMPETITION... AND THEY HAVE *DEFILED* IT!
OH, UM... WHAT IS IT?
YOU HAVE A GUEST.
!

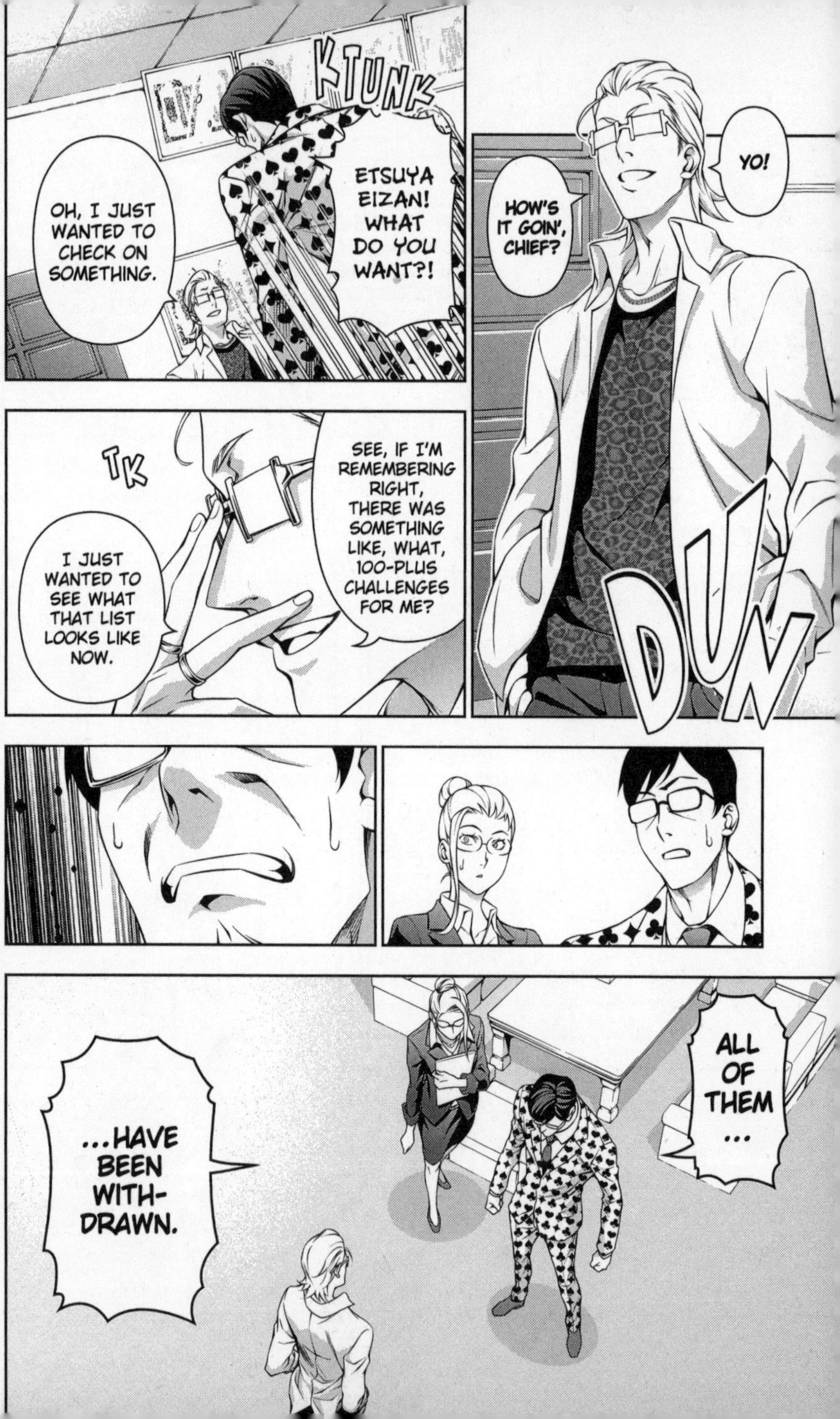
YO!
HOW'S IT GOIN', CHIEF?
DUN
KTUNK
ETSUYA EIZAN! WHAT DO YOU WANT?!
OH, I JUST WANTED TO CHECK ON SOMETHING.
SEE, IF I'M REMEMBERING RIGHT, THERE WAS SOMETHING LIKE, WHAT, 100-PLUS CHALLENGES FOR ME?
TK
I JUST WANTED TO SEE WHAT THAT LIST LOOKS LIKE NOW.
ALL OF THEM...
...HAVE BEEN WITH-DRAWN.

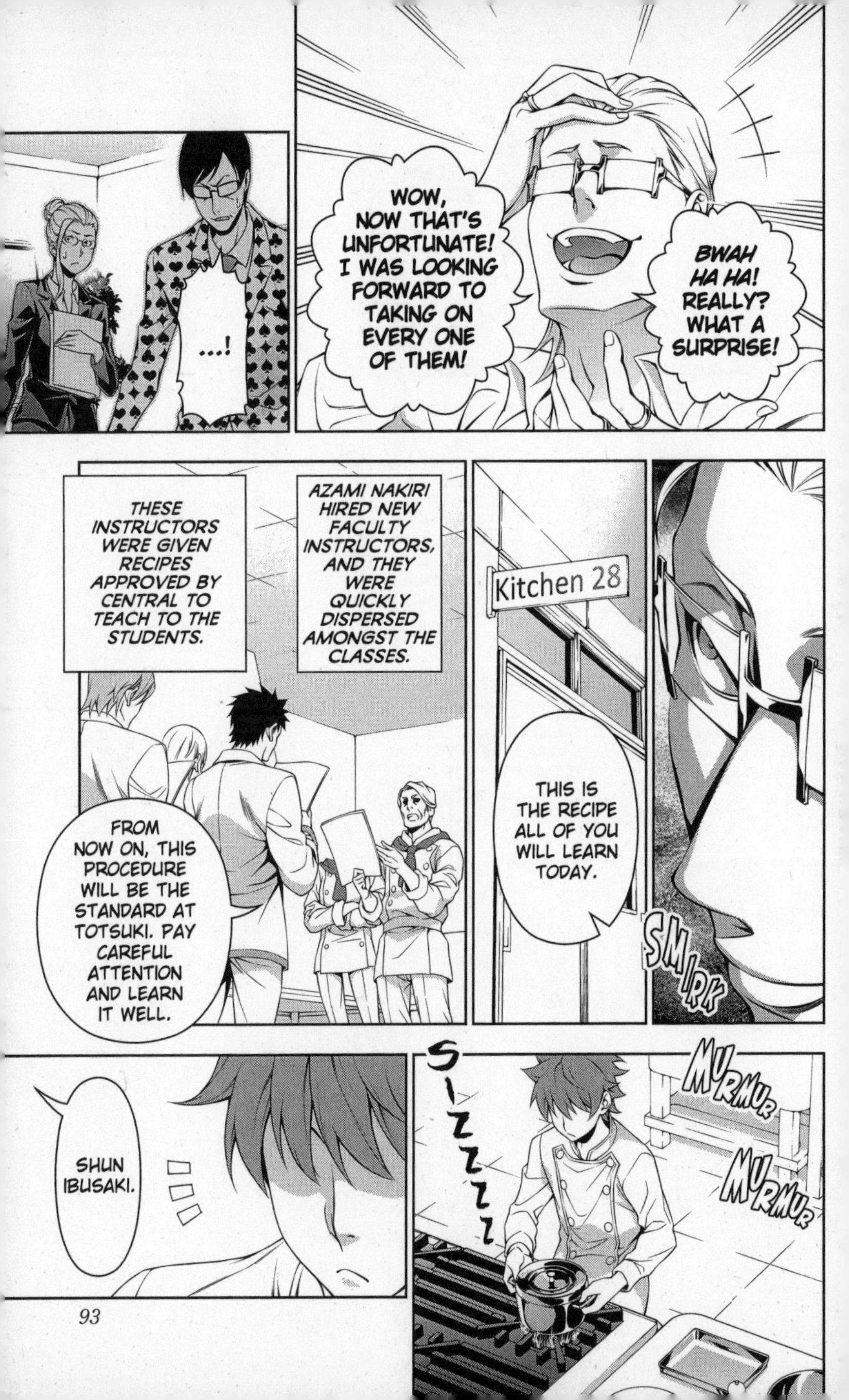
BWAH HA HA! REALLY? WHAT A SURPRISE!
WOW, NOW THAT'S UNFORTUNATE! I WAS LOOKING FORWARD TO TAKING ON EVERY ONE OF THEM!
...!
SMIRK
Kitchen 28
THIS IS THE RECIPE ALL OF YOU WILL LEARN TODAY.
AZAMI NAKIRI HIRED NEW FACULTY INSTRUCTORS, AND THEY WERE QUICKLY DISPERSED AMONGST THE CLASSES.
THESE INSTRUCTORS WERE GIVEN RECIPES APPROVED BY CENTRAL TO TEACH TO THE STUDENTS.
FROM NOW ON, THIS PROCEDURE WILL BE THE STANDARD AT TOTSUKI. PAY CAREFUL ATTENTION AND LEARN IT WELL.
MURMUR
MURMUR
SIZZZZZ
SHUN IBUSAKI.

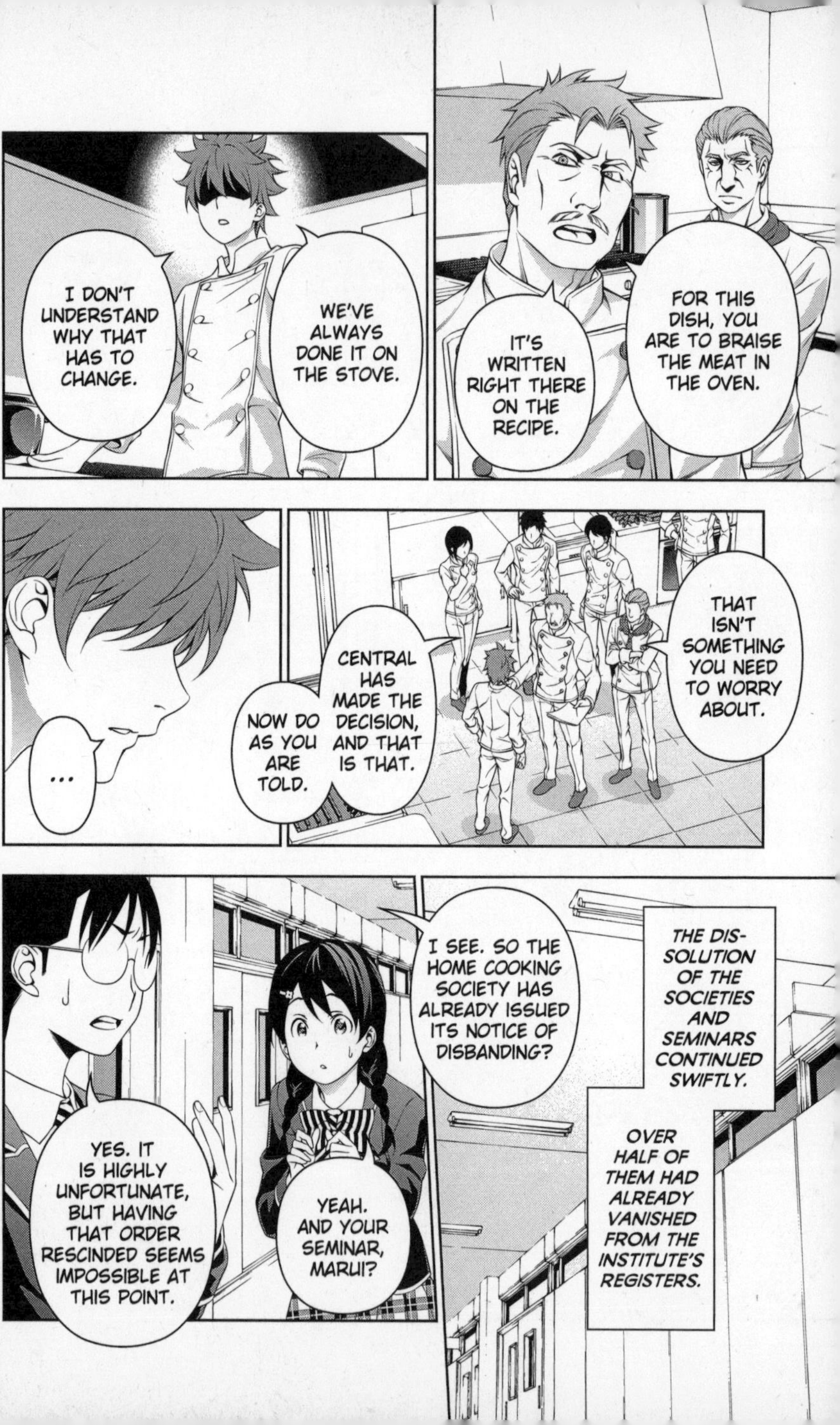
FOR THIS DISH, YOU ARE TO BRAISE THE MEAT IN THE OVEN.
IT'S WRITTEN RIGHT THERE ON THE RECIPE.
WE'VE ALWAYS DONE IT ON THE STOVE.
I DON'T UNDERSTAND WHY THAT HAS TO CHANGE.
THAT ISN'T SOMETHING YOU NEED TO WORRY ABOUT.
CENTRAL HAS MADE THE DECISION, AND THAT IS THAT.
NOW DO AS YOU ARE TOLD.
...
THE DISSOLUTION OF THE SOCIETIES AND SEMINARS CONTINUED SWIFTLY.
I SEE. SO THE HOME COOKING SOCIETY HAS ALREADY ISSUED ITS NOTICE OF DISBANDING?
OVER HALF OF THEM HAD ALREADY VANISHED FROM THE INSTITUTE'S REGISTERS.
YEAH. AND YOUR SEMINAR, MARUI?
YES. IT IS HIGHLY UNFORTUNATE, BUT HAVING THAT ORDER RESCINDED SEEMS IMPOSSIBLE AT THIS POINT.

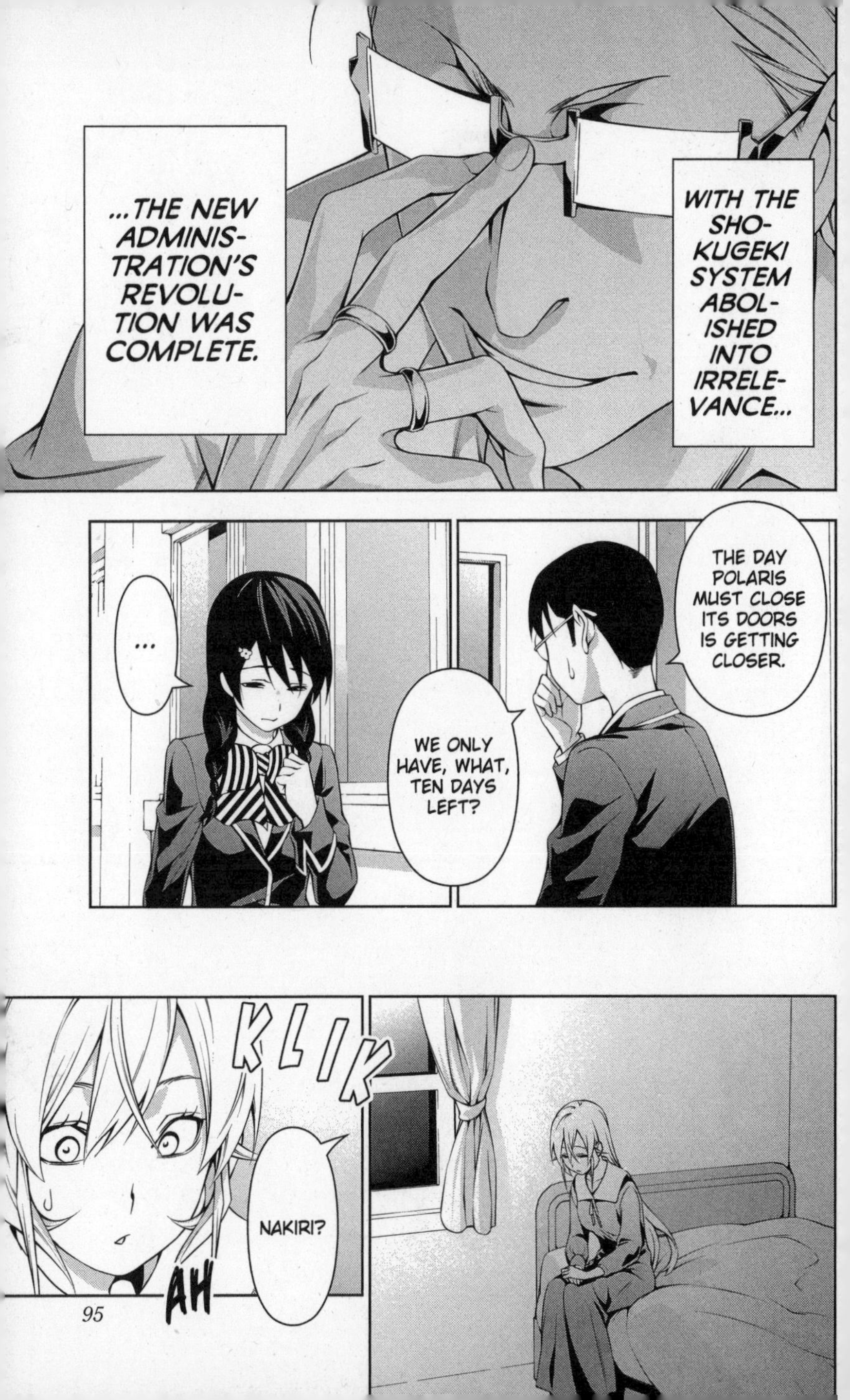
WITH THE SHOKUGEKI SYSTEM ABOLISHED INTO IRRELEVANCE...
...THE NEW ADMINISTRATION'S REVOLUTION WAS COMPLETE.
THE DAY POLARIS MUST CLOSE ITS DOORS IS GETTING CLOSER.
WE ONLY HAVE, WHAT, TEN DAYS LEFT?
...
KLIK
NAKIRI?
AH

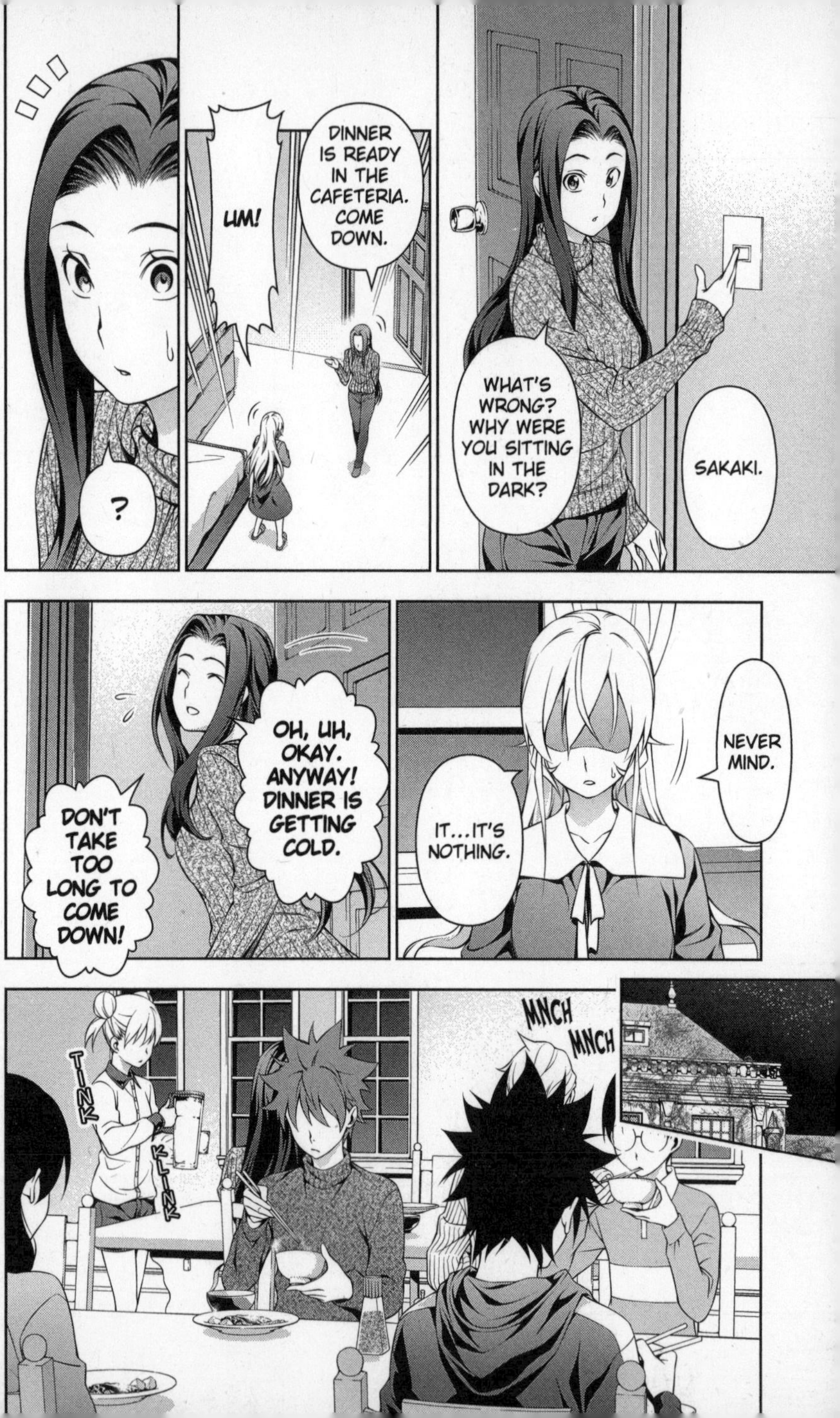
SAKAKI.
WHAT'S WRONG? WHY WERE YOU SITTING IN THE DARK?
DINNER IS READY IN THE CAFETERIA. COME DOWN.
UM!
?
NEVER MIND.
IT...IT'S NOTHING.
OH, UH, OKAY. ANYWAY! DINNER IS GETTING COLD.
DON'T TAKE TOO LONG TO COME DOWN!
MNCH MNCH
TINK
KLINK

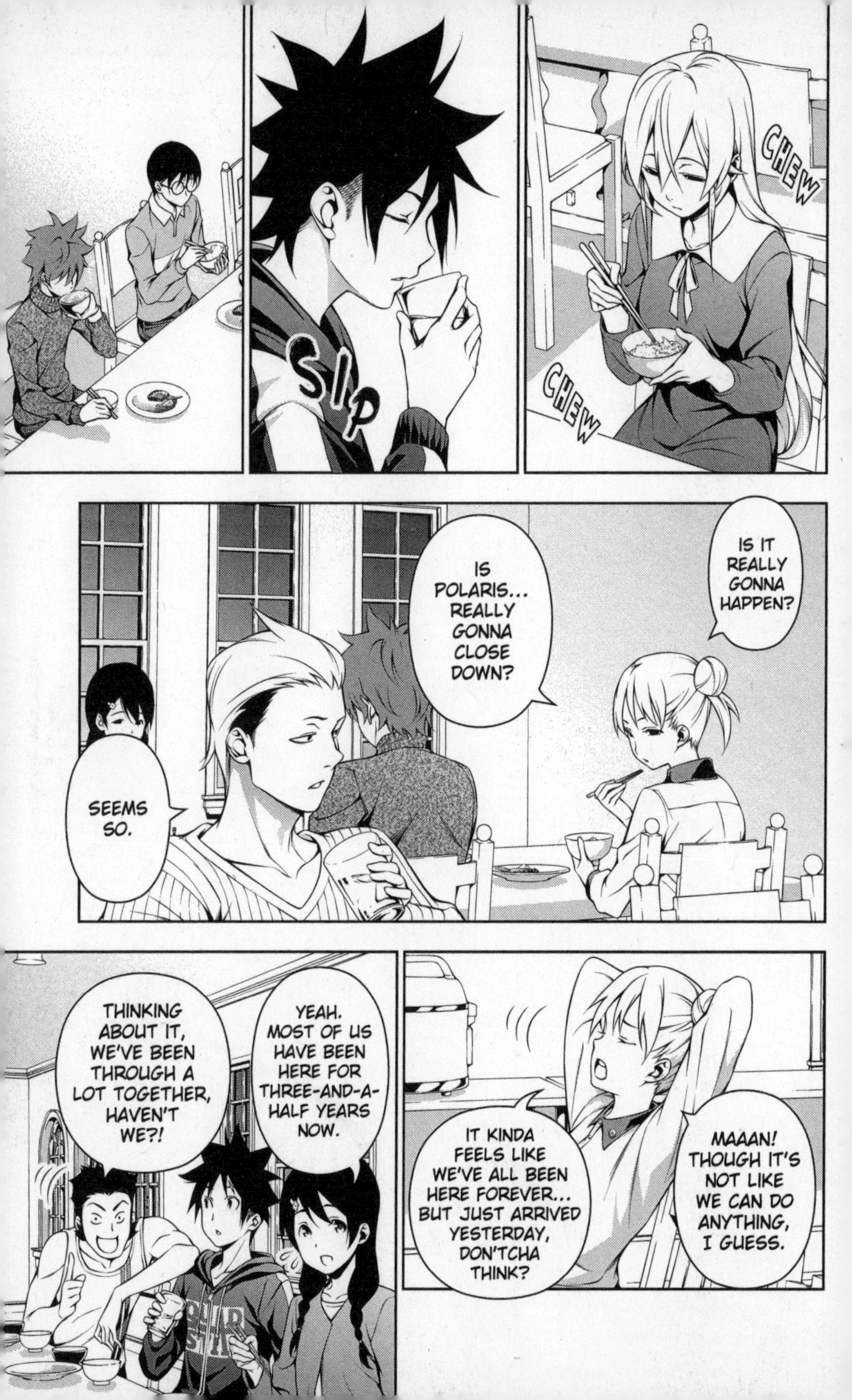
CHEW
CHEW
SIP
IS IT REALLY GONNA HAPPEN?
IS POLARIS... REALLY GONNA CLOSE DOWN?
SEEMS SO.
MAAAN! THOUGH IT'S NOT LIKE WE CAN DO ANYTHING, I GUESS.
IT KINDA FEELS LIKE WE'VE ALL BEEN HERE FOREVER... BUT JUST ARRIVED YESTERDAY, DON'TCHA THINK?
THINKING ABOUT IT, WE'VE BEEN THROUGH A LOT TOGETHER, HAVEN'T WE?!
YEAH. MOST OF US HAVE BEEN HERE FOR THREE-AND-A-HALF YEARS NOW.

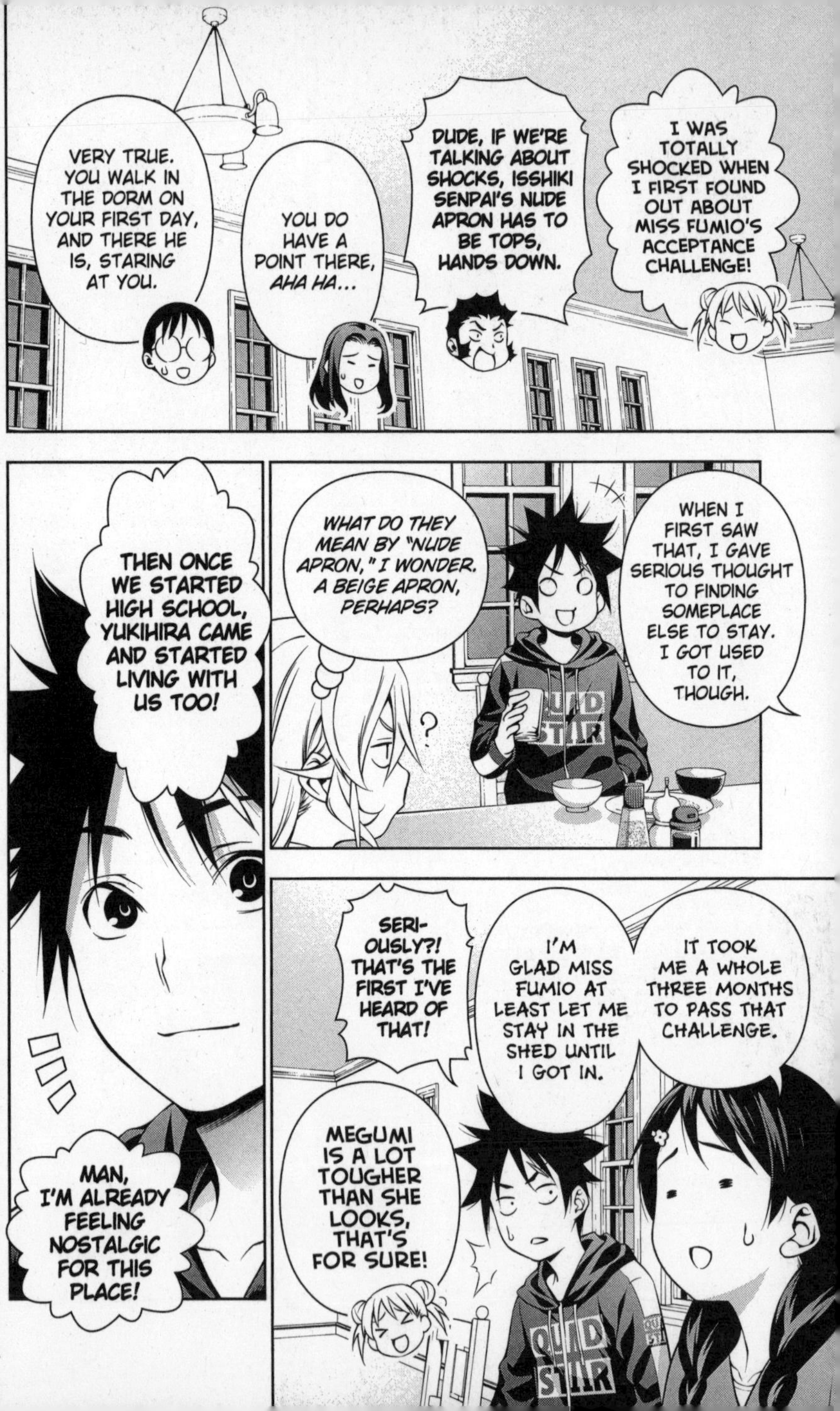
I WAS TOTALLY SHOCKED WHEN I FIRST FOUND OUT ABOUT MISS FUMIO'S ACCEPTANCE CHALLENGE!
DUDE, IF WE'RE TALKING ABOUT SHOCKS, ISSHIKI SENPAI'S NUDE APRON HAS TO BE TOPS, HANDS DOWN.
YOU DO HAVE A POINT THERE, *AHA HA...*
VERY TRUE. YOU WALK IN THE DORM ON YOUR FIRST DAY, AND THERE HE IS, STARING AT YOU.
WHEN I FIRST SAW THAT, I GAVE SERIOUS THOUGHT TO FINDING SOMEPLACE ELSE TO STAY. I GOT USED TO IT, THOUGH.
WHAT DO THEY MEAN BY "NUDE APRON," I WONDER. A BEIGE APRON, PERHAPS?
IT TOOK ME A WHOLE THREE MONTHS TO PASS THAT CHALLENGE.
I'M GLAD MISS FUMIO AT LEAST LET ME STAY IN THE SHED UNTIL I GOT IN.
SERIOUSLY?! THAT'S THE FIRST I'VE HEARD OF THAT!
MEGUMI IS A LOT TOUGHER THAN SHE LOOKS, THAT'S FOR SURE!
THEN ONCE WE STARTED HIGH SCHOOL, YUKIHIRA CAME AND STARTED LIVING WITH US TOO!
MAN, I'M ALREADY FEELING NOSTALGIC FOR THIS PLACE!

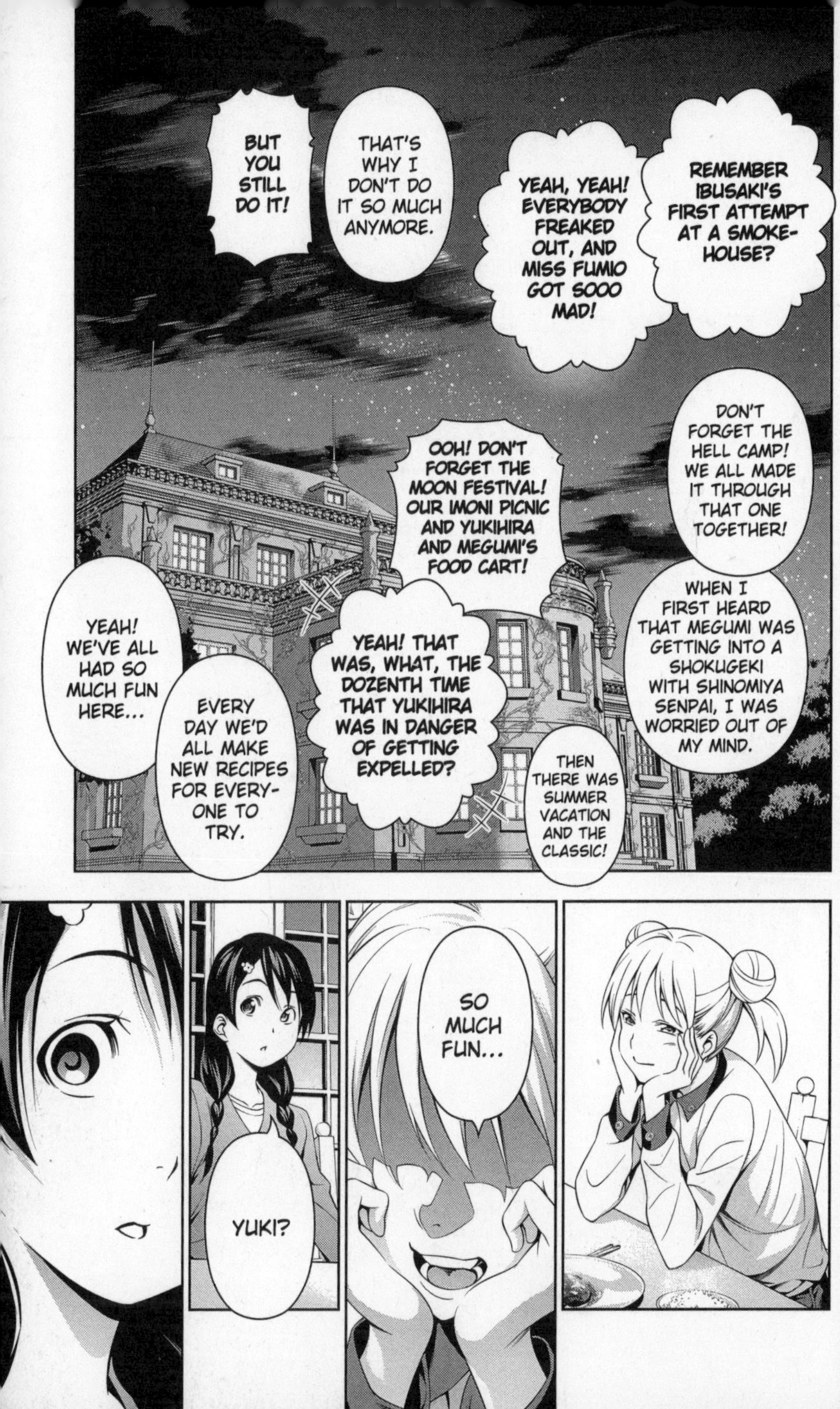
REMEMBER IBUSAKI'S FIRST ATTEMPT AT A SMOKE-HOUSE?
YEAH, YEAH! EVERYBODY FREAKED OUT, AND MISS FUMIO GOT SOOO MAD!
THAT'S WHY I DON'T DO IT SO MUCH ANYMORE.
BUT YOU STILL DO IT!
DON'T FORGET THE HELL CAMP! WE ALL MADE IT THROUGH THAT ONE TOGETHER!
OOH! DON'T FORGET THE MOON FESTIVAL! OUR IMONI PICNIC AND YUKIHIRA AND MEGUMI'S FOOD CART!
WHEN I FIRST HEARD THAT MEGUMI WAS GETTING INTO A SHOKUGEKI WITH SHINOMIYA SENPAI, I WAS WORRIED OUT OF MY MIND.
YEAH! THAT WAS, WHAT, THE DOZENTH TIME THAT YUKIHIRA WAS IN DANGER OF GETTING EXPELLED?
THEN THERE WAS SUMMER VACATION AND THE CLASSIC!
EVERY DAY WE'D ALL MAKE NEW RECIPES FOR EVERY-ONE TO TRY.
YEAH! WE'VE ALL HAD SO MUCH FUN HERE...
SO MUCH FUN...
YUKI?

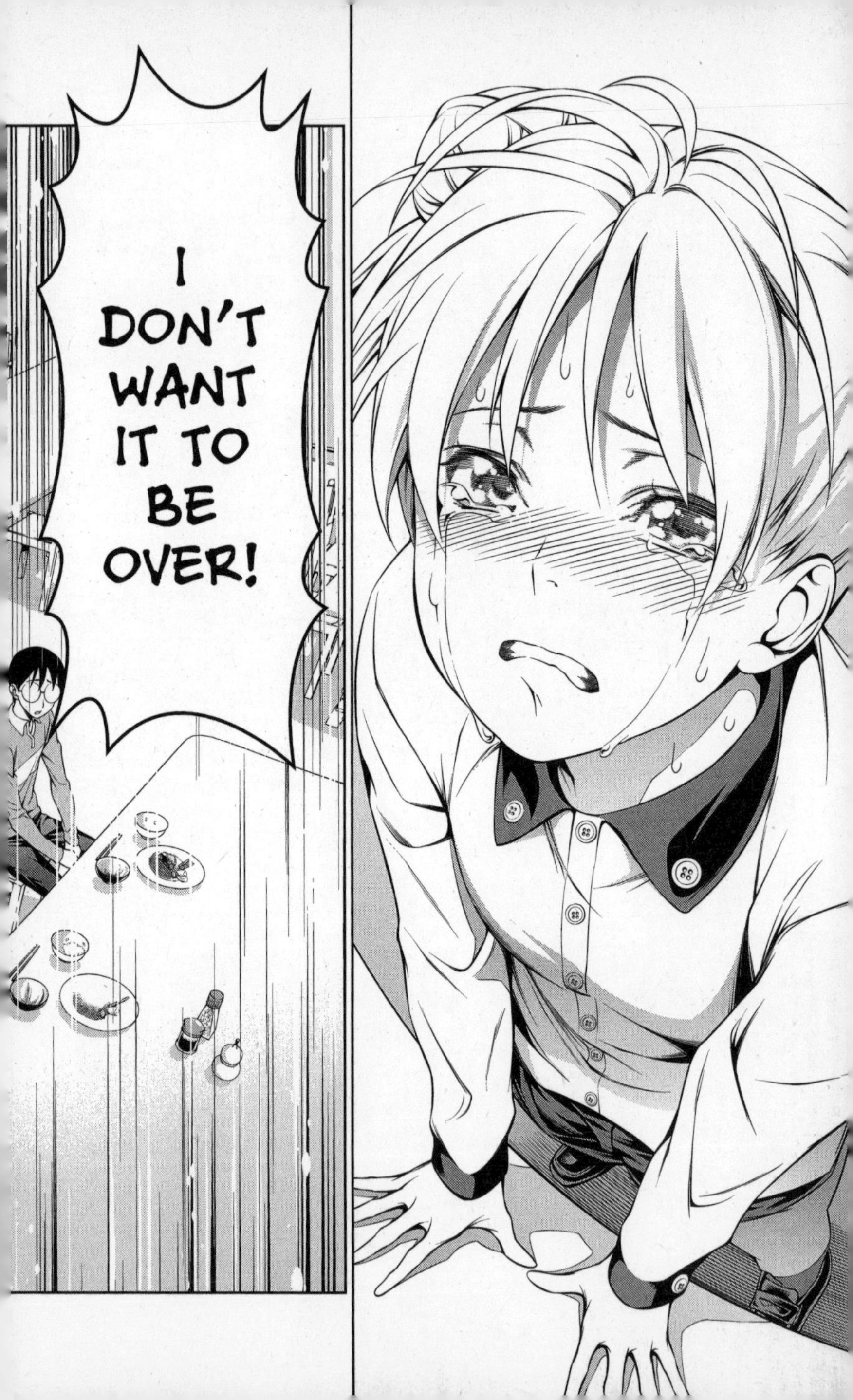
I DON'T WANT IT TO BE OVER!

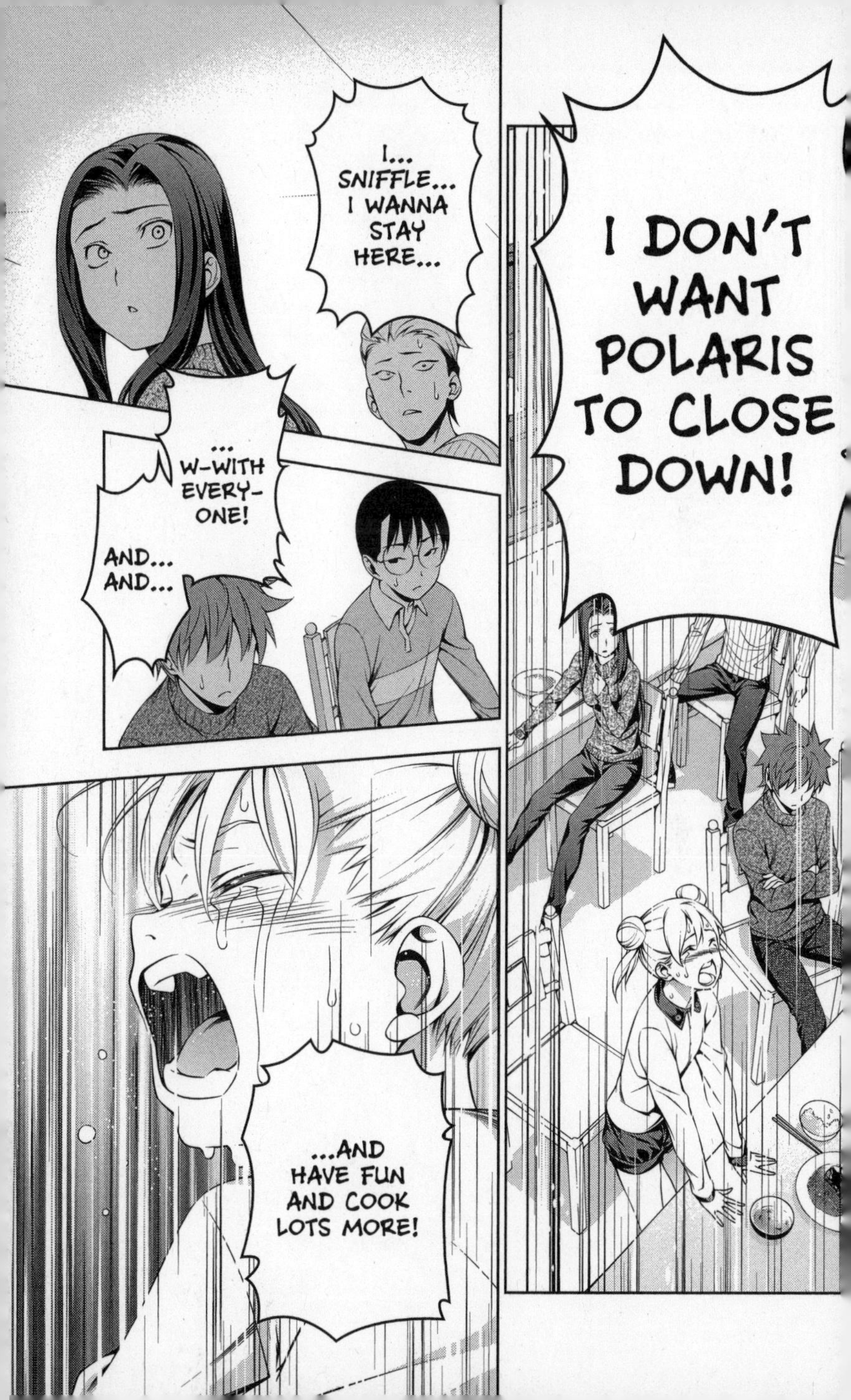
I... SNIFFLE... I WANNA STAY HERE...
...W-WITH EVERY-ONE!
AND... AND...
...AND HAVE FUN AND COOK LOTS MORE!
I DON'T WANT POLARIS TO CLOSE DOWN!

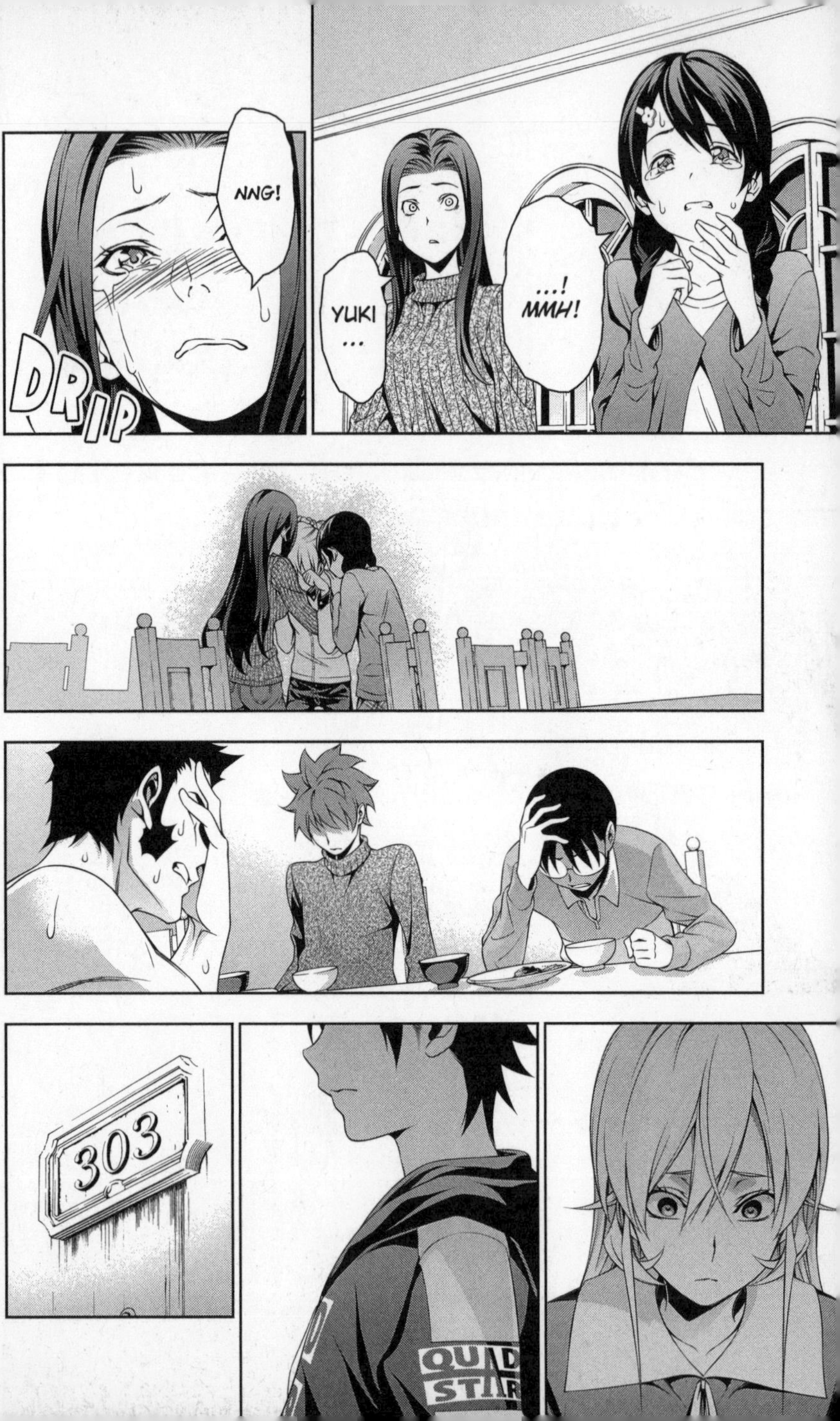
...! MMH!
YUKI ...
NNG!
DRIP
303

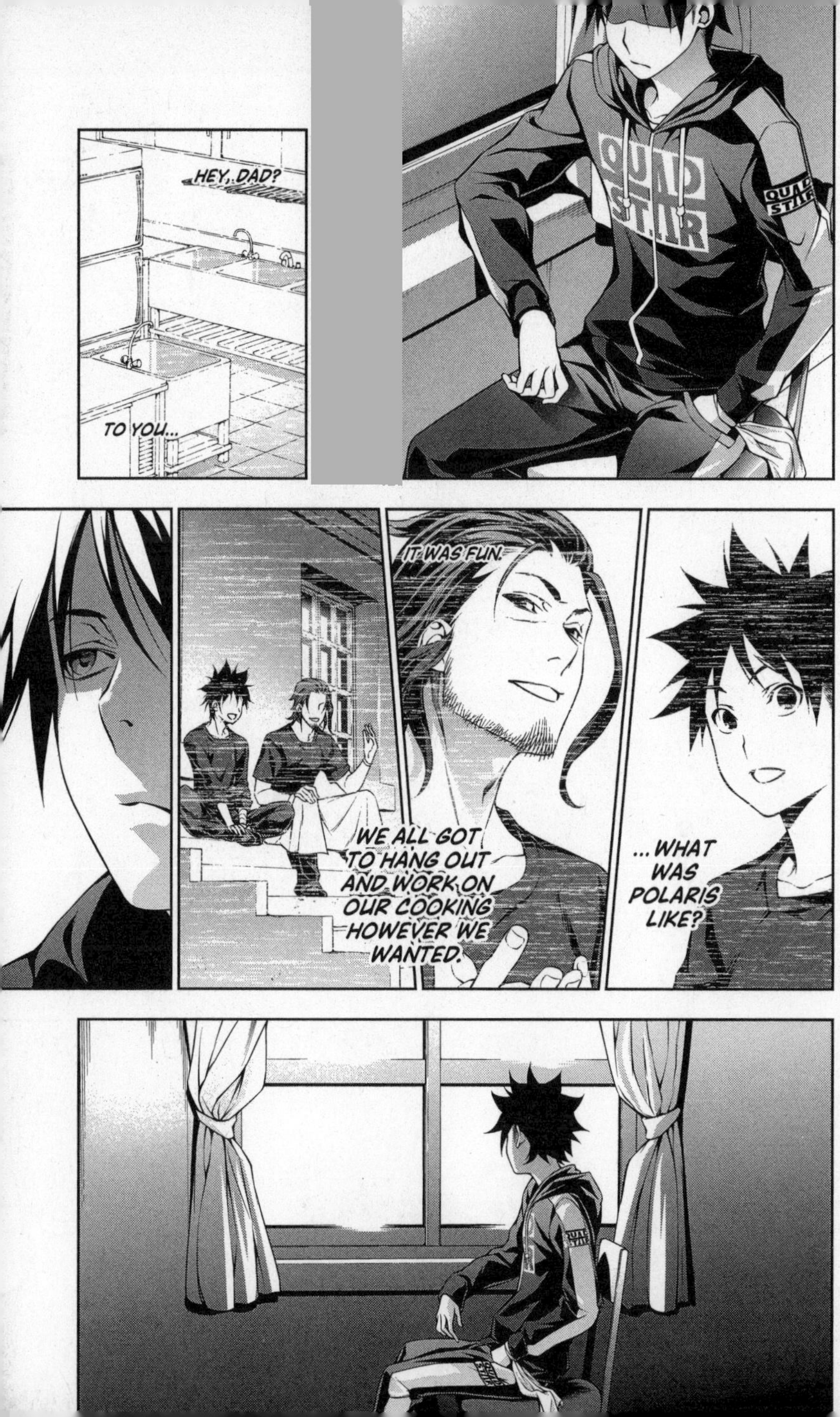
HEY, DAD?
TO YOU...
...WHAT WAS POLARIS LIKE?
IT WAS FUN.
WE ALL GOT TO HANG OUT AND WORK ON OUR COOKING HOWEVER WE WANTED.

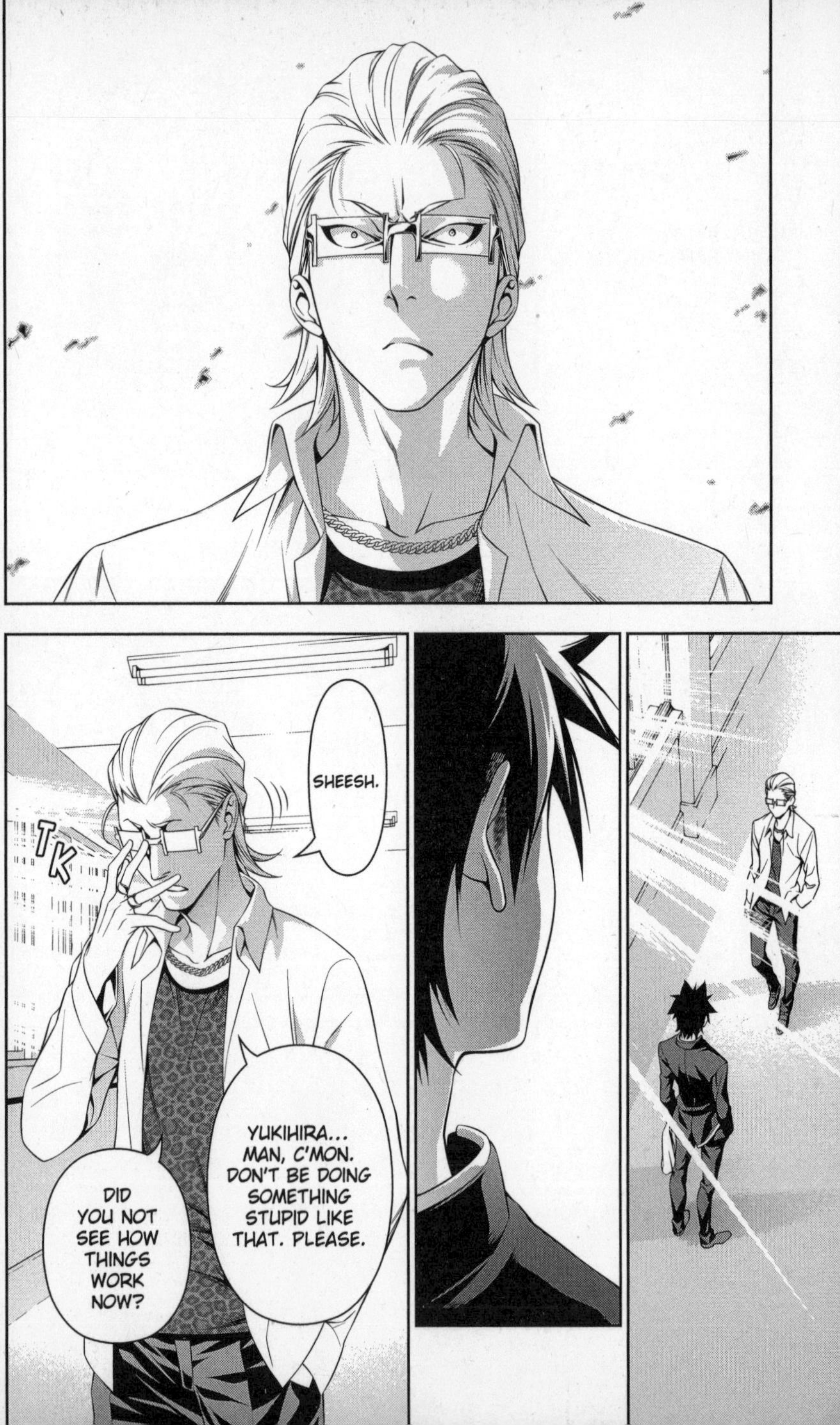
SHEESH.
TK
YUKIHIRA... MAN, C'MON. DON'T BE DOING SOMETHING STUPID LIKE THAT. PLEASE.
DID YOU NOT SEE HOW THINGS WORK NOW?

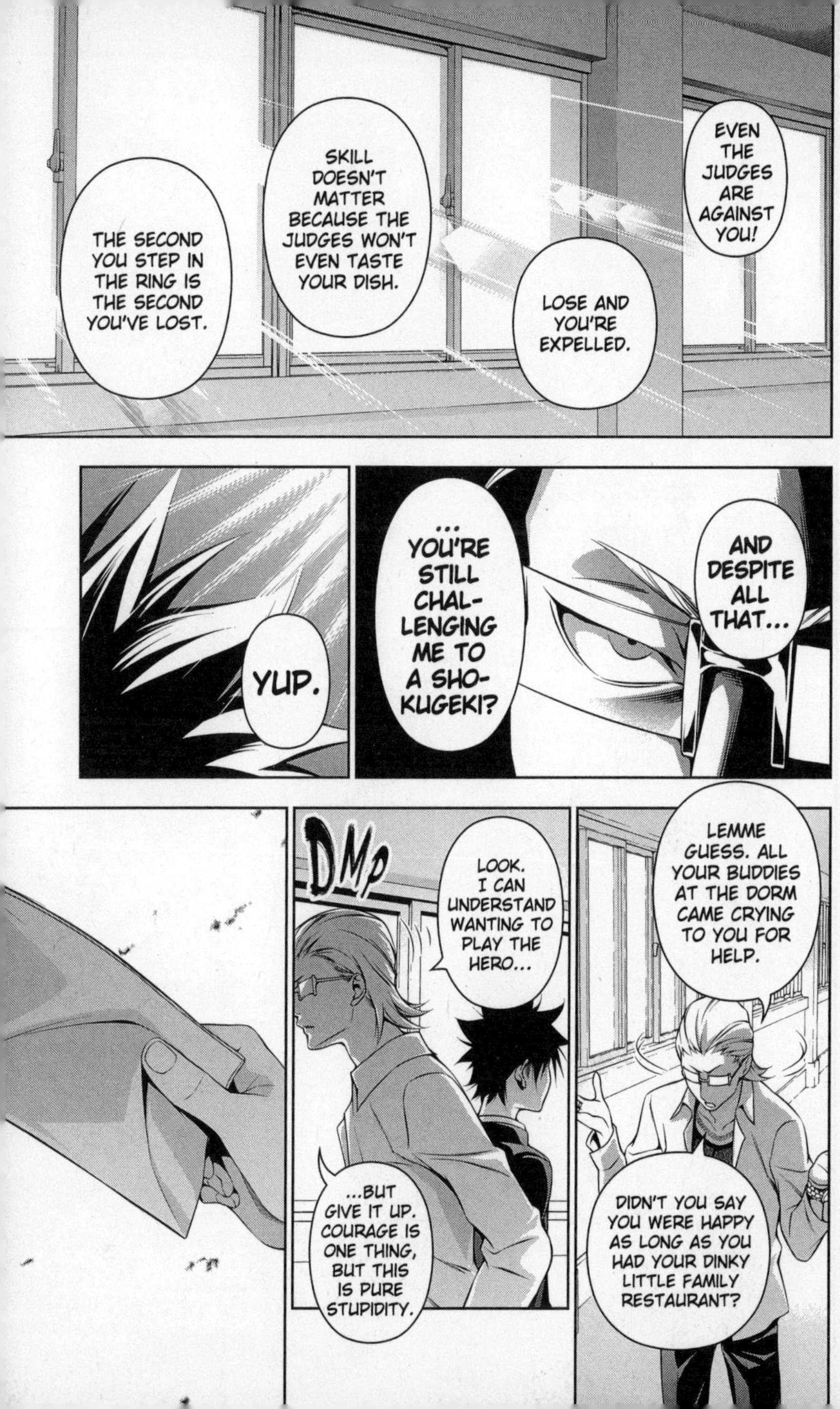
EVEN THE JUDGES ARE AGAINST YOU!
LOSE AND YOU'RE EXPELLED.
SKILL DOESN'T MATTER BECAUSE THE JUDGES WON'T EVEN TASTE YOUR DISH.
THE SECOND YOU STEP IN THE RING IS THE SECOND YOU'VE LOST.
AND DESPITE ALL THAT...
... YOU'RE STILL CHAL-LENGING ME TO A SHO-KUGEKI?
YUP.
LEMME GUESS. ALL YOUR BUDDIES AT THE DORM CAME CRYING TO YOU FOR HELP.
DIDN'T YOU SAY YOU WERE HAPPY AS LONG AS YOU HAD YOUR DINKY LITTLE FAMILY RESTAURANT?
DMP
LOOK. I CAN UNDERSTAND WANTING TO PLAY THE HERO...
...BUT GIVE IT UP. COURAGE IS ONE THING, BUT THIS IS PURE STUPIDITY.

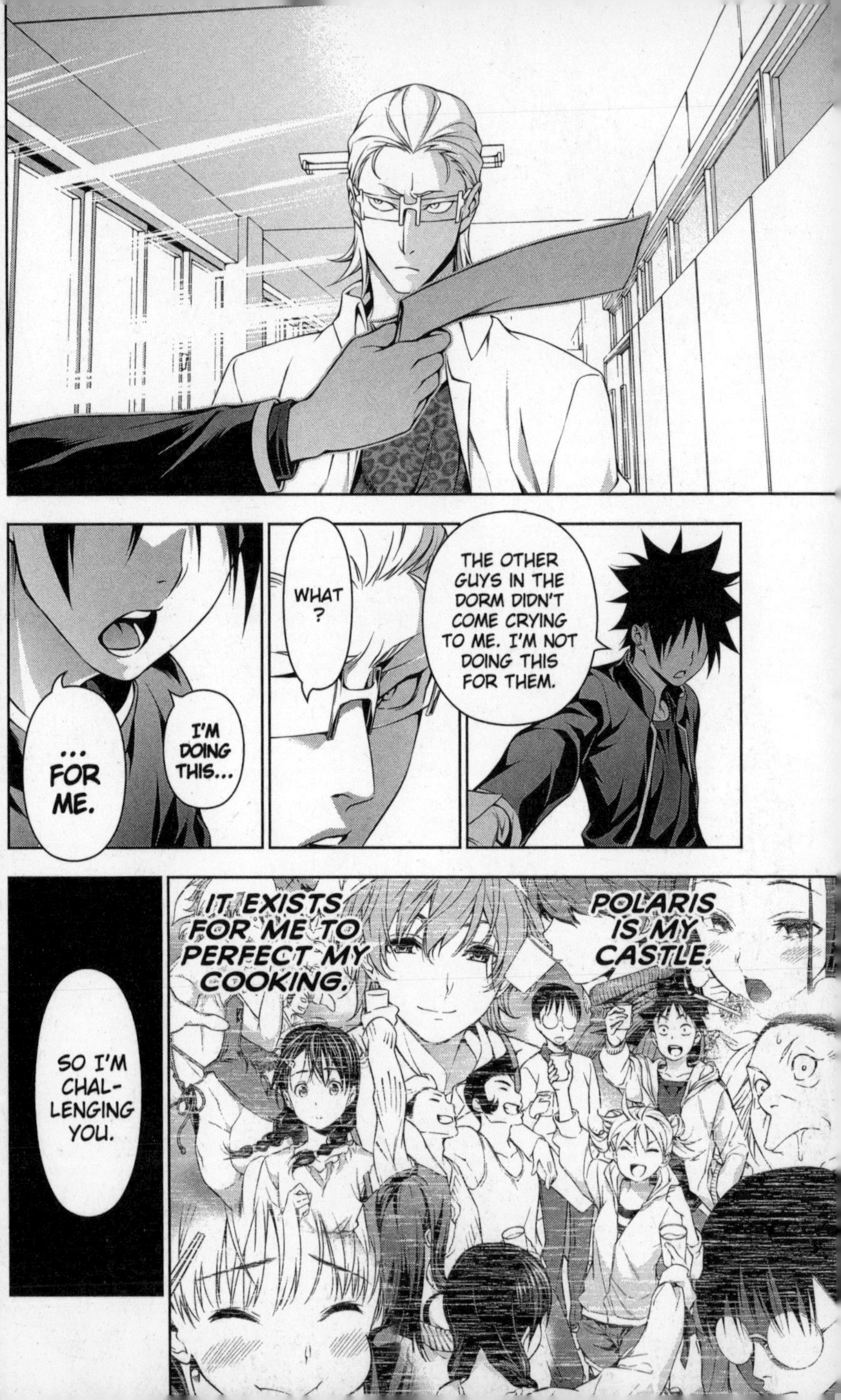
THE OTHER GUYS IN THE DORM DIDN'T COME CRYING TO ME. I'M NOT DOING THIS FOR THEM.
WHAT?
I'M DOING THIS...
...FOR ME.
POLARIS IS MY CASTLE.
IT EXISTS FOR ME TO PERFECT MY COOKING.
SO I'M CHAL-LENGING YOU.

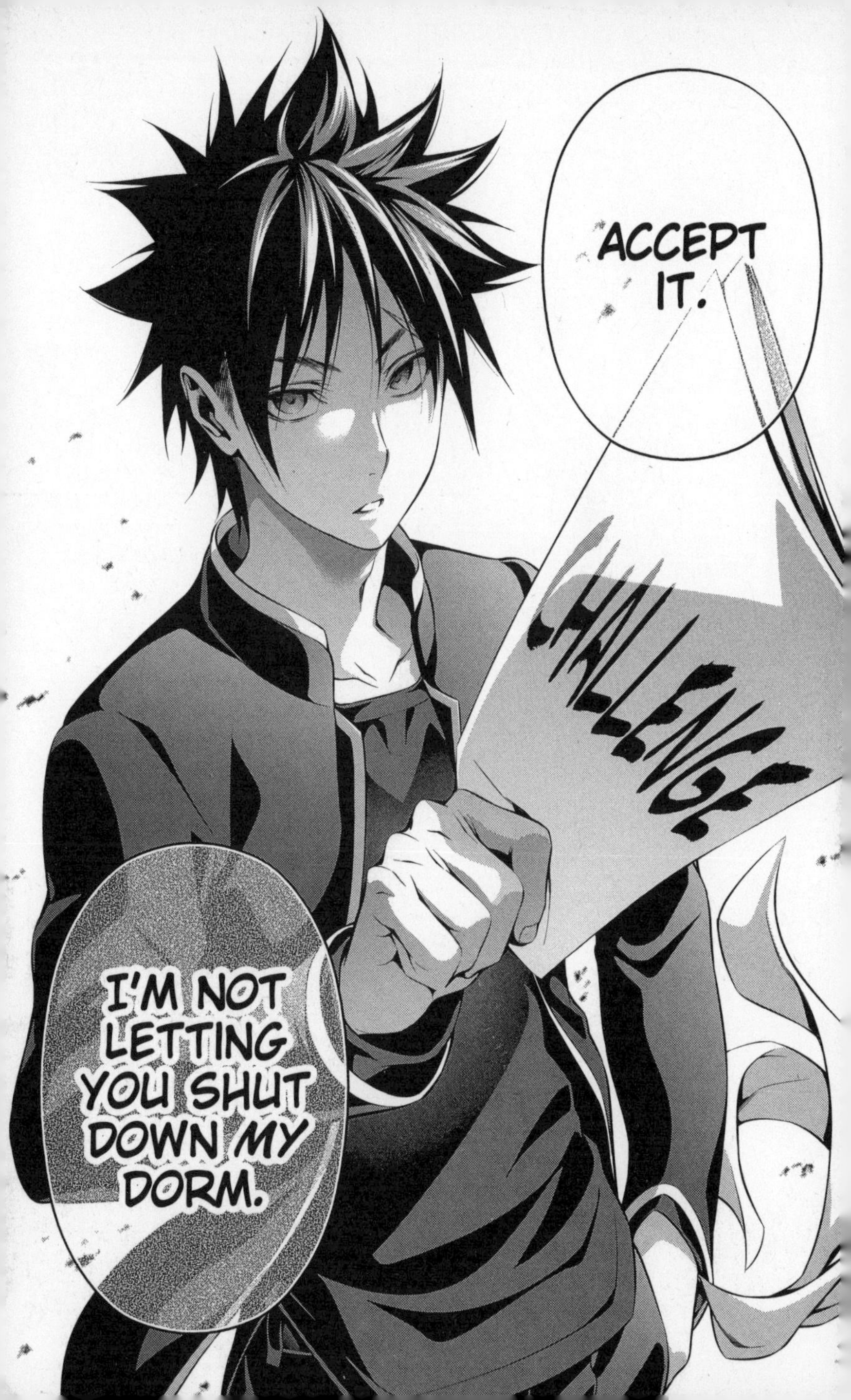
ACCEPT IT.
CHALLENGE!
I'M NOT LETTING YOU SHUT DOWN MY DORM.

Miss Erina's Splendid Days as a Runaway 5

-A DUTY INHERITED-

MEGUMI TADOKORO... PLEASE TAKE GOOD CARE OF MISS ERINA WHILE I AM NOT HERE.

UM... OKAY.

APPARENTLY, HISAKO'S BUTLER QUALITY HOMED IN ON MEGUMI'S MOTHERLY QUALITY.

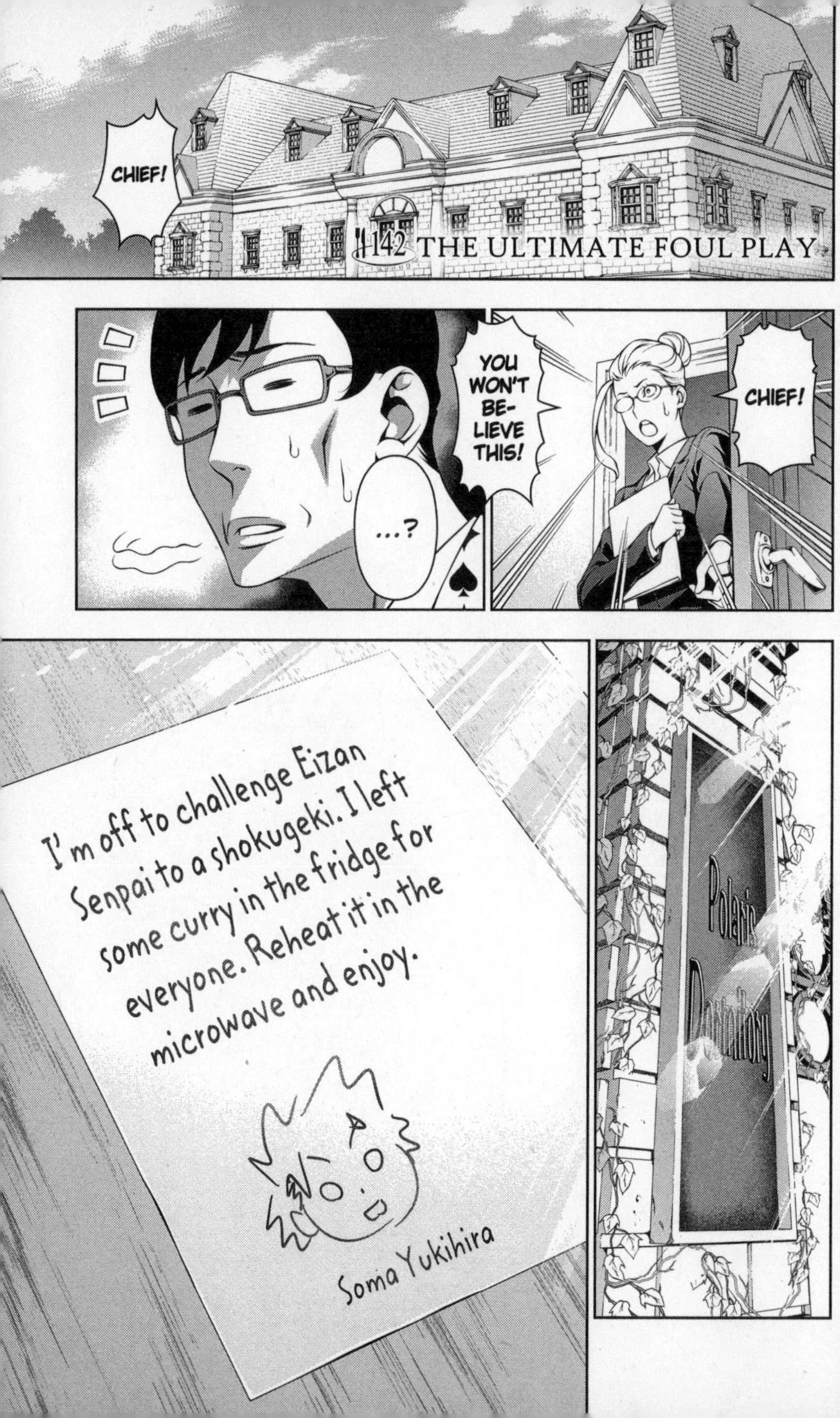
CHIEF!
142 THE ULTIMATE FOUL PLAY
CHIEF!
YOU WON'T BE- LIEVE THIS!
...?
I'm off to challenge Eizan Senpai to a shokugeki. I left some curry in the fridge for everyone. Reheat it in the microwave and enjoy.
Soma Yukihira

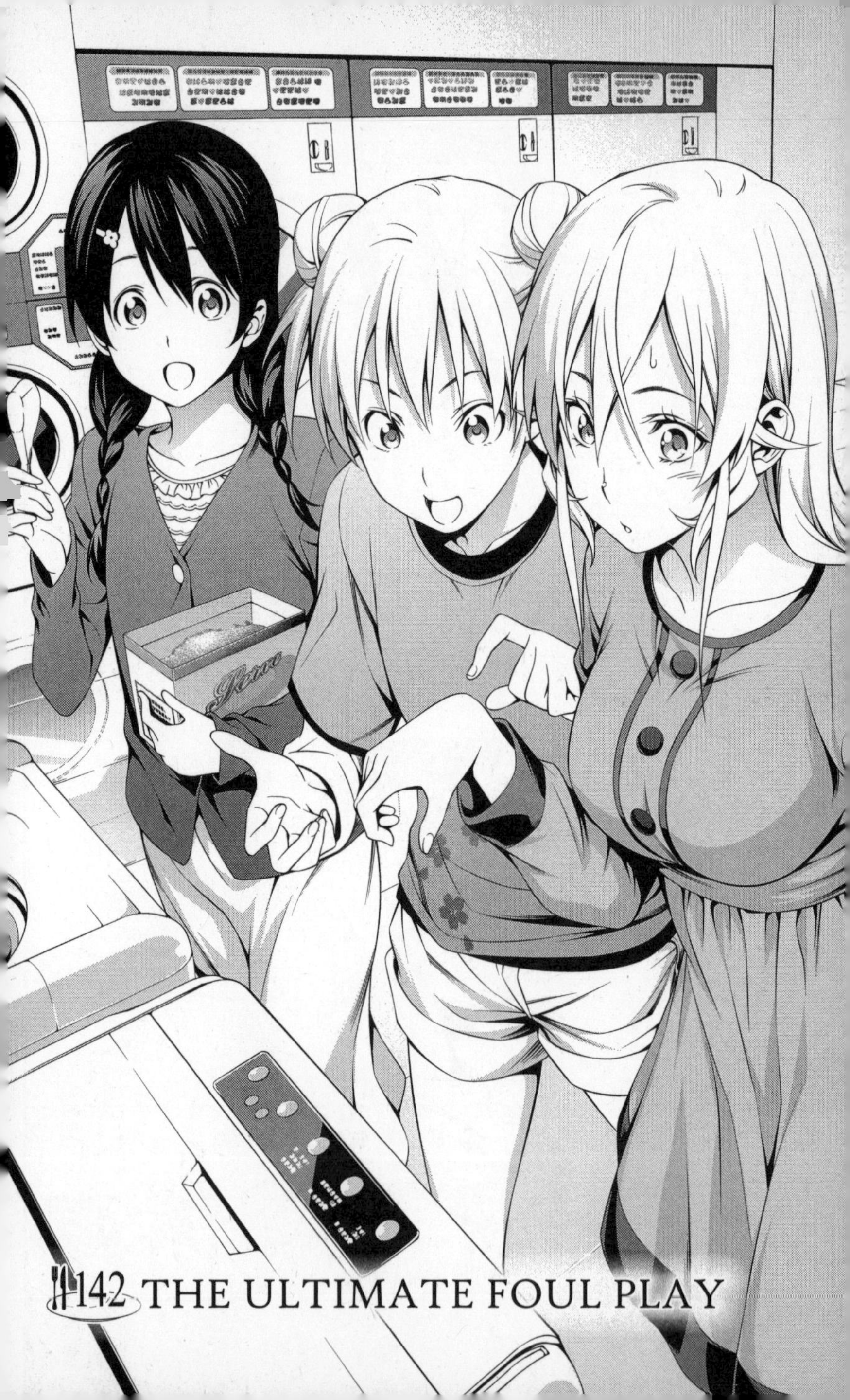

142 THE ULTIMATE FOUL PLAY

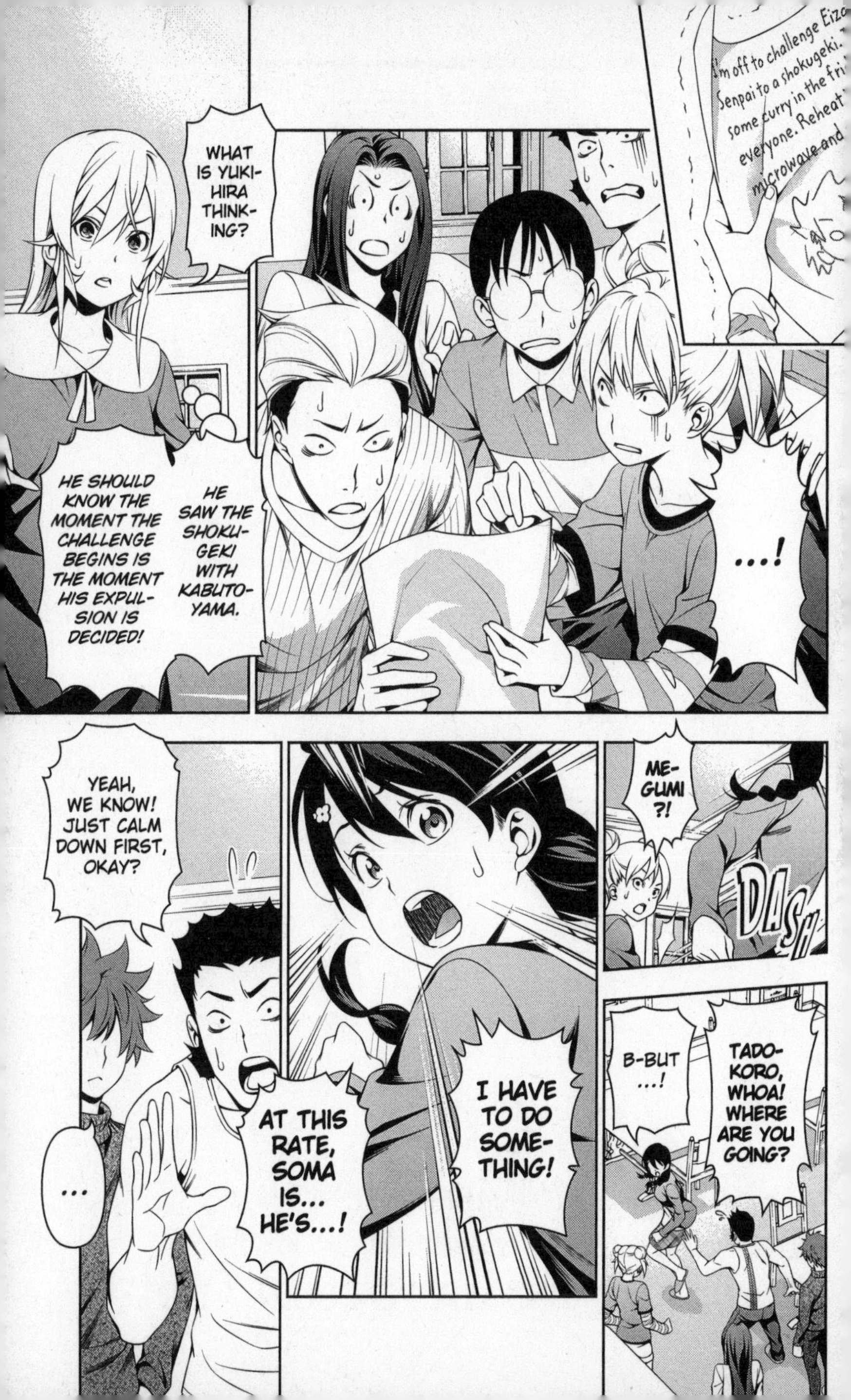
I'm off to challenge Eiza
Senpai to a shokugeki.
some curry in the fri
everyone. Reheat
microwave and
WHAT IS YUKIHIRA THINKING?
...!
HE SAW THE SHOKUGEKI WITH KABUTOYAMA.
HE SHOULD KNOW THE MOMENT THE CHALLENGE BEGINS IS THE MOMENT HIS EXPULSION IS DECIDED!
MEGUMI?!
DASH
TADOKORO, WHOA! WHERE ARE YOU GOING?
B-BUT...!
I HAVE TO DO SOMETHING!
AT THIS RATE, SOMA IS... HE'S...!
YEAH, WE KNOW! JUST CALM DOWN FIRST, OKAY?
...

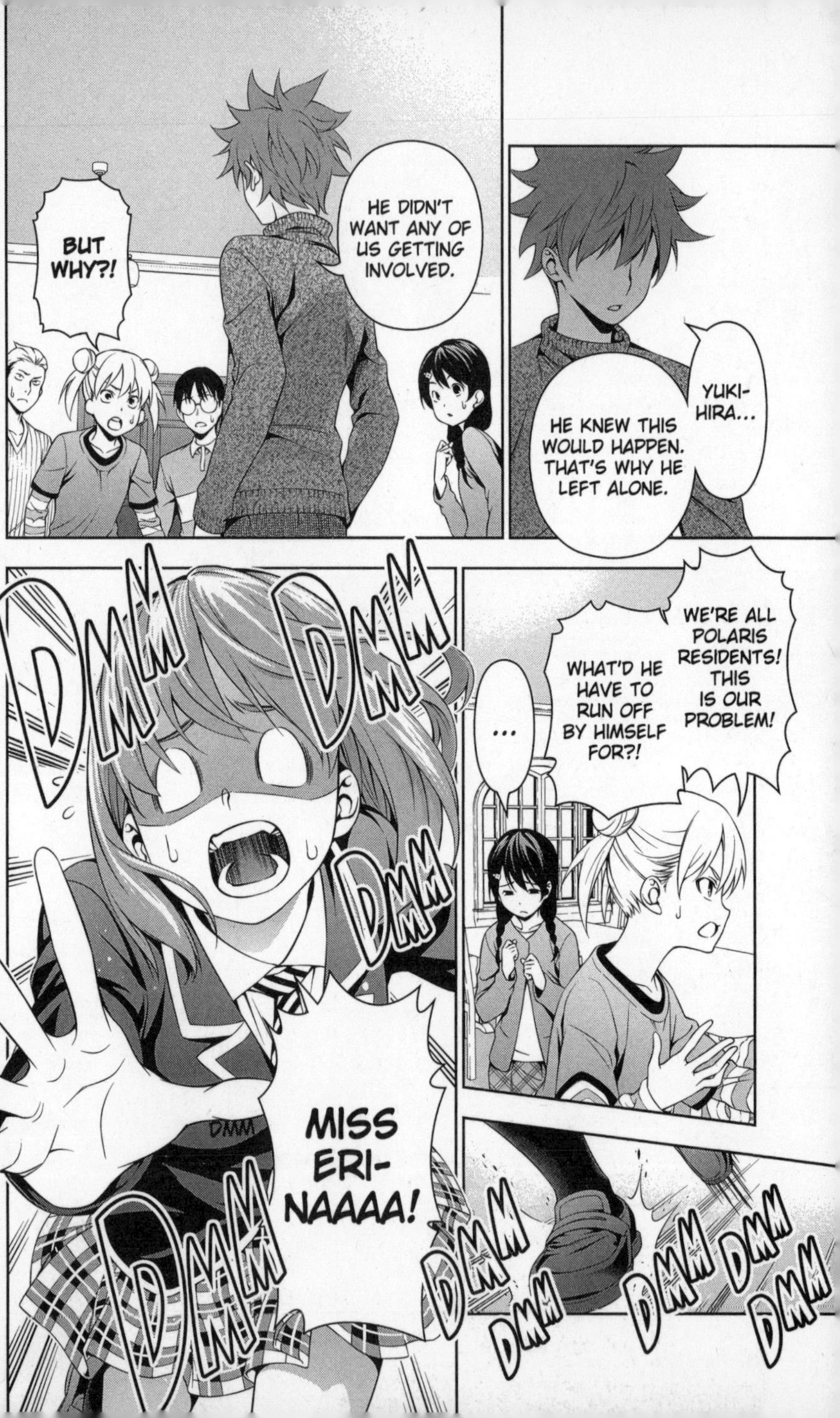
YUKI-HIRA...
HE KNEW THIS WOULD HAPPEN. THAT'S WHY HE LEFT ALONE.
HE DIDN'T WANT ANY OF US GETTING INVOLVED.
BUT WHY?!
WE'RE ALL POLARIS RESIDENTS! THIS IS OUR PROBLEM!
WHAT'D HE HAVE TO RUN OFF BY HIMSELF FOR?!
...
DMM DMM DMM
DMM
DMM
DMM DMM
DMM
DMM
DMM
MISS ERI-NAAAA!
DMM

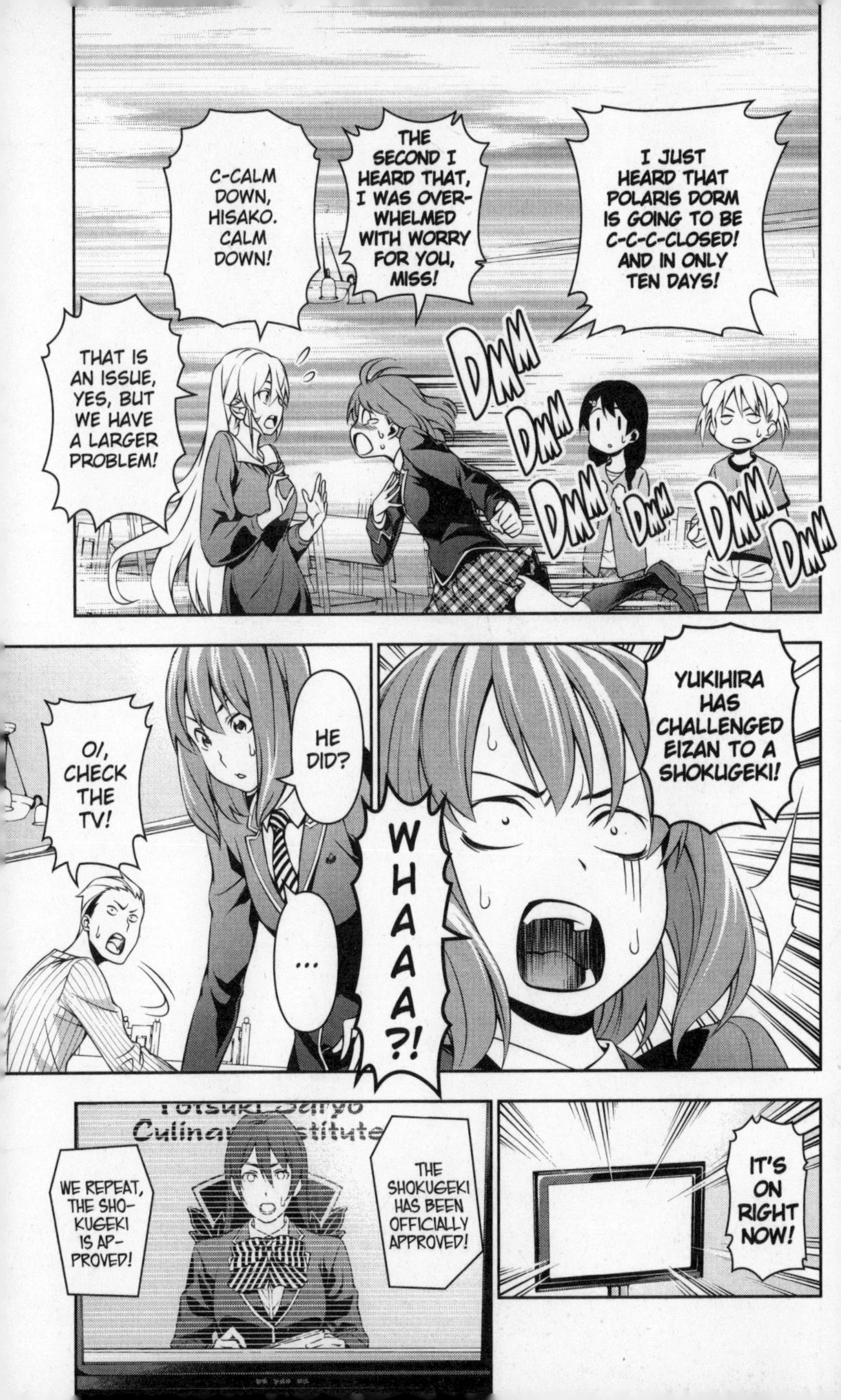
I JUST HEARD THAT POLARIS DORM IS GOING TO BE C-C-C-CLOSED! AND IN ONLY TEN DAYS!
THE SECOND I HEARD THAT, I WAS OVER-WHELMED WITH WORRY FOR YOU, MISS!
C-CALM DOWN, HISAKO. CALM DOWN!
DMM DMM DMM DMM DMM DMM
THAT IS AN ISSUE, YES, BUT WE HAVE A LARGER PROBLEM!
YUKIHIRA HAS CHALLENGED EIZAN TO A SHOKUGEKI!
WHAAAA?!
HE DID?
...
OI, CHECK THE TV!
IT'S ON RIGHT NOW!
THE SHOKUGEKI HAS BEEN OFFICIALLY APPROVED!
WE REPEAT, THE SHO-KUGEKI IS AP-PROVED!

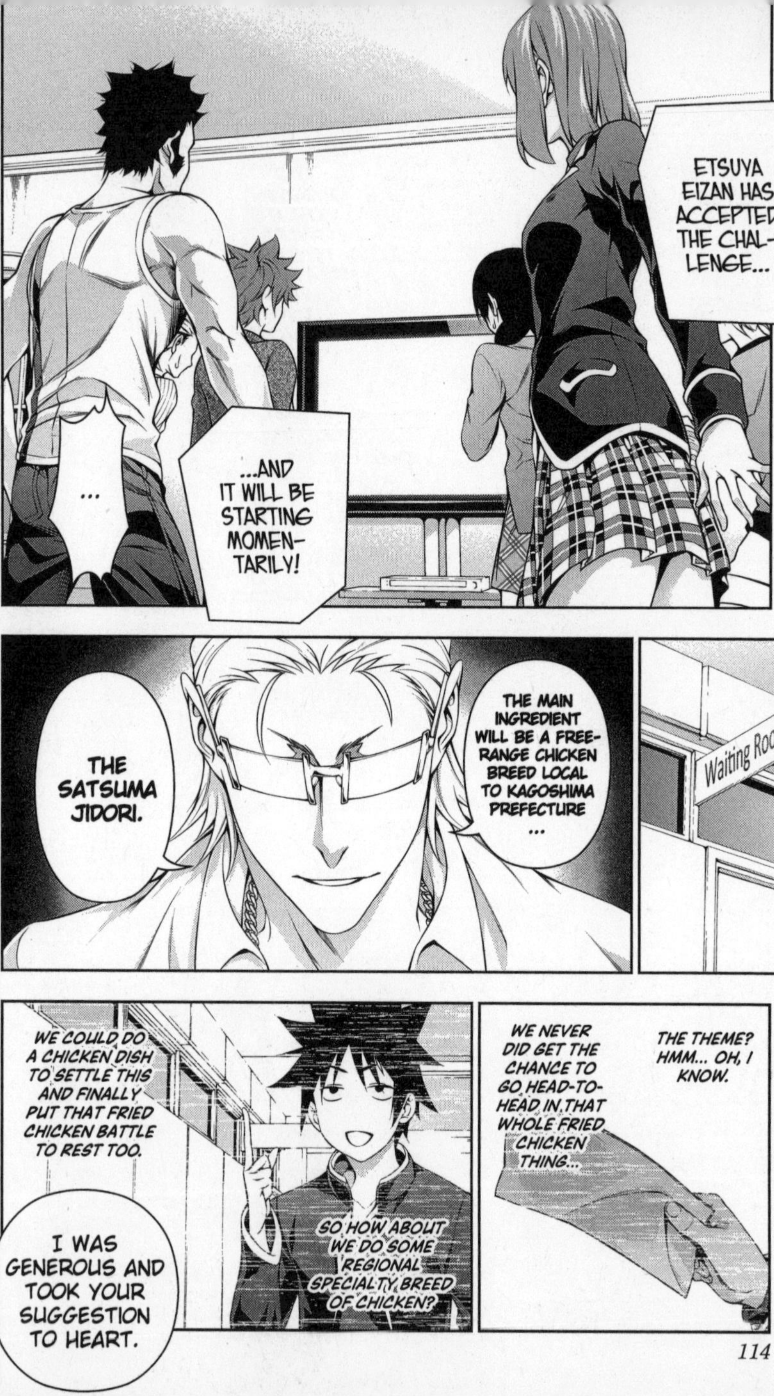
ETSUYA EIZAN HAS ACCEPTED THE CHALLENGE...
...AND IT WILL BE STARTING MOMENTARILY!
...
Waiting Room
THE MAIN INGREDIENT WILL BE A FREE-RANGE CHICKEN BREED LOCAL TO KAGOSHIMA PREFECTURE ...
THE SATSUMA JIDORI.
THE THEME? HMM... OH, I KNOW.
WE NEVER DID GET THE CHANCE TO GO HEAD-TO-HEAD IN THAT WHOLE FRIED CHICKEN THING...
WE COULD DO A CHICKEN DISH TO SETTLE THIS AND FINALLY PUT THAT FRIED CHICKEN BATTLE TO REST TOO.
SO HOW ABOUT WE DO SOME REGIONAL SPECIALTY BREED OF CHICKEN?
I WAS GENEROUS AND TOOK YOUR SUGGESTION TO HEART.

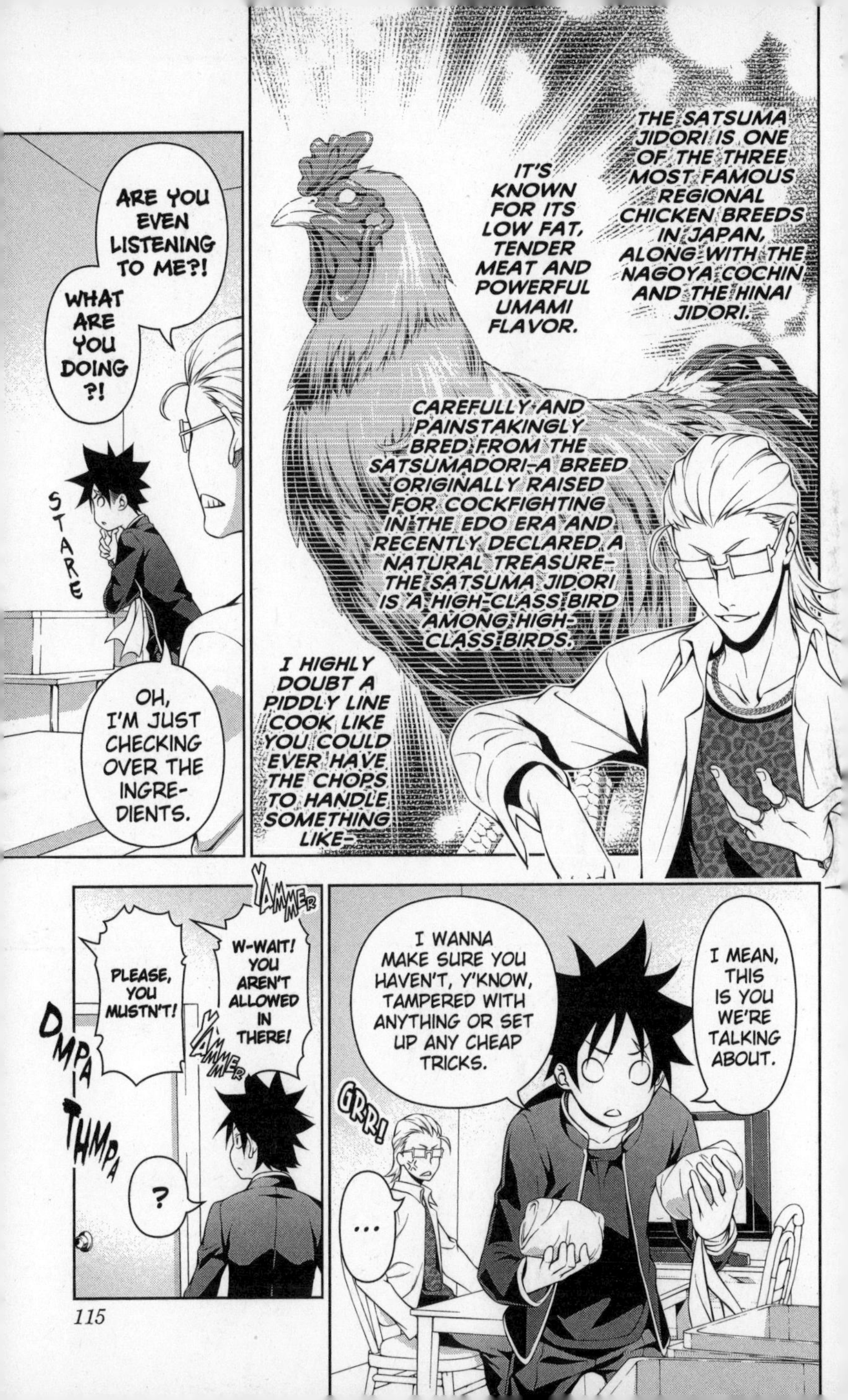
THE SATSUMA JIDORI IS ONE OF THE THREE MOST FAMOUS REGIONAL CHICKEN BREEDS IN JAPAN, ALONG WITH THE NAGOYA COCHIN AND THE HINAI JIDORI.
IT'S KNOWN FOR ITS LOW FAT, TENDER MEAT AND POWERFUL UMAMI FLAVOR.
CAREFULLY AND PAINSTAKINGLY BRED FROM THE SATSUMADORI—A BREED ORIGINALLY RAISED FOR COCKFIGHTING IN THE EDO ERA AND RECENTLY DECLARED A NATURAL TREASURE—THE SATSUMA JIDORI IS A HIGH-CLASS BIRD AMONG HIGH-CLASS BIRDS.
I HIGHLY DOUBT A PIDDLY LINE COOK LIKE YOU COULD EVER HAVE THE CHOPS TO HANDLE SOMETHING LIKE—
ARE YOU EVEN LISTENING TO ME?!
WHAT ARE YOU DOING?!
STARE
OH, I'M JUST CHECKING OVER THE INGREDIENTS.
I MEAN, THIS IS YOU WE'RE TALKING ABOUT.
I WANNA MAKE SURE YOU HAVEN'T, Y'KNOW, TAMPERED WITH ANYTHING OR SET UP ANY CHEAP TRICKS.
GRR!
...
YAMMER
W-WAIT! YOU AREN'T ALLOWED IN THERE!
PLEASE, YOU MUSTN'T!
YAMMER
DMPA
THMPA
?

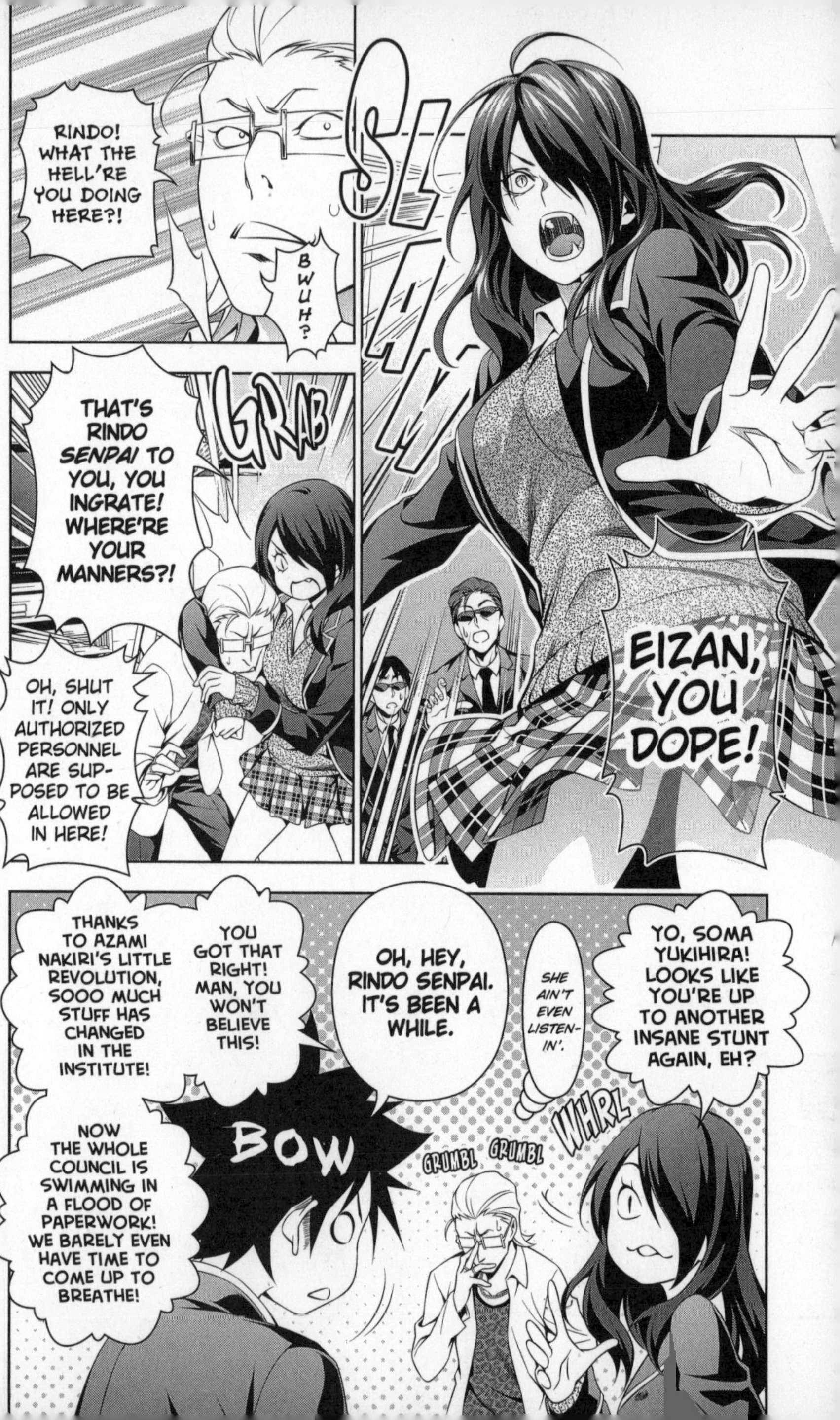
SLAM
EIZAN, YOU DOPE!
RINDO! WHAT THE HELL'RE YOU DOING HERE?!
BWUH?
GRAB
THAT'S RINDO *SENPAI* TO YOU, YOU INGRATE! WHERE'RE YOUR MANNERS?!
OH, SHUT IT! ONLY AUTHORIZED PERSONNEL ARE SUP-POSED TO BE ALLOWED IN HERE!
YO, SOMA YUKIHIRA! LOOKS LIKE YOU'RE UP TO ANOTHER INSANE STUNT AGAIN, EH?
SHE AIN'T EVEN LISTEN-IN'.
WHRL
OH, HEY, RINDO SENPAI. IT'S BEEN A WHILE.
YOU GOT THAT RIGHT! MAN, YOU WON'T BELIEVE THIS!
THANKS TO AZAMI NAKIRI'S LITTLE REVOLUTION, SOOO MUCH STUFF HAS CHANGED IN THE INSTITUTE!
GRUMBL GRUMBL
BOW
NOW THE WHOLE COUNCIL IS SWIMMING IN A FLOOD OF PAPERWORK! WE BARELY EVEN HAVE TIME TO COME UP TO BREATHE!

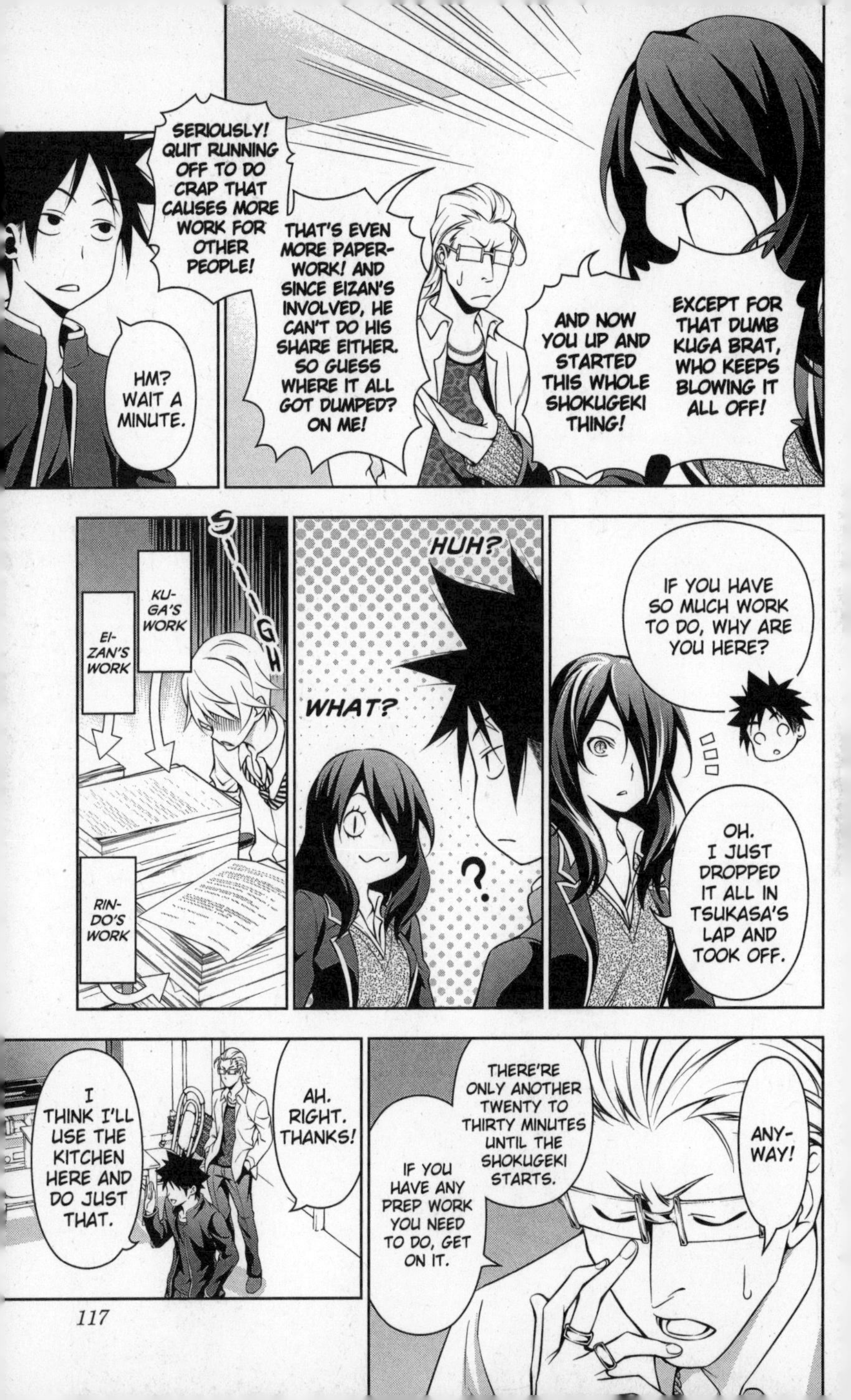
EXCEPT FOR THAT DUMB KUGA BRAT, WHO KEEPS BLOWING IT ALL OFF!
AND NOW YOU UP AND STARTED THIS WHOLE SHOKUGEKI THING!
THAT'S EVEN MORE PAPERWORK! AND SINCE EIZAN'S INVOLVED, HE CAN'T DO HIS SHARE EITHER. SO GUESS WHERE IT ALL GOT DUMPED? ON ME!
SERIOUSLY! QUIT RUNNING OFF TO DO CRAP THAT CAUSES MORE WORK FOR OTHER PEOPLE!
HM? WAIT A MINUTE.
IF YOU HAVE SO MUCH WORK TO DO, WHY ARE YOU HERE?
OH. I JUST DROPPED IT ALL IN TSUKASA'S LAP AND TOOK OFF.
HUH?
WHAT?
SIGH
KU-GA'S WORK
EI-ZAN'S WORK
RIN-DO'S WORK
ANY-WAY!
THERE'RE ONLY ANOTHER TWENTY TO THIRTY MINUTES UNTIL THE SHOKUGEKI STARTS.
IF YOU HAVE ANY PREP WORK YOU NEED TO DO, GET ON IT.
AH. RIGHT. THANKS!
I THINK I'LL USE THE KITCHEN HERE AND DO JUST THAT.

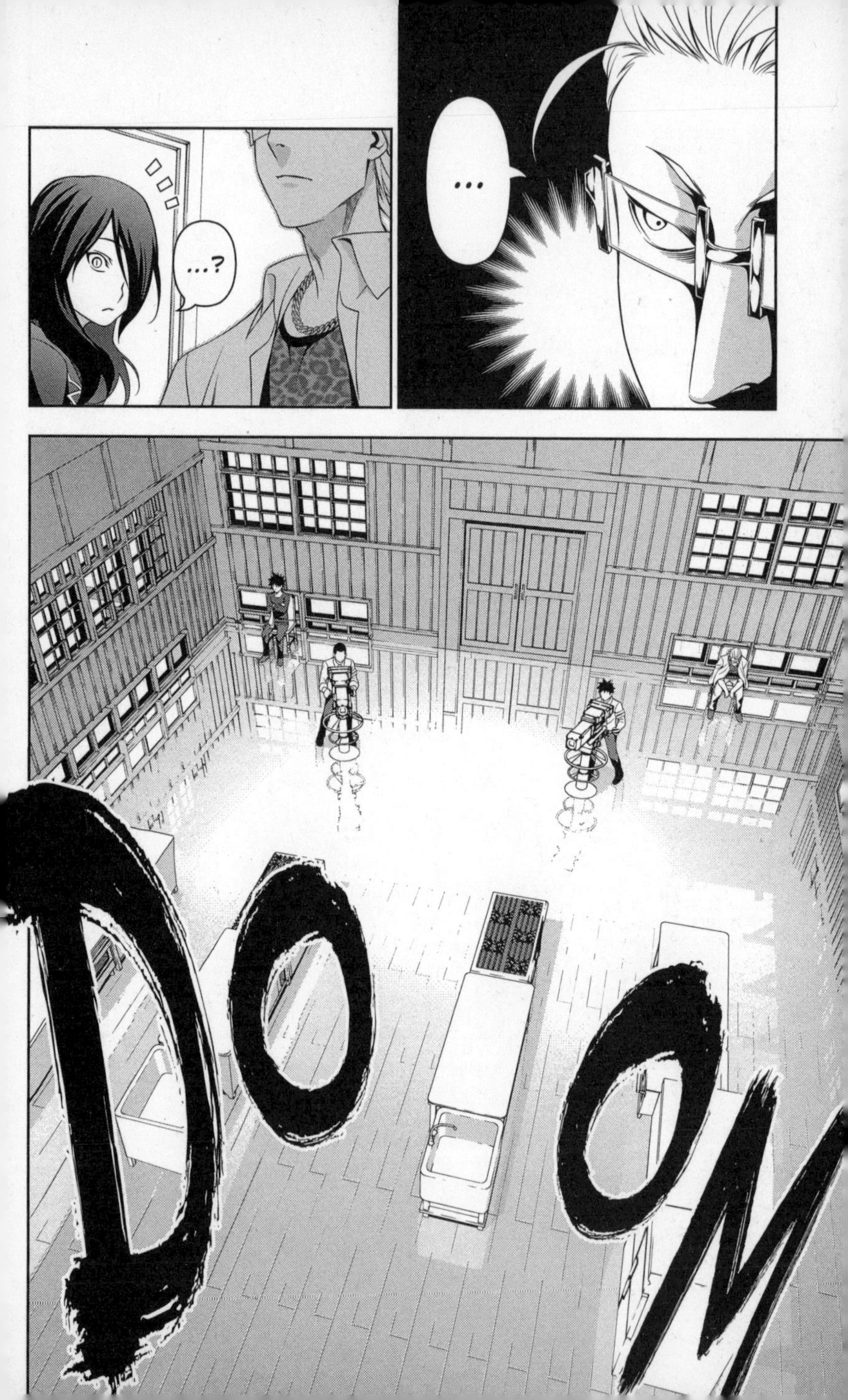
...
...?
DOOM

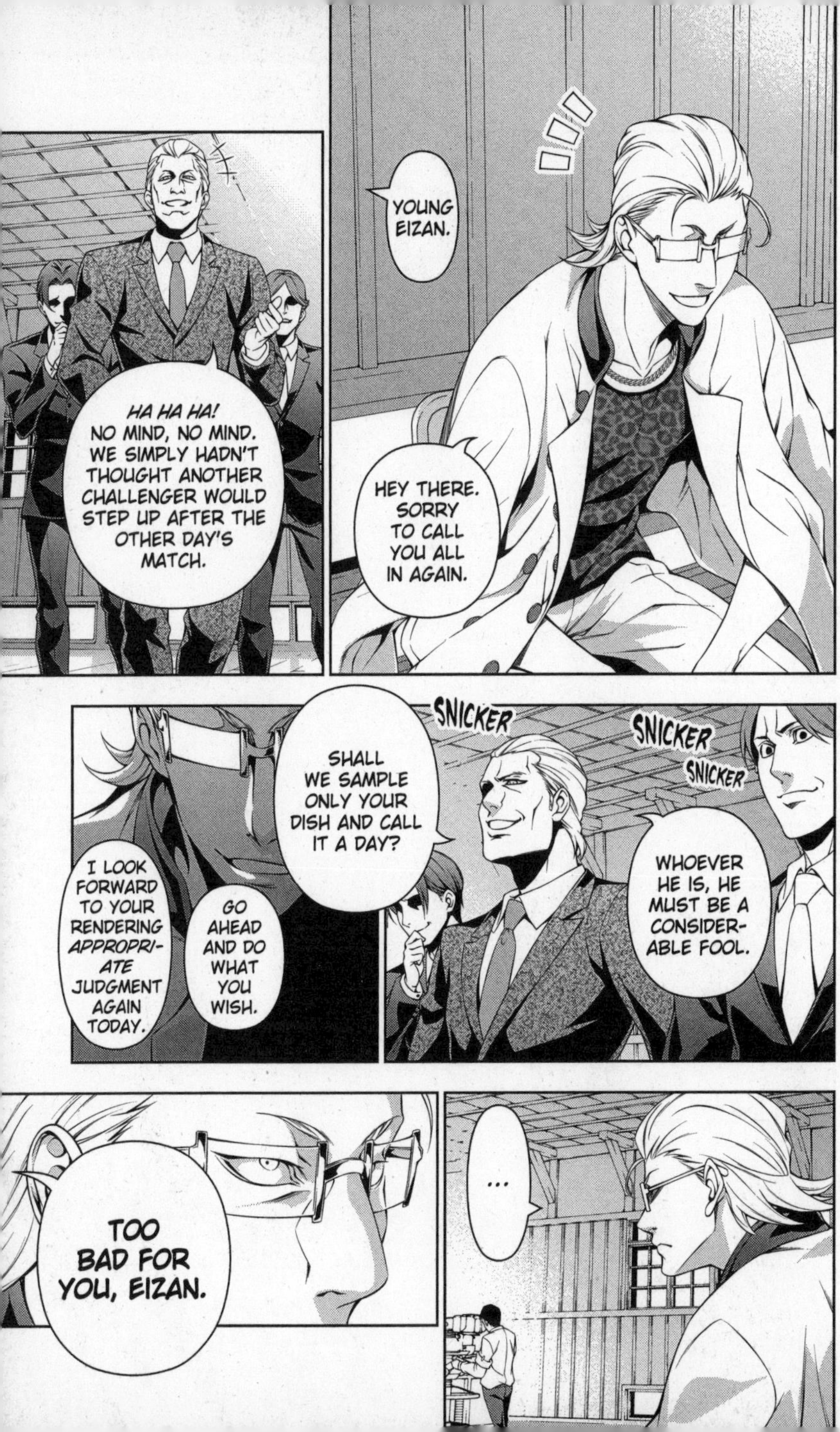
YOUNG EIZAN.
HEY THERE. SORRY TO CALL YOU ALL IN AGAIN.
HA HA HA! NO MIND, NO MIND. WE SIMPLY HADN'T THOUGHT ANOTHER CHALLENGER WOULD STEP UP AFTER THE OTHER DAY'S MATCH.
SNICKER
SNICKER
SNICKER
WHOEVER HE IS, HE MUST BE A CONSIDER-ABLE FOOL.
SHALL WE SAMPLE ONLY YOUR DISH AND CALL IT A DAY?
GO AHEAD AND DO WHAT YOU WISH.
I LOOK FORWARD TO YOUR RENDERING *APPROPRI-ATE* JUDGMENT AGAIN TODAY.
...
TOO BAD FOR YOU, EIZAN.

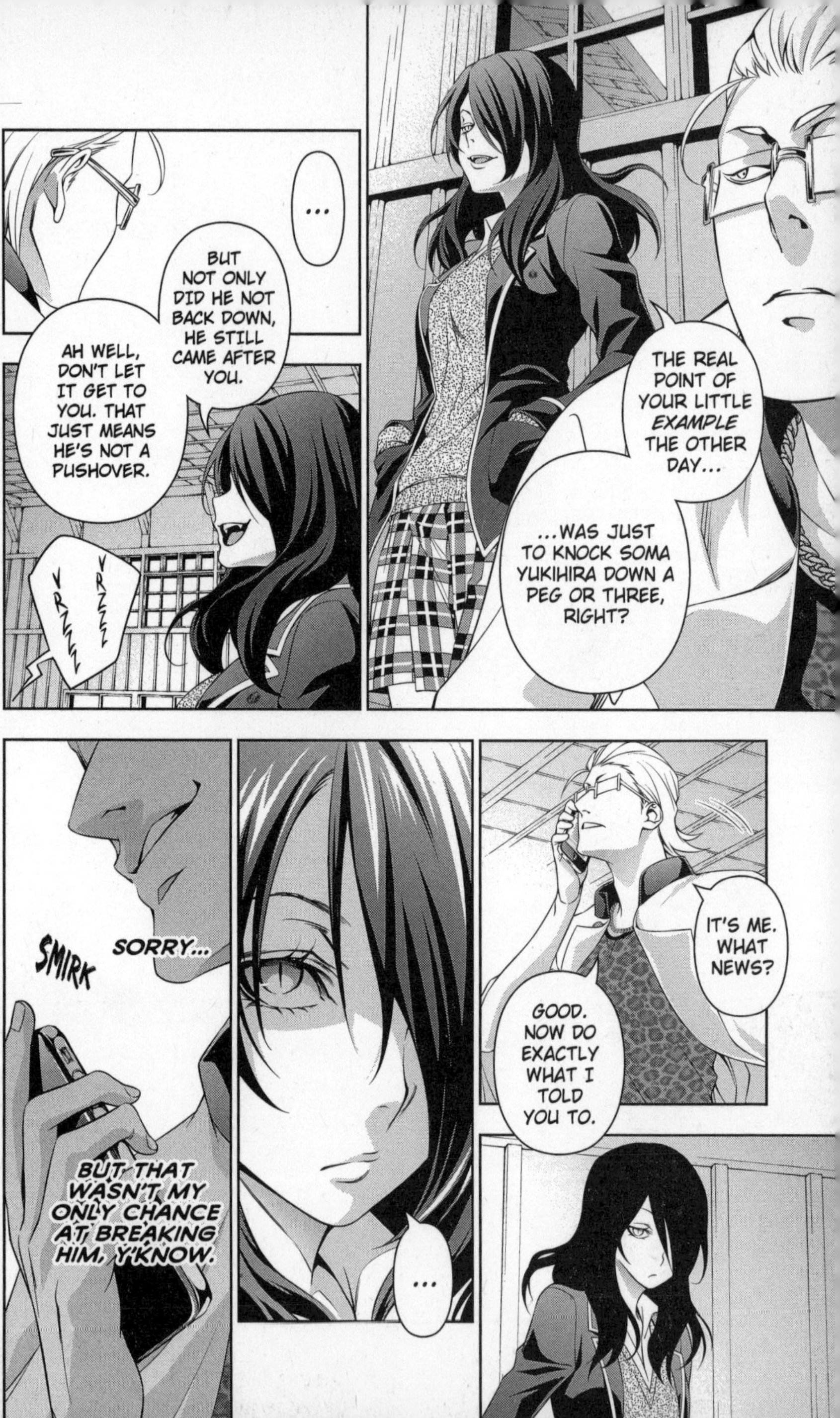
THE REAL POINT OF YOUR LITTLE *EXAMPLE* THE OTHER DAY...
...WAS JUST TO KNOCK SOMA YUKIHIRA DOWN A PEG OR THREE, RIGHT?
...
BUT NOT ONLY DID HE NOT BACK DOWN, HE STILL CAME AFTER YOU.
AH WELL, DON'T LET IT GET TO YOU. THAT JUST MEANS HE'S NOT A PUSHOVER.
VRZZZZ
VRZZZ
IT'S ME. WHAT NEWS?
GOOD. NOW DO EXACTLY WHAT I TOLD YOU TO.
...
SMIRK
SORRY...
BUT THAT WASN'T MY ONLY CHANCE AT BREAKING HIM, Y'KNOW.

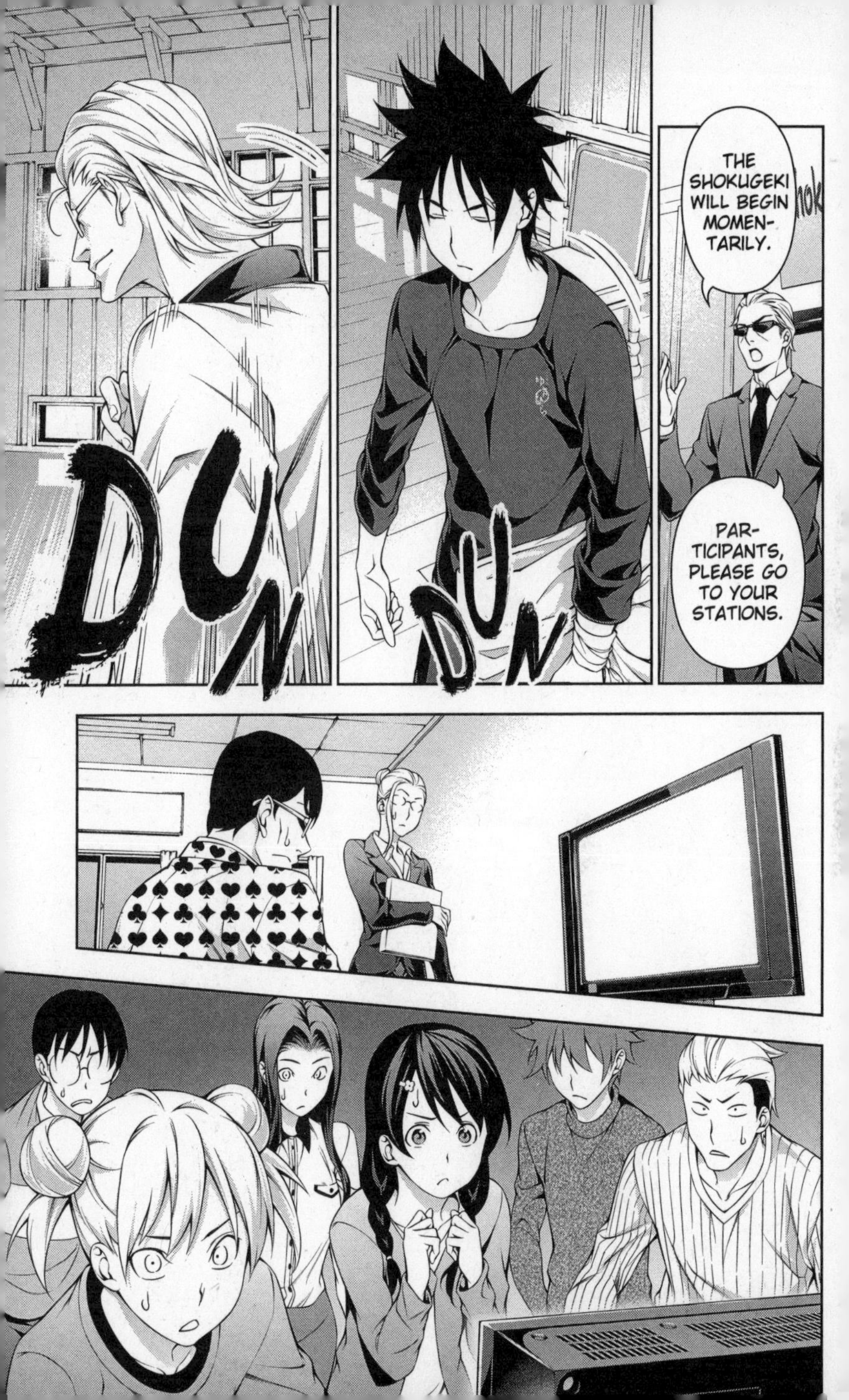
THE SHOKUGEKI WILL BEGIN MOMEN-TARILY.
PAR-TICIPANTS, PLEASE GO TO YOUR STATIONS.
DUN
DUN

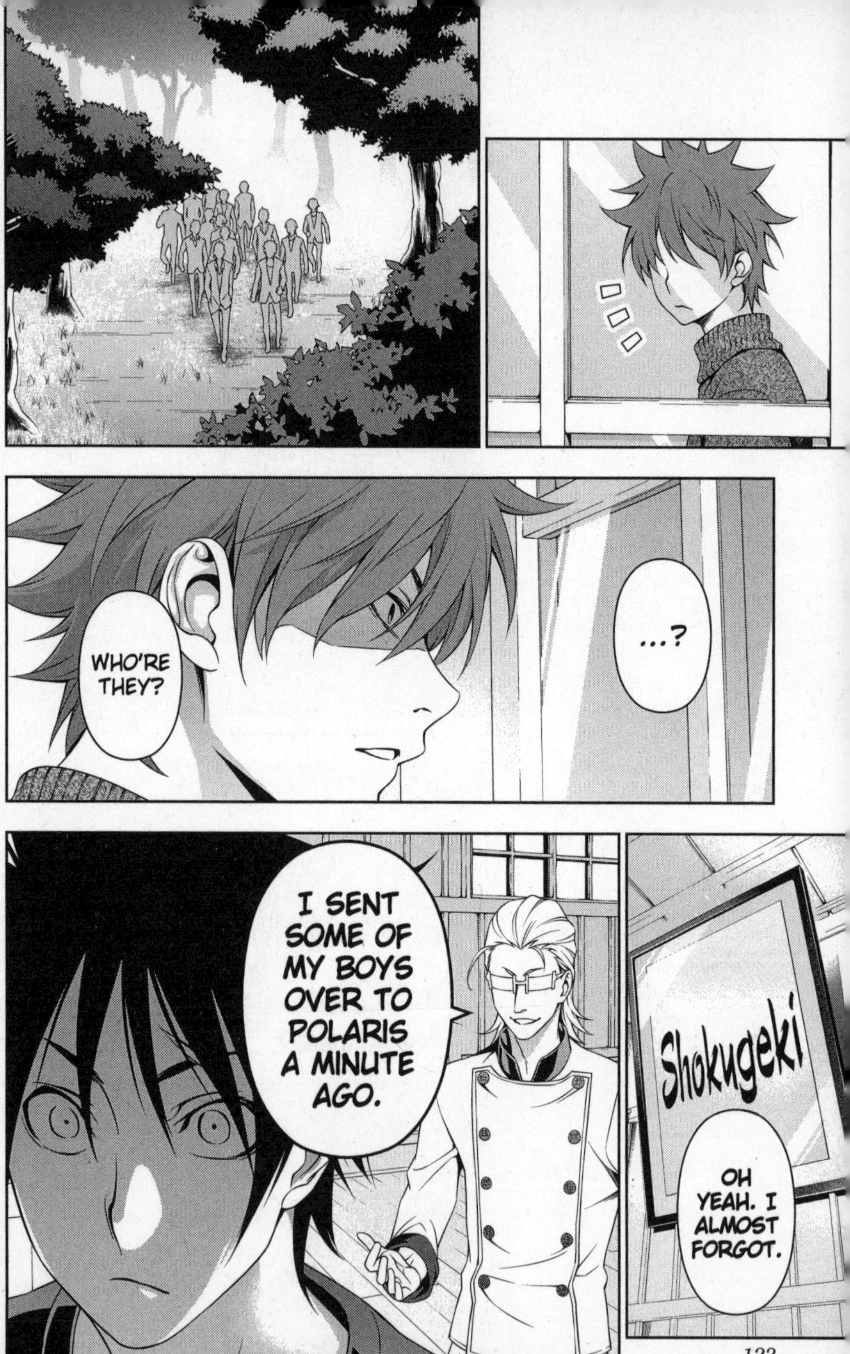
...?
WHO'RE THEY?
Shokugeki
OH YEAH. I ALMOST FORGOT.
I SENT SOME OF MY BOYS OVER TO POLARIS A MINUTE AGO.

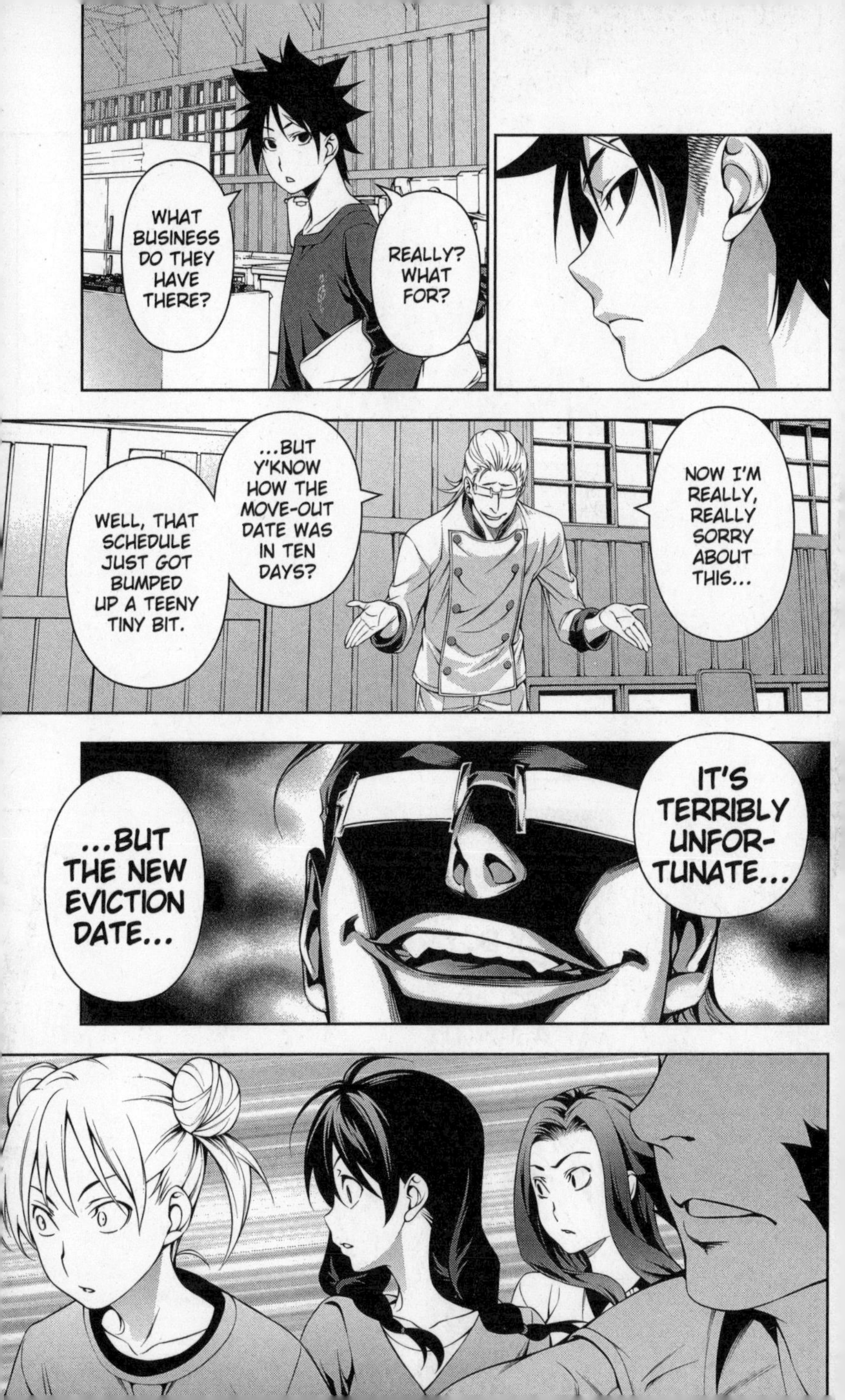
REALLY? WHAT FOR?
WHAT BUSINESS DO THEY HAVE THERE?
NOW I'M REALLY, REALLY SORRY ABOUT THIS...
...BUT Y'KNOW HOW THE MOVE-OUT DATE WAS IN TEN DAYS?
WELL, THAT SCHEDULE JUST GOT BUMPED UP A TEENY TINY BIT.
IT'S TERRIBLY UNFOR-TUNATE...
...BUT THE NEW EVICTION DATE...

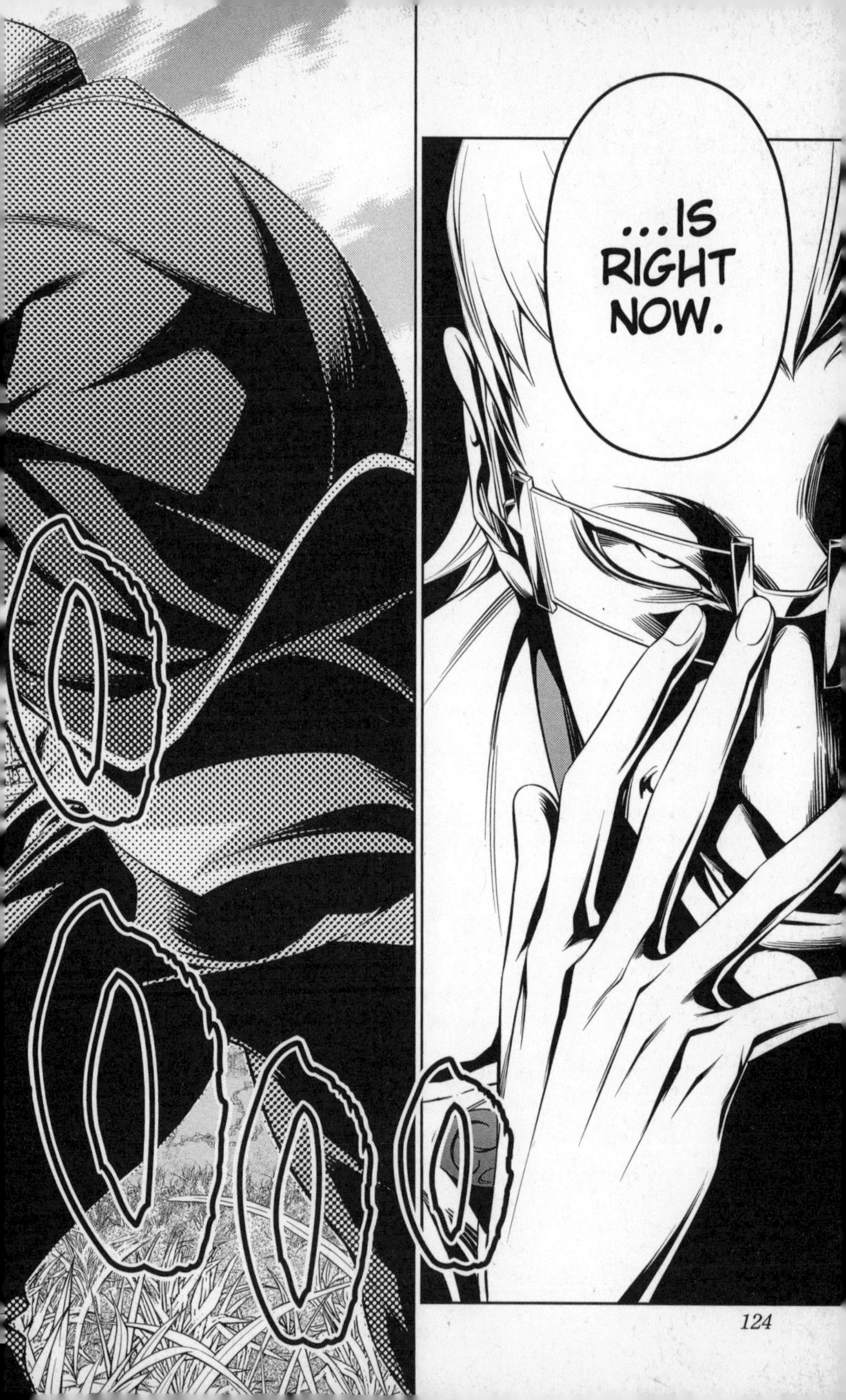
...IS RIGHT NOW.

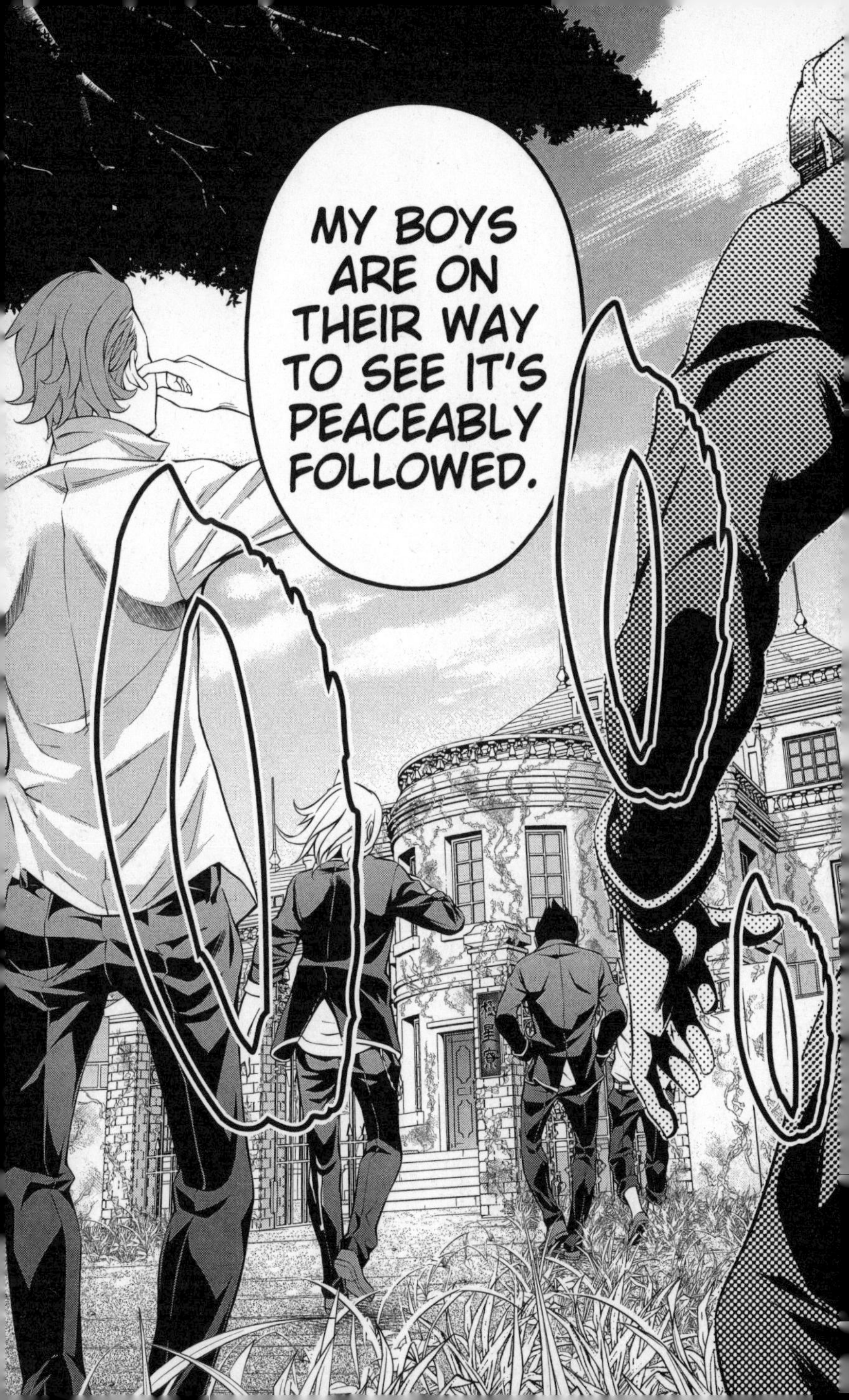
MY BOYS ARE ON THEIR WAY TO SEE IT'S PEACEABLY FOLLOWED.

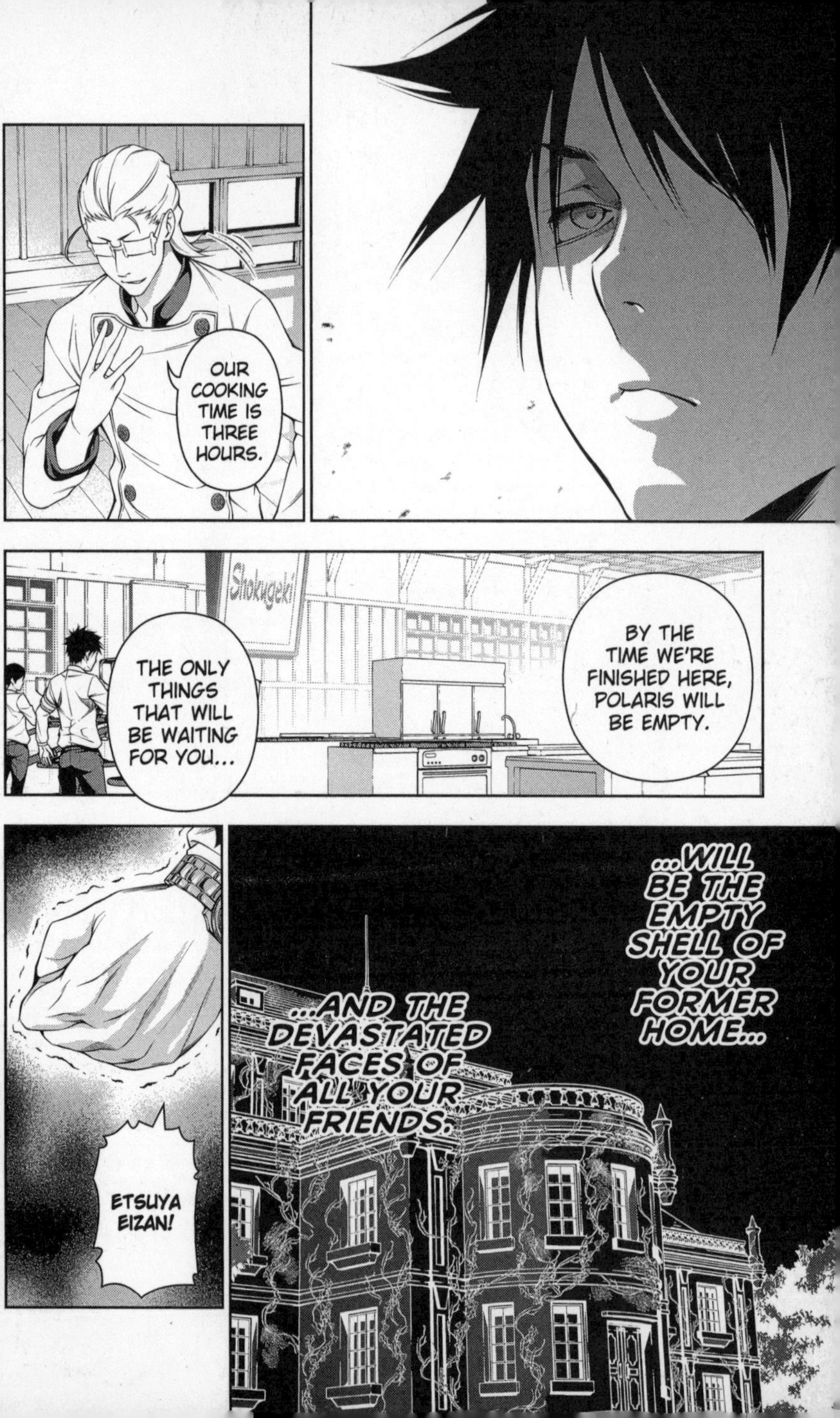
OUR COOKING TIME IS THREE HOURS.
BY THE TIME WE'RE FINISHED HERE, POLARIS WILL BE EMPTY.
Shokugeki
THE ONLY THINGS THAT WILL BE WAITING FOR YOU...
...WILL BE THE EMPTY SHELL OF YOUR FORMER HOME...
...AND THE DEVASTATED FACES OF ALL YOUR FRIENDS.
ETSUYA EIZAN!

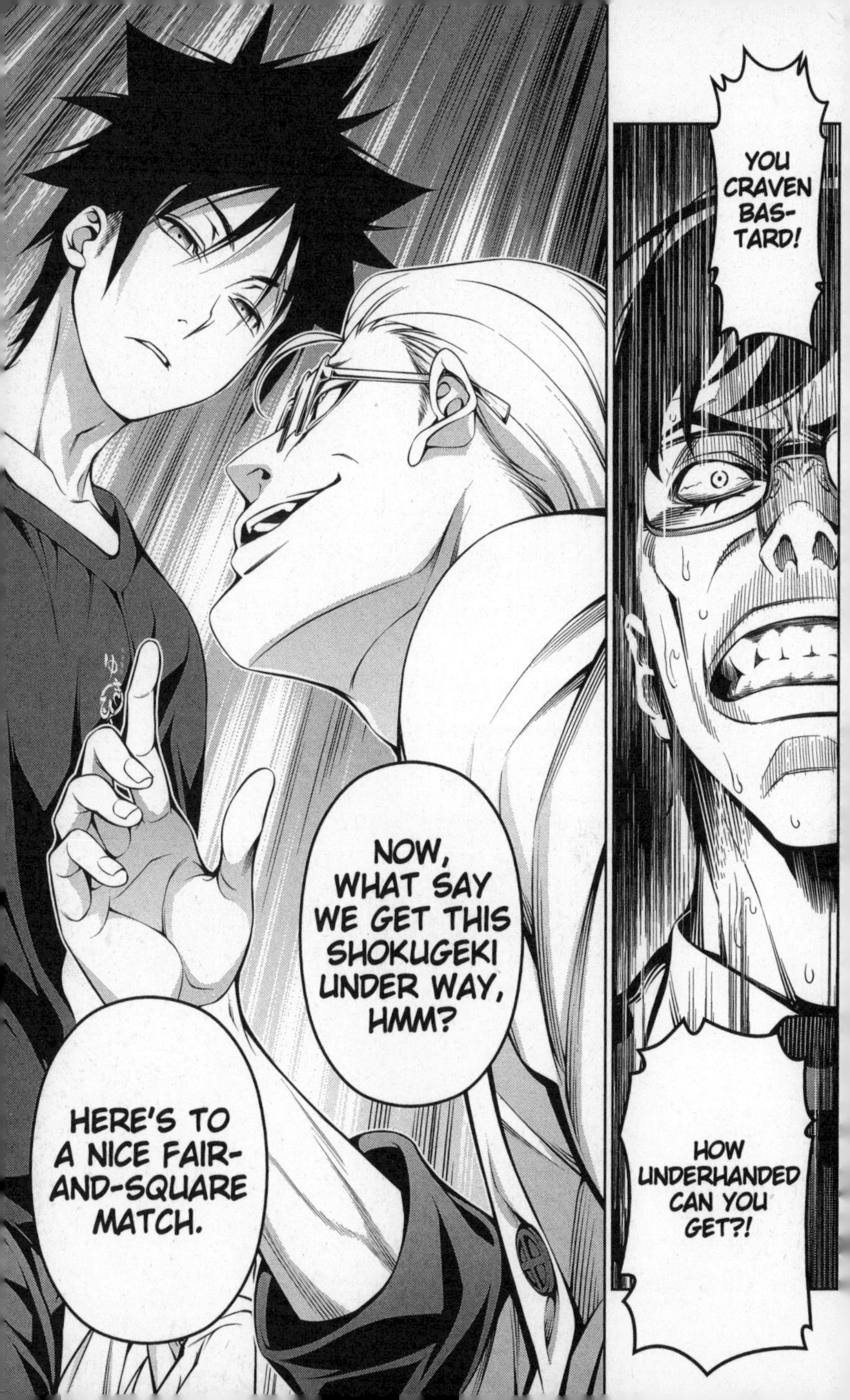
YOU CRAVEN BAS-TARD!
HOW UNDERHANDED CAN YOU GET?!
NOW, WHAT SAY WE GET THIS SHOKUGEKI UNDER WAY, HMM?
HERE'S TO A NICE FAIR-AND-SQUARE MATCH.

Miss Erina's Splendid Days as a Runaway 6

~STRANGE CHOICES LOOM~

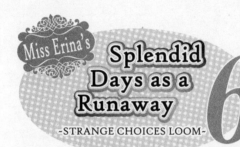

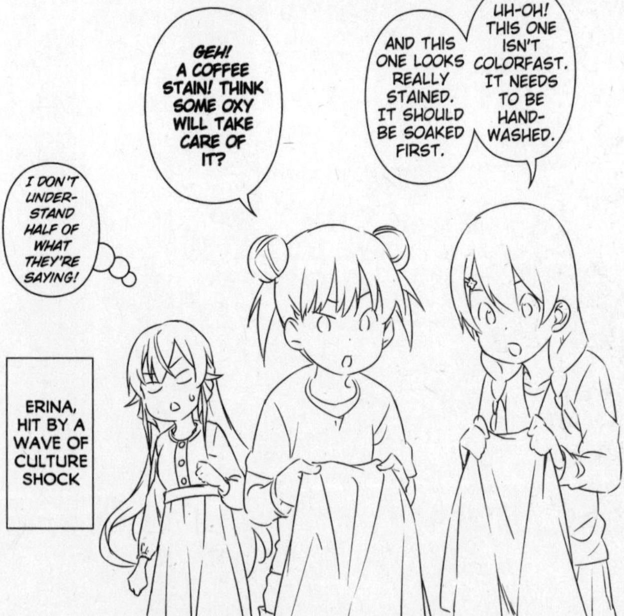

UH-OH! THIS ONE ISN'T COLORFAST. IT NEEDS TO BE HAND-WASHED.
AND THIS ONE LOOKS REALLY STAINED. IT SHOULD BE SOAKED FIRST.
GEH! A COFFEE STAIN! THINK SOME OXY WILL TAKE CARE OF IT?
I DON'T UNDER-STAND HALF OF WHAT THEY'RE SAYING!
ERINA, HIT BY A WAVE OF CULTURE SHOCK

143 THE OPENING VOLLEY IS SHOT

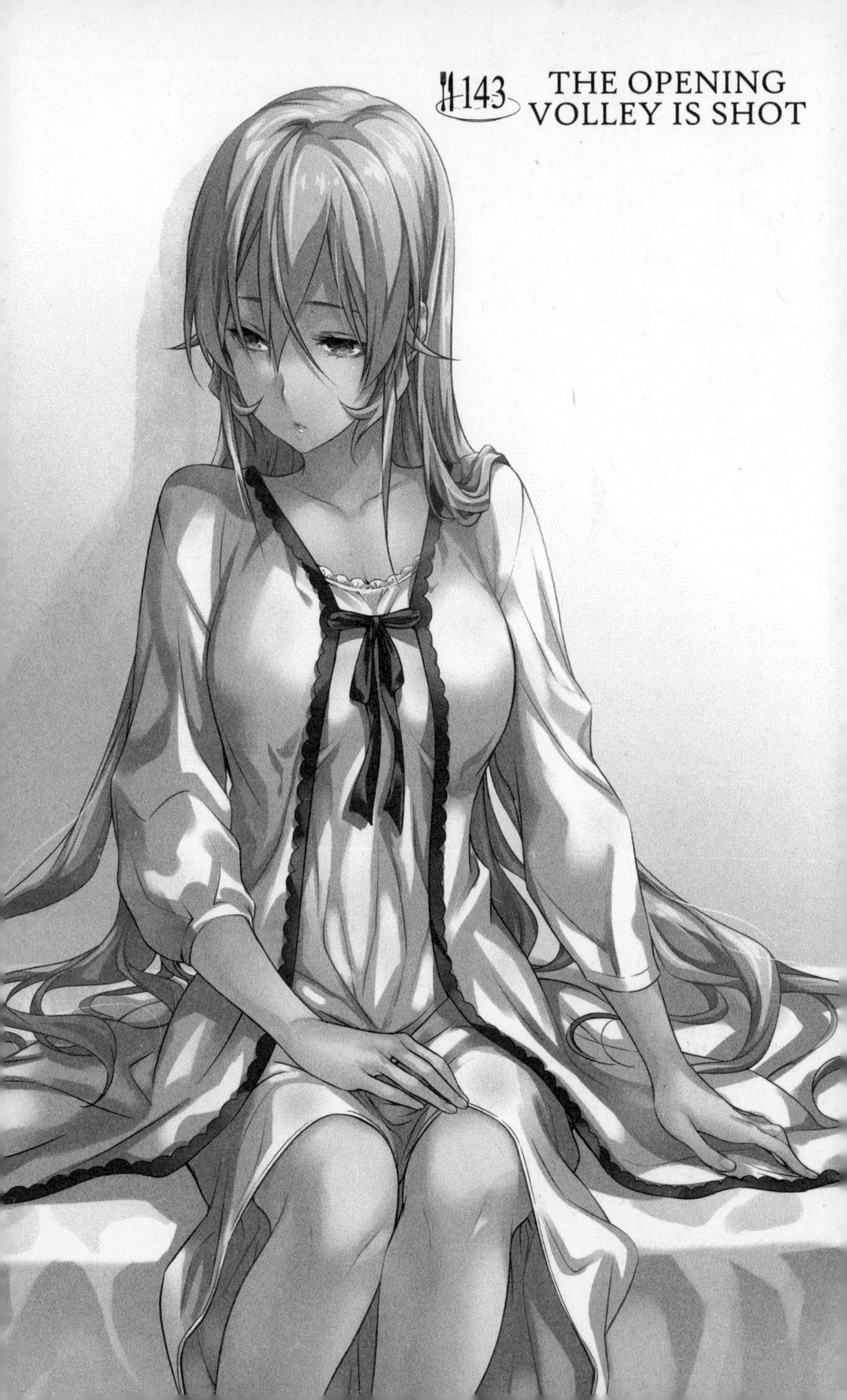

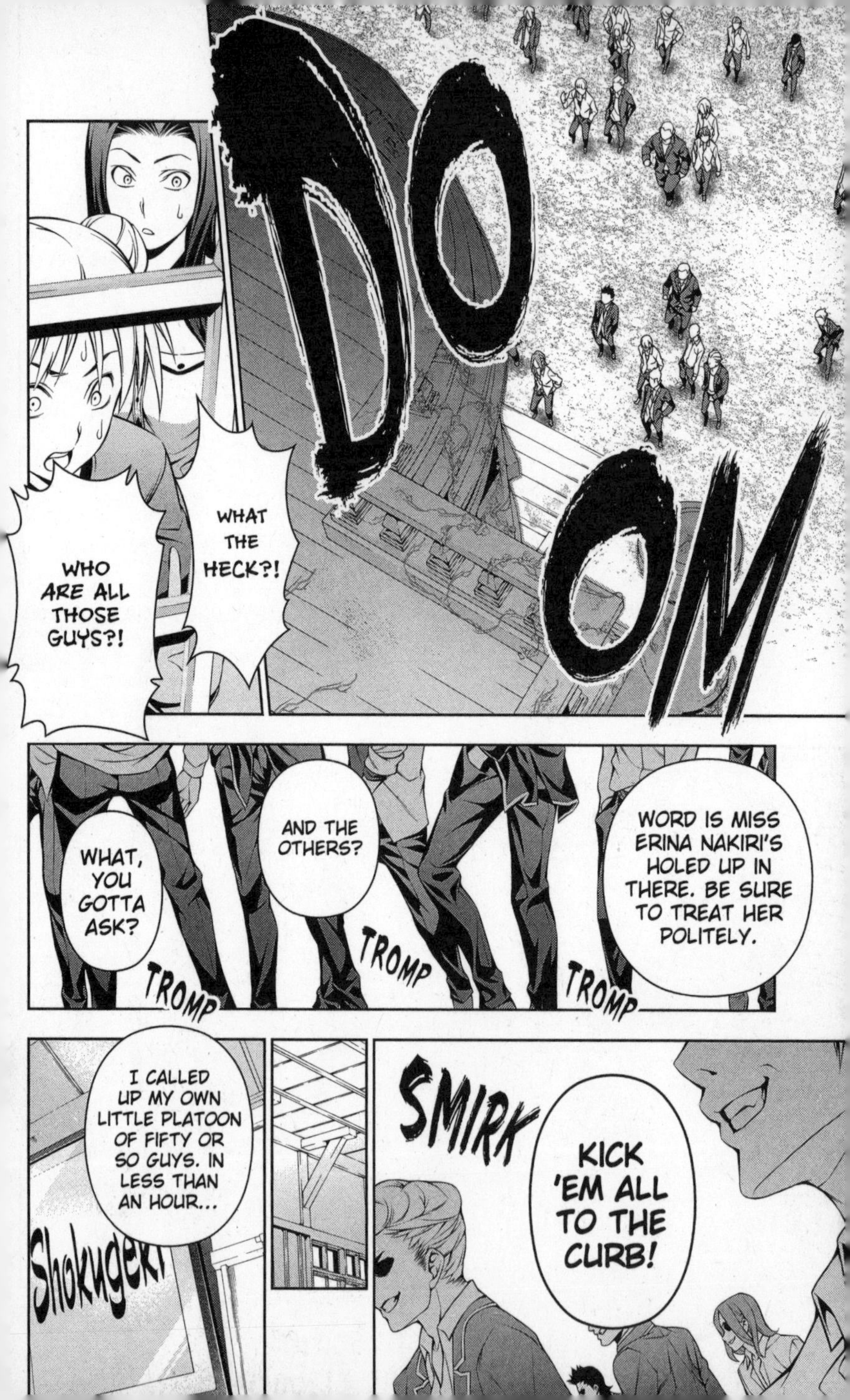
DOOOM
WHAT THE HECK?!
WHO ARE ALL THOSE GUYS?!
WORD IS MISS ERINA NAKIRI'S HOLED UP IN THERE. BE SURE TO TREAT HER POLITELY.
TROMP
AND THE OTHERS?
TROMP
WHAT, YOU GOTTA ASK?
TROMP
SMIRK
KICK 'EM ALL TO THE CURB!
I CALLED UP MY OWN LITTLE PLATOON OF FIFTY OR SO GUYS. IN LESS THAN AN HOUR...
Shokugeki

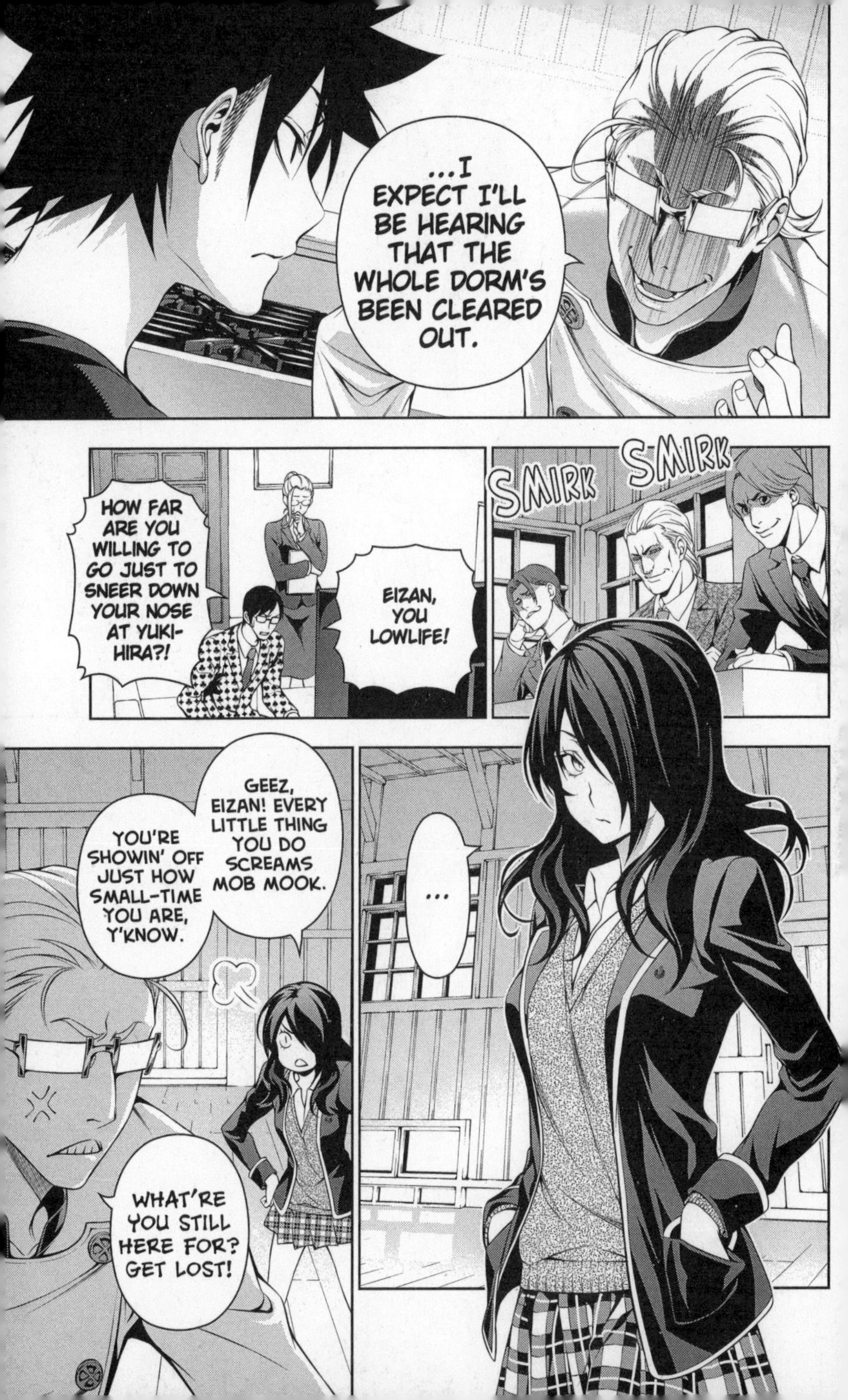
...I EXPECT I'LL BE HEARING THAT THE WHOLE DORM'S BEEN CLEARED OUT.
SMIRK
SMIRK
EIZAN, YOU LOWLIFE!
HOW FAR ARE YOU WILLING TO GO JUST TO SNEER DOWN YOUR NOSE AT YUKI-HIRA?!
...
GEEZ, EIZAN! EVERY LITTLE THING YOU DO SCREAMS MOB MOOK.
YOU'RE SHOWIN' OFF JUST HOW SMALL-TIME YOU ARE, Y'KNOW.
WHAT'RE YOU STILL HERE FOR? GET LOST!

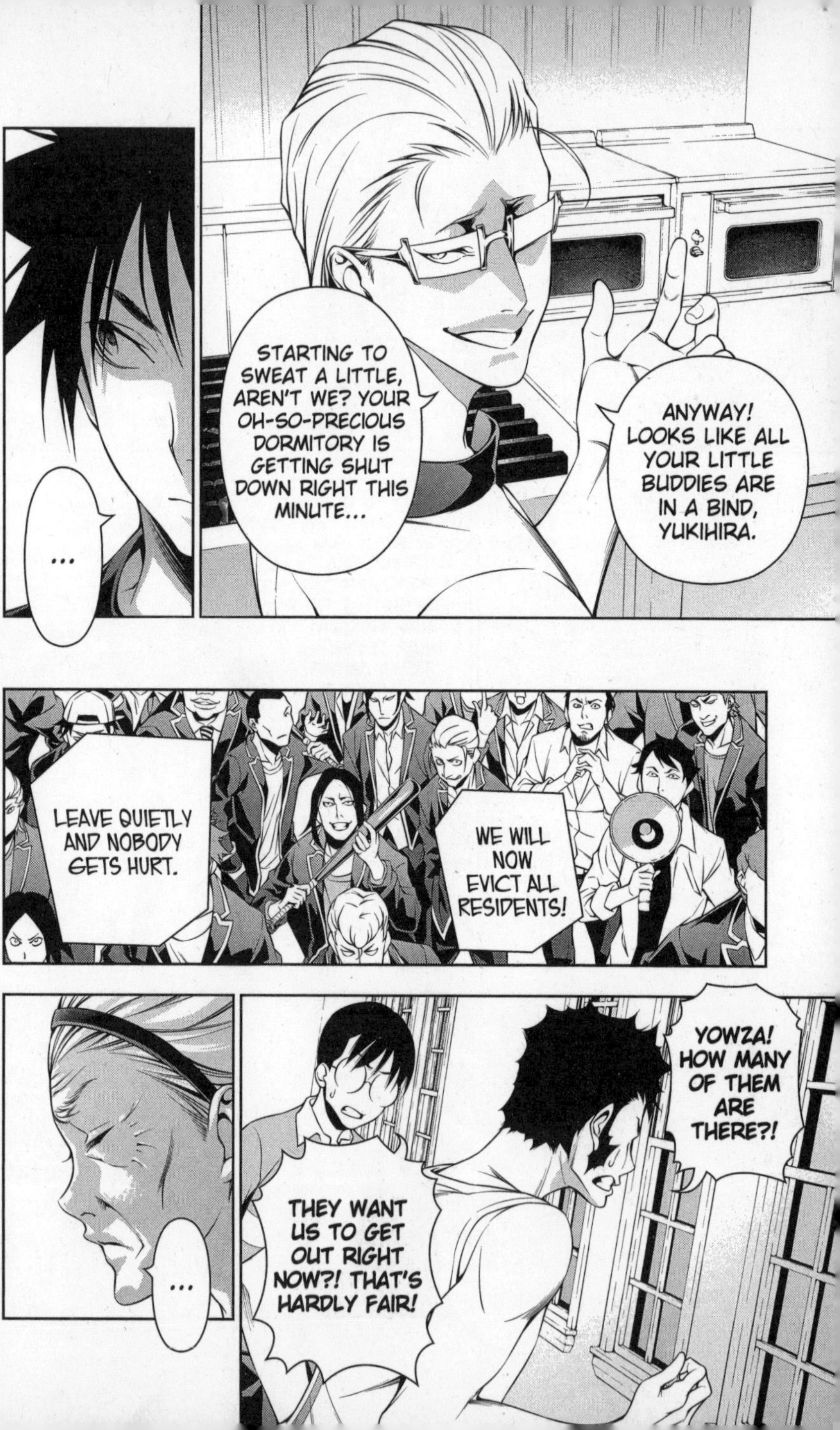
ANYWAY! LOOKS LIKE ALL YOUR LITTLE BUDDIES ARE IN A BIND, YUKIHIRA.
STARTING TO SWEAT A LITTLE, AREN'T WE? YOUR OH-SO-PRECIOUS DORMITORY IS GETTING SHUT DOWN RIGHT THIS MINUTE...
...
WE WILL NOW EVICT ALL RESIDENTS!
LEAVE QUIETLY AND NOBODY GETS HURT.
YOWZA! HOW MANY OF THEM ARE THERE?!
THEY WANT US TO GET OUT RIGHT NOW?! THAT'S HARDLY FAIR!
...

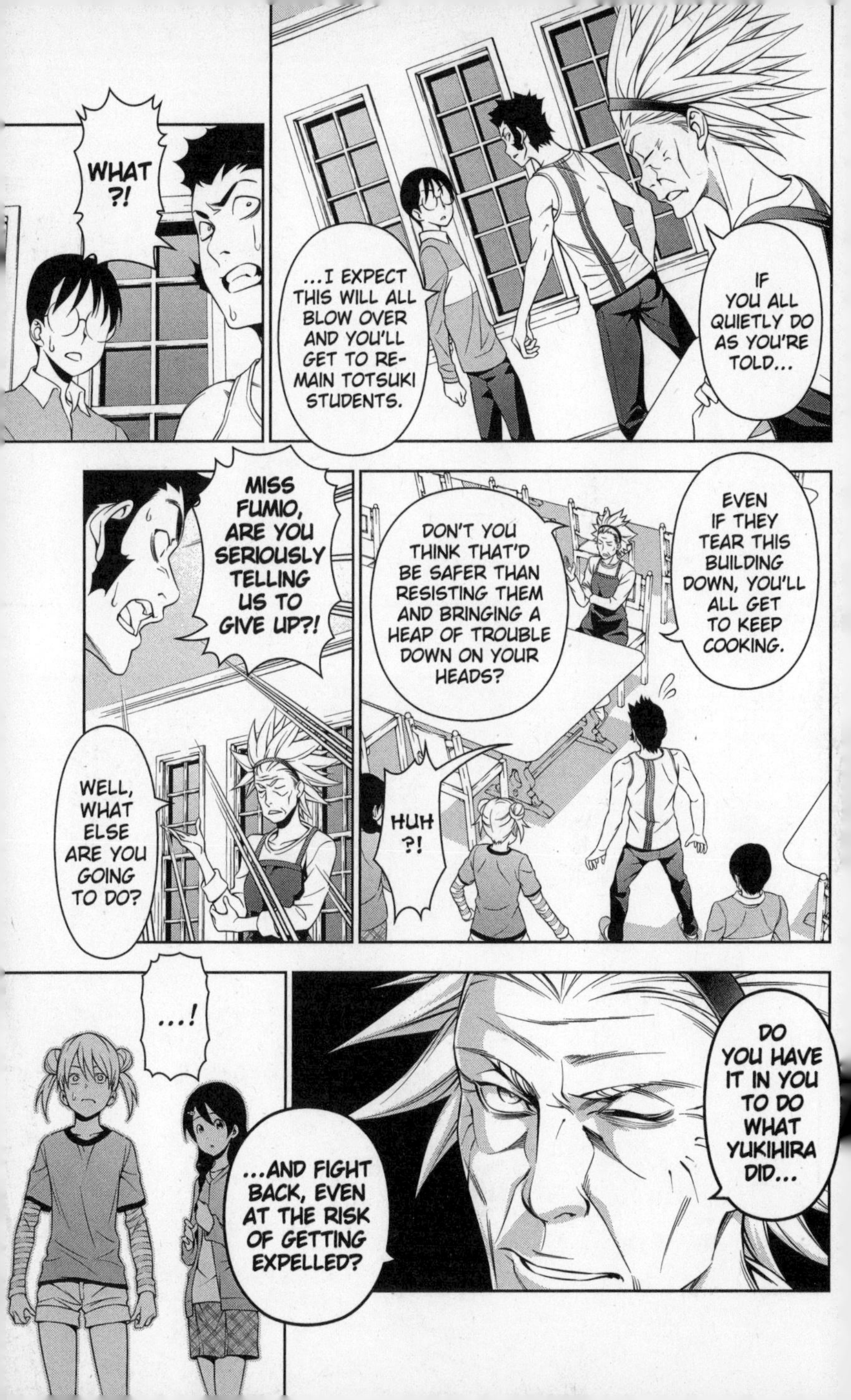
IF YOU ALL QUIETLY DO AS YOU'RE TOLD...
...I EXPECT THIS WILL ALL BLOW OVER AND YOU'LL GET TO RE-MAIN TOTSUKI STUDENTS.
WHAT?!
EVEN IF THEY TEAR THIS BUILDING DOWN, YOU'LL ALL GET TO KEEP COOKING.
DON'T YOU THINK THAT'D BE SAFER THAN RESISTING THEM AND BRINGING A HEAP OF TROUBLE DOWN ON YOUR HEADS?
HUH?!
MISS FUMIO, ARE YOU SERIOUSLY TELLING US TO GIVE UP?!
WELL, WHAT ELSE ARE YOU GOING TO DO?
DO YOU HAVE IT IN YOU TO DO WHAT YUKIHIRA DID...
...AND FIGHT BACK, EVEN AT THE RISK OF GETTING EXPELLED?
...!

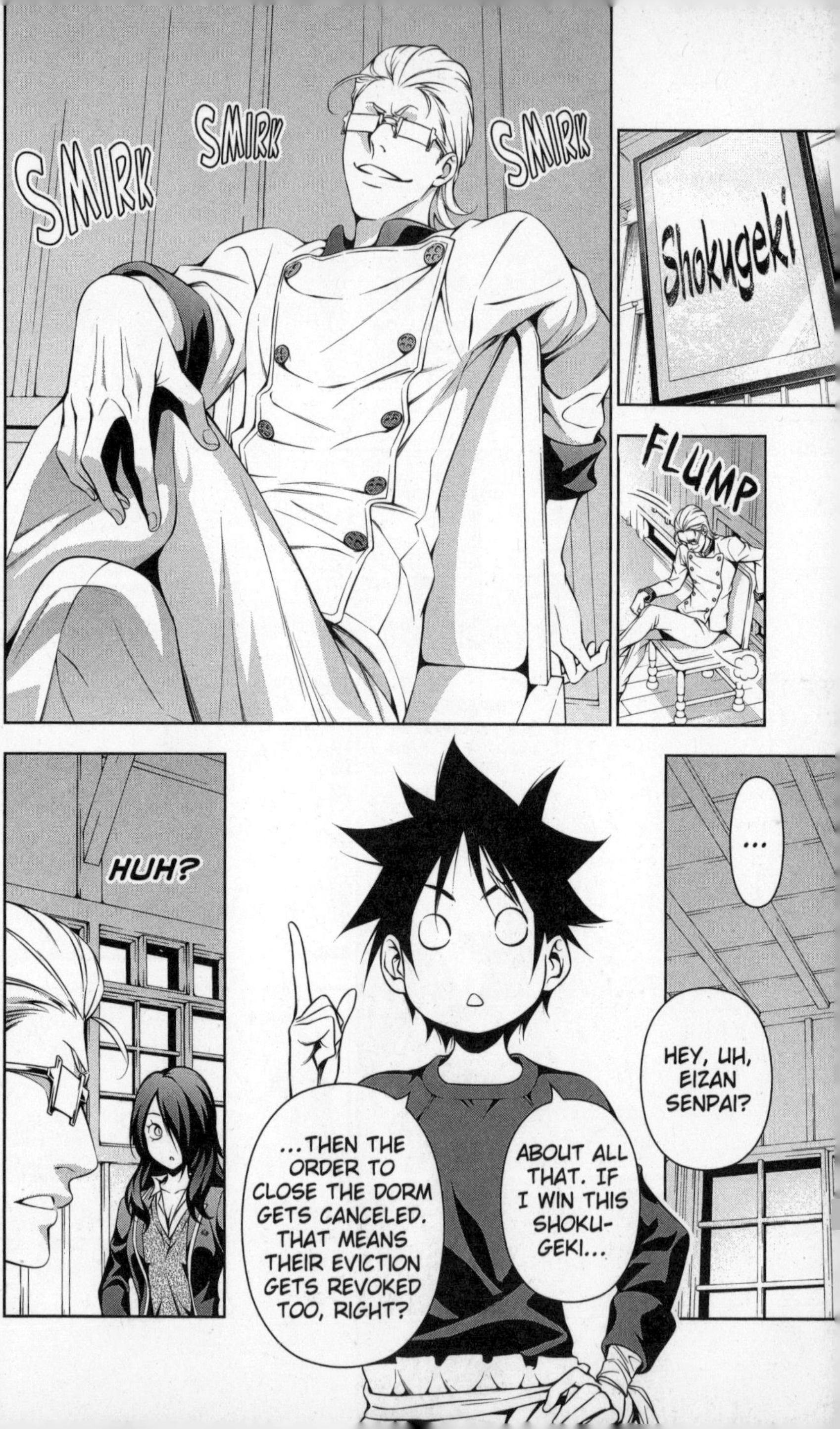
Shokugeki
FLUMP
SMIRK
SMIRK
SMIRK
...
HEY, UH, EIZAN SENPAI?
ABOUT ALL THAT. IF I WIN THIS SHOKU-GEKI...
...THEN THE ORDER TO CLOSE THE DORM GETS CANCELED. THAT MEANS THEIR EVICTION GETS REVOKED TOO, RIGHT?
HUH?

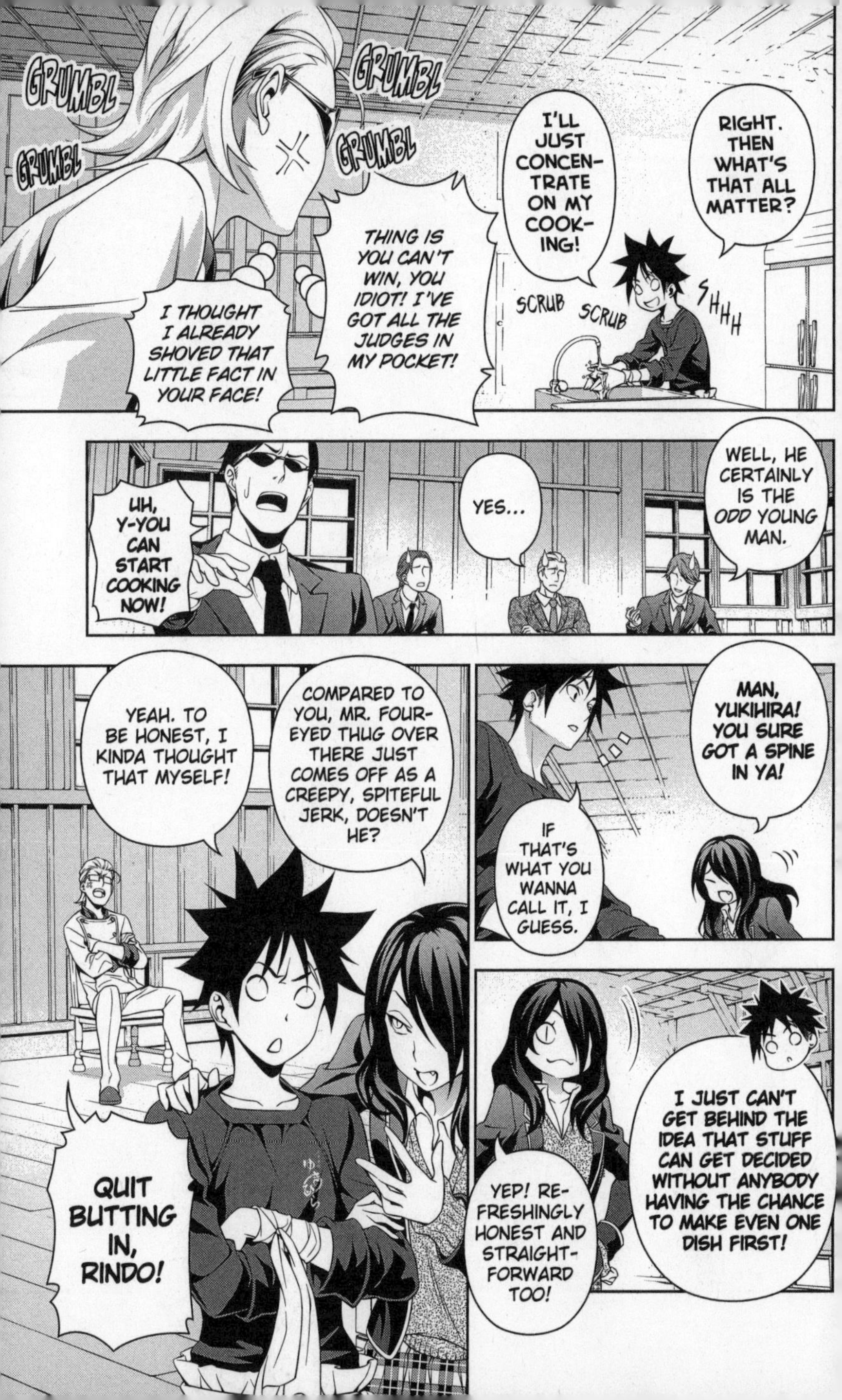
RIGHT. THEN WHAT'S THAT ALL MATTER?
I'LL JUST CONCEN-TRATE ON MY COOK-ING!
SHHH
SCRUB SCRUB
GRUMBL
GRUMBL
GRUMBL
GRUMBL
THING IS YOU CAN'T WIN, YOU IDIOT! I'VE GOT ALL THE JUDGES IN MY POCKET!
I THOUGHT I ALREADY SHOVED THAT LITTLE FACT IN YOUR FACE!
WELL, HE CERTAINLY IS THE ODD YOUNG MAN.
YES...
UH, Y-YOU CAN START COOKING NOW!
MAN, YUKIHIRA! YOU SURE GOT A SPINE IN YA!
IF THAT'S WHAT YOU WANNA CALL IT, I GUESS.
I JUST CAN'T GET BEHIND THE IDEA THAT STUFF CAN GET DECIDED WITHOUT ANYBODY HAVING THE CHANCE TO MAKE EVEN ONE DISH FIRST!
YEP! RE-FRESHINGLY HONEST AND STRAIGHT-FORWARD TOO!
COMPARED TO YOU, MR. FOUR-EYED THUG OVER THERE JUST COMES OFF AS A CREEPY, SPITEFUL JERK, DOESN'T HE?
YEAH. TO BE HONEST, I KINDA THOUGHT THAT MYSELF!
QUIT BUTTING IN, RINDO!

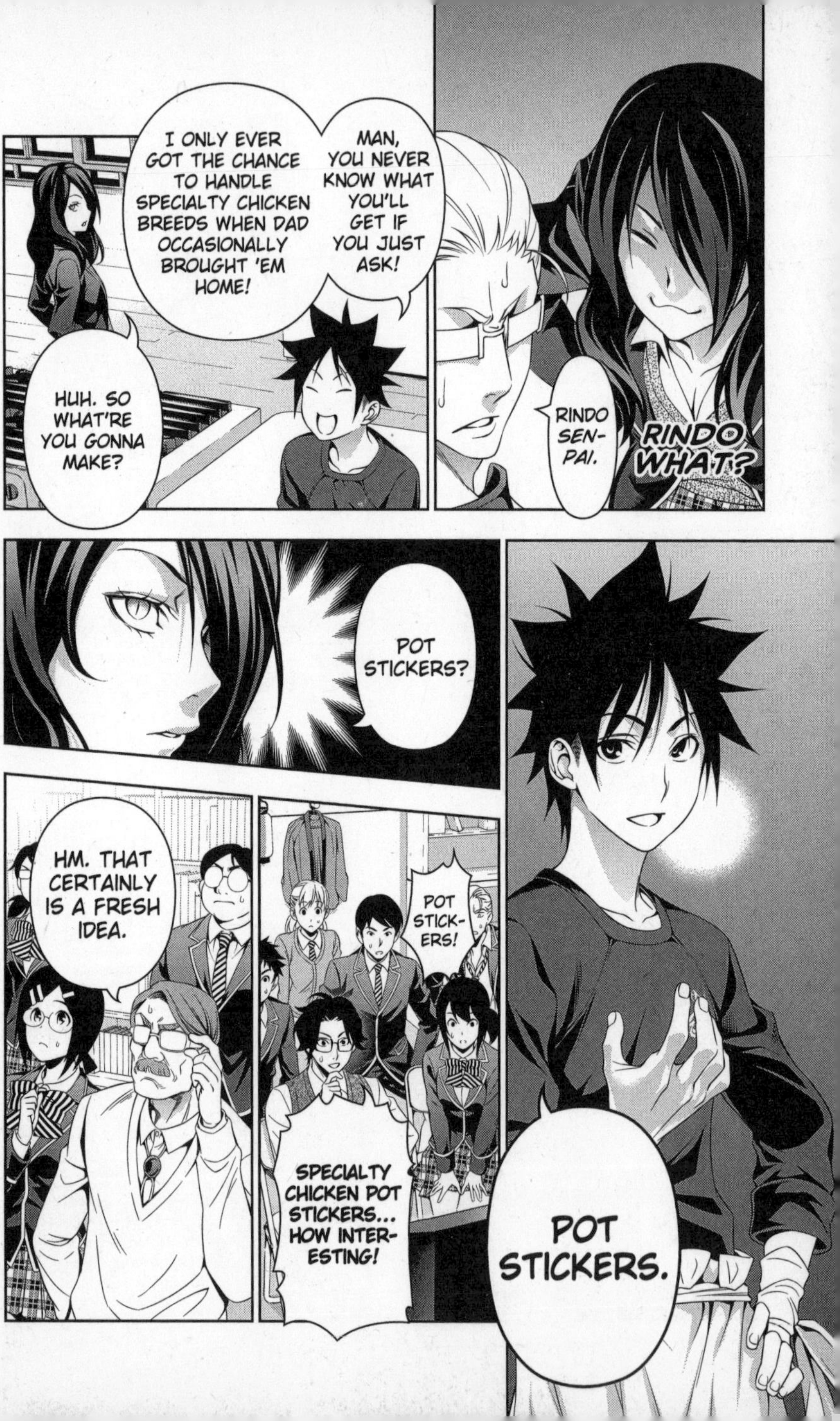
RINDO WHAT?
RINDO SEN-PAI.
MAN, YOU NEVER KNOW WHAT YOU'LL GET IF YOU JUST ASK!
I ONLY EVER GOT THE CHANCE TO HANDLE SPECIALTY CHICKEN BREEDS WHEN DAD OCCASIONALLY BROUGHT 'EM HOME!
HUH. SO WHAT'RE YOU GONNA MAKE?
POT STICKERS.
POT STICKERS?
POT STICK-ERS!
SPECIALTY CHICKEN POT STICKERS... HOW INTER-ESTING!
HM. THAT CERTAINLY IS A FRESH IDEA.

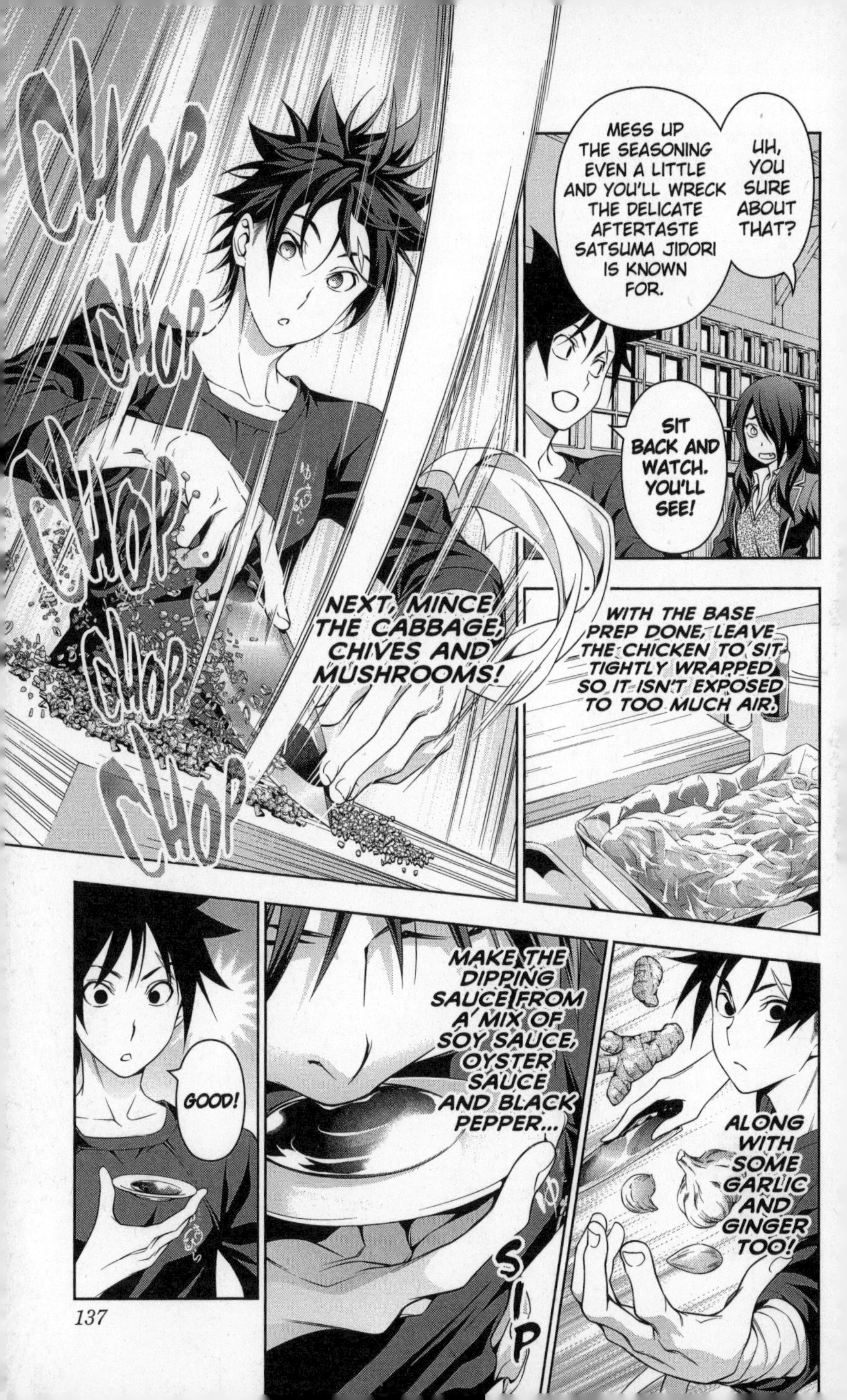
UH, YOU SURE ABOUT THAT?
MESS UP THE SEASONING EVEN A LITTLE AND YOU'LL WRECK THE DELICATE AFTERTASTE SATSUMA JIDORI IS KNOWN FOR.
SIT BACK AND WATCH. YOU'LL SEE!
WITH THE BASE PREP DONE, LEAVE THE CHICKEN TO SIT TIGHTLY WRAPPED SO IT ISN'T EXPOSED TO TOO MUCH AIR.
CHOP
CHOP
CHOP
CHOP
CHOP
NEXT, MINCE THE CABBAGE, CHIVES AND MUSHROOMS!
ALONG WITH SOME GARLIC AND GINGER TOO!
MAKE THE DIPPING SAUCE FROM A MIX OF SOY SAUCE, OYSTER SAUCE AND BLACK PEPPER...
SIP
GOOD!

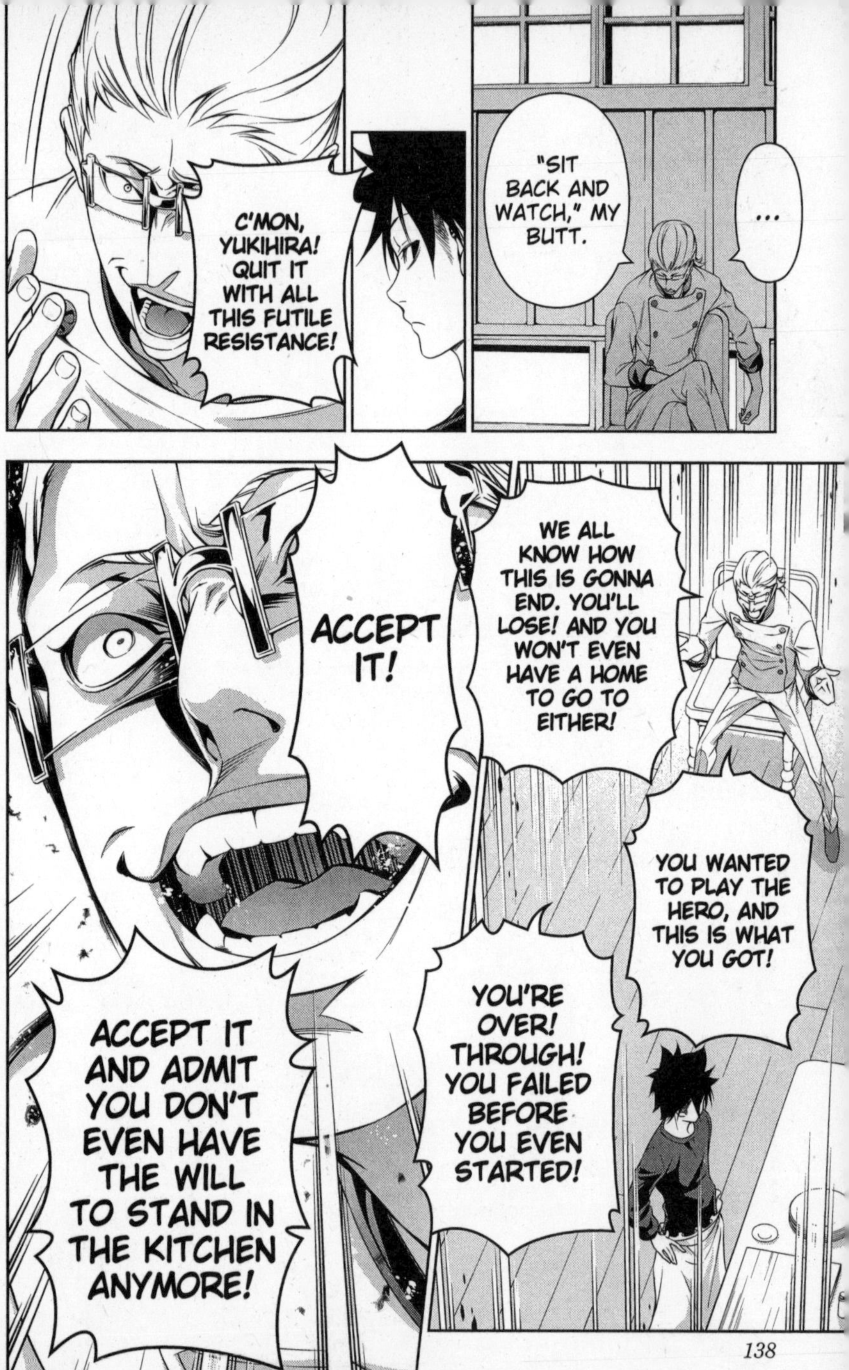
...
"SIT BACK AND WATCH," MY BUTT.
C'MON, YUKIHIRA! QUIT IT WITH ALL THIS FUTILE RESISTANCE!
WE ALL KNOW HOW THIS IS GONNA END. YOU'LL LOSE! AND YOU WON'T EVEN HAVE A HOME TO GO TO EITHER!
YOU WANTED TO PLAY THE HERO, AND THIS IS WHAT YOU GOT!
YOU'RE OVER! THROUGH! YOU FAILED BEFORE YOU EVEN STARTED!
ACCEPT IT!
ACCEPT IT AND ADMIT YOU DON'T EVEN HAVE THE WILL TO STAND IN THE KITCHEN ANYMORE!

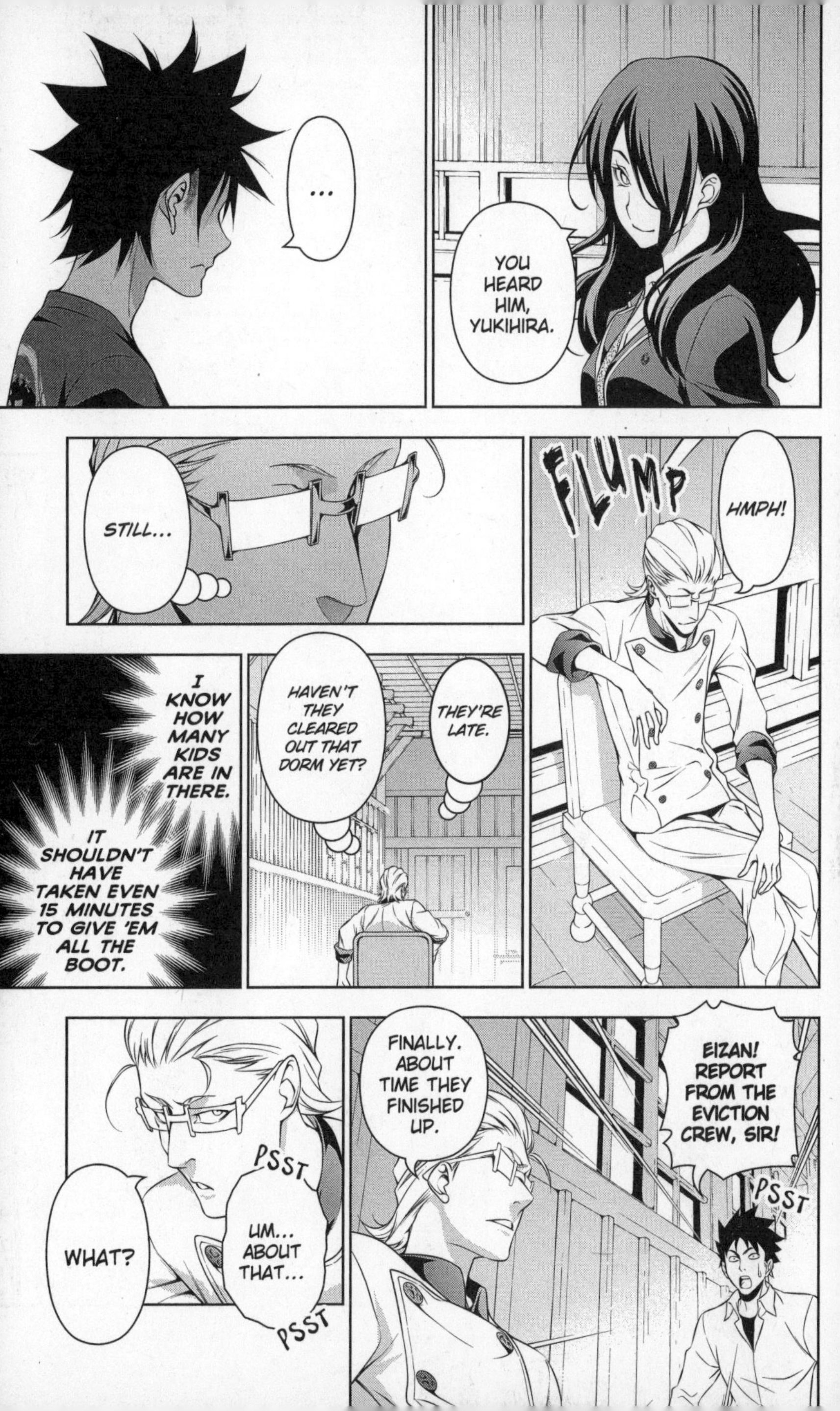
YOU HEARD HIM, YUKIHIRA.
...
FLUMP
HMPH!
STILL...
THEY'RE LATE.
HAVEN'T THEY CLEARED OUT THAT DORM YET?
I KNOW HOW MANY KIDS ARE IN THERE.
IT SHOULDN'T HAVE TAKEN EVEN 15 MINUTES TO GIVE 'EM ALL THE BOOT.
EIZAN! REPORT FROM THE EVICTION CREW, SIR!
PSST
FINALLY. ABOUT TIME THEY FINISHED UP.
PSST
UM... ABOUT THAT...
PSST
WHAT?

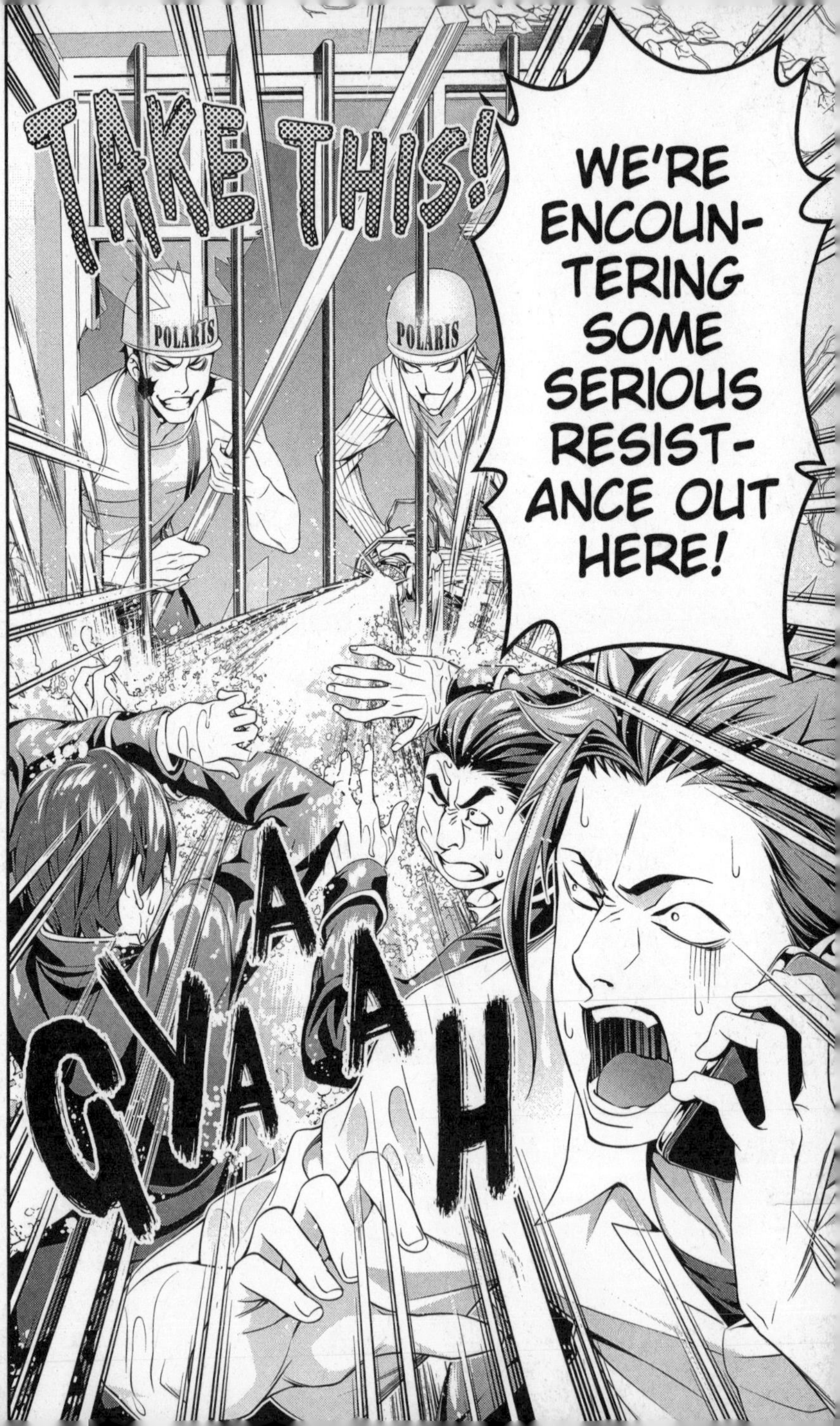
WE'RE ENCOUN-TERING SOME SERIOUS RESIST-ANCE OUT HERE!
TAKE THIS!
POLARIS
POLARIS
GYAAAAH

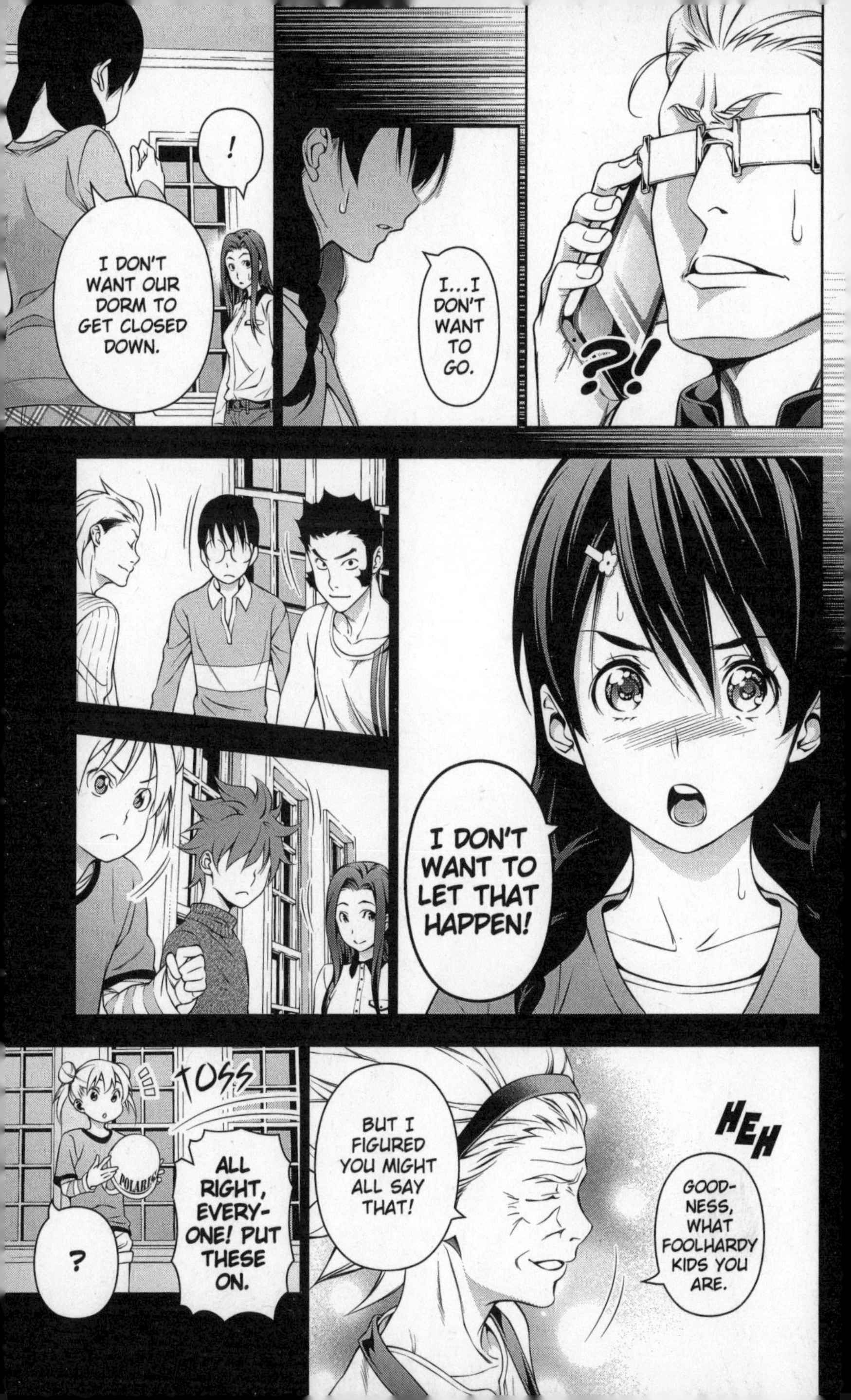
?!
I...I DON'T WANT TO GO.
!
I DON'T WANT OUR DORM TO GET CLOSED DOWN.
I DON'T WANT TO LET THAT HAPPEN!
HEH
GOOD-NESS, WHAT FOOLHARDY KIDS YOU ARE.
BUT I FIGURED YOU MIGHT ALL SAY THAT!
TOSS
ALL RIGHT, EVERY-ONE! PUT THESE ON.
?

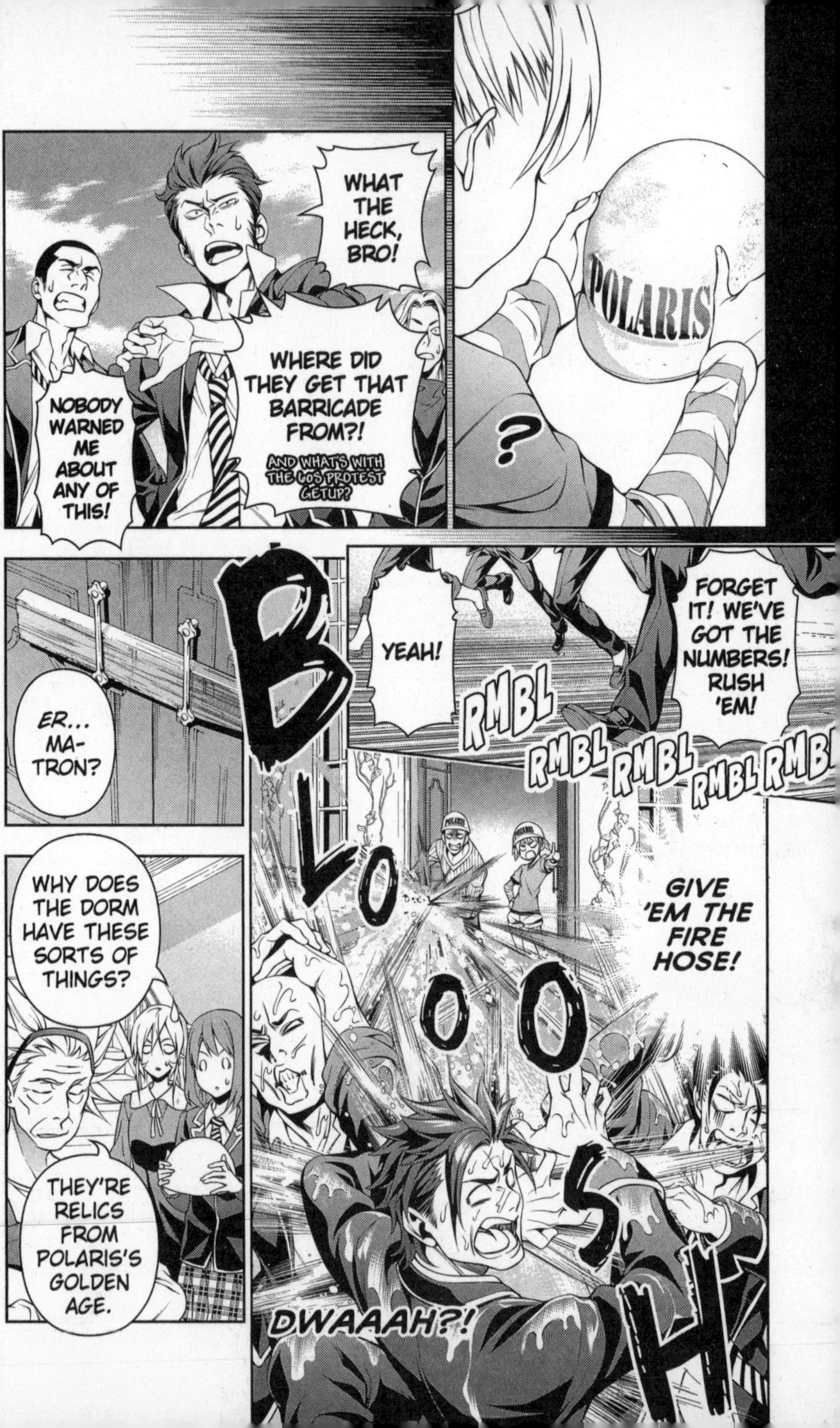
POLARIS
?
WHAT THE HECK, BRO!
WHERE DID THEY GET THAT BARRICADE FROM?!
AND WHAT'S WITH THE 60S PROTEST GETUP?
NOBODY WARNED ME ABOUT ANY OF THIS!
FORGET IT! WE'VE GOT THE NUMBERS! RUSH 'EM!
YEAH!
RMBL RMBL RMBL RMBL RMBL
BLOOOSH
GIVE 'EM THE FIRE HOSE!
POLARIS
DWAAAH?!
ER... MA-TRON?
WHY DOES THE DORM HAVE THESE SORTS OF THINGS?
THEY'RE RELICS FROM POLARIS'S GOLDEN AGE.

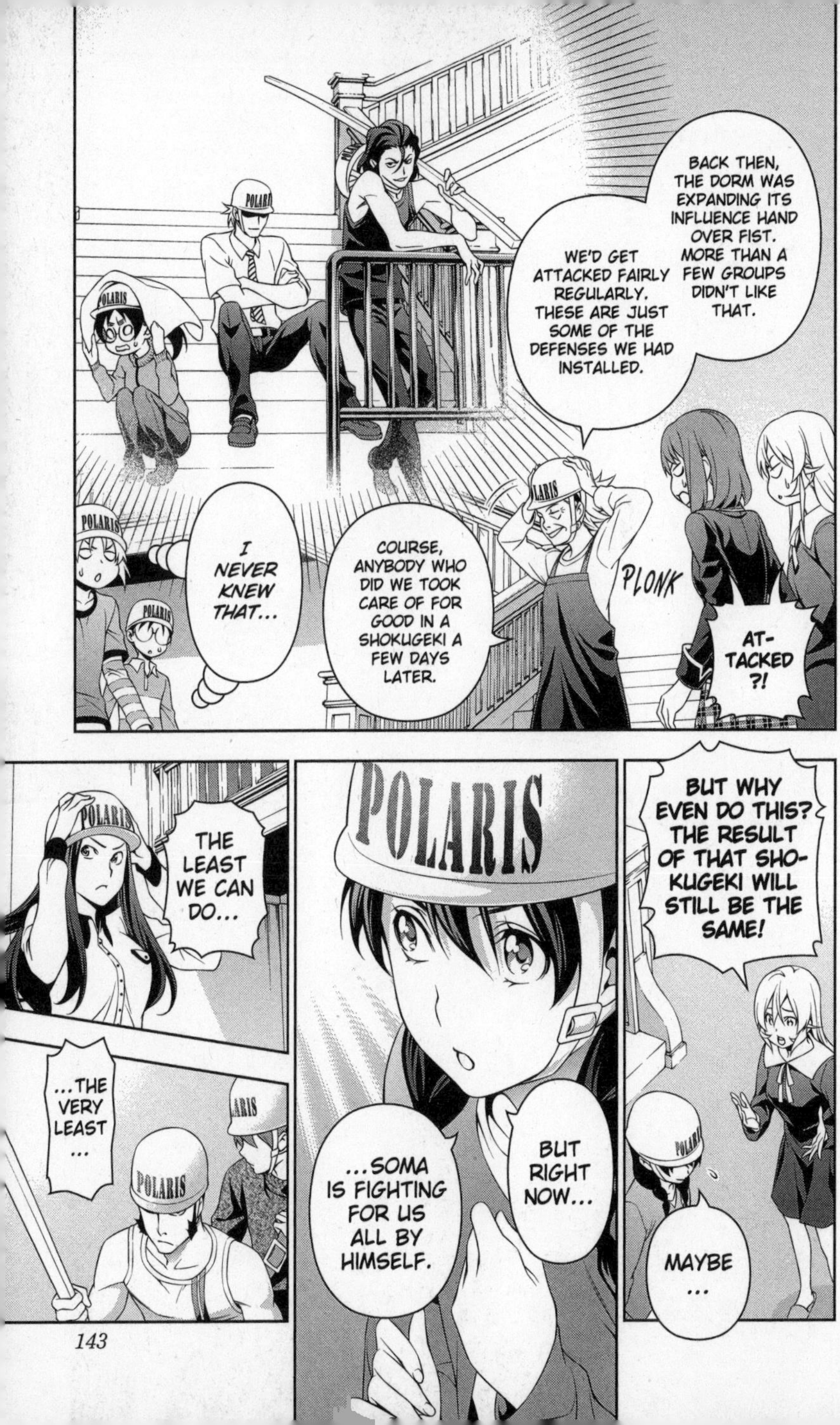
BACK THEN, THE DORM WAS EXPANDING ITS INFLUENCE HAND OVER FIST. MORE THAN A FEW GROUPS DIDN'T LIKE THAT.
WE'D GET ATTACKED FAIRLY REGULARLY. THESE ARE JUST SOME OF THE DEFENSES WE HAD INSTALLED.
AT-TACKED?!
PLONK
COURSE, ANYBODY WHO DID WE TOOK CARE OF FOR GOOD IN A SHOKUGEKI A FEW DAYS LATER.
I NEVER KNEW THAT...
BUT WHY EVEN DO THIS? THE RESULT OF THAT SHO-KUGEKI WILL STILL BE THE SAME!
MAYBE...
BUT RIGHT NOW...
...SOMA IS FIGHTING FOR US ALL BY HIMSELF.
THE LEAST WE CAN DO...
...THE VERY LEAST...

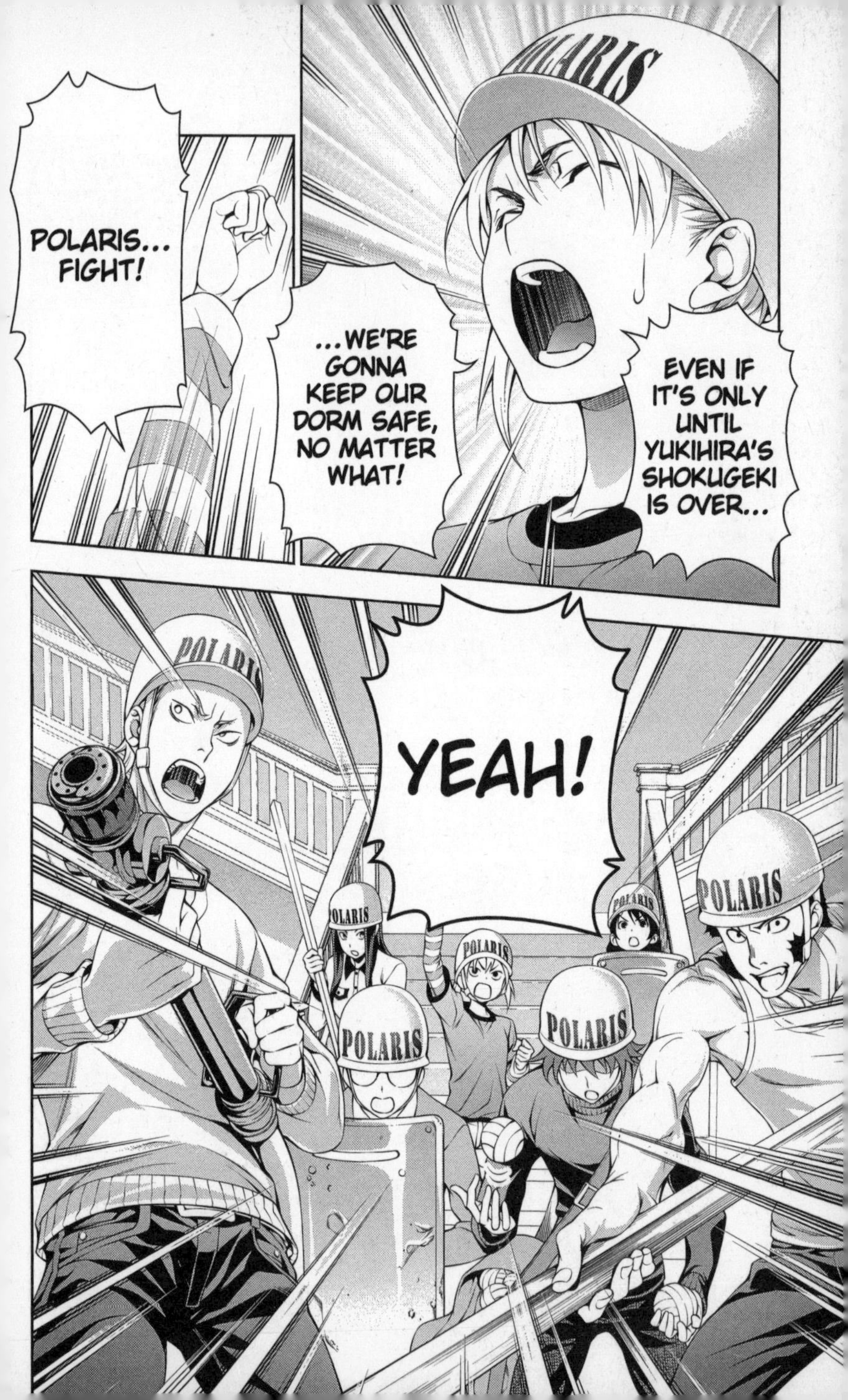
EVEN IF IT'S ONLY UNTIL YUKIHIRA'S SHOKUGEKI IS OVER...
...WE'RE GONNA KEEP OUR DORM SAFE, NO MATTER WHAT!
POLARIS... FIGHT!
YEAH!

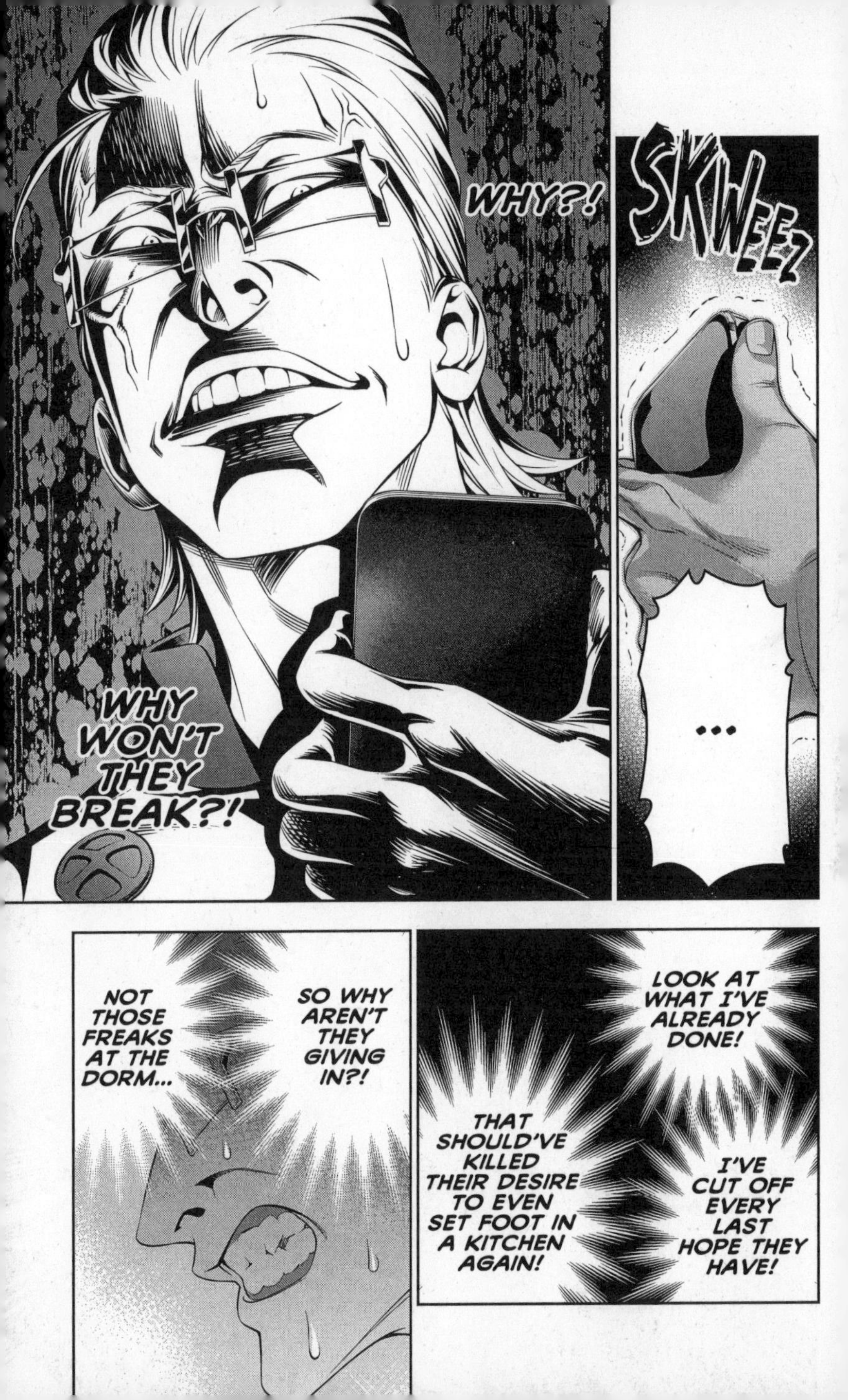
SKWEEZ
...
WHY?!
WHY WON'T THEY BREAK?!
LOOK AT WHAT I'VE ALREADY DONE!
I'VE CUT OFF EVERY LAST HOPE THEY HAVE!
THAT SHOULD'VE KILLED THEIR DESIRE TO EVEN SET FOOT IN A KITCHEN AGAIN!
SO WHY AREN'T THEY GIVING IN?!
NOT THOSE FREAKS AT THE DORM...

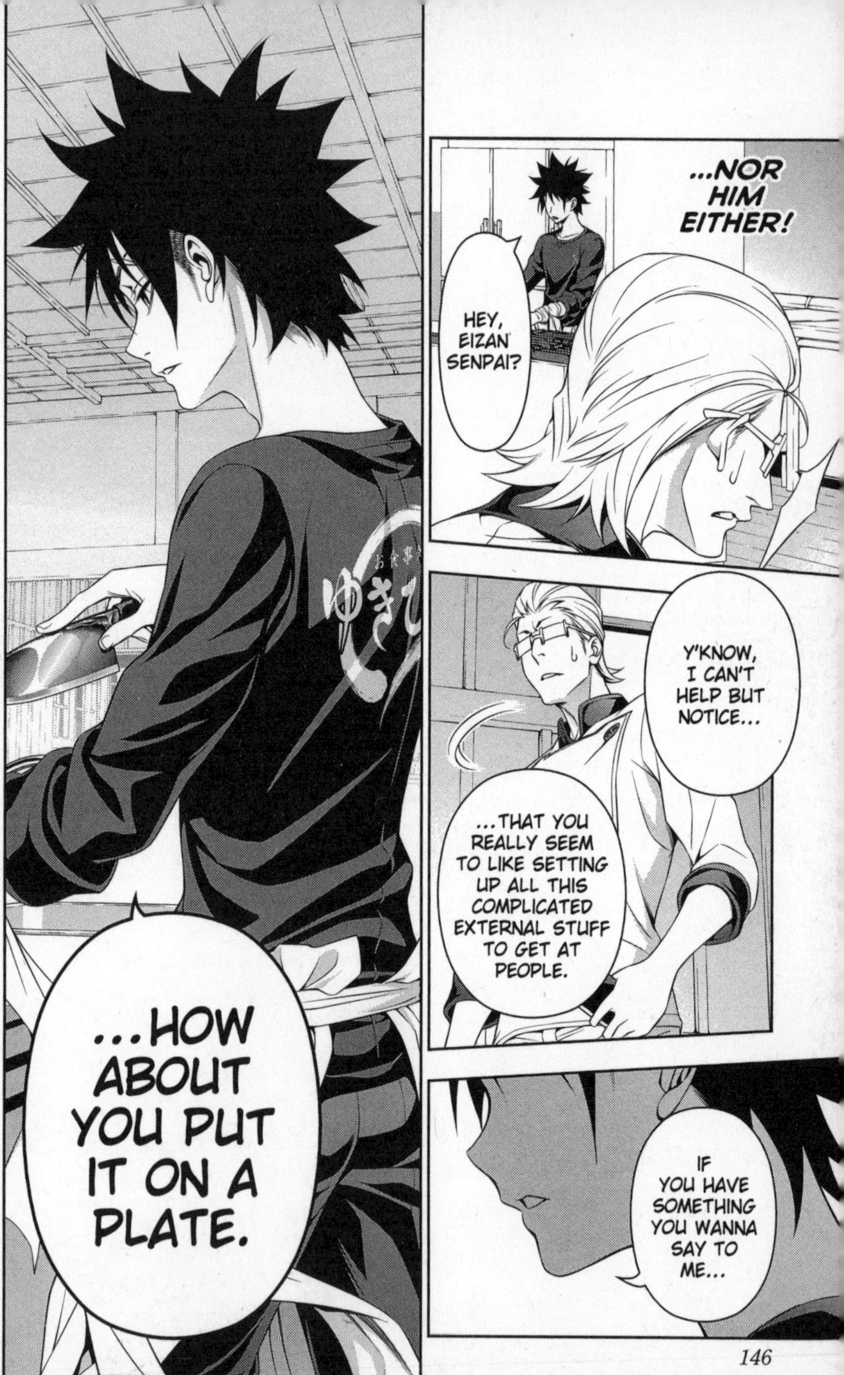
...NOR HIM EITHER!
HEY, EIZAN SENPAI?
Y'KNOW, I CAN'T HELP BUT NOTICE...
...THAT YOU REALLY SEEM TO LIKE SETTING UP ALL THIS COMPLICATED EXTERNAL STUFF TO GET AT PEOPLE.
IF YOU HAVE SOMETHING YOU WANNA SAY TO ME...
...HOW ABOUT YOU PUT IT ON A PLATE.

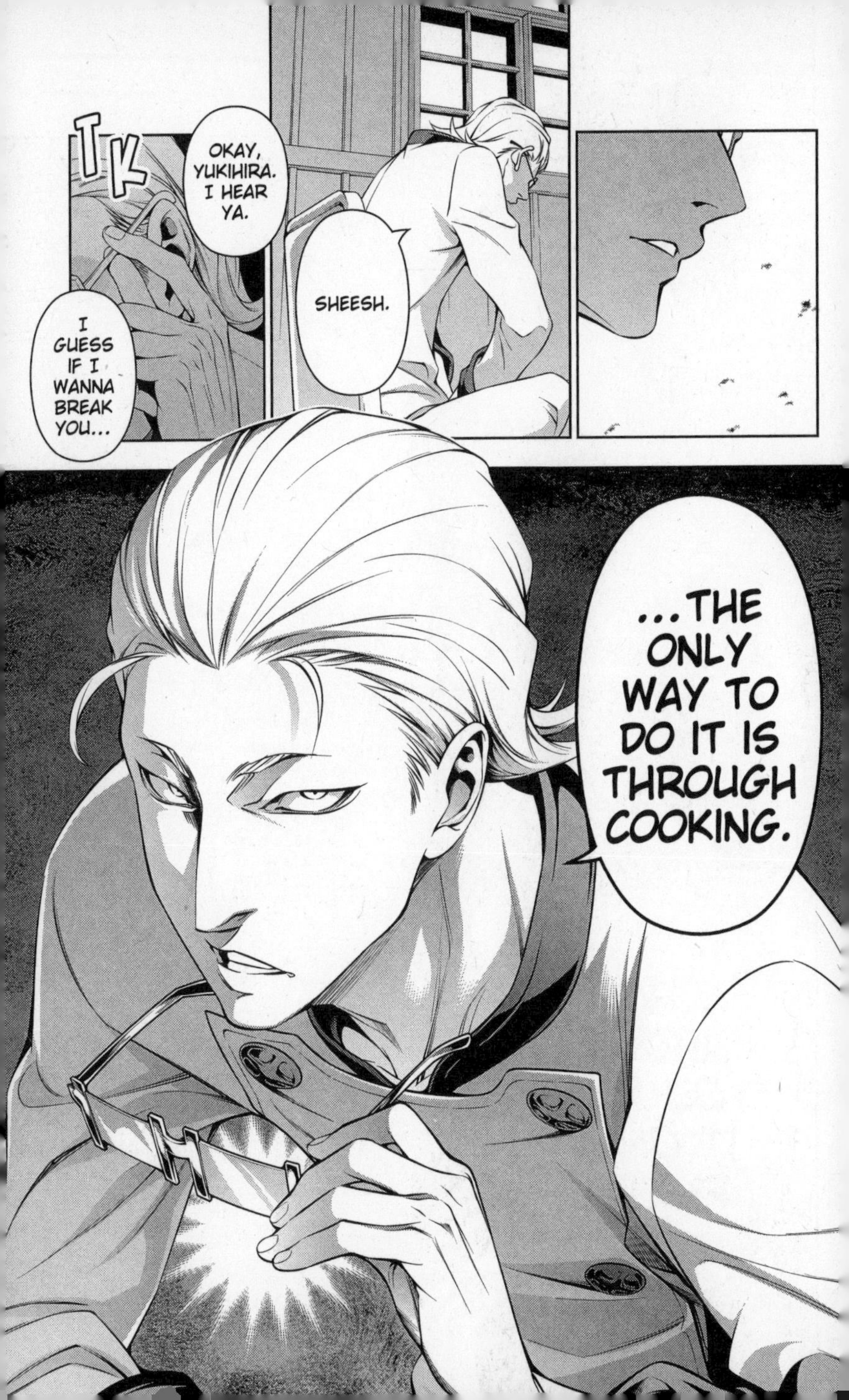
SHEESH.
OKAY, YUKIHIRA. I HEAR YA.
TK
I GUESS IF I WANNA BREAK YOU...
...THE ONLY WAY TO DO IT IS THROUGH COOKING.

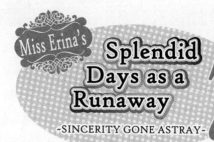

Miss Erina's

Splendid Days as a Runaway 7

~SINCERITY GONE ASTRAY~

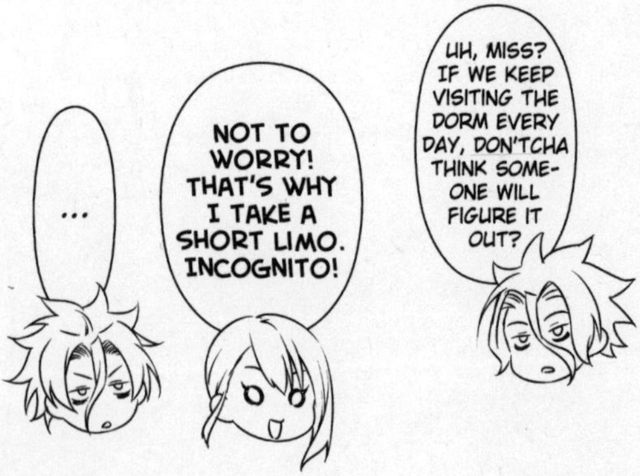

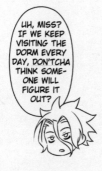

UH, MISS? IF WE KEEP VISITING THE DORM EVERY DAY, DON'TCHA THINK SOME-ONE WILL FIGURE IT OUT?
NOT TO WORRY! THAT'S WHY I TAKE A SHORT LIMO. INCOGNITO!
...

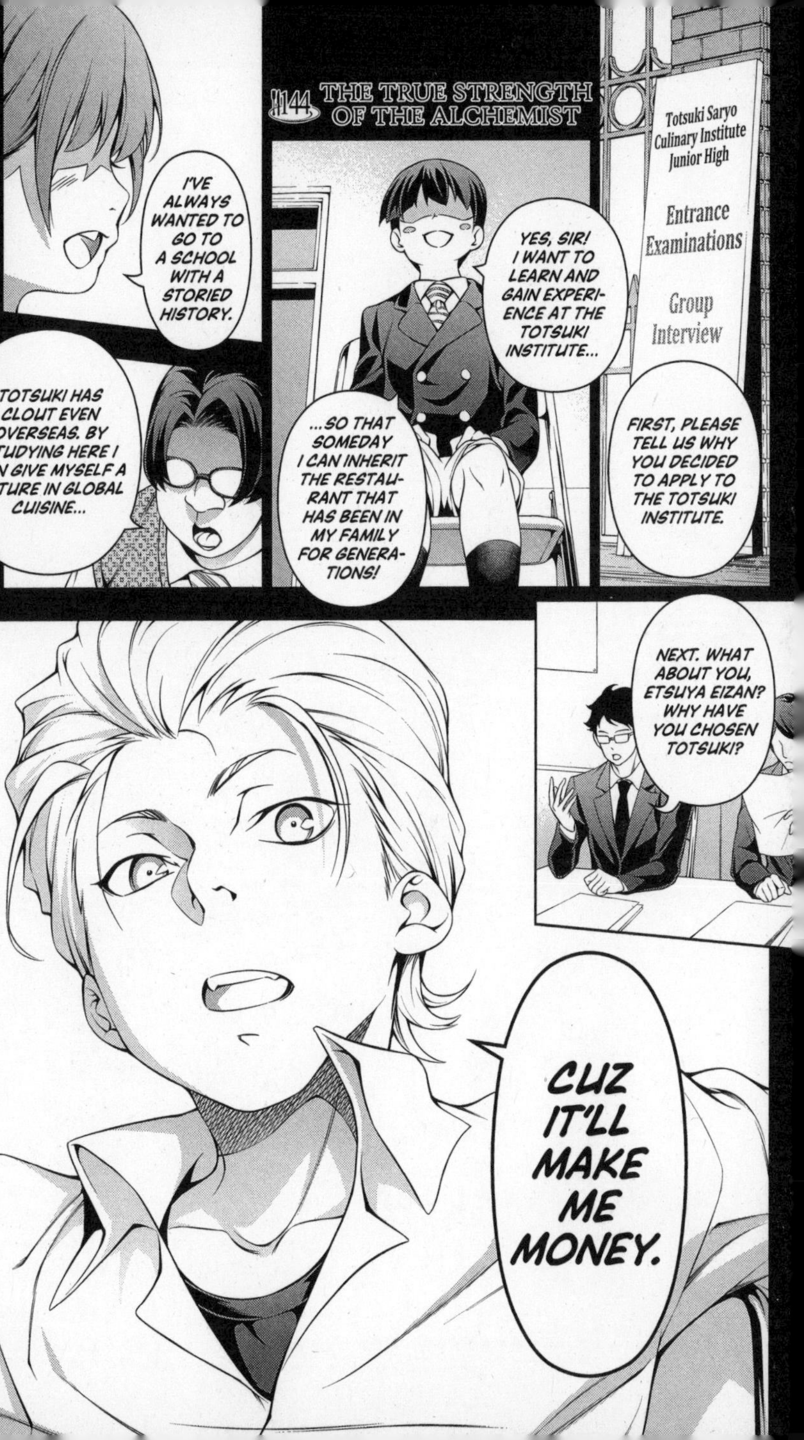
Totsuki Saryo Culinary Institute Junior High
Entrance Examinations
Group Interview
FIRST, PLEASE TELL US WHY YOU DECIDED TO APPLY TO THE TOTSUKI INSTITUTE.
144 THE TRUE STRENGTH OF THE ALCHEMIST
YES, SIR! I WANT TO LEARN AND GAIN EXPERIENCE AT THE TOTSUKI INSTITUTE...
...SO THAT SOMEDAY I CAN INHERIT THE RESTAURANT THAT HAS BEEN IN MY FAMILY FOR GENERATIONS!
I'VE ALWAYS WANTED TO GO TO A SCHOOL WITH A STORIED HISTORY.
TOTSUKI HAS CLOUT EVEN OVERSEAS. BY STUDYING HERE I CAN GIVE MYSELF A FUTURE IN GLOBAL CUISINE...
NEXT. WHAT ABOUT YOU, ETSUYA EIZAN? WHY HAVE YOU CHOSEN TOTSUKI?
CUZ IT'LL MAKE ME MONEY.

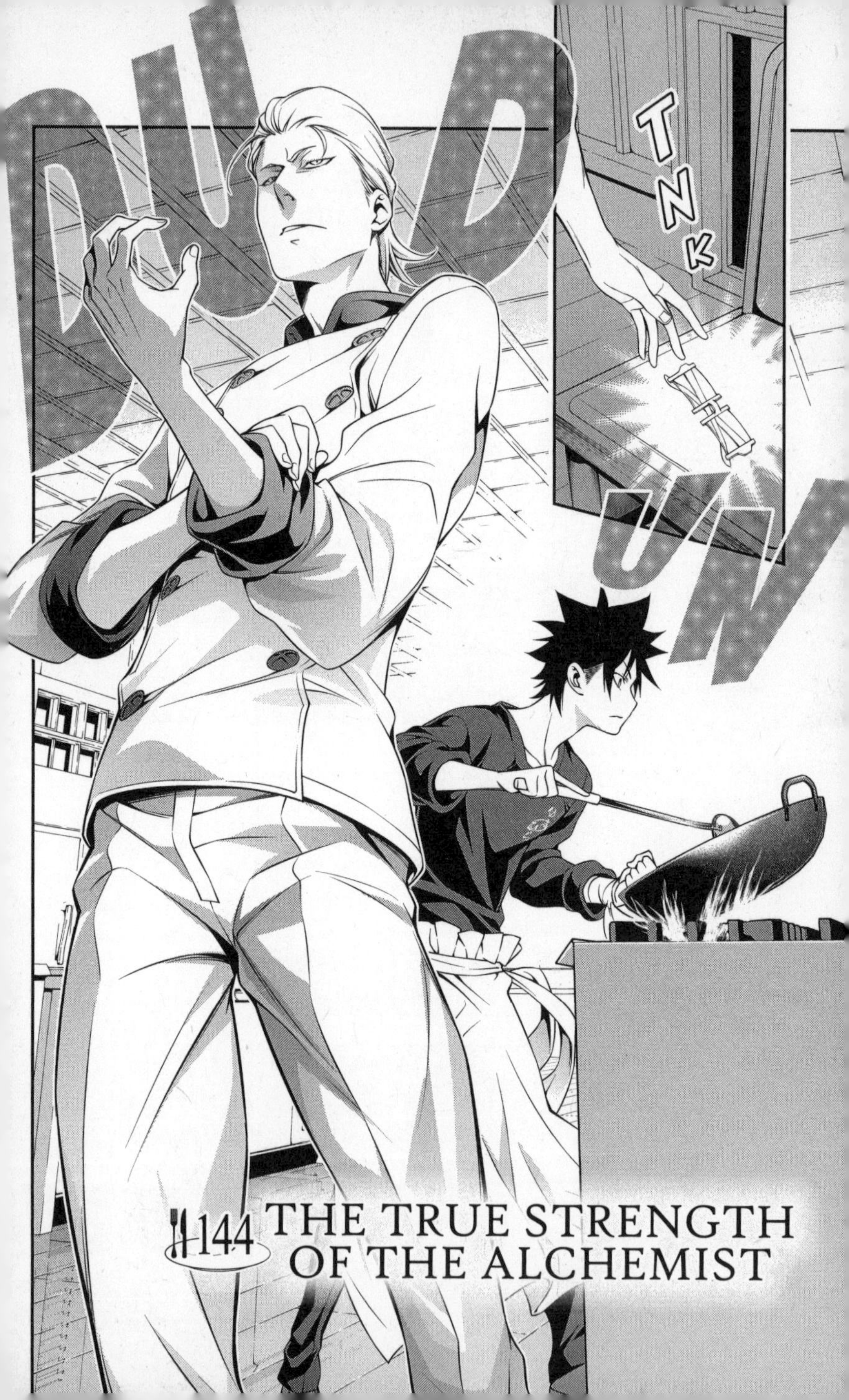
TNK

144 THE TRUE STRENGTH OF THE ALCHEMIST

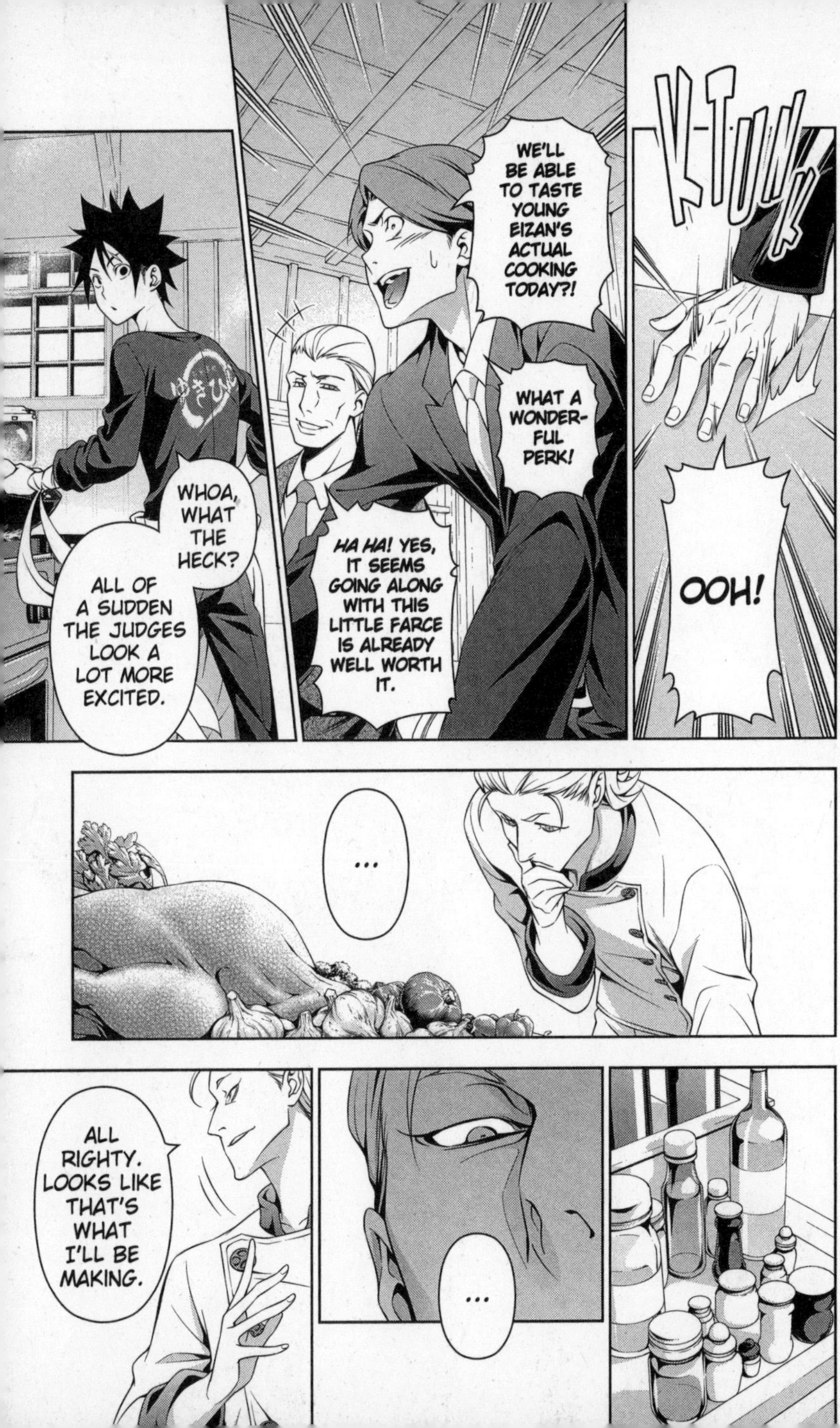
K-TUNK
OOH!
WE'LL BE ABLE TO TASTE YOUNG EIZAN'S ACTUAL COOKING TODAY?!
WHAT A WONDERFUL PERK!
HA HA! YES, IT SEEMS GOING ALONG WITH THIS LITTLE FARCE IS ALREADY WELL WORTH IT.
WHOA, WHAT THE HECK?
ALL OF A SUDDEN THE JUDGES LOOK A LOT MORE EXCITED.
...
...
ALL RIGHTY. LOOKS LIKE THAT'S WHAT I'LL BE MAKING.

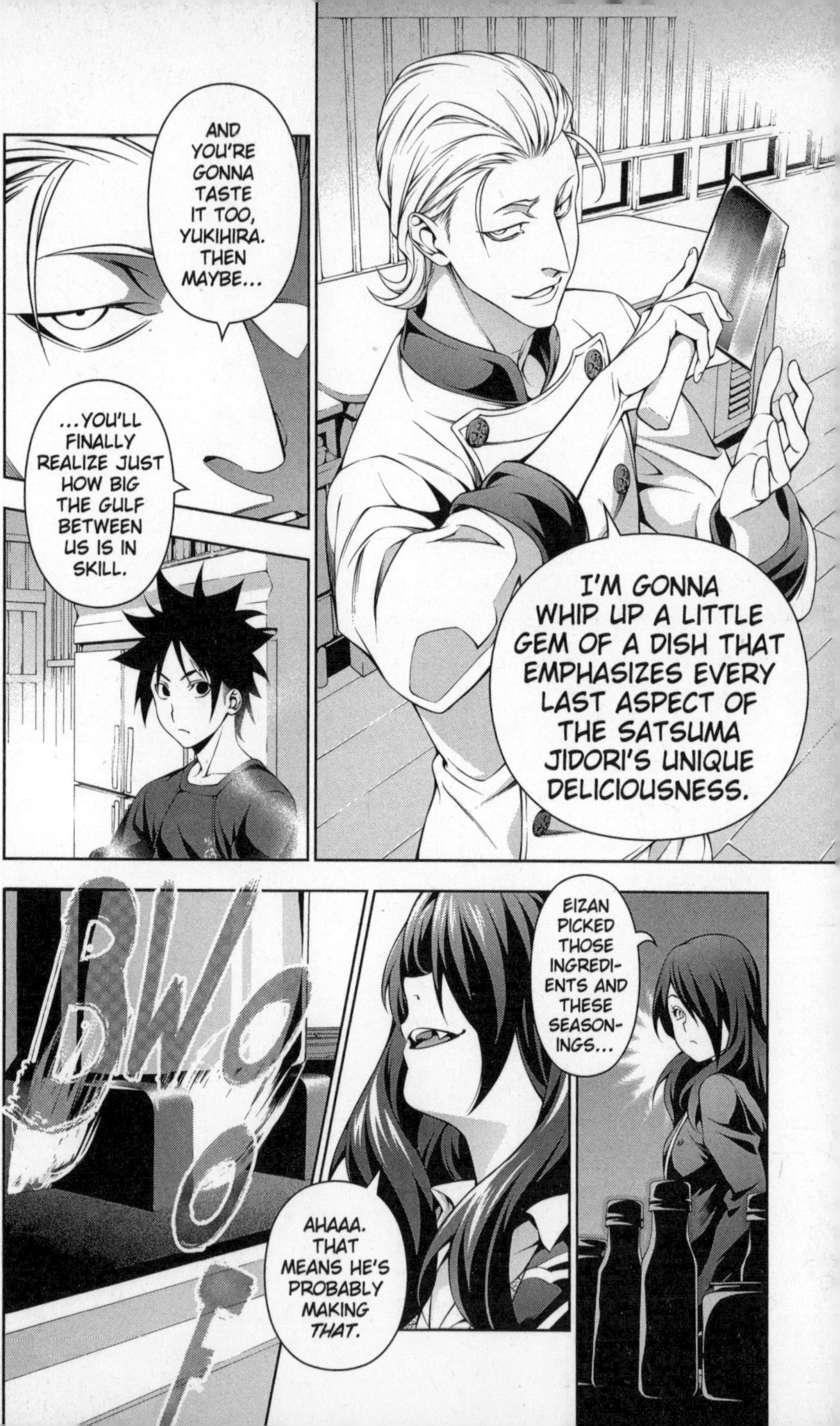
I'M GONNA WHIP UP A LITTLE GEM OF A DISH THAT EMPHASIZES EVERY LAST ASPECT OF THE SATSUMA JIDORI'S UNIQUE DELICIOUSNESS.
AND YOU'RE GONNA TASTE IT TOO, YUKIHIRA. THEN MAYBE...
...YOU'LL FINALLY REALIZE JUST HOW BIG THE GULF BETWEEN US IS IN SKILL.
EIZAN PICKED THOSE INGREDI-ENTS AND THESE SEASON-INGS...
AHAAA. THAT MEANS HE'S PROBABLY MAKING *THAT*.
BWOO

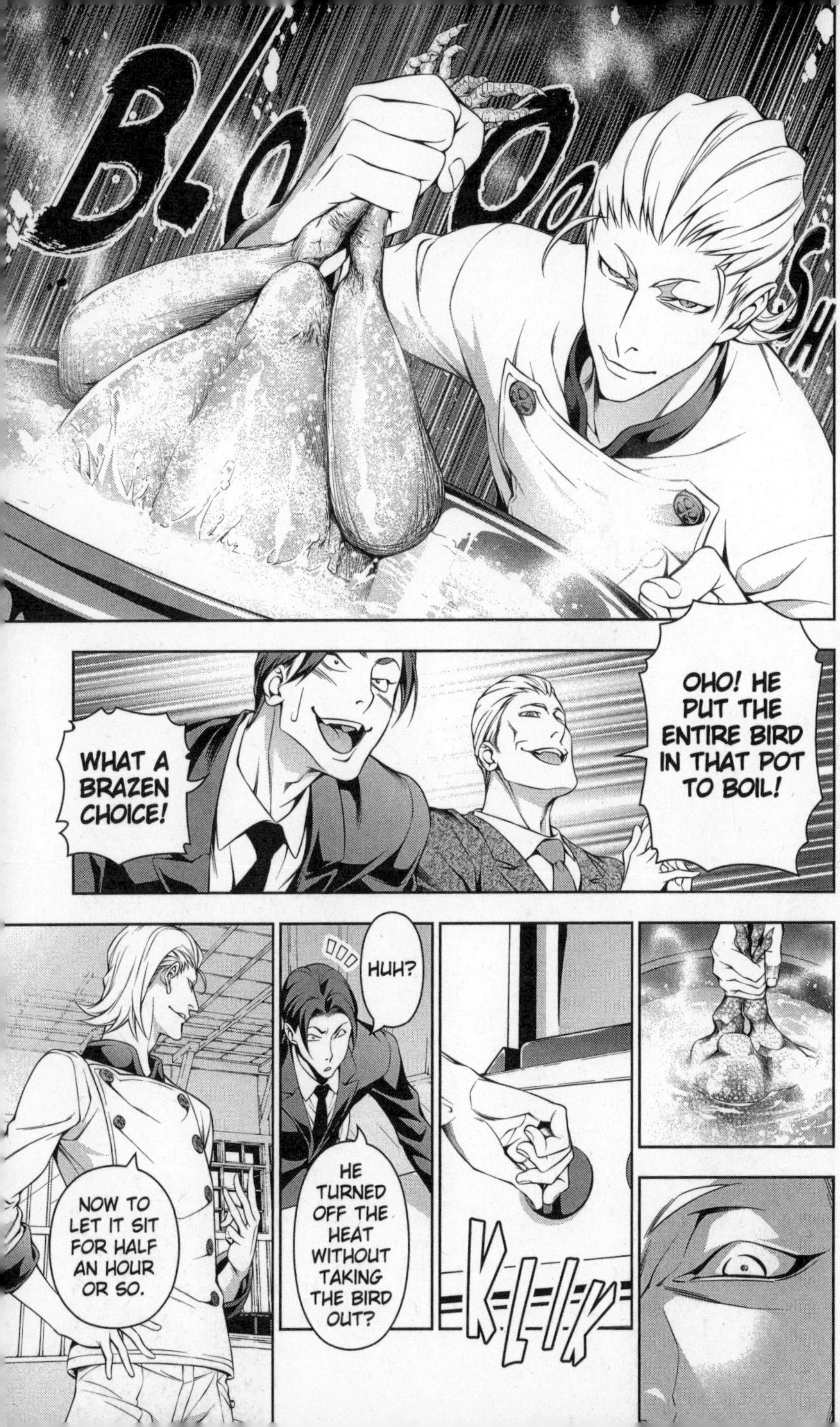
BLOOOOOSH
OHO! HE PUT THE ENTIRE BIRD IN THAT POT TO BOIL!
WHAT A BRAZEN CHOICE!
KLIK
HUH?
HE TURNED OFF THE HEAT WITHOUT TAKING THE BIRD OUT?
NOW TO LET IT SIT FOR HALF AN HOUR OR SO.

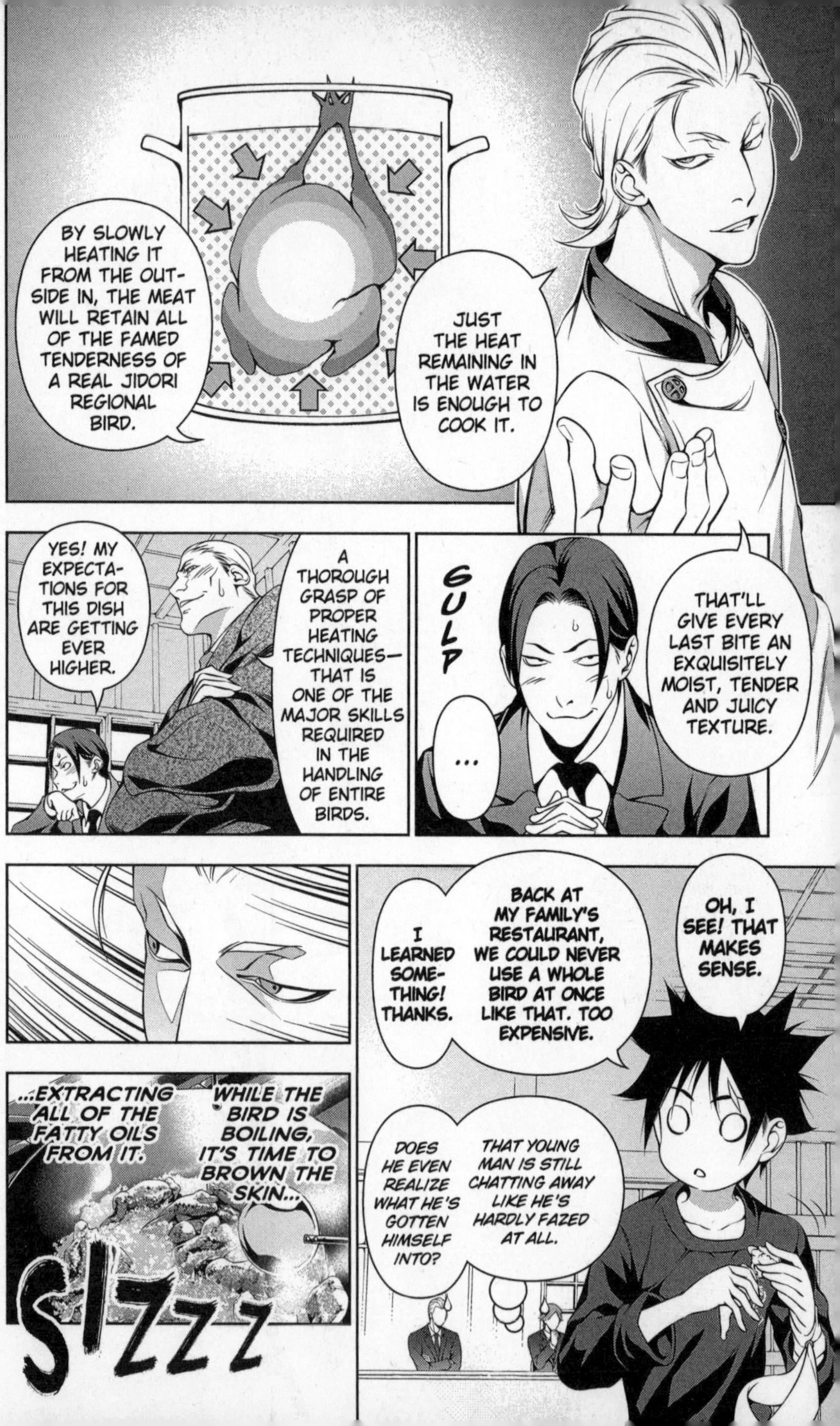
JUST THE HEAT REMAINING IN THE WATER IS ENOUGH TO COOK IT.
BY SLOWLY HEATING IT FROM THE OUT-SIDE IN, THE MEAT WILL RETAIN ALL OF THE FAMED TENDERNESS OF A REAL JIDORI REGIONAL BIRD.
THAT'LL GIVE EVERY LAST BITE AN EXQUISITELY MOIST, TENDER AND JUICY TEXTURE.
GULP
...
A THOROUGH GRASP OF PROPER HEATING TECHNIQUES—THAT IS ONE OF THE MAJOR SKILLS REQUIRED IN THE HANDLING OF ENTIRE BIRDS.
YES! MY EXPECTA-TIONS FOR THIS DISH ARE GETTING EVER HIGHER.
OH, I SEE! THAT MAKES SENSE.
BACK AT MY FAMILY'S RESTAURANT, WE COULD NEVER USE A WHOLE BIRD AT ONCE LIKE THAT. TOO EXPENSIVE.
I LEARNED SOME-THING! THANKS.
THAT YOUNG MAN IS STILL CHATTING AWAY LIKE HE'S HARDLY FAZED AT ALL.
DOES HE EVEN REALIZE WHAT HE'S GOTTEN HIMSELF INTO?
WHILE THE BIRD IS BOILING, IT'S TIME TO BROWN THE SKIN...
...EXTRACTING ALL OF THE FATTY OILS FROM IT.
SIZZZ

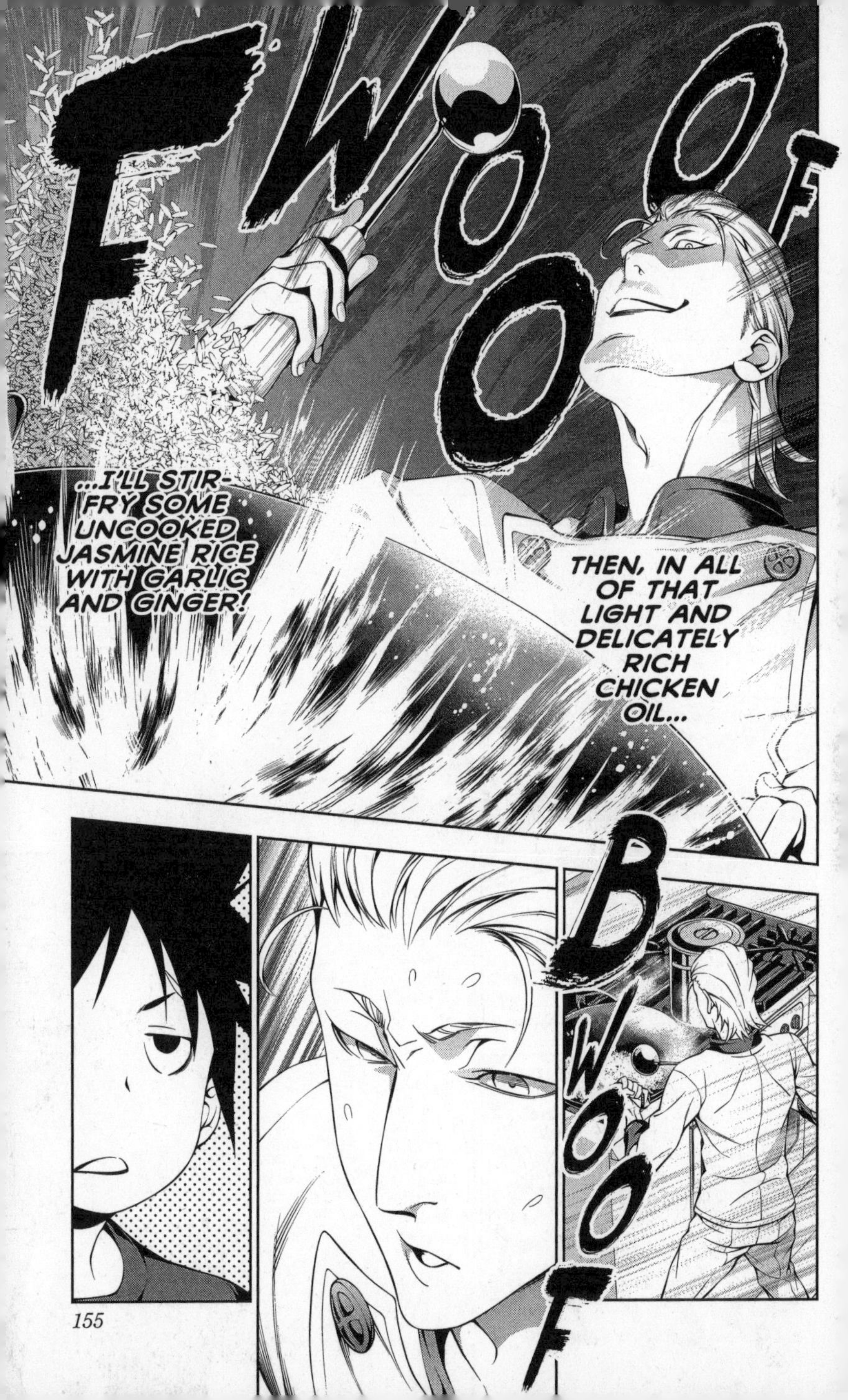
FWOOOF
THEN, IN ALL OF THAT LIGHT AND DELICATELY RICH CHICKEN OIL...
...I'LL STIR-FRY SOME UNCOOKED JASMINE RICE WITH GARLIC AND GINGER!
BWOOOF

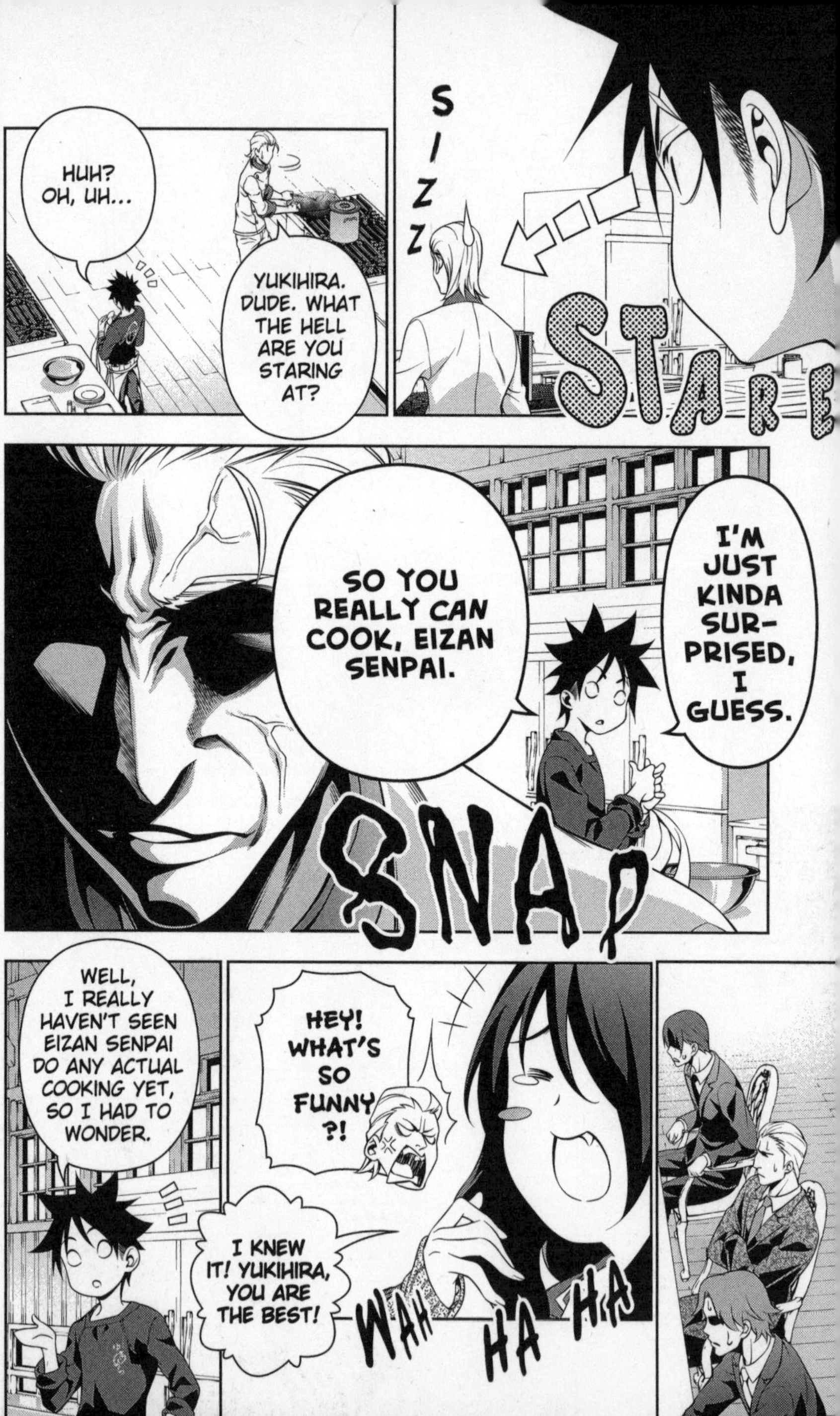
...
S
I
Z
Z
STARE
YUKIHIRA. DUDE. WHAT THE HELL ARE YOU STARING AT?
HUH? OH, UH...
I'M JUST KINDA SUR-PRISED, I GUESS.
SO YOU REALLY CAN COOK, EIZAN SENPAI.
SNAP
HEY! WHAT'S SO FUNNY?!
I KNEW IT! YUKIHIRA, YOU ARE THE BEST!
WAH HA HA
WELL, I REALLY HAVEN'T SEEN EIZAN SENPAI DO ANY ACTUAL COOKING YET, SO I HAD TO WONDER.

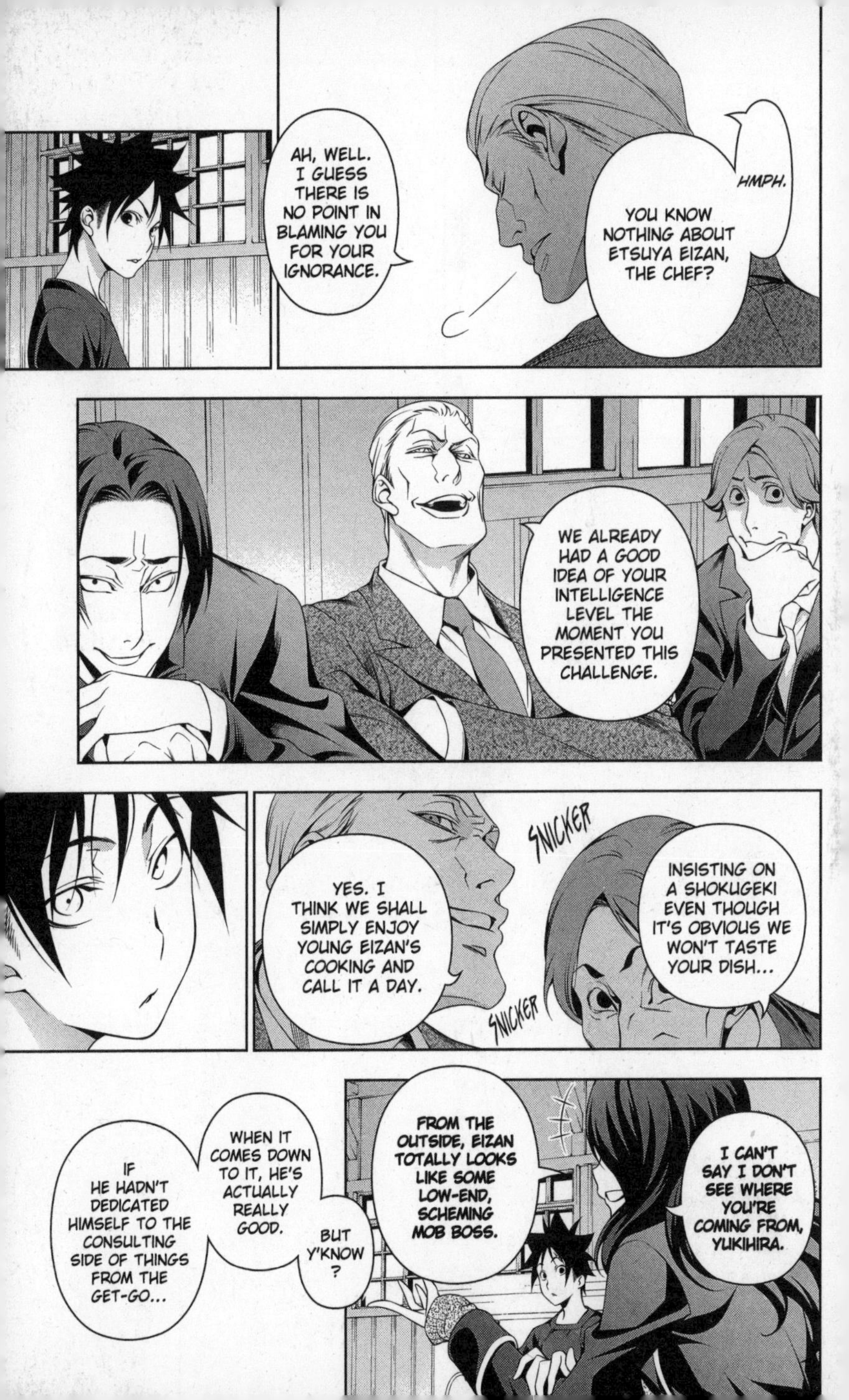
HMPH.
YOU KNOW NOTHING ABOUT ETSUYA EIZAN, THE CHEF?
AH, WELL. I GUESS THERE IS NO POINT IN BLAMING YOU FOR YOUR IGNORANCE.
WE ALREADY HAD A GOOD IDEA OF YOUR INTELLIGENCE LEVEL THE MOMENT YOU PRESENTED THIS CHALLENGE.
SNICKER
INSISTING ON A SHOKUGEKI EVEN THOUGH IT'S OBVIOUS WE WON'T TASTE YOUR DISH...
YES. I THINK WE SHALL SIMPLY ENJOY YOUNG EIZAN'S COOKING AND CALL IT A DAY.
SNICKER
I CAN'T SAY I DON'T SEE WHERE YOU'RE COMING FROM, YUKIHIRA.
FROM THE OUTSIDE, EIZAN TOTALLY LOOKS LIKE SOME LOW-END, SCHEMING MOB BOSS.
BUT Y'KNOW?
WHEN IT COMES DOWN TO IT, HE'S ACTUALLY REALLY GOOD.
IF HE HADN'T DEDICATED HIMSELF TO THE CONSULTING SIDE OF THINGS FROM THE GET-GO...

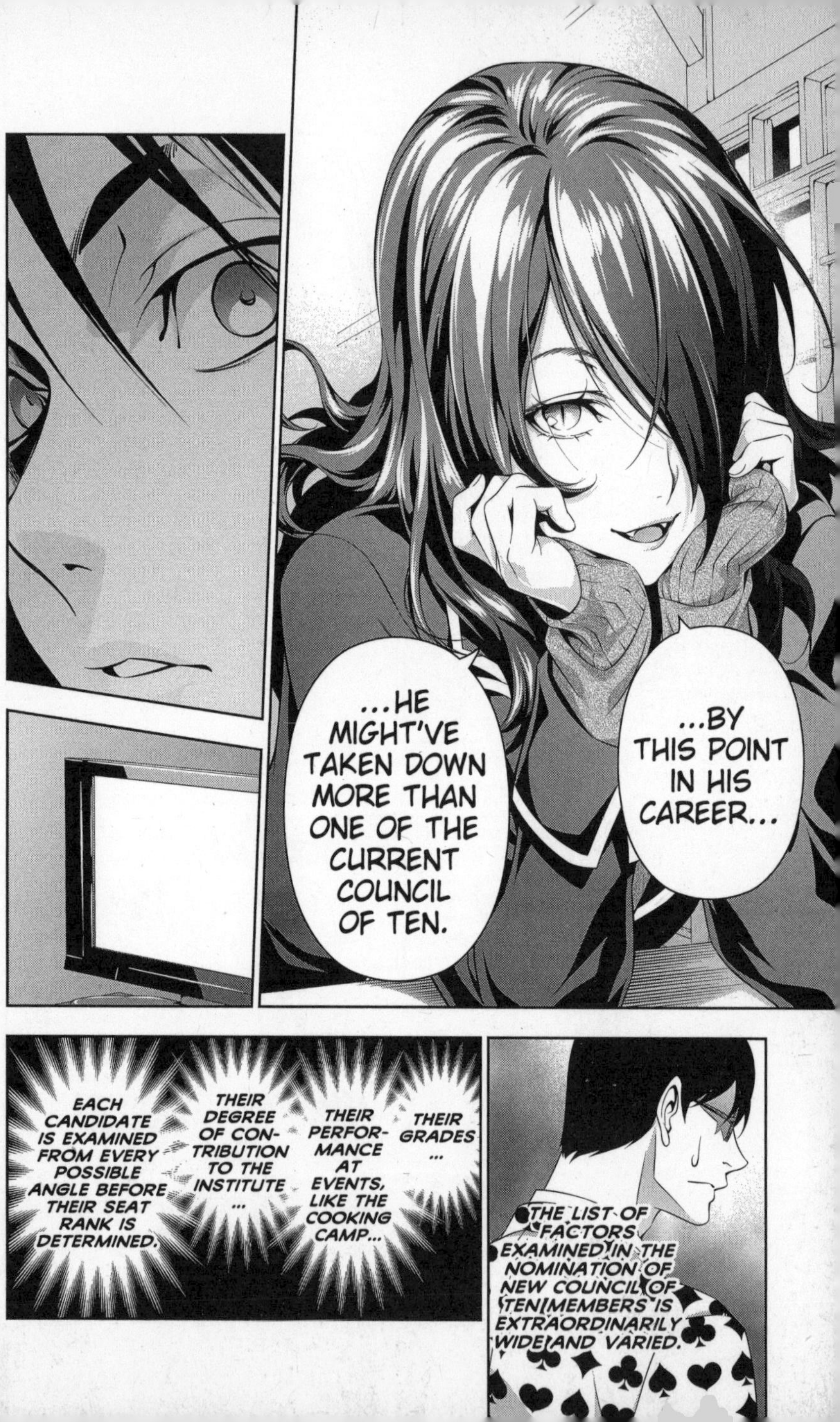
...BY THIS POINT IN HIS CAREER...
...HE MIGHT'VE TAKEN DOWN MORE THAN ONE OF THE CURRENT COUNCIL OF TEN.
THE LIST OF FACTORS EXAMINED IN THE NOMINATION OF NEW COUNCIL OF TEN MEMBERS IS EXTRAORDINARILY WIDE AND VARIED.
THEIR GRADES...
THEIR PERFORMANCE AT EVENTS, LIKE THE COOKING CAMP...
THEIR DEGREE OF CONTRIBUTION TO THE INSTITUTE...
EACH CANDIDATE IS EXAMINED FROM EVERY POSSIBLE ANGLE BEFORE THEIR SEAT RANK IS DETERMINED.

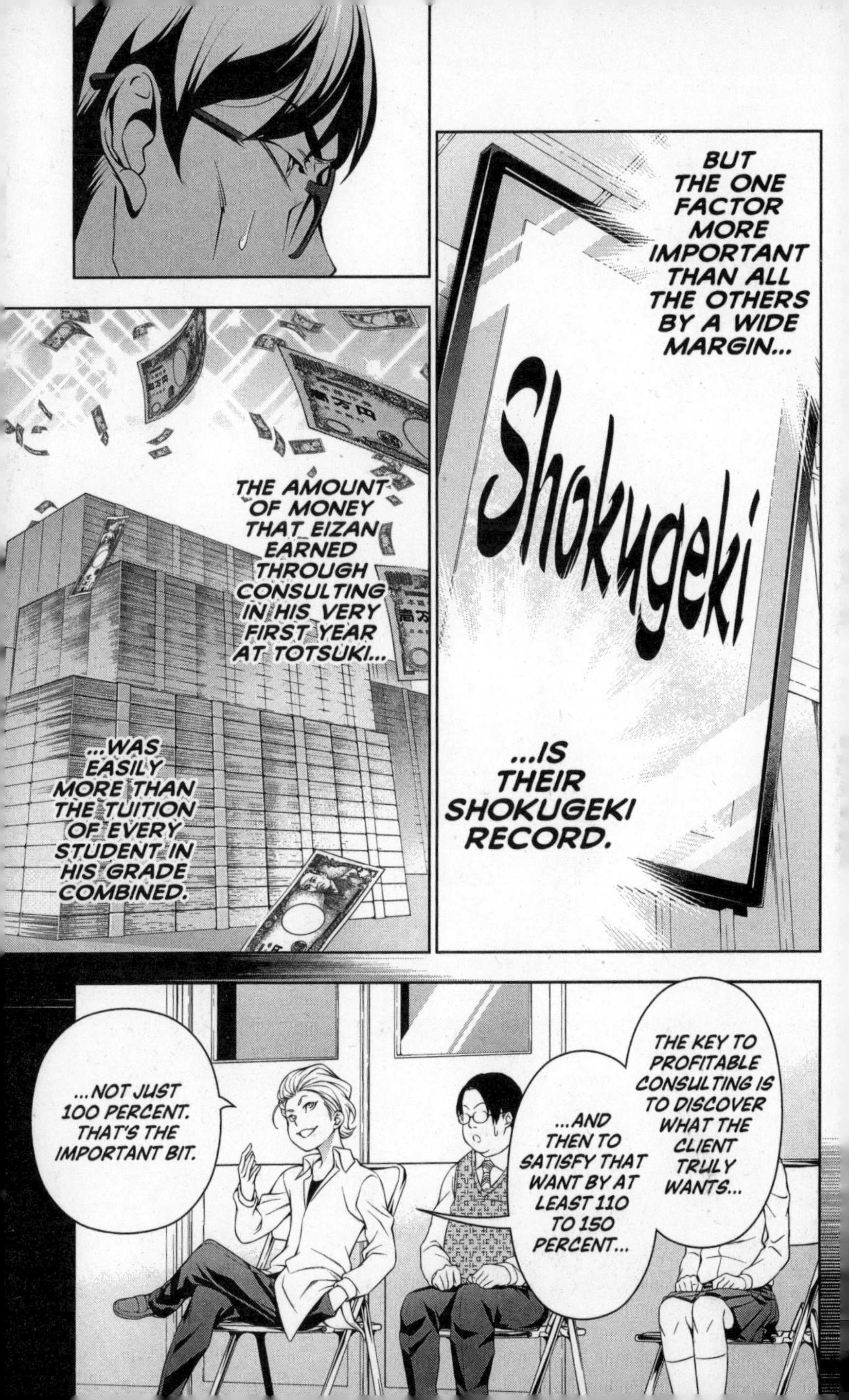
THE AMOUNT OF MONEY THAT EIZAN EARNED THROUGH CONSULTING IN HIS VERY FIRST YEAR AT TOTSUKI...
...WAS EASILY MORE THAN THE TUITION OF EVERY STUDENT IN HIS GRADE COMBINED.
BUT THE ONE FACTOR MORE IMPORTANT THAN ALL THE OTHERS BY A WIDE MARGIN...
Shokugeki
...IS THEIR SHOKUGEKI RECORD.
THE KEY TO PROFITABLE CONSULTING IS TO DISCOVER WHAT THE CLIENT TRULY WANTS...
...AND THEN TO SATISFY THAT WANT BY AT LEAST 110 TO 150 PERCENT...
...NOT JUST 100 PERCENT. THAT'S THE IMPORTANT BIT.

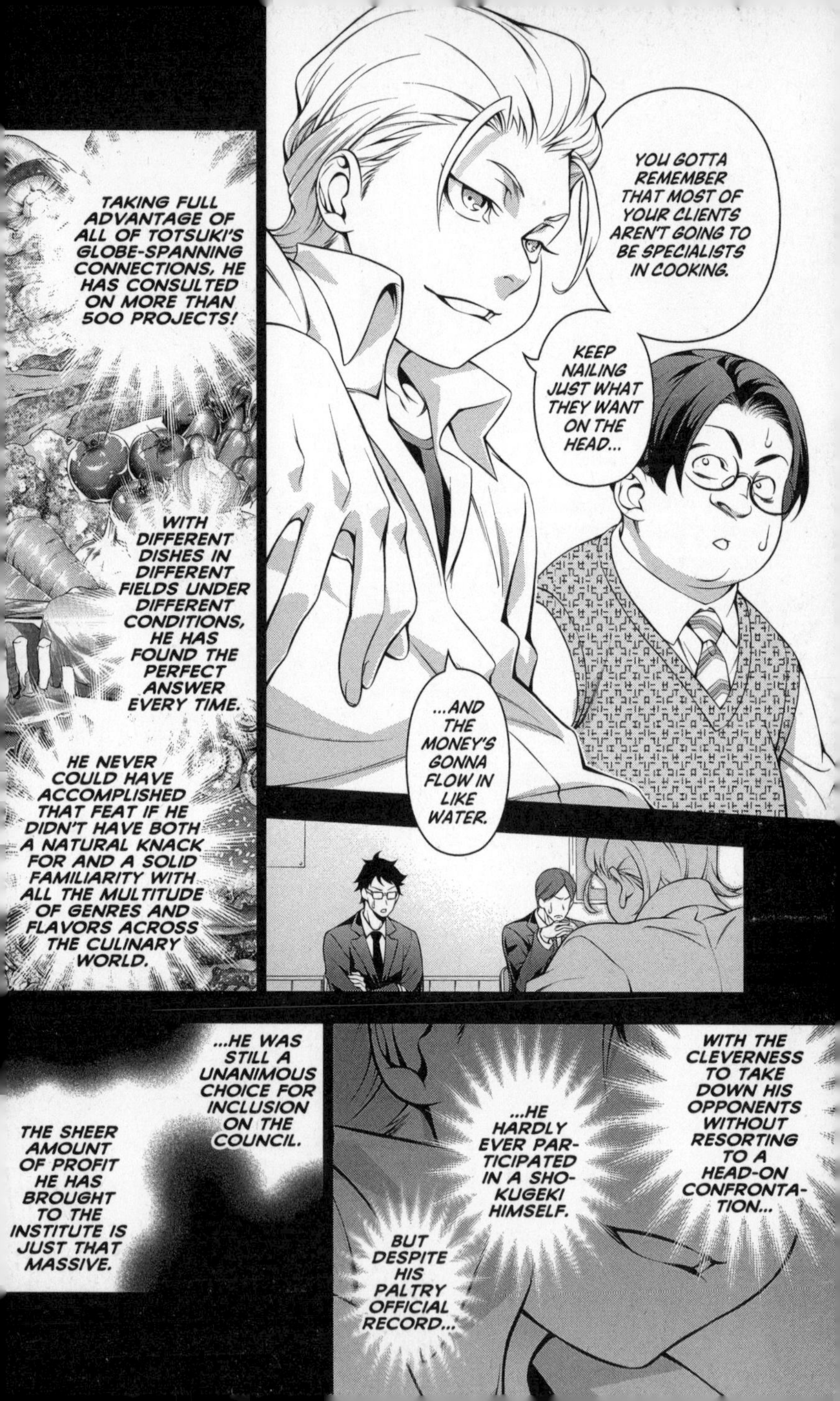
YOU GOTTA REMEMBER THAT MOST OF YOUR CLIENTS AREN'T GOING TO BE SPECIALISTS IN COOKING.
KEEP NAILING JUST WHAT THEY WANT ON THE HEAD...
...AND THE MONEY'S GONNA FLOW IN LIKE WATER.
TAKING FULL ADVANTAGE OF ALL OF TOTSUKI'S GLOBE-SPANNING CONNECTIONS, HE HAS CONSULTED ON MORE THAN 500 PROJECTS!
WITH DIFFERENT DISHES IN DIFFERENT FIELDS UNDER DIFFERENT CONDITIONS, HE HAS FOUND THE PERFECT ANSWER EVERY TIME.
HE NEVER COULD HAVE ACCOMPLISHED THAT FEAT IF HE DIDN'T HAVE BOTH A NATURAL KNACK FOR AND A SOLID FAMILIARITY WITH ALL THE MULTITUDE OF GENRES AND FLAVORS ACROSS THE CULINARY WORLD.
WITH THE CLEVERNESS TO TAKE DOWN HIS OPPONENTS WITHOUT RESORTING TO A HEAD-ON CONFRONTA-TION...
...HE HARDLY EVER PAR-TICIPATED IN A SHO-KUGEKI HIMSELF.
BUT DESPITE HIS PALTRY OFFICIAL RECORD...
...HE WAS STILL A UNANIMOUS CHOICE FOR INCLUSION ON THE COUNCIL.
THE SHEER AMOUNT OF PROFIT HE HAS BROUGHT TO THE INSTITUTE IS JUST THAT MASSIVE.

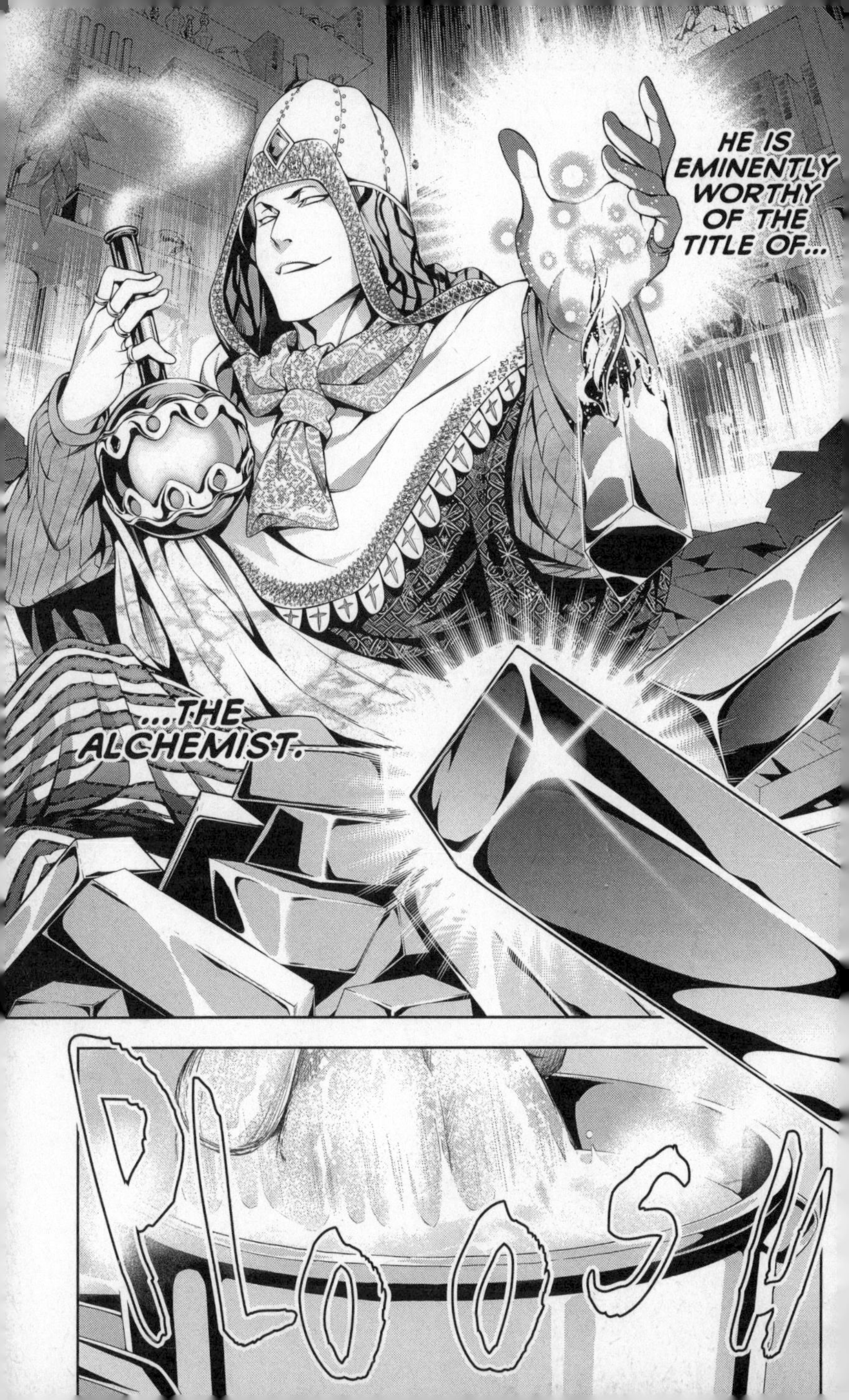
HE IS EMINENTLY WORTHY OF THE TITLE OF...
...THE ALCHEMIST.
PLOOSH

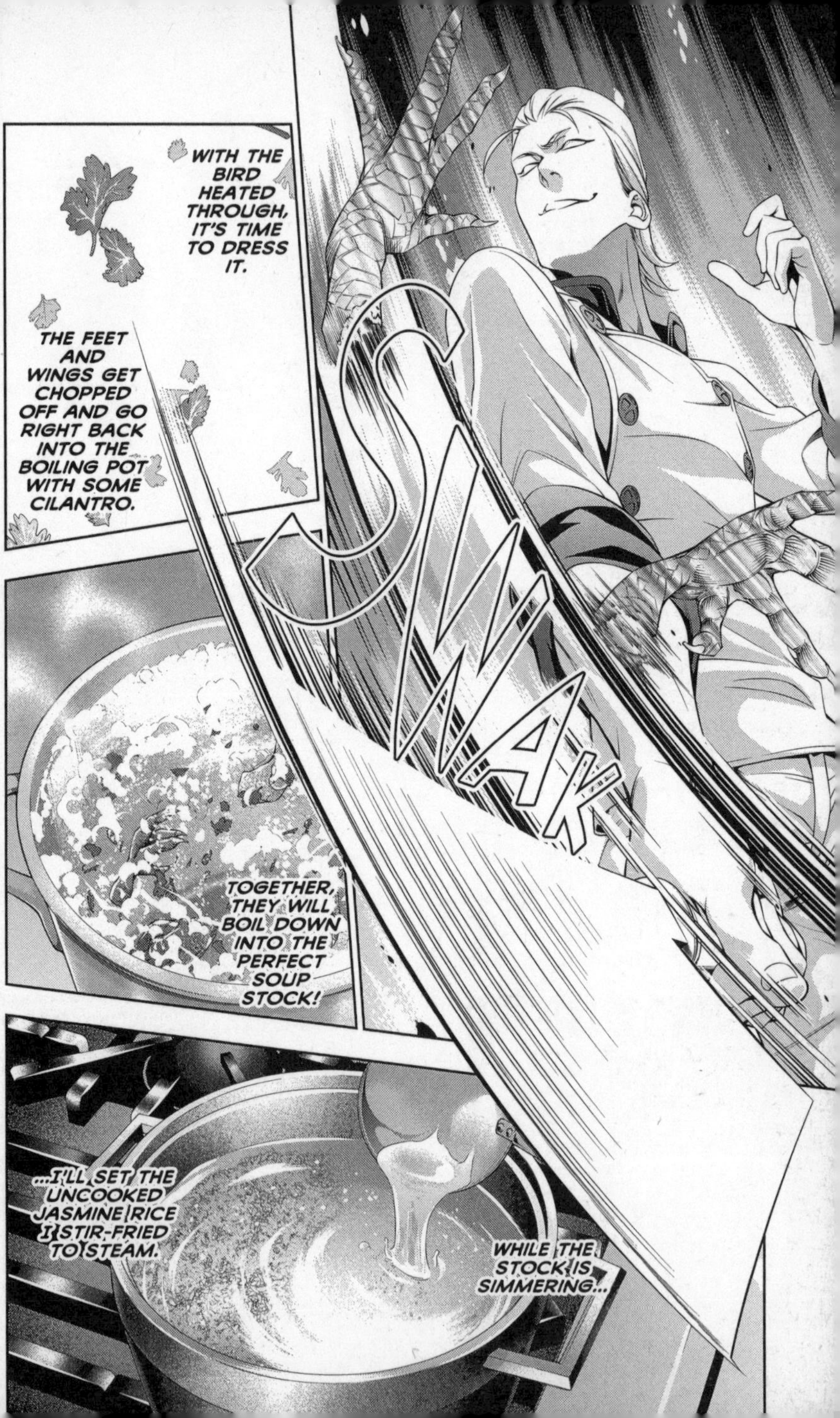
SWAK
WITH THE BIRD HEATED THROUGH, IT'S TIME TO DRESS IT.
THE FEET AND WINGS GET CHOPPED OFF AND GO RIGHT BACK INTO THE BOILING POT WITH SOME CILANTRO.
TOGETHER, THEY WILL BOIL DOWN INTO THE PERFECT SOUP STOCK!
WHILE THE STOCK IS SIMMERING...
...I'LL SET THE UNCOOKED JASMINE RICE I STIR-FRIED TO STEAM.

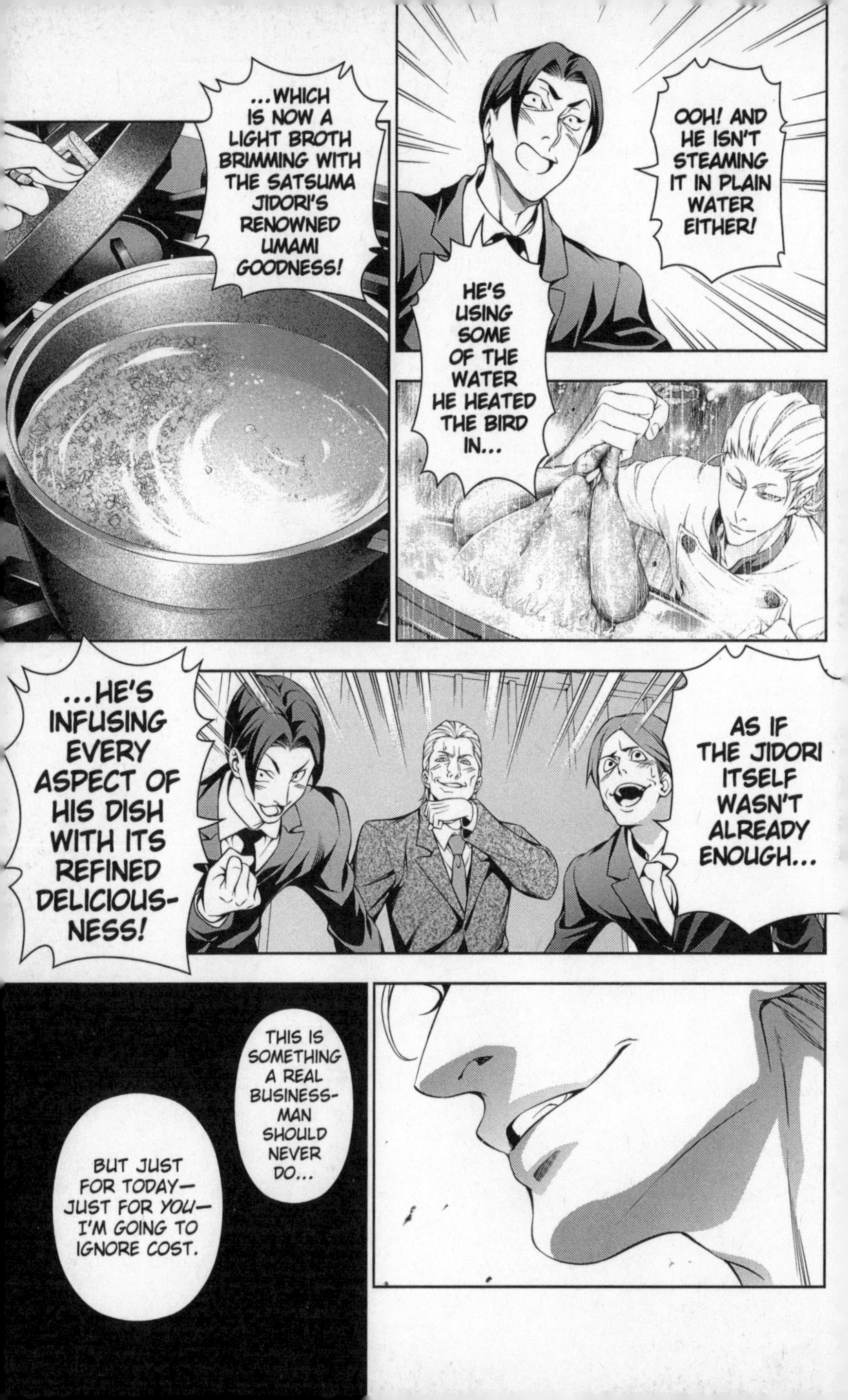
OOH! AND HE ISN'T STEAMING IT IN PLAIN WATER EITHER!
HE'S USING SOME OF THE WATER HE HEATED THE BIRD IN...
...WHICH IS NOW A LIGHT BROTH BRIMMING WITH THE SATSUMA JIDORI'S RENOWNED UMAMI GOODNESS!
AS IF THE JIDORI ITSELF WASN'T ALREADY ENOUGH...
...HE'S INFUSING EVERY ASPECT OF HIS DISH WITH ITS REFINED DELICIOUS-NESS!
THIS IS SOMETHING A REAL BUSINESS-MAN SHOULD NEVER DO...
BUT JUST FOR TODAY— JUST FOR *YOU*— I'M GOING TO IGNORE COST.

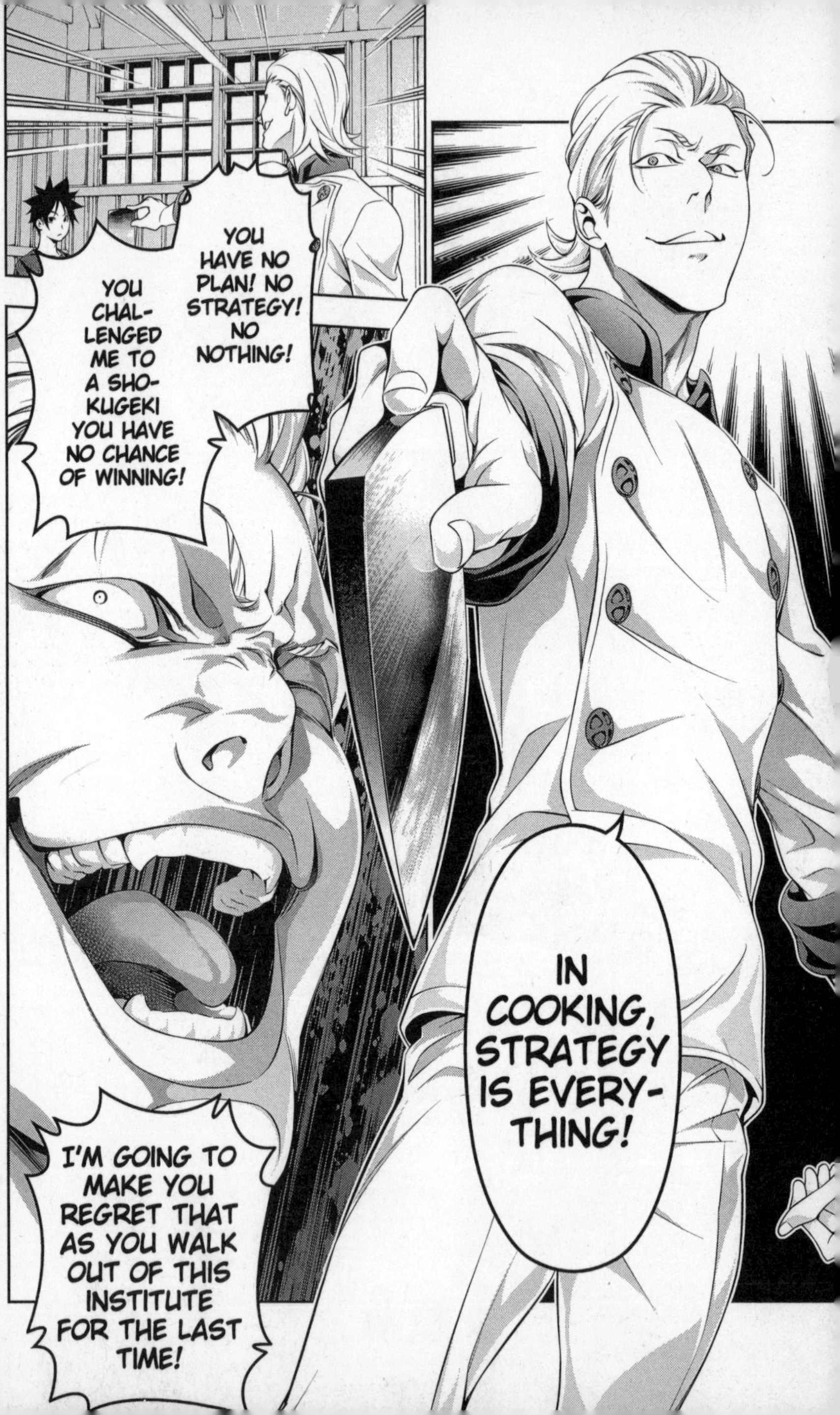
YOU HAVE NO PLAN! NO STRATEGY! NO NOTHING!
YOU CHALLENGED ME TO A SHOKUGEKI YOU HAVE NO CHANCE OF WINNING!
IN COOKING, STRATEGY IS EVERYTHING!
I'M GOING TO MAKE YOU REGRET THAT AS YOU WALK OUT OF THIS INSTITUTE FOR THE LAST TIME!

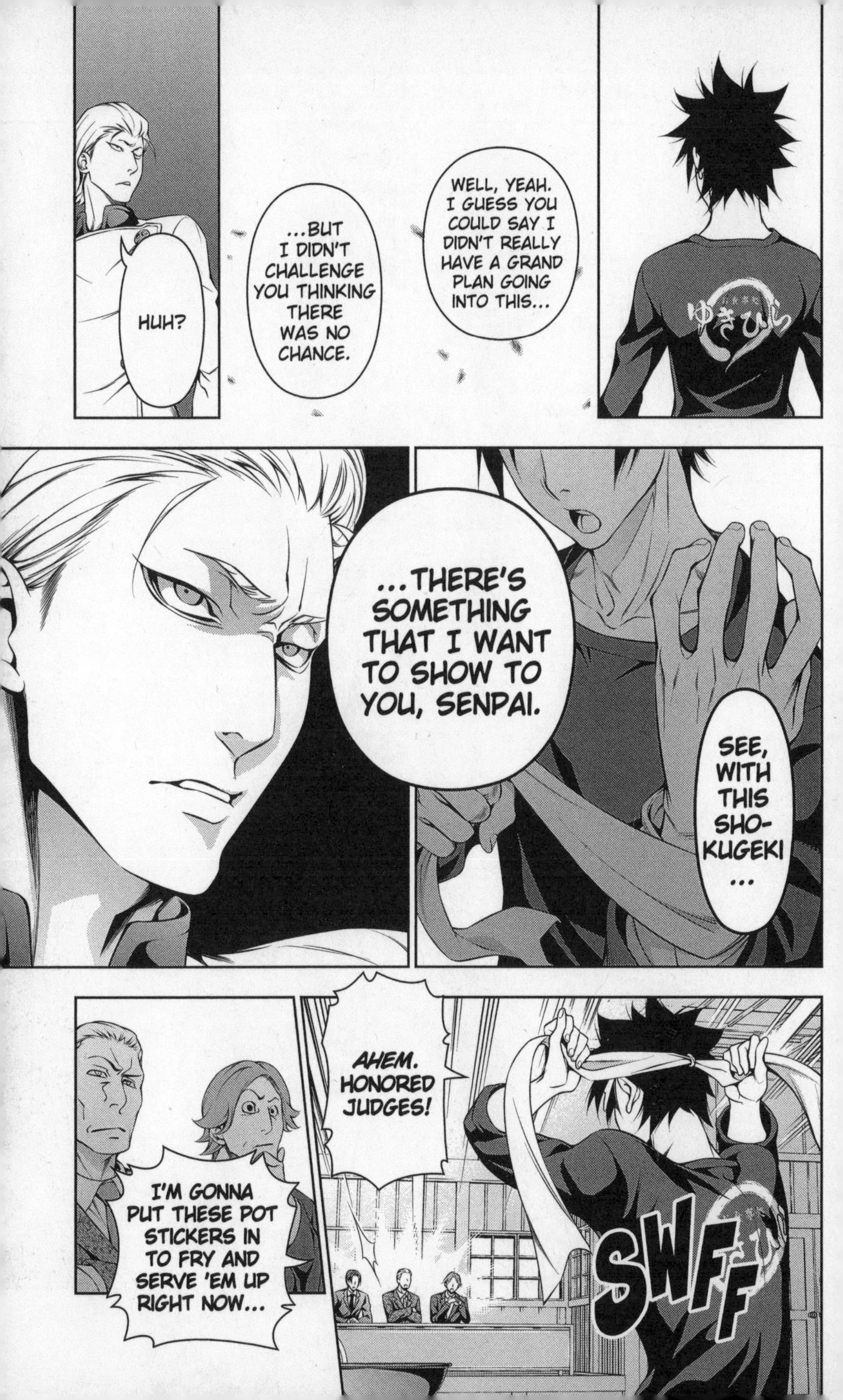
WELL, YEAH. I GUESS YOU COULD SAY I DIDN'T REALLY HAVE A GRAND PLAN GOING INTO THIS...
...BUT I DIDN'T CHALLENGE YOU THINKING THERE WAS NO CHANCE.
HUH?
SEE, WITH THIS SHO-KUGEKI...
...THERE'S SOMETHING THAT I WANT TO SHOW TO YOU, SENPAI.
AHEM. HONORED JUDGES!
SWFF
I'M GONNA PUT THESE POT STICKERS IN TO FRY AND SERVE 'EM UP RIGHT NOW...

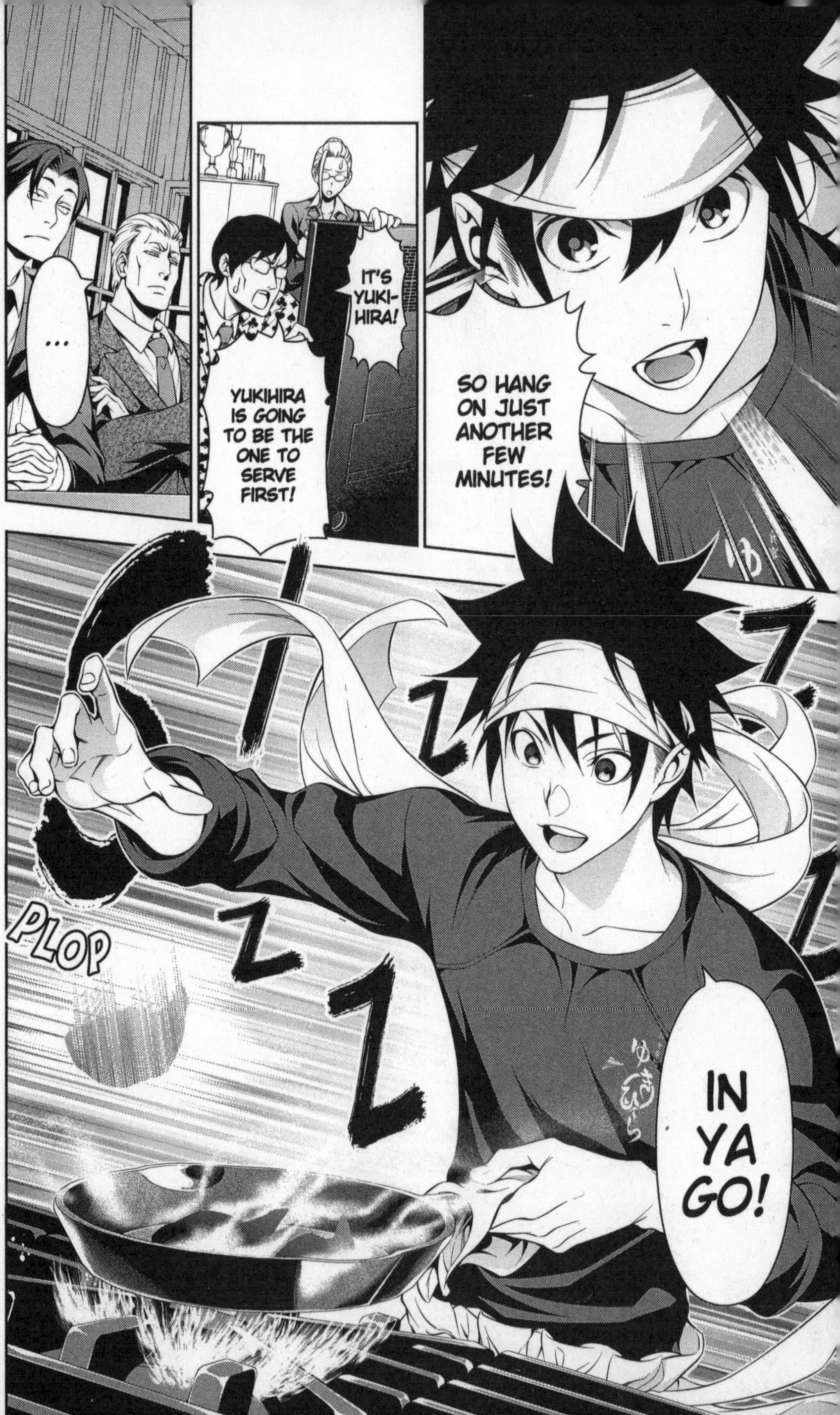
SO HANG ON JUST ANOTHER FEW MINUTES!
IT'S YUKI-HIRA!
YUKIHIRA IS GOING TO BE THE ONE TO SERVE FIRST!
...
IN YA GO!
PLOP

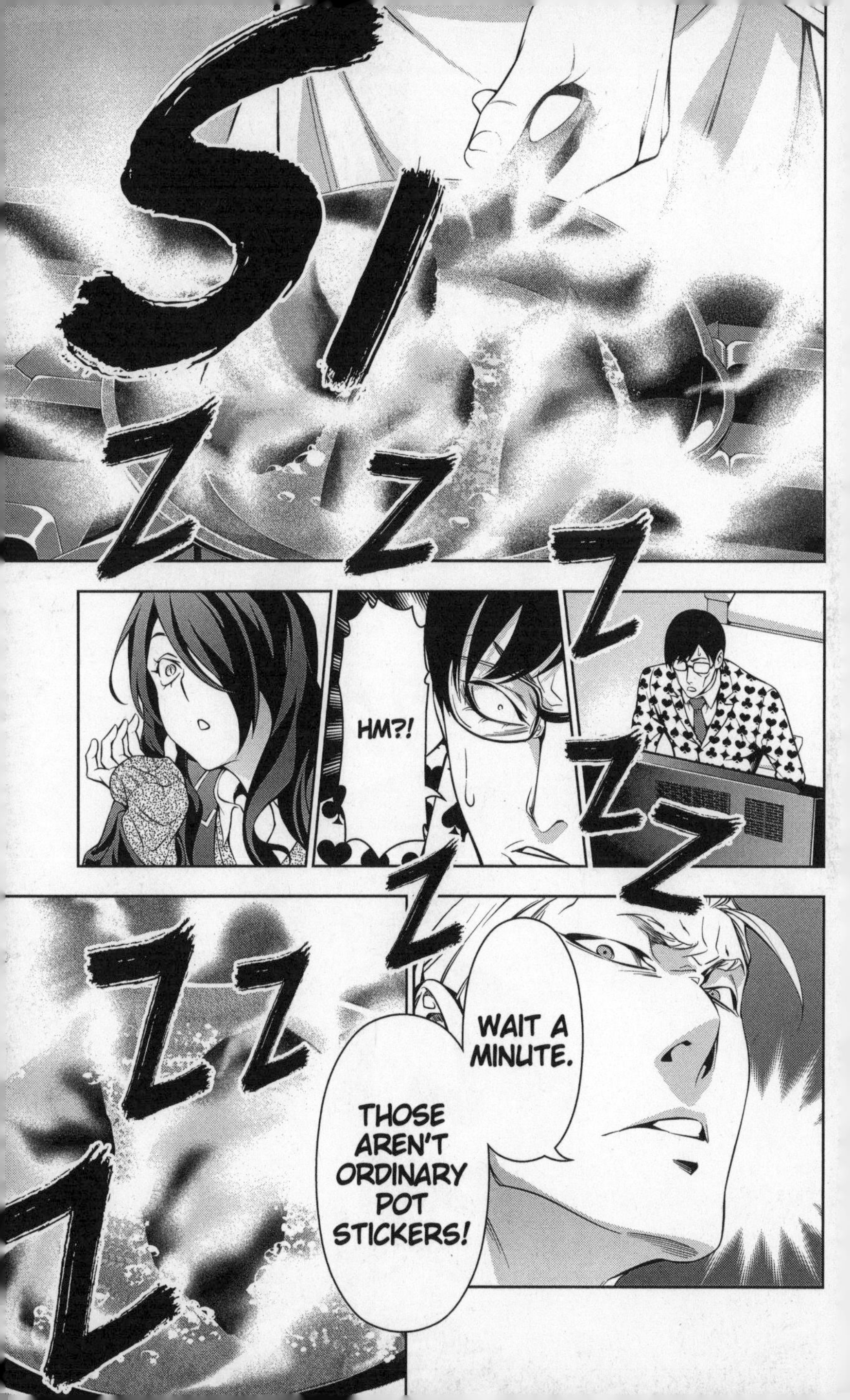
SIZZZZZZZZ
HM?!
WAIT A MINUTE.
THOSE AREN'T ORDINARY POT STICKERS!

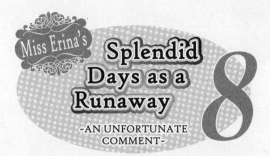

Miss Erina's Splendid Days as a Runaway 8

~AN UNFORTUNATE COMMENT~

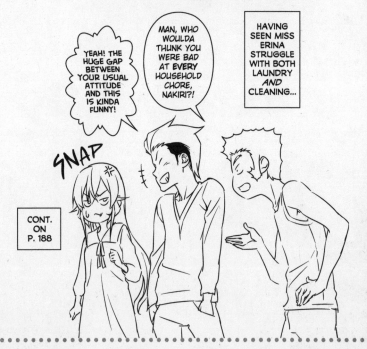

HAVING SEEN MISS ERINA STRUGGLE WITH BOTH LAUNDRY *AND* CLEANING...
MAN, WHO WOULDA THUNK YOU WERE BAD AT EVERY HOUSEHOLD CHORE, NAKIRI?!
YEAH! THE HUGE GAP BETWEEN YOUR USUAL ATTITUDE AND THIS IS KINDA FUNNY!
SNAP

CONT. ON P. 188

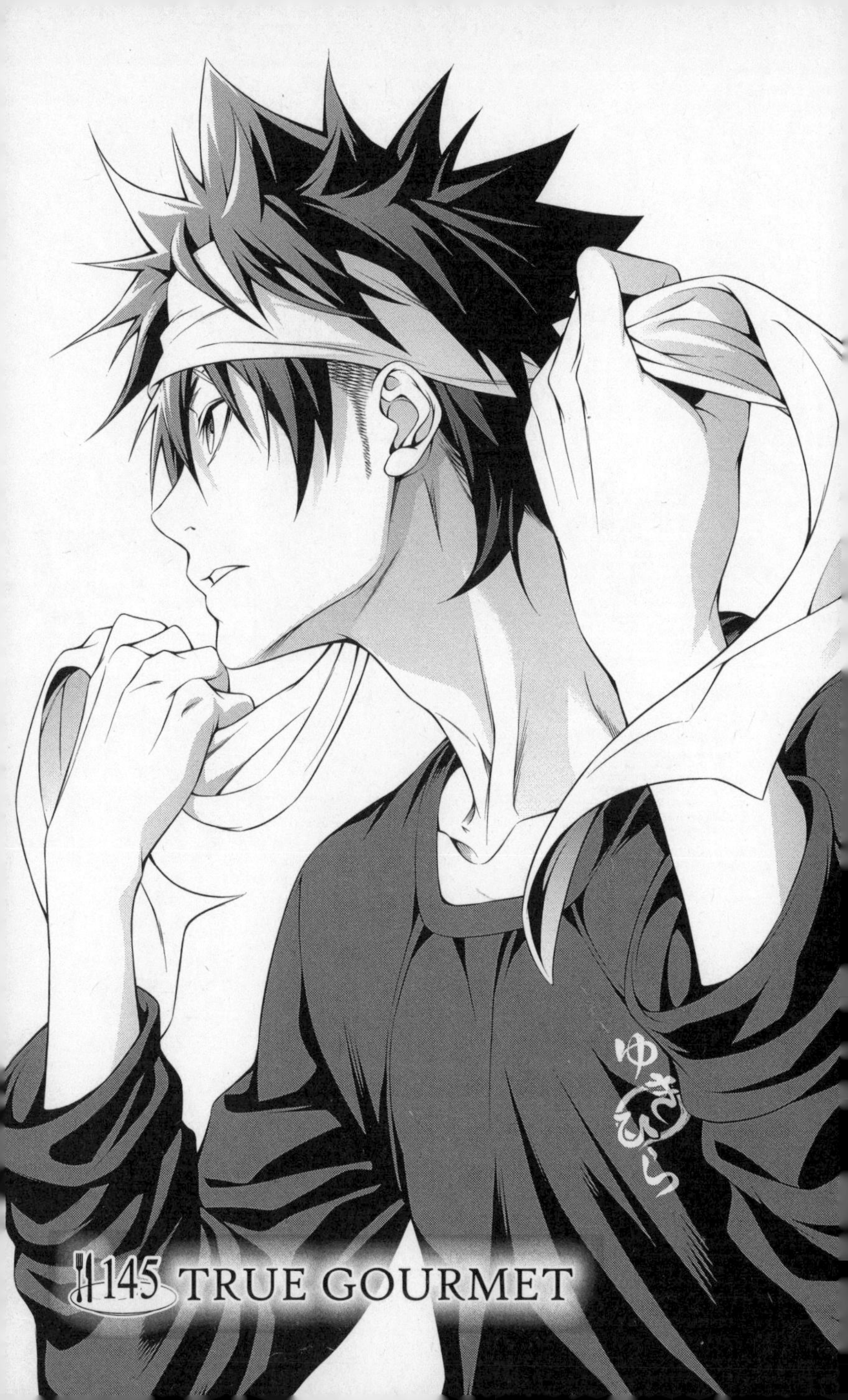
ゆきひら

145 TRUE GOURMET

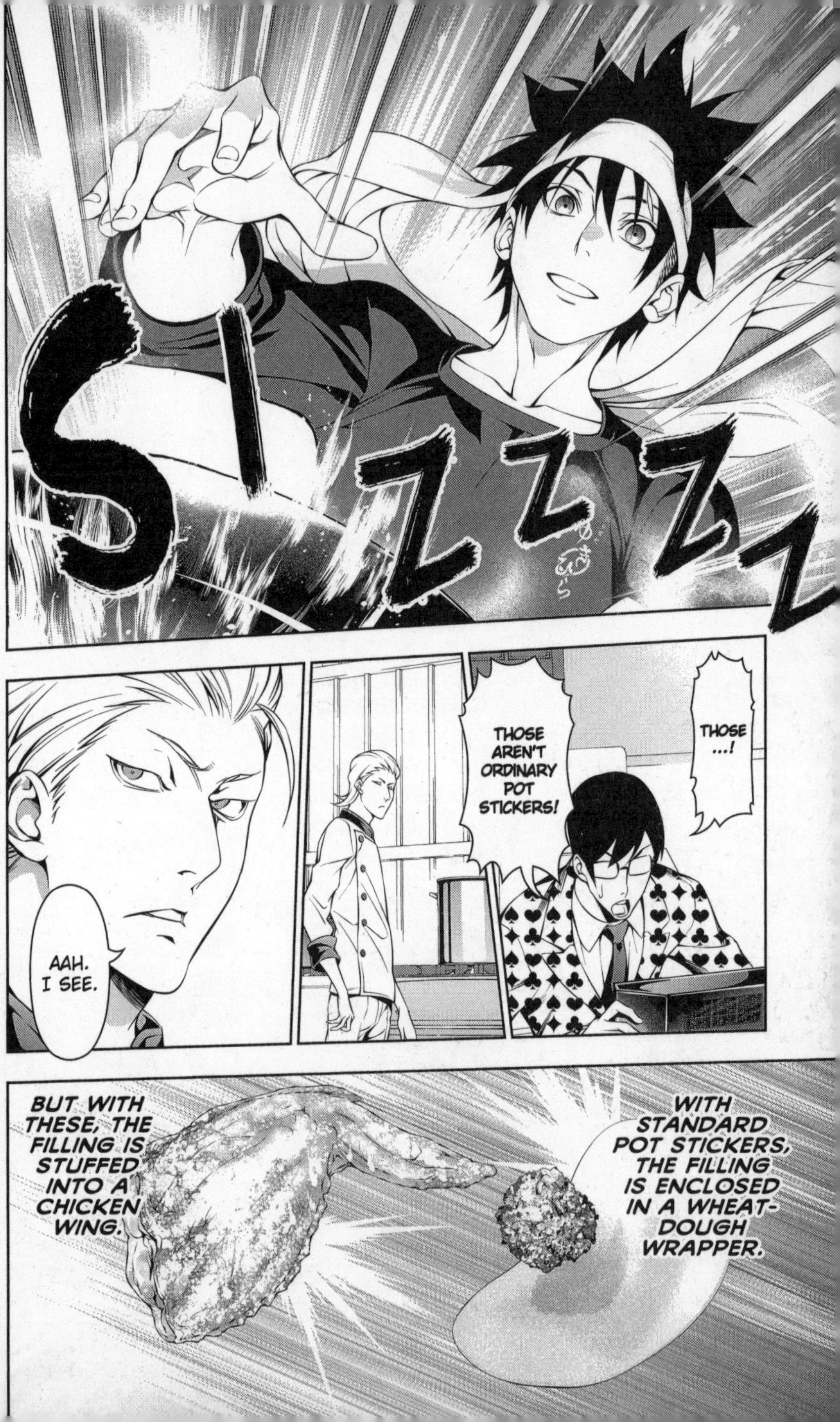
SIZZZZ
THOSE ...!
THOSE AREN'T ORDINARY POT STICKERS!
AAH. I SEE.
WITH STANDARD POT STICKERS, THE FILLING IS ENCLOSED IN A WHEAT-DOUGH WRAPPER.
BUT WITH THESE, THE FILLING IS STUFFED INTO A CHICKEN WING.

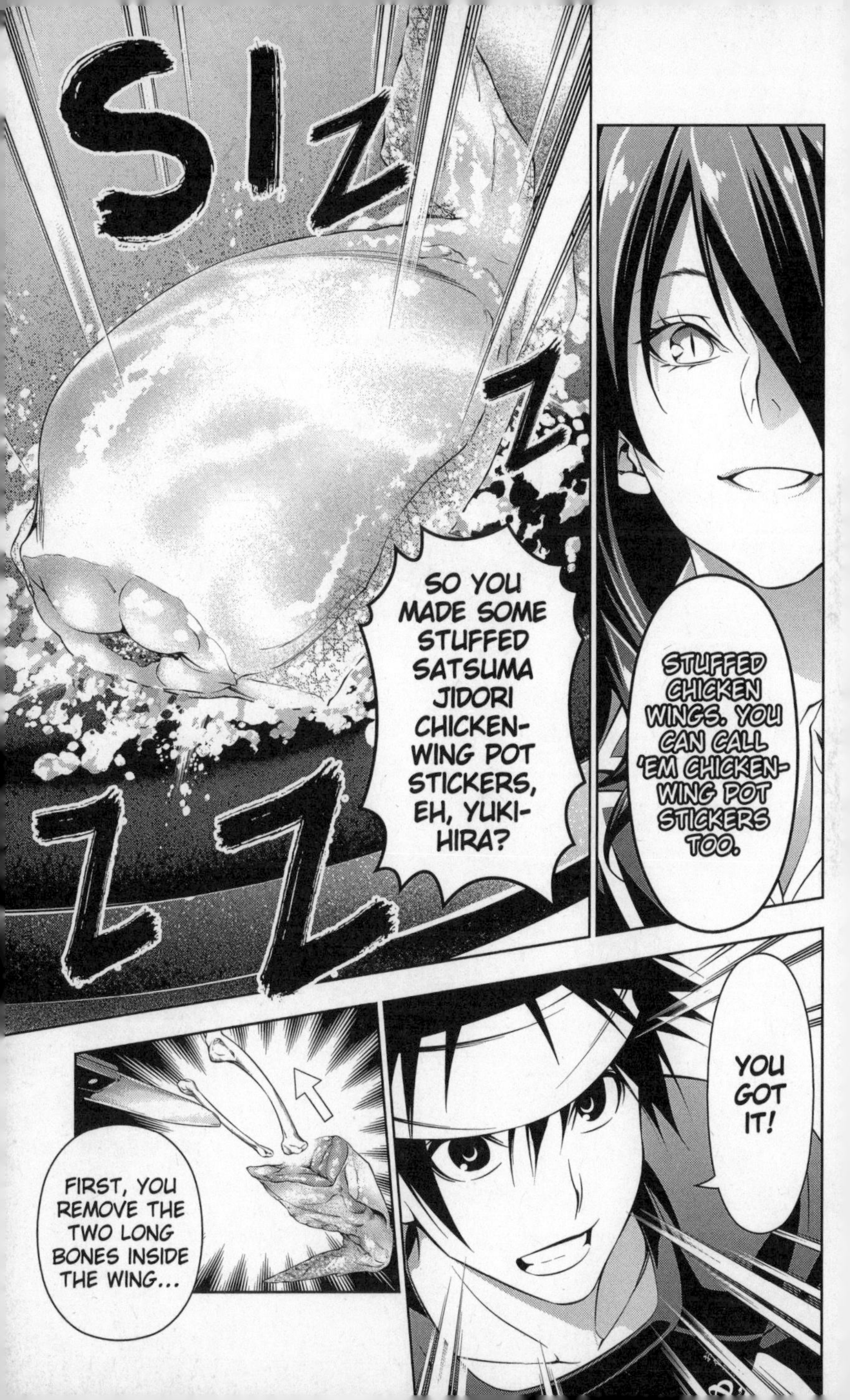
SIZZZZ
STUFFED CHICKEN WINGS. YOU CAN CALL 'EM CHICKEN-WING POT STICKERS TOO.
SO YOU MADE SOME STUFFED SATSUMA JIDORI CHICKEN-WING POT STICKERS, EH, YUKIHIRA?
YOU GOT IT!
FIRST, YOU REMOVE THE TWO LONG BONES INSIDE THE WING...

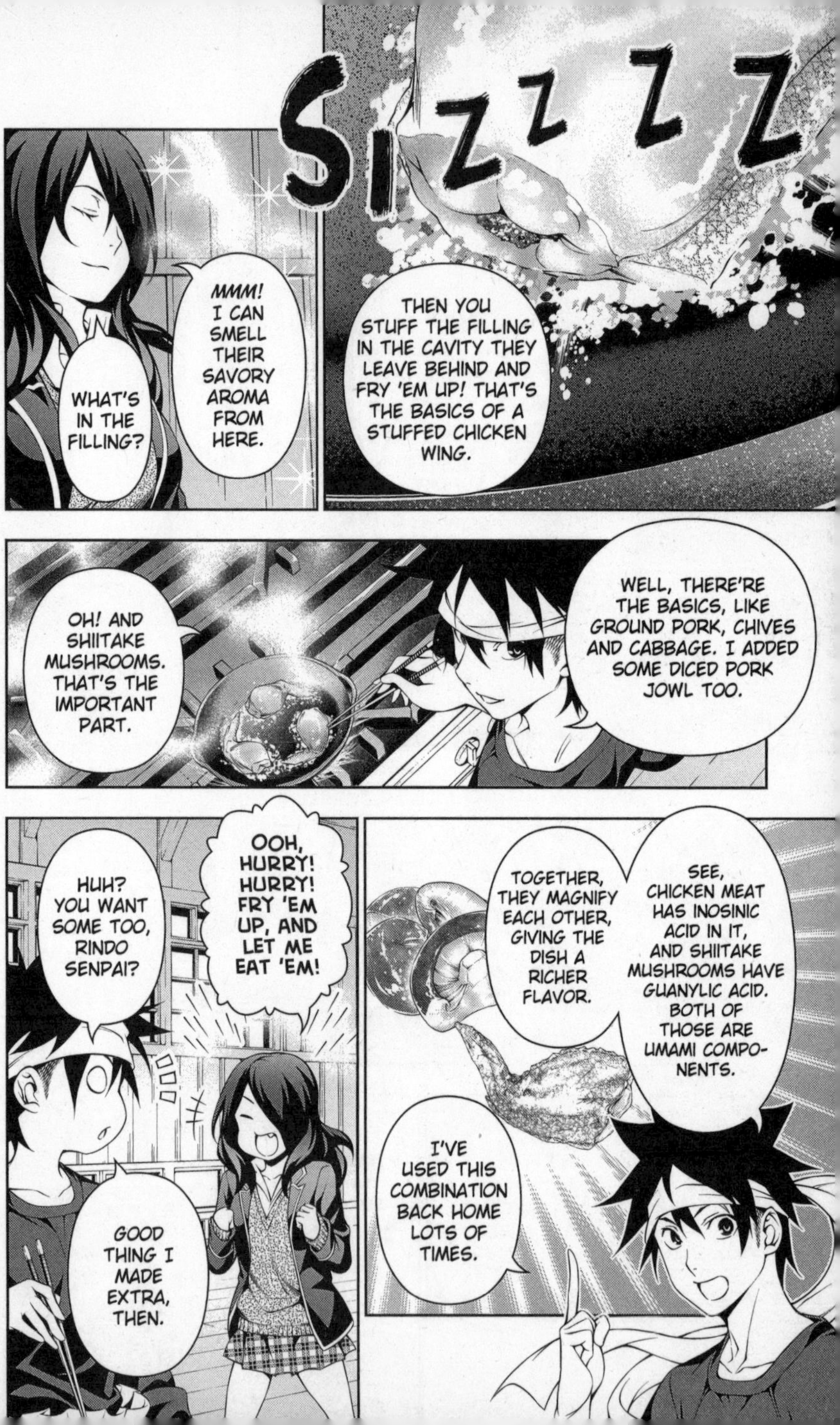
SIZZZZ
THEN YOU STUFF THE FILLING IN THE CAVITY THEY LEAVE BEHIND AND FRY 'EM UP! THAT'S THE BASICS OF A STUFFED CHICKEN WING.
MMM! I CAN SMELL THEIR SAVORY AROMA FROM HERE.
WHAT'S IN THE FILLING?
WELL, THERE'RE THE BASICS, LIKE GROUND PORK, CHIVES AND CABBAGE. I ADDED SOME DICED PORK JOWL TOO.
OH! AND SHIITAKE MUSHROOMS. THAT'S THE IMPORTANT PART.
SEE, CHICKEN MEAT HAS INOSINIC ACID IN IT, AND SHIITAKE MUSHROOMS HAVE GUANYLIC ACID. BOTH OF THOSE ARE UMAMI COMPO-NENTS.
TOGETHER, THEY MAGNIFY EACH OTHER, GIVING THE DISH A RICHER FLAVOR.
I'VE USED THIS COMBINATION BACK HOME LOTS OF TIMES.
OOH, HURRY! HURRY! FRY 'EM UP, AND LET ME EAT 'EM!
HUH? YOU WANT SOME TOO, RINDO SENPAI?
GOOD THING I MADE EXTRA, THEN.

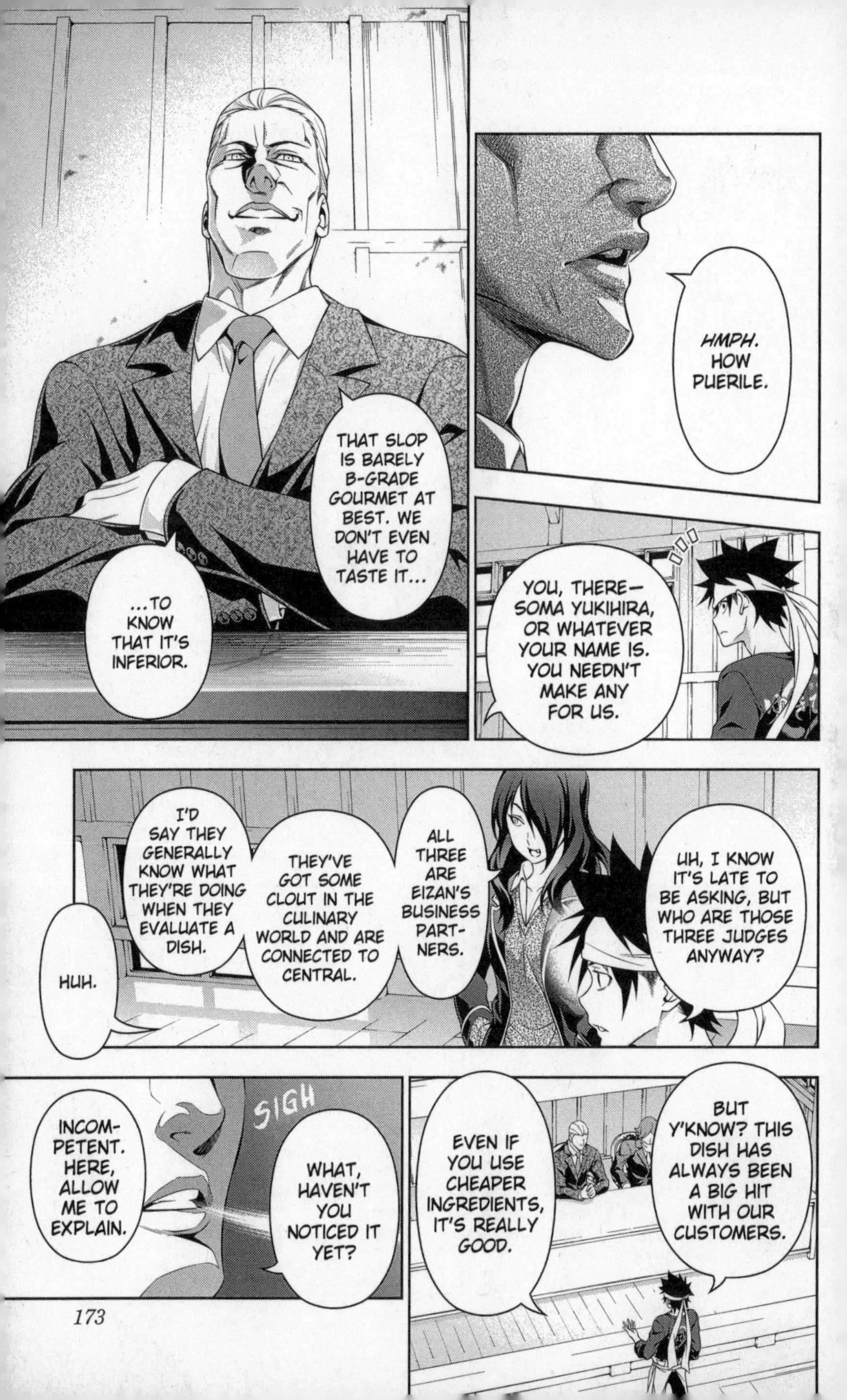
HMPH. HOW PUERILE.
YOU, THERE— SOMA YUKIHIRA, OR WHATEVER YOUR NAME IS. YOU NEEDN'T MAKE ANY FOR US.
THAT SLOP IS BARELY B-GRADE GOURMET AT BEST. WE DON'T EVEN HAVE TO TASTE IT...
...TO KNOW THAT IT'S INFERIOR.
UH, I KNOW IT'S LATE TO BE ASKING, BUT WHO ARE THOSE THREE JUDGES ANYWAY?
ALL THREE ARE EIZAN'S BUSINESS PART- NERS.
THEY'VE GOT SOME CLOUT IN THE CULINARY WORLD AND ARE CONNECTED TO CENTRAL.
I'D SAY THEY GENERALLY KNOW WHAT THEY'RE DOING WHEN THEY EVALUATE A DISH.
HUH.
BUT Y'KNOW? THIS DISH HAS ALWAYS BEEN A BIG HIT WITH OUR CUSTOMERS.
EVEN IF YOU USE CHEAPER INGREDIENTS, IT'S REALLY GOOD.
WHAT, HAVEN'T YOU NOTICED IT YET?
SIGH
INCOM- PETENT. HERE, ALLOW ME TO EXPLAIN.

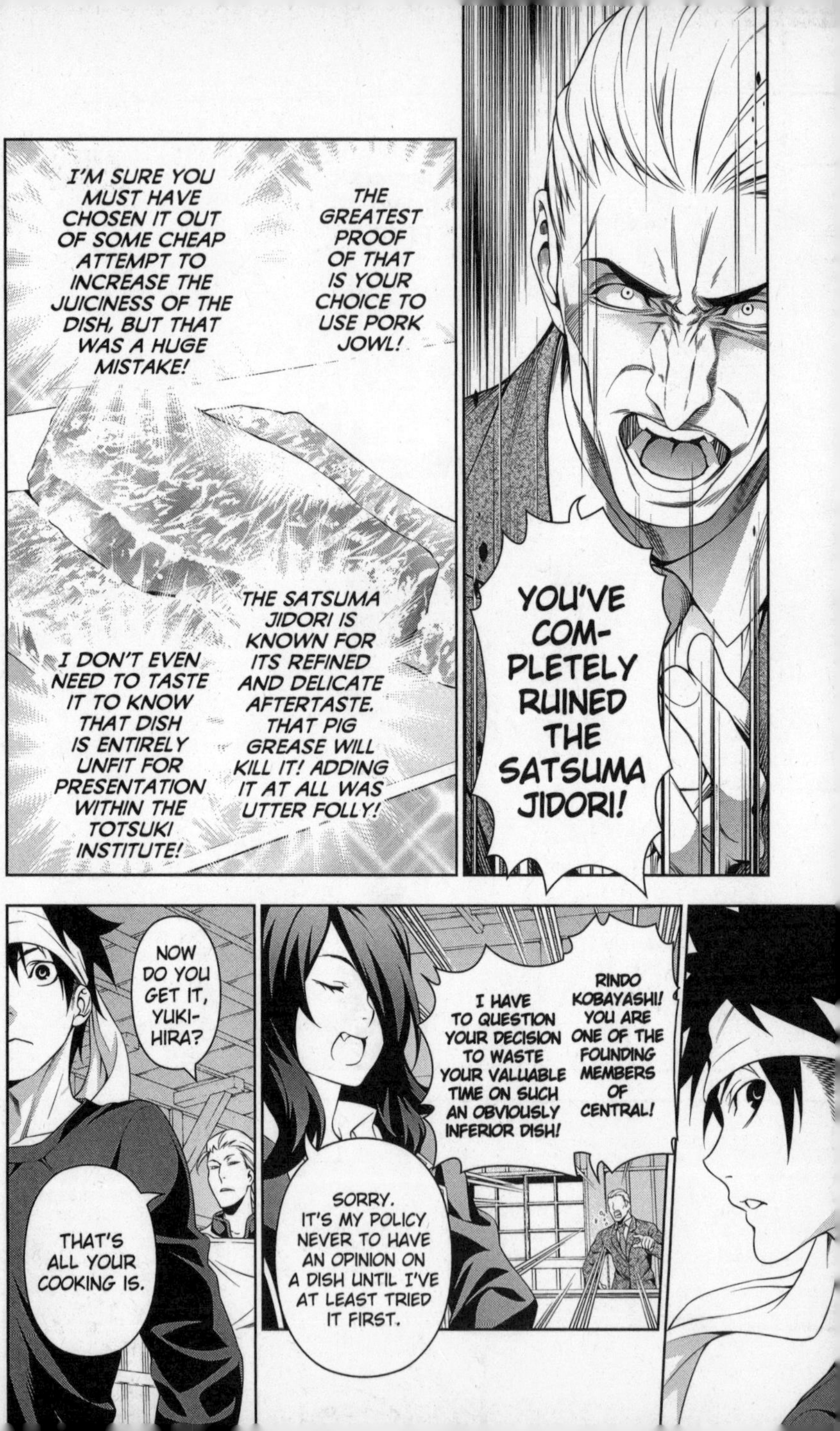
YOU'VE COM-PLETELY RUINED THE SATSUMA JIDORI!
THE GREATEST PROOF OF THAT IS YOUR CHOICE TO USE PORK JOWL!
I'M SURE YOU MUST HAVE CHOSEN IT OUT OF SOME CHEAP ATTEMPT TO INCREASE THE JUICINESS OF THE DISH, BUT THAT WAS A HUGE MISTAKE!
THE SATSUMA JIDORI IS KNOWN FOR ITS REFINED AND DELICATE AFTERTASTE. THAT PIG GREASE WILL KILL IT! ADDING IT AT ALL WAS UTTER FOLLY!
I DON'T EVEN NEED TO TASTE IT TO KNOW THAT DISH IS ENTIRELY UNFIT FOR PRESENTATION WITHIN THE TOTSUKI INSTITUTE!
RINDO KOBAYASHI! YOU ARE ONE OF THE FOUNDING MEMBERS OF CENTRAL!
I HAVE TO QUESTION YOUR DECISION TO WASTE YOUR VALUABLE TIME ON SUCH AN OBVIOUSLY INFERIOR DISH!
SORRY. IT'S MY POLICY NEVER TO HAVE AN OPINION ON A DISH UNTIL I'VE AT LEAST TRIED IT FIRST.
NOW DO YOU GET IT, YUKI-HIRA?
THAT'S ALL YOUR COOKING IS.

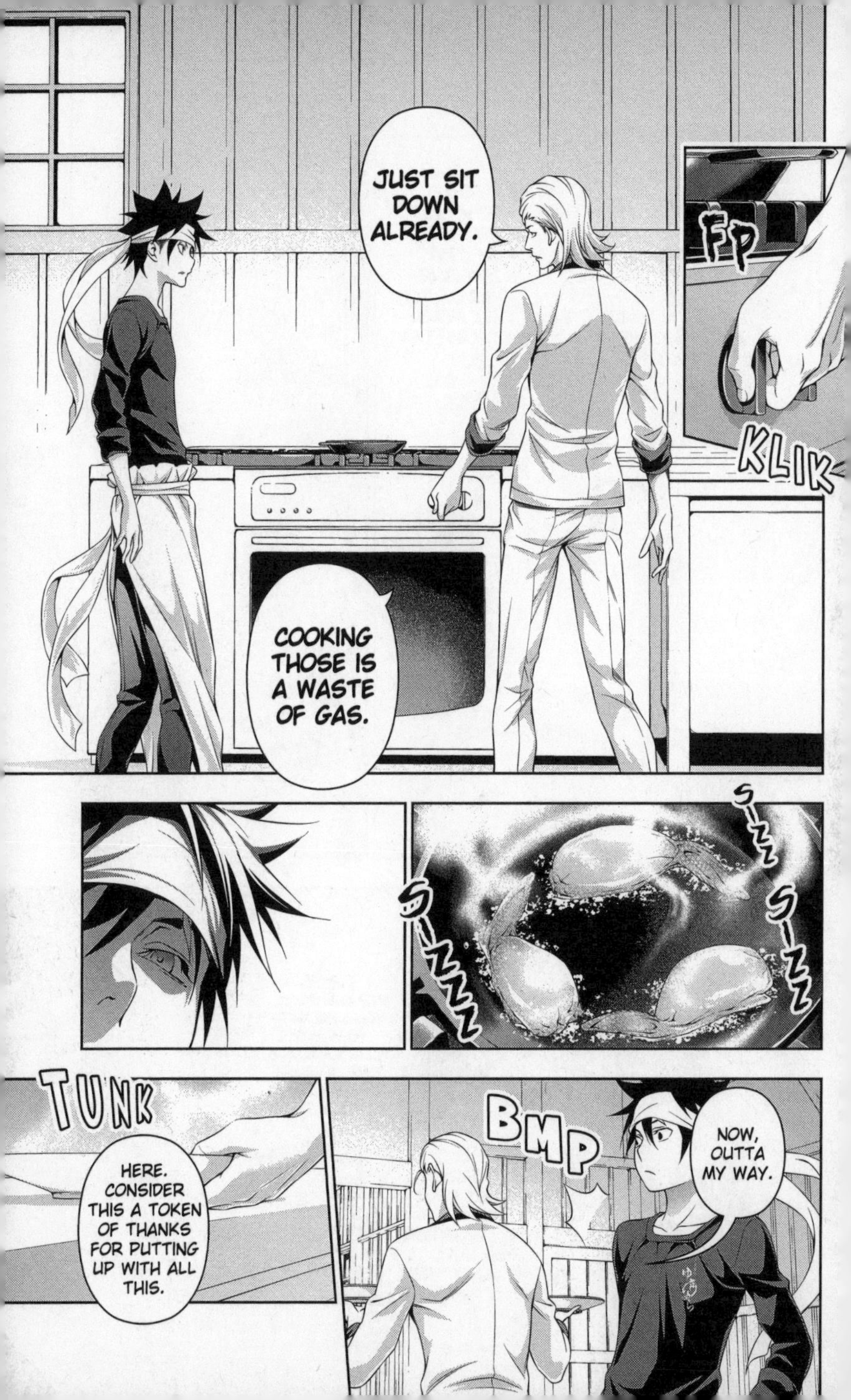
Fp
KLIK
JUST SIT DOWN ALREADY.
COOKING THOSE IS A WASTE OF GAS.
S-ZZZ
S-ZZZ
S-ZZZZ
BMP
NOW, OUTTA MY WAY.
TUNK
HERE. CONSIDER THIS A TOKEN OF THANKS FOR PUTTING UP WITH ALL THIS.

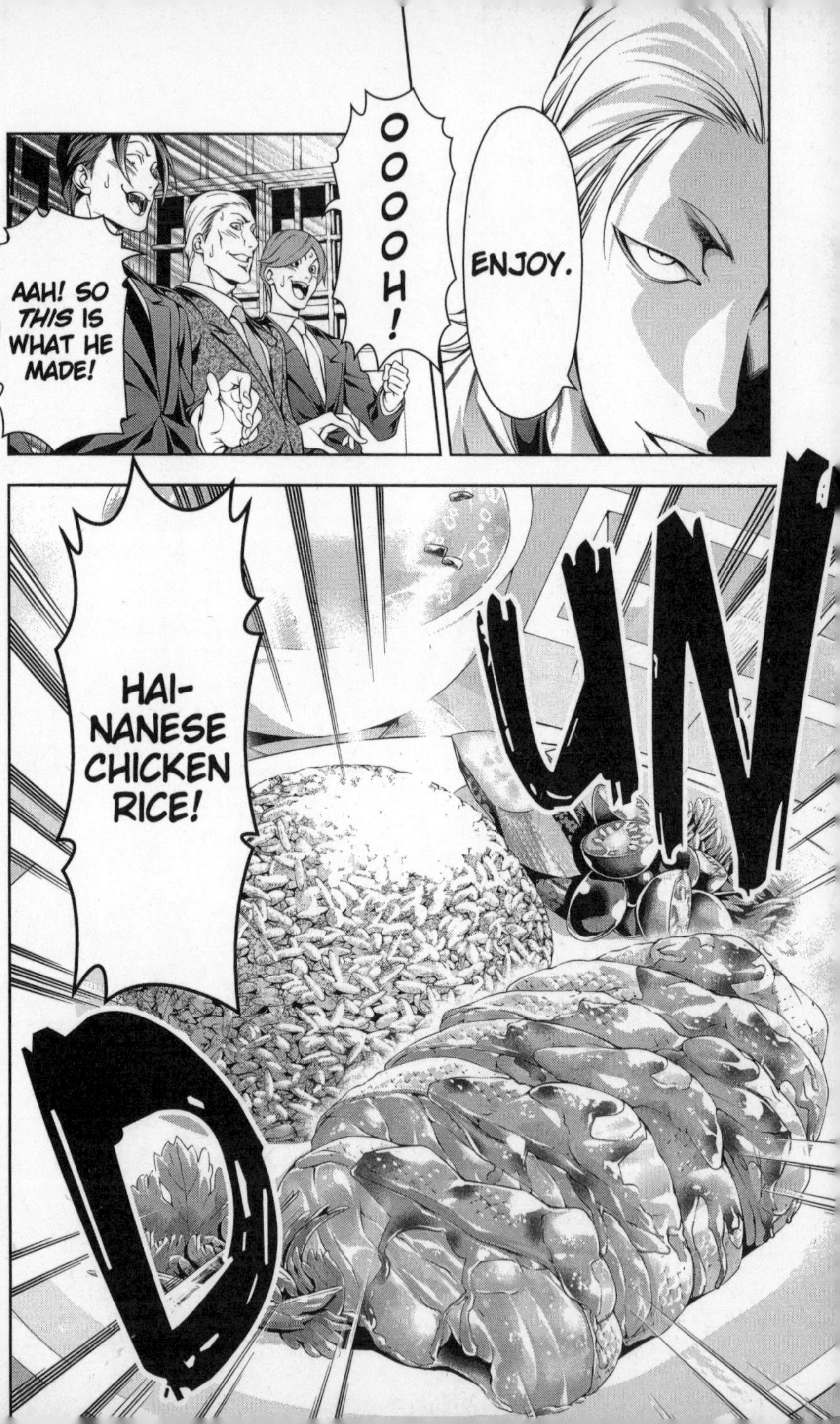
ENJOY.
OOOOOH!
AAH! SO THIS IS WHAT HE MADE!
HAI-NANESE CHICKEN RICE!
DUN

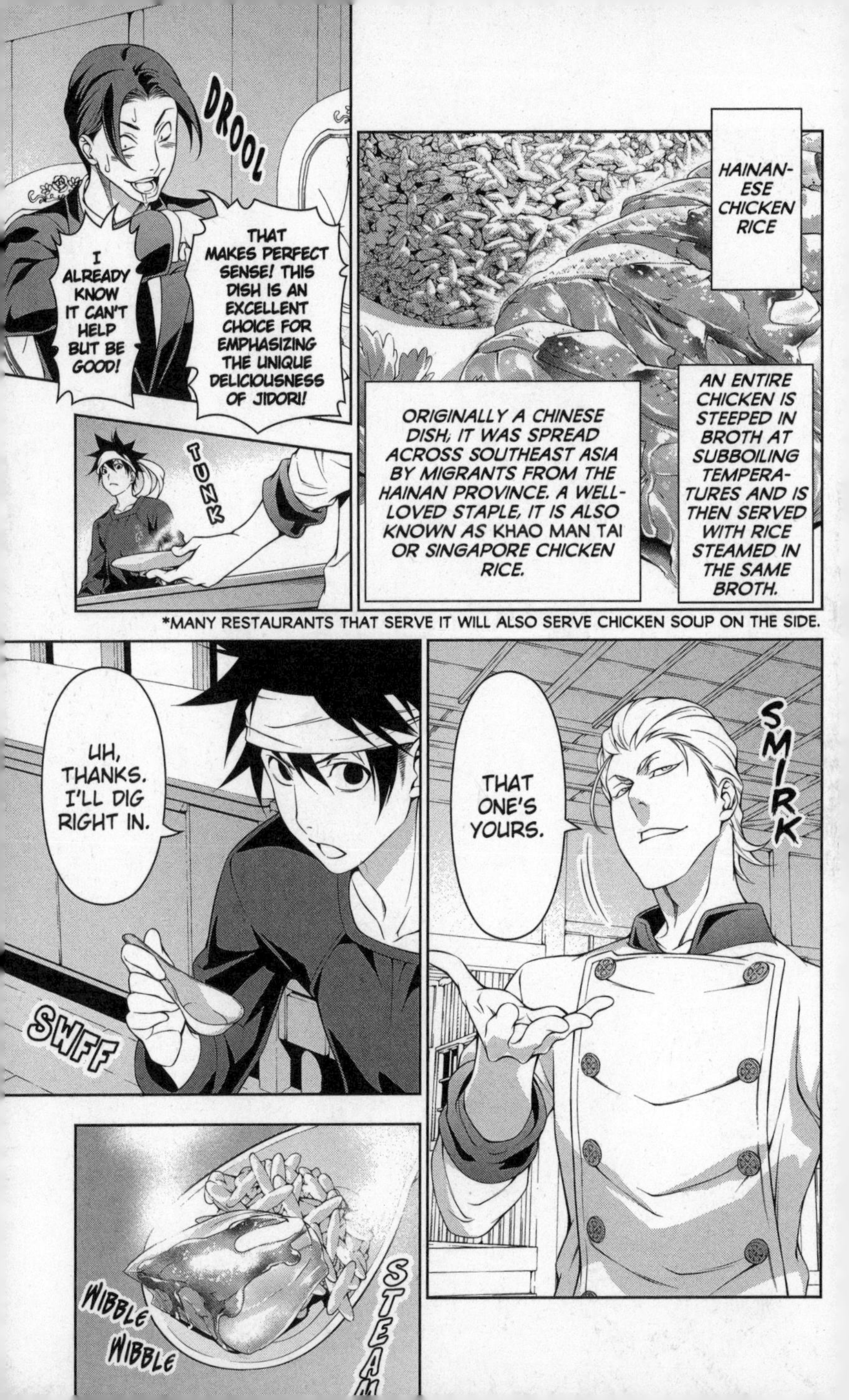
HAINANESE CHICKEN RICE
AN ENTIRE CHICKEN IS STEEPED IN BROTH AT SUBBOILING TEMPERATURES AND IS THEN SERVED WITH RICE STEAMED IN THE SAME BROTH.
ORIGINALLY A CHINESE DISH; IT WAS SPREAD ACROSS SOUTHEAST ASIA BY MIGRANTS FROM THE HAINAN PROVINCE. A WELL-LOVED STAPLE, IT IS ALSO KNOWN AS KHAO MAN TAI OR SINGAPORE CHICKEN RICE.
DROOL
THAT MAKES PERFECT SENSE! THIS DISH IS AN EXCELLENT CHOICE FOR EMPHASIZING THE UNIQUE DELICIOUSNESS OF JIDORI!
I ALREADY KNOW IT CAN'T HELP BUT BE GOOD!
TUNK
SMIRK
THAT ONE'S YOURS.
UH, THANKS. I'LL DIG RIGHT IN.
SWFF
STEAM
WIBBLE WIBBLE

*MANY RESTAURANTS THAT SERVE IT WILL ALSO SERVE CHICKEN SOUP ON THE SIDE.

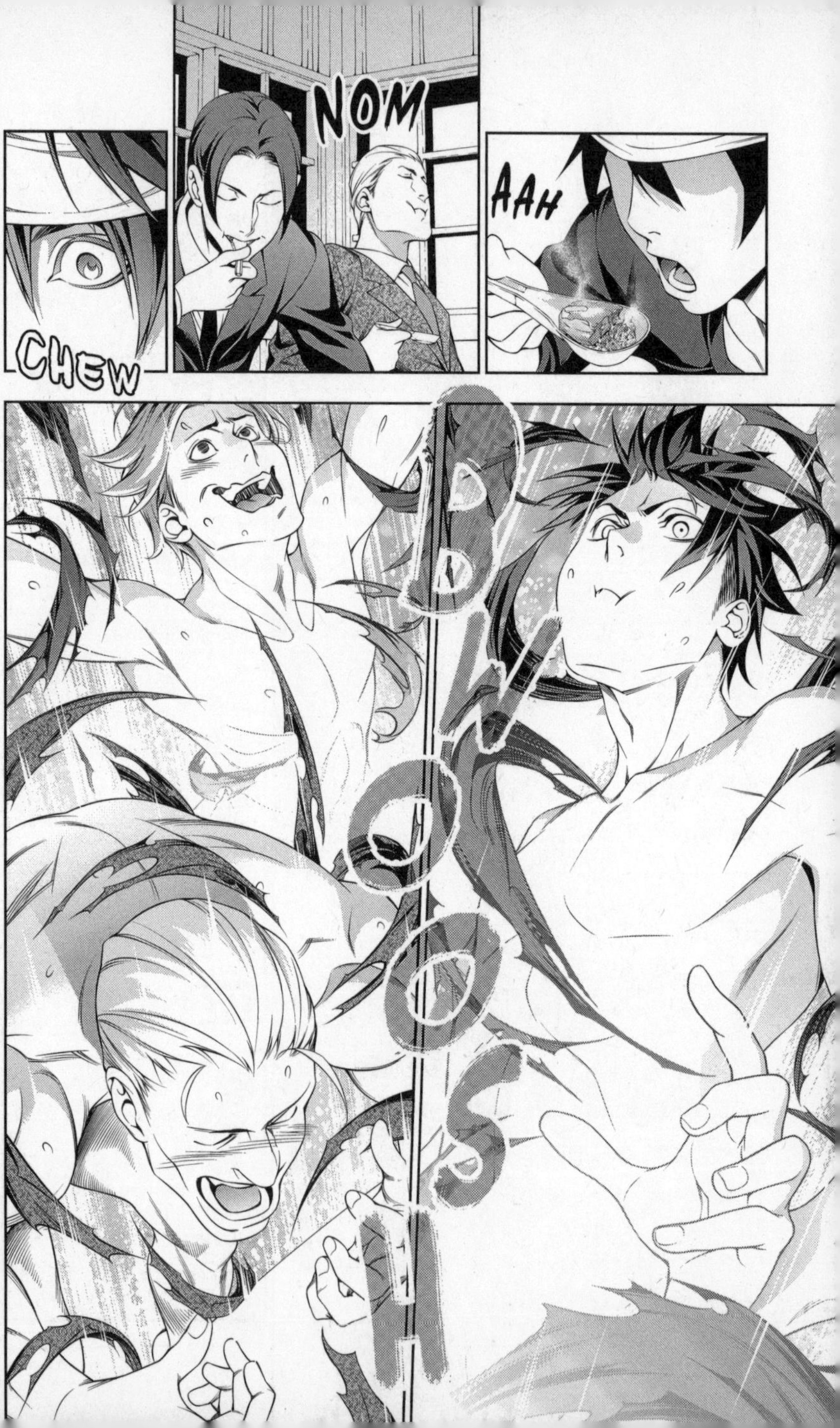
AAH
NOM
CHEW
BWOOS

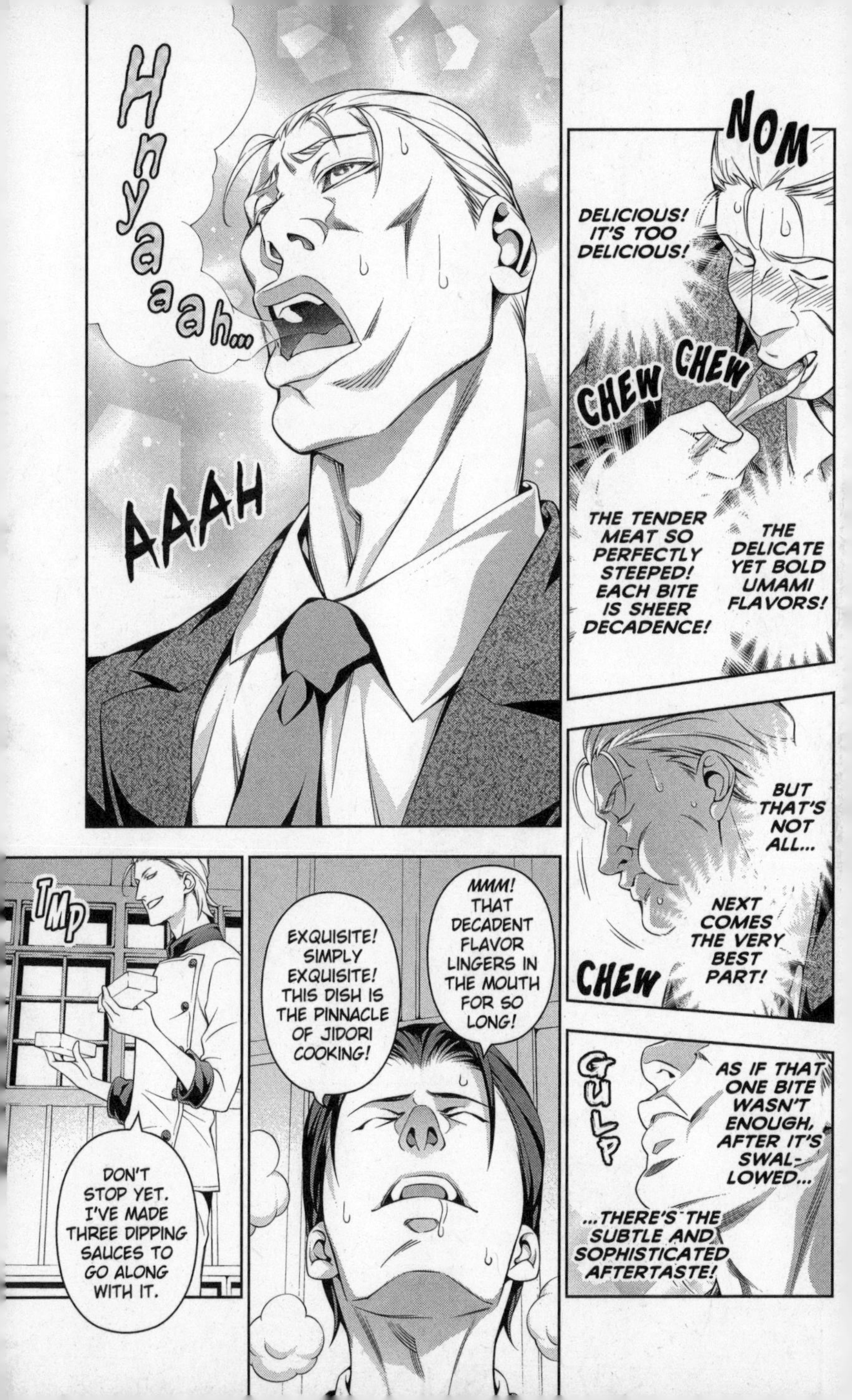
NOM
DELICIOUS! IT'S TOO DELICIOUS!
CHEW CHEW
THE DELICATE YET BOLD UMAMI FLAVORS!
THE TENDER MEAT SO PERFECTLY STEEPED! EACH BITE IS SHEER DECADENCE!
BUT THAT'S NOT ALL...
NEXT COMES THE VERY BEST PART!
CHEW
GULP
AS IF THAT ONE BITE WASN'T ENOUGH, AFTER IT'S SWAL-LOWED...
...THERE'S THE SUBTLE AND SOPHISTICATED AFTERTASTE!
Hnyaaaah...
AAAH
MMM! THAT DECADENT FLAVOR LINGERS IN THE MOUTH FOR SO LONG!
EXQUISITE! SIMPLY EXQUISITE! THIS DISH IS THE PINNACLE OF JIDORI COOKING!
TMP
DON'T STOP YET. I'VE MADE THREE DIPPING SAUCES TO GO ALONG WITH IT.

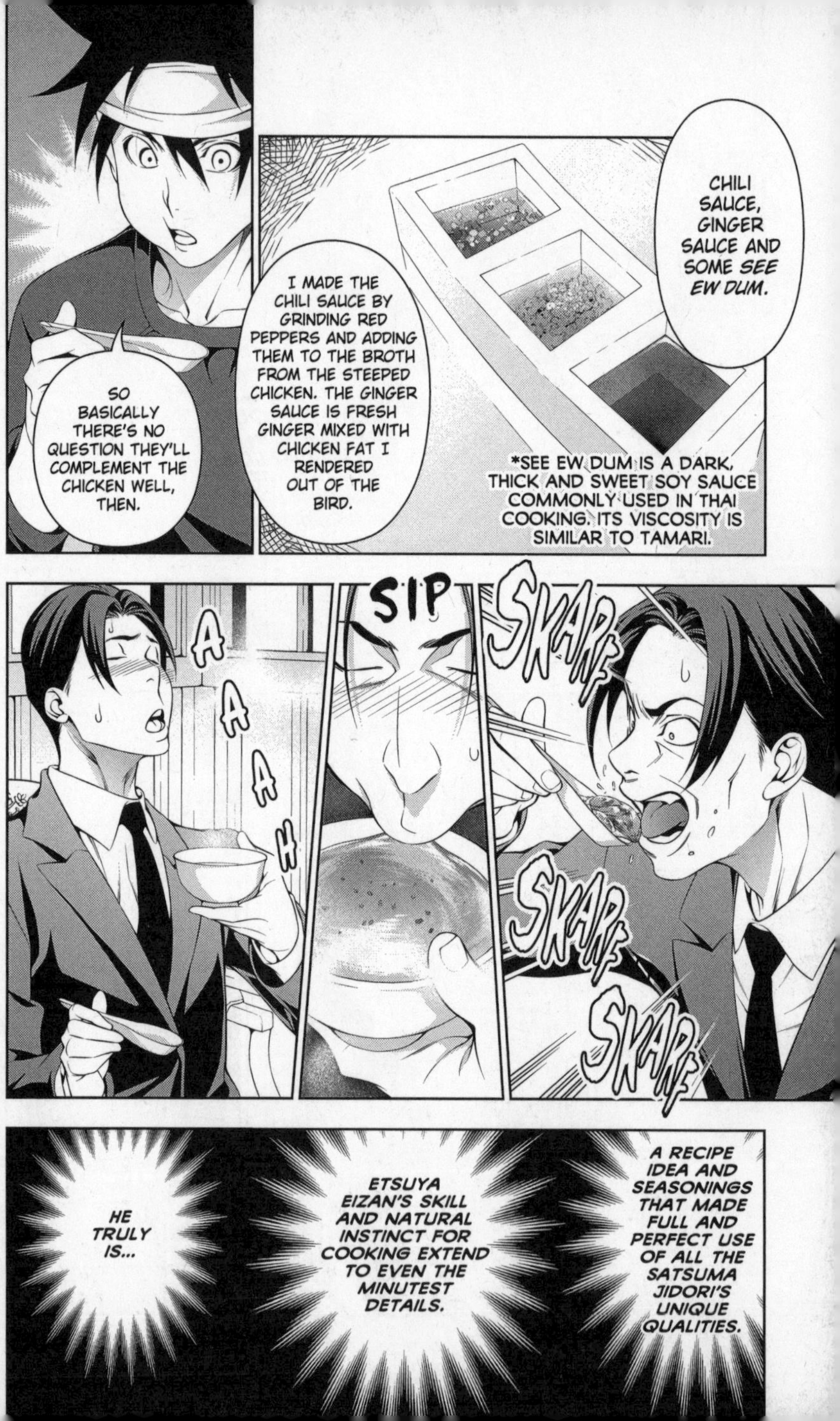
CHILI SAUCE, GINGER SAUCE AND SOME *SEE EW DUM.*
I MADE THE CHILI SAUCE BY GRINDING RED PEPPERS AND ADDING THEM TO THE BROTH FROM THE STEEPED CHICKEN. THE GINGER SAUCE IS FRESH GINGER MIXED WITH CHICKEN FAT I RENDERED OUT OF THE BIRD.
*SEE EW DUM IS A DARK, THICK AND SWEET SOY SAUCE COMMONLY USED IN THAI COOKING. ITS VISCOSITY IS SIMILAR TO TAMARI.
SO BASICALLY THERE'S NO QUESTION THEY'LL COMPLEMENT THE CHICKEN WELL, THEN.
SKARF
SKARF
SKARF
SIP
AAAH
A RECIPE IDEA AND SEASONINGS THAT MADE FULL AND PERFECT USE OF ALL THE SATSUMA JIDORI'S UNIQUE QUALITIES.
ETSUYA EIZAN'S SKILL AND NATURAL INSTINCT FOR COOKING EXTEND TO EVEN THE MINUTEST DETAILS.
HE TRULY IS...

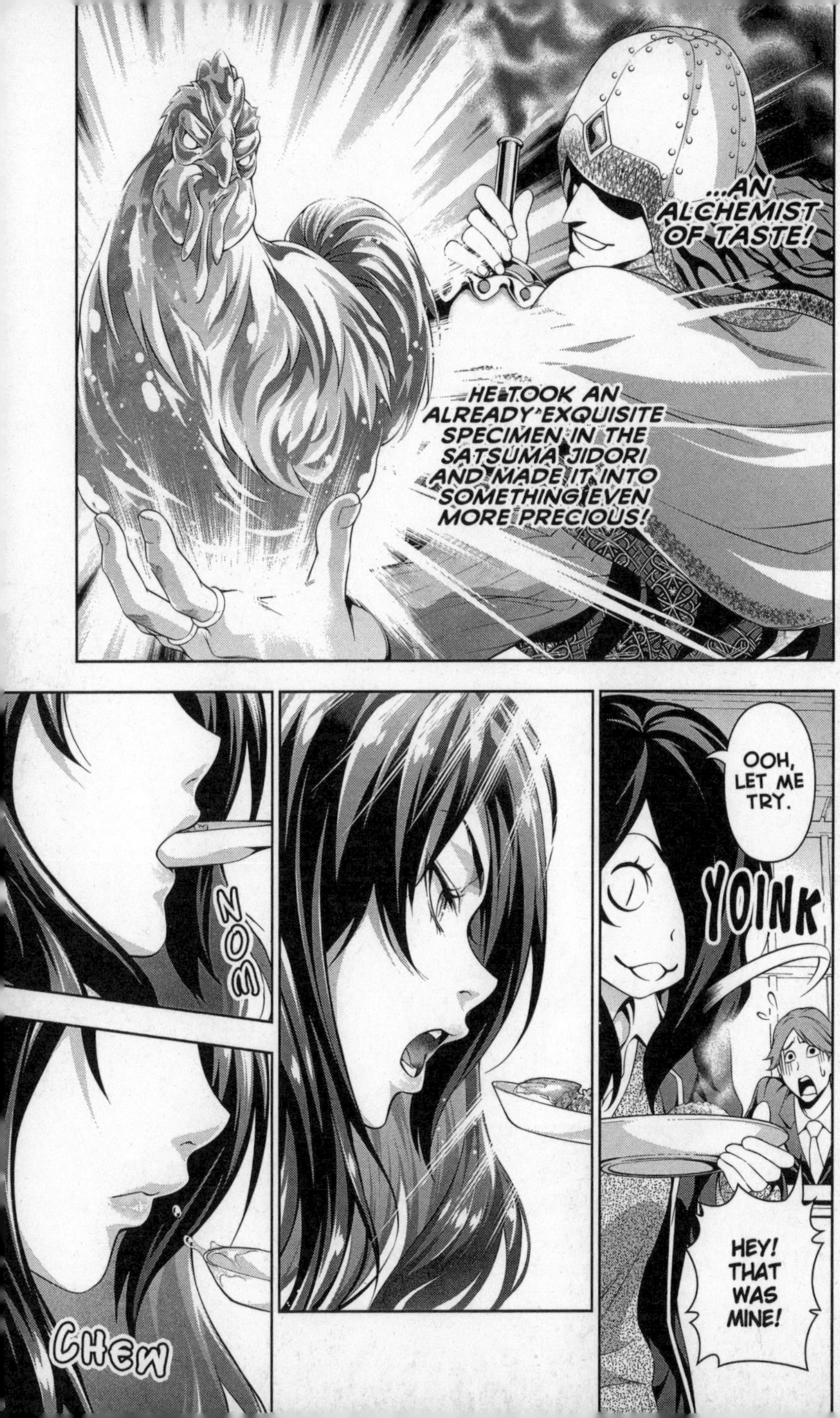
...AN ALCHEMIST OF TASTE!
HE TOOK AN ALREADY EXQUISITE SPECIMEN IN THE SATSUMA JIDORI AND MADE IT INTO SOMETHING EVEN MORE PRECIOUS!
OOH, LET ME TRY.
YOINK
HEY! THAT WAS MINE!
NOM
CHEW

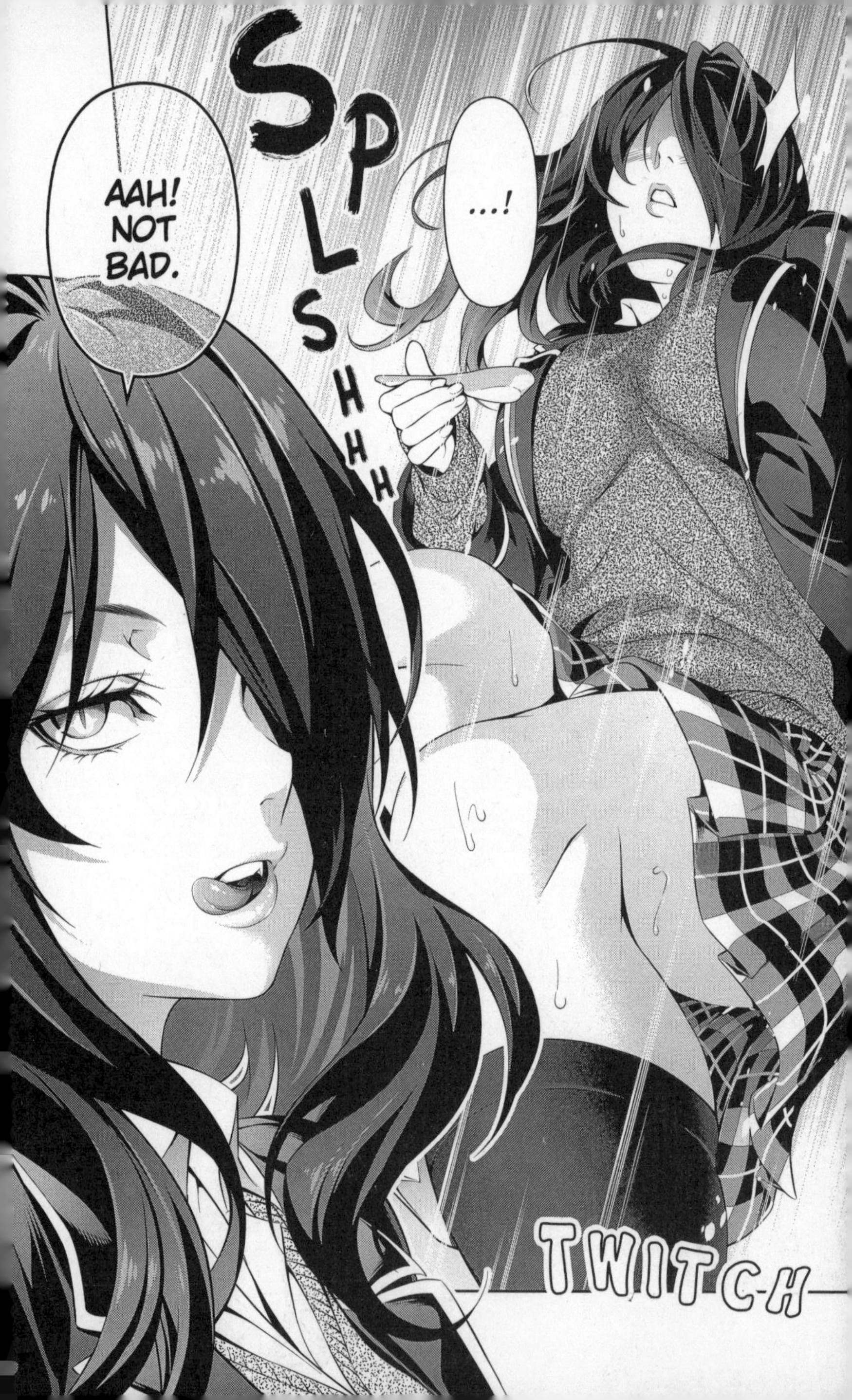
...!
SPLSHHH
AAH! NOT BAD.
TWITCH

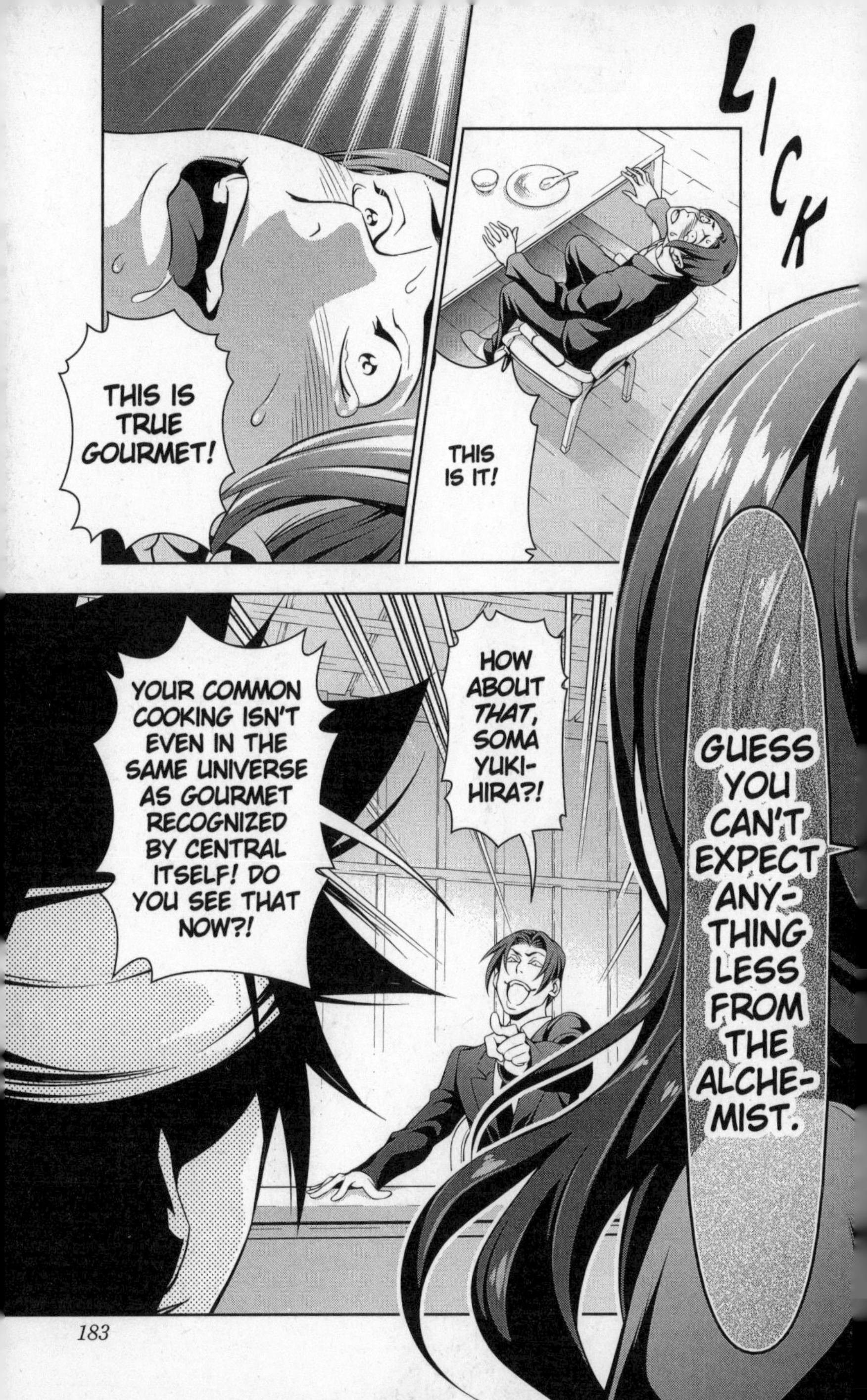
LICK
THIS IS IT!
THIS IS TRUE GOURMET!
HOW ABOUT *THAT*, SOMA YUKIHIRA?!
YOUR COMMON COOKING ISN'T EVEN IN THE SAME UNIVERSE AS GOURMET RECOGNIZED BY CENTRAL ITSELF! DO YOU SEE THAT NOW?!
GUESS YOU CAN'T EXPECT ANYTHING LESS FROM THE ALCHEMIST.

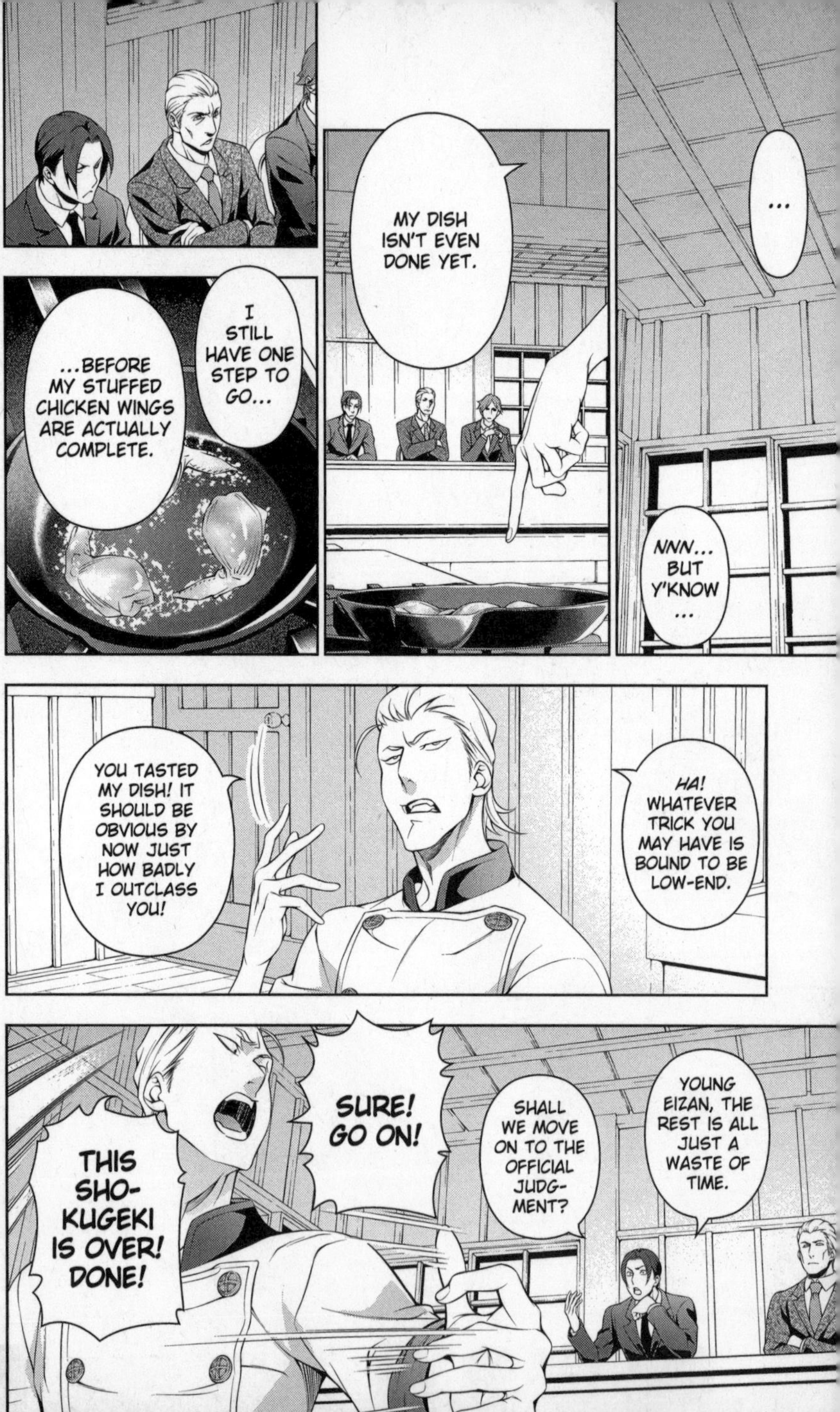
...
NNN... BUT Y'KNOW...
MY DISH ISN'T EVEN DONE YET.
I STILL HAVE ONE STEP TO GO...
...BEFORE MY STUFFED CHICKEN WINGS ARE ACTUALLY COMPLETE.
HA! WHATEVER TRICK YOU MAY HAVE IS BOUND TO BE LOW-END.
YOU TASTED MY DISH! IT SHOULD BE OBVIOUS BY NOW JUST HOW BADLY I OUTCLASS YOU!
YOUNG EIZAN, THE REST IS ALL JUST A WASTE OF TIME.
SHALL WE MOVE ON TO THE OFFICIAL JUDGMENT?
SURE! GO ON!
THIS SHOKUGEKI IS OVER! DONE!

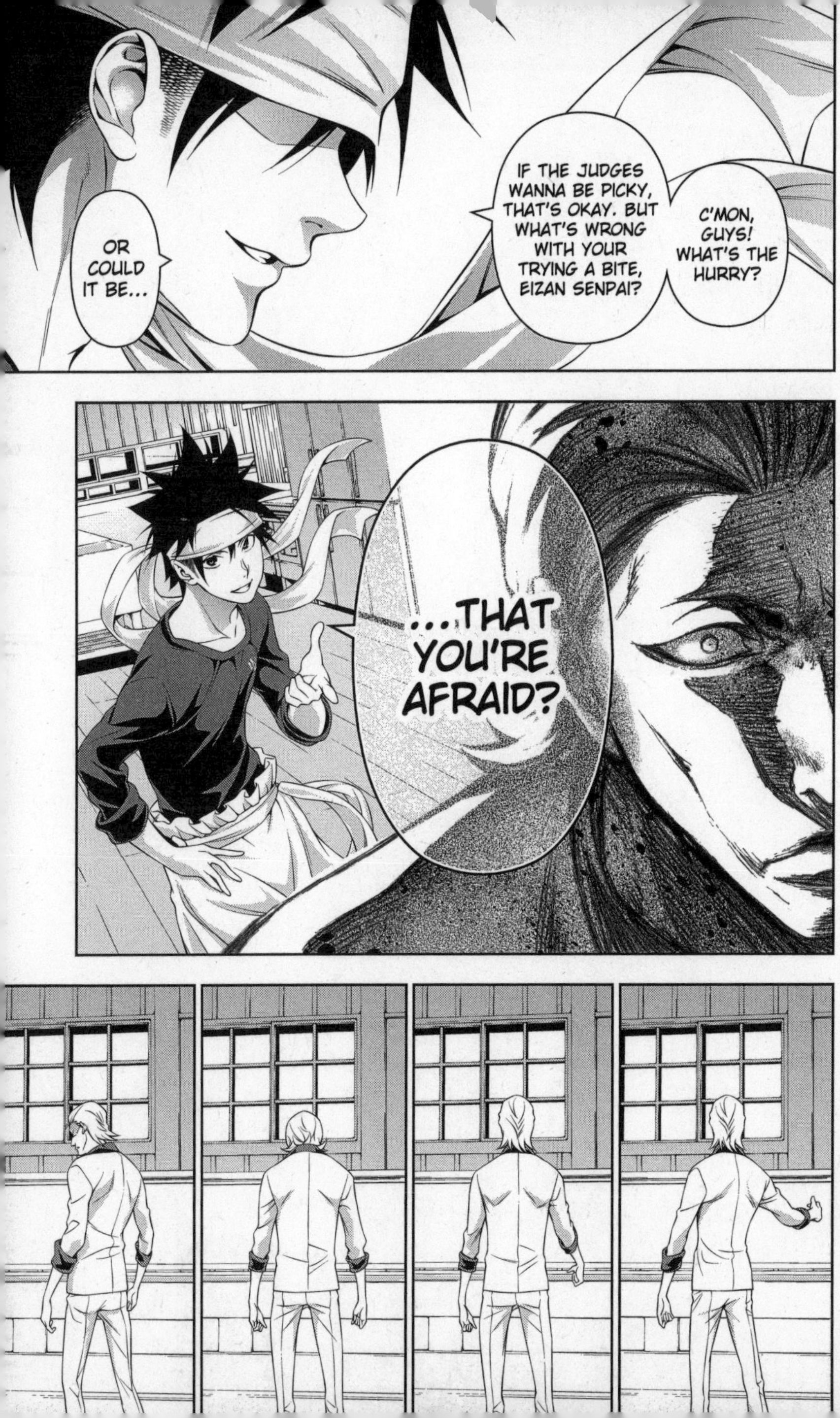
C'MON, GUYS! WHAT'S THE HURRY?
IF THE JUDGES WANNA BE PICKY, THAT'S OKAY. BUT WHAT'S WRONG WITH YOUR TRYING A BITE, EIZAN SENPAI?
OR COULD IT BE...
...THAT YOU'RE AFRAID?

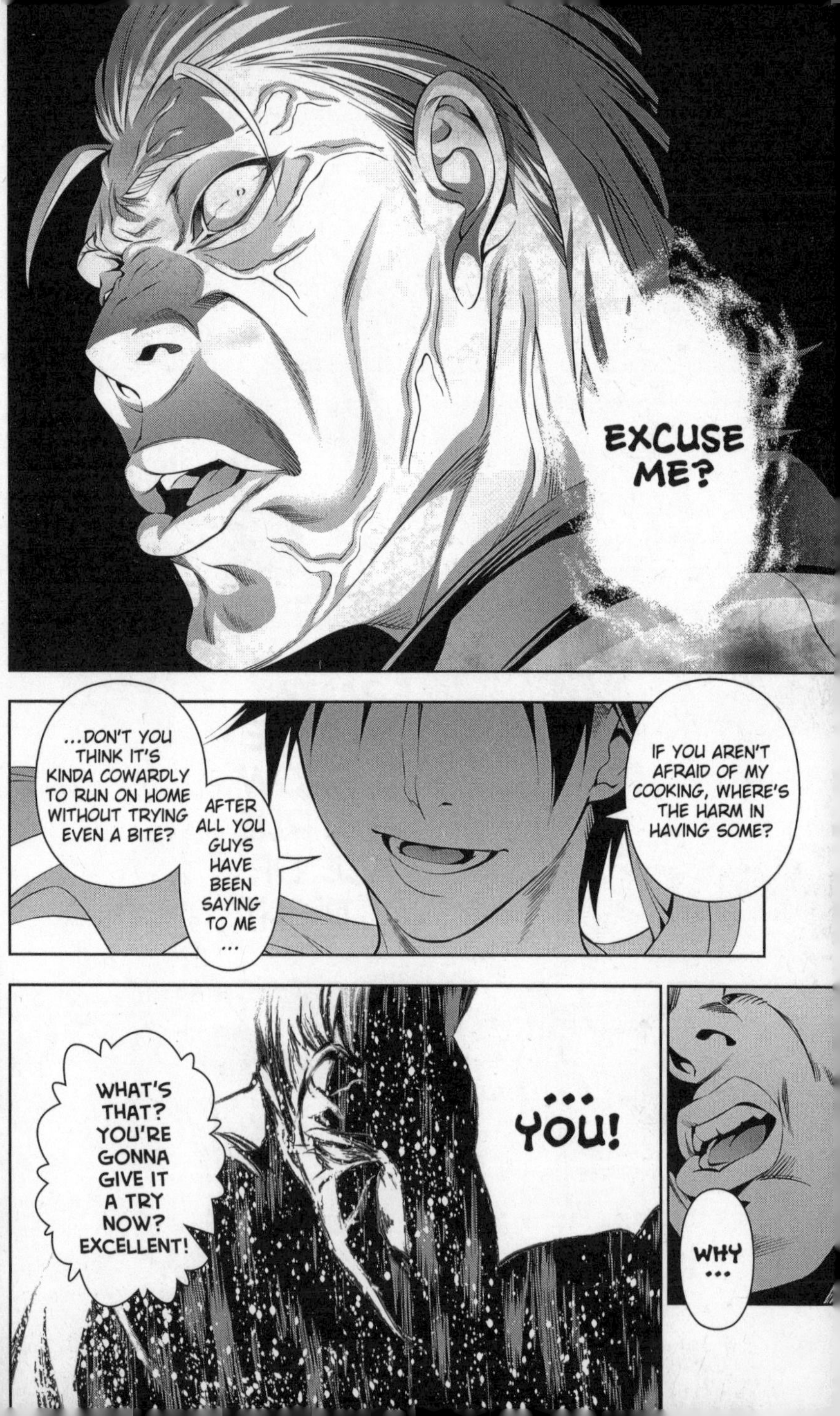
EXCUSE ME?
IF YOU AREN'T AFRAID OF MY COOKING, WHERE'S THE HARM IN HAVING SOME?
AFTER ALL YOU GUYS HAVE BEEN SAYING TO ME ...
...DON'T YOU THINK IT'S KINDA COWARDLY TO RUN ON HOME WITHOUT TRYING EVEN A BITE?
WHY ...
... YOU!
WHAT'S THAT? YOU'RE GONNA GIVE IT A TRY NOW? EXCELLENT!

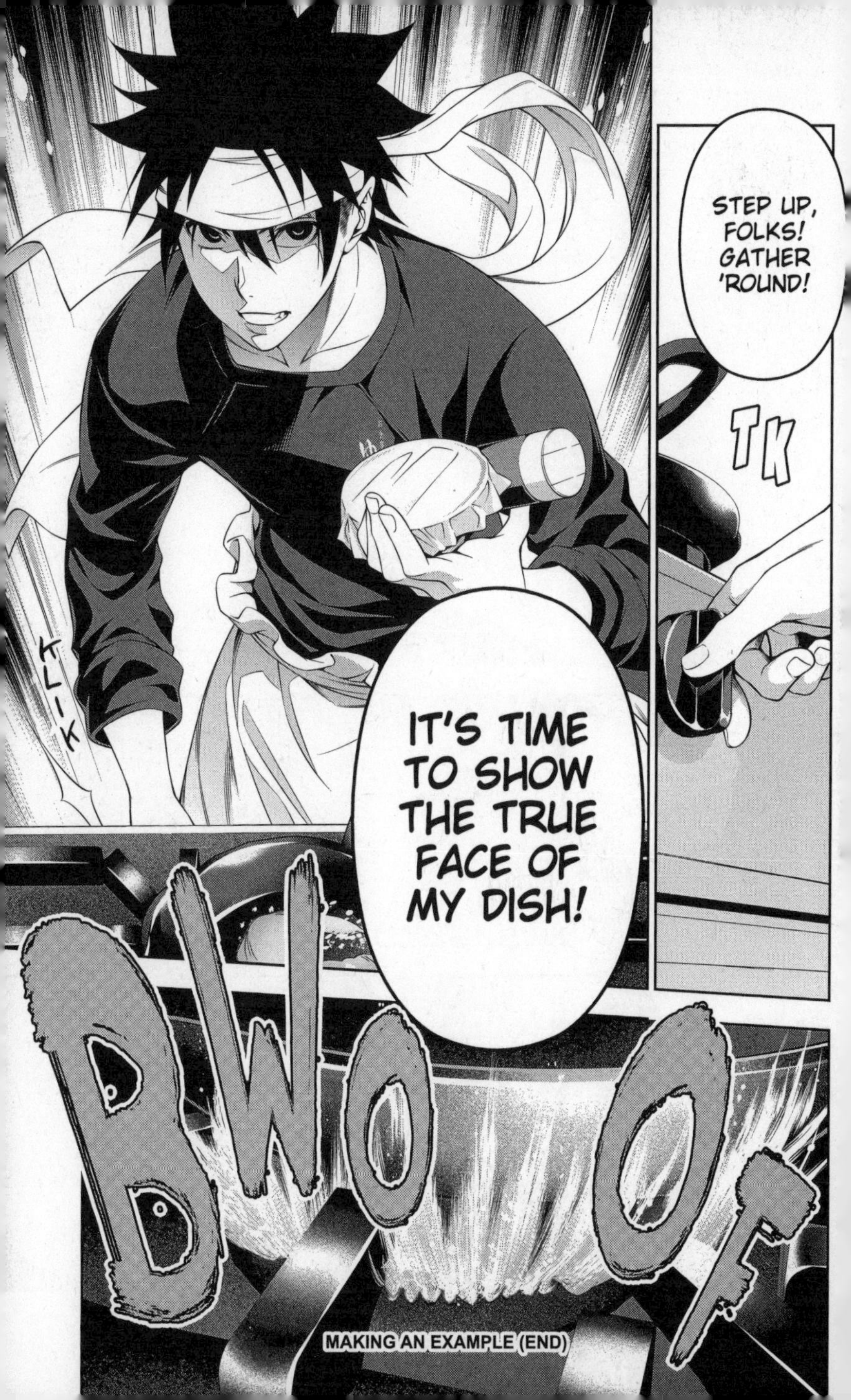
STEP UP, FOLKS! GATHER 'ROUND!
TK
IT'S TIME TO SHOW THE TRUE FACE OF MY DISH!
KLIK
BWOOF
MAKING AN EXAMPLE (END)

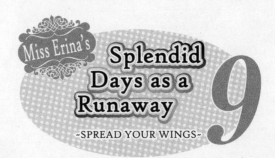

Miss Erina's

Splendid Days as a Runaway 9

~SPREAD YOUR WINGS~

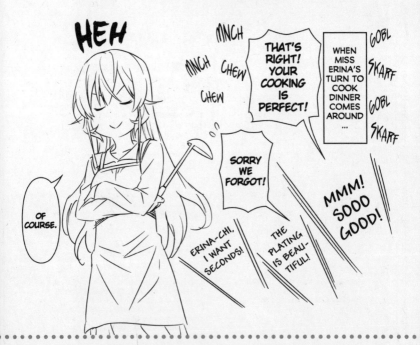

WHEN MISS ERINA'S TURN TO COOK DINNER COMES AROUND ...
GOBL
SKARF
GOBL
SKARF
THAT'S RIGHT! YOUR COOKING IS PERFECT!
MNCH
CHEW
MNCH
CHEW
HEH
MMM! SOOO GOOD!
SORRY WE FORGOT!
THE PLATING IS BEAU-TIFUL!
ERINA-CHI, I WANT SECONDS!
OF COURSE.

ARTIST: YUTO TSUKUDA   RECIPE BY: YUKI MORISAKI

VOLUME 17
SPECIAL SUPPLEMENT!

EIZAN'S SPECIAL RECIPE
HAINANESE
CHICKEN & RICE

SMIRK

SMIRK

SMIRK

SMIRK

LOVED BY HIS FAN CLUB...

ETSUYA EIZAN, A MAN
OF MANY FACES

INGREDIENTS
(SERVES 2)

2 CHICKEN THIGHS
2 CUPS UNCOOKED RICE

1 TEASPOON EACH SALT, SUGAR,
FRESHLY GRATED GINGER,
FRESHLY GRATED GARLIC AND
NAM PLA

1 TABLESPOON EACH CHICKEN
BOUILLON, COOKING SAKE

TOMATO, CUCUMBER, CILANTRO,
PEPPER

<3 DIPPING SAUCES>

★ **SWEET CHILI SAUCE**
AS DESIRED

★ **SWEET SOY SAUCE**
2 TABLESPOONS SOY SAUCE
1 TABLESPOON SUGAR
1 TABLESPOON CANOLA OIL

★ **GINGER SAUCE**
1 TEASPOON GRATED GINGER
2 TABLESPOONS CANOLA OIL
½ TABLESPOON LEMON JUICE
½ TEASPOON SALT

RUB THE CHICKEN THIGHS WITH THE SALT,
PEPPER AND SUGAR. DRIZZLE WITH COOKING
SAKE, AND LET REST FOR 10 MINUTES.

THOROUGHLY RINSE THE RICE, AND THEN
SUBMERGE IT IN WATER AND LET SOAK FOR
20 MINUTES. DRAIN AND SET TO THE SIDE.

3

POUR THE RICE FROM (2) INTO A RICE COOKER, AND ADD A LITTLE LESS WATER THAN NORMALLY NEEDED
FOR COOKING 2 CUPS OF RICE. STIR IN THE CHICKEN BOUILLON, GRATED GINGER, GRATED GARLIC AND
NAM PLA. PLACE THE CHICKEN THIGHS SKIN-SIDE DOWN ON TOP OF THE RICE MIXTURE, AND THEN STEAM
AS NORMAL.

ONCE THE RICE HAS STEAMED, PROMPTLY
REMOVE THE CHICKEN THIGHS AND CUT
THEM INTO 2 CM STRIPS. STIR THE RICE
THOROUGHLY TO MIX AND FLUFF.

USE A SMALL BOWL OR MOLD TO PLATE
THE RICE. ARRANGE THE CHICKEN ON THE
PLATE. DECORATE WITH TOMATO WEDGES,
CUCUMBER SLICES AND CHOPPED CILANTRO.
MIX THE THREE SAUCES, SET THEM IN
DIPPING BOWLS TO THE SIDE, AND DONE!

Miss Erina's Splendid Days as a Runaway

~RISING FEELINGS~

10

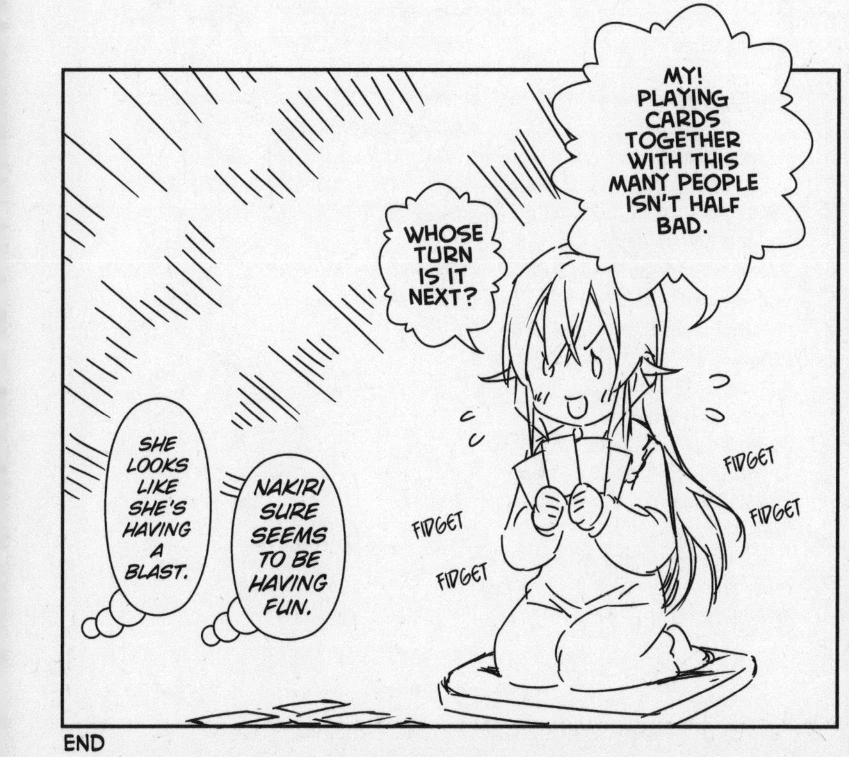
MY! PLAYING CARDS TOGETHER WITH THIS MANY PEOPLE ISN'T HALF BAD.
WHOSE TURN IS IT NEXT?
FIDGET
FIDGET
FIDGET
FIDGET
NAKIRI SURE SEEMS TO BE HAVING FUN.
SHE LOOKS LIKE SHE'S HAVING A BLAST.

END

You're Reading in the Wrong Direction!!

1
2
3
1
2
3
4
5
6

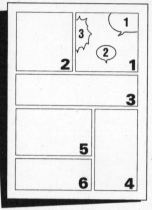

Whoops! Guess what? You're starting at the wrong end of the comic!

...It's true! In keeping with the original Japanese format, **Food Wars!** is meant to be read from right to left, starting in the upper-right corner.

Unlike English, which is read from left to right, Japanese is read from right to left, meaning that action, sound effects and word-balloon order are completely reversed... something which can make readers unfamiliar with Japanese feel pretty backwards themselves. For this reason, manga or Japanese comics published in the U.S. in English have sometimes been published "flopped"—that is, printed in exact reverse order, as though seen from the other side of a mirror.

By flopping pages, U.S. publishers can avoid confusing readers, but the compromise is not without its downside. For one thing, a character in a flopped manga series who once wore in the original Japanese version a T-shirt emblazoned with "M A Y" (as in "the merry month of") now wears one which reads "Y A M"! Additionally, many manga creators in Japan are themselves unhappy with the process, as some feel the mirror-imaging of their art skews their original intentions.

We are proud to bring you Yuto Tsukuda and Shun Saeki's **Food Wars!** in the original unflopped format.

For now, though, turn to the other side of the book and let the adventure begin...!

—Editor

KUGA!
DAMN IT, KUGA! IT'S RINDO SENPAI! YOU PICK UP YOUR PHONE THIS MINUTE.
JUST HOW LONG DO YOU PLAN ON POUTING? ANSWER YOUR PHONE! ANSWER IT!
LEAVING FREQUENT, RATHER DEMANDING PHONE MESSAGES

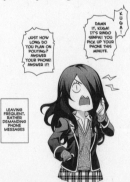